Lecture Notes in Computer Science 7415

Commenced Publication in 1973
Founding and Former Series Editors:
Gerhard Goos, Juris Hartmanis, and Jan van Leeuwen

Daniel Lassiter   Marija Slavkovik (Eds.)

New Directions in Logic, Language and Computation

ESSLLI 2010 and ESSLLI 2011
Student Sessions
Selected Papers

 Springer

Volume Editors

Daniel Lassiter
Stanford University
Department of Psychology
420 Jordan Hall
450 Serra Mall
Stanford, CA 94305, USA
E-mail: danlassiter@stanford.edu

Marija Slavkovik
University of Luxembourg
6, Rue Richard Coudenhove Kalergi
1359 Luxembourg
E-mail: marija.slavkovik@uni.lu

ISSN 0302-9743   e-ISSN 1611-3349
ISBN 978-3-642-31466-7   e-ISBN 978-3-642-31467-4
DOI 10.1007/978-3-642-31467-4
Springer Heidelberg Dordrecht London New York

Library of Congress Control Number: 2012940850

CR Subject Classification (1998): F.4.1, I.2.3-4, I.2.7, D.3.2

LNCS Sublibrary: SL 1 – Theoretical Computer Science and General Issues

Typesetting: Camera-ready by author, data conversion by Scientific Publishing Services, Chennai, India

Printed on acid-free paper

Springer is part of Springer Science+Business Media (www.springer.com)

Preface

We are happy to present you with the second volume of selected papers from the Student Sessions of the European Summer Schools in Logic, Language and Information (ESSLLI), in what we hope will develop into a biannual tradition. This collection contains revised and expanded version of papers presented at the Student Sessions of the 22nd and 23rd ESSLLI, held respectively in 2010 in Copenhagen, Denmark, and in 2011 in Ljubljana, Slovenia. ESSLLI has taken place every year since 1989 under the auspices of FoLLI, the Association for Logic, Language and Information. Since 1996, the Student Session has provided a forum in which promising young scholars can present their work in a friendly and supportive environment and get constructive feedback from expert reviewers and audiences from diverse areas.

Many papers from previous Student Sessions have represented original perspectives and lasting insights from promising young researchers. In recognition of this, a volume of selected best papers from 2008 and 2009 appeared for the first time in early 2011 as a *Lecture Notes in Computer Science* volume (*Interfaces: Explorations in Logic, Language, and Computation*, ed. Thomas Icard and Reinhard Muskens). We hope that with this follow-up volume we may encourage promising young researchers in future years to submit high-quality work to the Student Session.

We received 49 submissions in the 2010 Student Session, out of which 16 were selected for oral and 11 for poster presentations. In the 2011 Student Session we received 53 submissions out of which 16 were selected for oral and 6 for poster presentation. Out of the 32 papers selected for oral presentations, we selected 15 that were extended and reviewed again for inclusion in this volume.

We would like to thank those without whom the Student Session and this volume would not have been possible: our hard-working Program Committees, the helpful audiences, and especially the main ESSLLI organizers and the many expert reviewers who generously took time to help select these papers and sharpen the insights that they contain.

April 2012

Daniel Lassiter
Marija Slavkovik

Organization

Program Committee 2010

Jens Ulrik Hansen	Roskilde University, Denmark
Szymon Klarman	Vrije Universiteit Amsterdam, The Netherlands
Ekaterina Lebedeva	INRIA Nancy, University Henri - Poincare, France
Pierre Lison	DFKI Saarbrücken, Germany
Mingya Liu	University of Göttingen, Germany
Marija Slavkovik	University of Luxembourg
Natalia Vinogradova	Bordeaux-1 University, France

Program Committee 2011

Anna Chernilovskaya	Utrecht University, The Netherlands
Hanna de Vries	Utrecht University, The Netherlands
Janez Kranjc	Jozef Stefan Institute, Slovenia
Daniel Lassiter	New York University, USA
Daphne Theijssen	Radboud University Nijmegen, The Netherlands
Sander Wubben	Tilburg University, The Netherlands
Fan Yang	University of Helsinki, Finland

Table of Contents

Predicting the Position of Attributive Adjectives in the French NP

Gwendoline Fox[1] and Juliette Thuilier[2]

[1] University of Paris 3 - Sorbonne Nouvelle (ILPGA) and EA 1483
[2] Univ Paris Diderot, Sorbonne Paris Cité, ALPAGE, UMR-I 001 INRIA

1   Introduction

French displays the possibility of both pre-nominal and post-nominal ordering of adjectives within the noun phrase (NP).

(1)   un **magnifique** tableau / un tableau **magnifique**
       a   magnificent painting / a   painting magnificient
       "a magnificient painting"

While all adjectives may alternate in position, the choice between both orders is not as free as suggested in (1):

(2)   a.   un **beau** tableau / ??un tableau **beau**
            a nice   painting / a   painting nice
        b.   un très **beau** tableau / un tableau très **beau**
            a very nice   painting / a painting very nice
            "a (very) nice painting"
        c.   *un **beau** à couper le   souffle tableau / un tableau **beau** à
            a   nice to cut   the breath painting / a painting nice   to
            couper le   souffle
            cut   the breath
            "a breathtakingly beautiful painting"

The examples in (2) show that the positionning of attributive adjectives is a complex phenomenon: unlike *magnifique*, the adjective *beau* cannot be placed freely when it is the only element of the adjectival phrase (AP). It is strongly preferred in anteposition (2-a). The addition of the pre-adjectival adverb *très* gives more flexibility and equally allows both orders (2-b) whereas the use of a post-adjectival modifier constrains the placement to postposition (2-c).

    The phenomenon of adjective alternation has been widely studied in French linguistics ([1], [2], [3], [4], [5], [6], [7] among others). Many constraints were proposed on different dimensions of the language: phonology, morphology, syntax, semantics[1], discourse and pragmatics. Only one of them is categorical in the

---

[1] In some cases, alternation leads to meaning differences for the adjective (see for instance [1], [3], [7]). The decision between the different possible accounts of how these differences could be generated is beyond the scope of this article. We thus leave aside these semantic considerations and focus here on the form of the adjective.

D. Lassiter and M. Slavkovik (Eds.): ESSLLI Student Sessions, LNCS 7415, pp. 1–15, 2012.
© Springer-Verlag Berlin Heidelberg 2012

sense that it imposes a specific position to any attributive adjective: the presence of a post-adjectival complement (3) or modifier (2-c) only allows postposition of the adjective.

(3)   un homme **fier**   de son fils / *un **fier**   de son fils homme
       a   man   proud of his son / a   proud of his son man
       "a man proud of his son"

The other constraints participating in the alternation between anteposition and postposition are not categorical. For instance, as noted in the corpus studies of [2] and [3], length is a preferential constraint: short adjectives tend to be anteposed to the noun. The sequence "un magnifique tableau" in (1) illustrates that this rule can be violated whether one considers the length of the adjective alone: *magnifique* has 3 syllables, or the relative length between the adjective and the noun (3 > 2).

Although the above-mentioned works have enabled to identify the constraints playing a role in the placement of adjectives, most are based on introspection and only examine a few of these constraints. It is thus very difficult to evaluate the actual impact of each of them in usage, and therefore to estimate their respective weight in the speaker's choice for one position over the other. This paper aims to get a better grasp of the general picture of the phenomenon. To do so, we present along the same lines as [8], [9] and [10], a quantitative study, based on two corpora: the French Tree Bank (henceforth FTB) and the Est-Républicain corpus (henceforth ER). We propose a regression model based on interpretable constraints and compare the prediction capacities of different subsets in order to determine what kind of informations are the most reliable to account for the placement of adjectives.

The paper is organised as follows. We present in section 2 the methodological aspects of our study : constitution of the datatable and presentation of the statistical model. In section 3, we describe the variables derived from the constraints found in the literature. Section 4 is dedicated to the comparison of the models based on the different subsets of variables and to the interpretation of the results.

2   Methodology

Building the Datatable. The first step of this work is to collect the data concerning adjectives and capture the constraints found in the literature. The study is based on the functionally annotated subset of the FTB corpus [11][2], which contains 12,351 sentences, 24,098 word types and 385,458 tokens. It is, for the moment, the only existing treebank for French. We extracted all the occurrences of attributive adjectives from this corpus[3], and filtered out numeral adjectives[4],

---

[2] This subset corresponds to the part that was manually corrected.
[3] We identified attributive adjectives using the following pattern in the treebank: an adjective occuring with a nominal head within a NP is an attributive adjective.
[4] Cardinal numerals such as *trois* 'three', *vingt* 'twenty', *soixante* 'sixty'... are sometimes annotated as adjectives in the FTB.

adjectives appearing in dates[5], abbreviations[6] and incorrectly annotated occurrences. We also discarded the 438 adjectives occurring with a post-adjectival dependent since postposition is obligatory in this case, regardless of the values of other constraints that we consider (see (2-c) and (3)). The remaining adjectives constitute the basis of the datatable, to which we have added information on the position of each adjective with respect to the noun it modifies, and 10 other variables that we describe in section 3.

Three variables of our study are based on frequency counts: FREQ, COLLOCANT and COLLOCPOST. They were extracted from the ER corpus for more reliable counts. The raw corpus contains 147,934,722 tokens, and is available on the ATILF website[7]. It was tagged and lemmatized with the *Morfette* system [12] adapted for French. We used ER for these constraints because it is around 380 times larger than FTB. We therefore consider that frequency in ER is a better estimator of the probability of use of an adjective. Also, we use here a log transformed value of the frequency to reduce the range of values of this variable. More precisely, the three variables take the following value: *log(frequency in ER + 1)*, in order to avoid a null value in case an adjectival lemma or noun-adjective combination is absent from ER.

Presentation of the Datatable. The datatable contains 14,804 occurrences corresponding to 1,920 adjectival lemmas. 4,227 (28.6%) tokens appear in anteposition, and 10,577 (71.4%) in postposition. Table 1 shows that the adjectival lemmas displaying occurrences in both positions represent only 9.5% of all lemmas, yet these few lemmas correspond to 5,473 occurrences, i.e. 37.0% of the datatable, which means that very few adjectives actually alternate in usage but they are highly frequent.

Note that among the alternating adjectives (occurring in both positions), the ratio between anteposed and postposed occurrences is the reverse from that of all adjectives: there are 3,727 anteposed (68,1%) and 1,746 postposed (31,9%) adjectives. Alternating adjectives thus show a preference for anteposition. The general pattern is therefore that postposed adjectives tend to be infrequent lemmas occurring only in postposition, whereas alternating adjectives tend to be frequent and to prefer anteposition.

Table 1. Distribution of adjectival lemmas and tokens according to position

	anteposed	postposed	both positions	Overall
number of lemmas	125	1613	182	1920
	6.5%	84.0%	9.5%	100%
tokens	500	8831	5473	14804
	3.4%	59.7%	37.0%	100%

---

[5] Examples of dates containing adjectives: "$[13]_{ADJ}$ $[mars]_N$", "$[lundi]_N$ $[31]_{ADJ}$".

[6] Nouns or adjectives are viewed as abbreviations if their last letter is a capital letter.

[7] *http://www.cnrtl.fr/corpus/estrepublicain/*

Statistical Inference and Logistic Regression. We used logistic regression models [13] to estimate the distribution of adjective positions using the variables from the datatable. Formally, a logistic regression is a function for which values can be interpreted as conditional probabilities. Its analytical form is as follows:

$$\pi_{\text{ante}} = \frac{e^{\beta \mathbf{X}}}{1 + e^{\beta \mathbf{X}}} \tag{1}$$

where, in our case, π_{ante} is the probability for the adjective to be anteposed and β corresponds to the abbreviation of the sequence of regression coefficients α, β_0... β_n, respectively associated with the predicting variables X_0... X_n. Given a scatter plot, the calculation of regression consists in the maximum likelihood estimation of α and β_i parameters for each variable in a *logit* space.

This type of modelling consists in the combining of several explicative variables (binary or continuous) to predict the behaviour of a single binary variable, here the position of the adjective. More precisely, we estimate the probability of anteposition as a function of 10 variables. Given one adjectival occurrence and the value of the 10 explanatory variables attributed to this occurrence, the model gives the probability of anteposition of the occurrence. Here, the model predicts postposition if the probabilty is below 0.5, and anteposition if it is higher or equal to 0.5. The accuracy gives the proportion of data that is correctly predicted according to this threshold. However, this measure does not evaluate completely satisfactorily the predictive power of the model because the threshold is arbitrary and does not account for the fact that a probability of 0.55 is different from a probability of 0.95. We therefore use an additional measure: the area under the ROC curve (AUC) [14], [15]. This measure gives the discrimination capacity of the model for all the pairs of opposite responses. A model with an AUC probability close to 0.5 indicates random predictions, and a value of 1, perfect prediction. It is usually considered that a model with an AUC value equal or above 0.8 has some utility in predicting the value of the dependent variable [14, p. 247].

The methodology of this paper consists in the comparison of models based on different constraint clusters, in order to evaluate their respective relevance. The comparisons take as reference a baseline model that does not contain any explanatory variables and systematically predicts postposition. Its accuracy is of 71.4% ($\sigma = 0.019$), which corresponds to the proportion of postposed adjectives in the datatable. Moreover, for the baseline model, AUC = 0.5, given that this model does not discriminate anteposition and postposition.

3   Variables

The variables we use in our logistic regression models are derived from the constraints found in the literature on attributive adjectives in French. They are summarized in table 2. Each model is based on different sets of constraints according to specific properties. The first set (COORD and ADV) concerns the syntactic environment of the adjective, the second is based on the lexical properties

Table 2. Summary table of variables and their values (*bool* = boolean and *real* = real number)

Variables	Types	Description
COORD	*bool*	adjective in coordination or not
ADV	*bool*	adjective with pre-modifying adverb or not
DERIVED	*bool*	derived adjective or not
NATIO	*bool*	adjective of nationality or not
INDEF	*bool*	indefinite adjective or not
ADJ-LENGTH	*real*	length of the adjective in syllables (log scale)
AP-LENGTH	*real*	length of the AP in syllables (log scale)
FREQ	*real*	adjective frequency in the ER corpus (log scale)
COLLOCANT	*real*	score for the adjective-noun bigram (log scale)
COLLOCPOST	*real*	score for the noun adjective bigram (log scale)

of the adjectival item (DERIVED, NATIO and INDEF), the third one on constraints linked to cognitive processing (ADJ-LENGTH, AP-LENGTH and FREQ). Finally, the fourth group examines collocationnal effects of the Noun - Adjective combination (COLLOCANT and COLLOCPOST).

3.1 Syntactic Variables

The variables based on syntactic properties rely on the idea that the internal structure of the AP has an influence on the placement of adjectives. As seen in the introduction, one of them, i.e. the presence of a post-adjectival dependent, is categorical and is therefore not integrated in our study. It suggests however that the syntactic environment of the adjective may have an important role in its positioning. We thus propose here two other constraints related to different internal structures within the AP.

Coordination (COORD). In a competence account of attributive position like in [6], the position of coordinated adjectives is not restricted, as can be seen in example (4) (from [6]).

(4)   une **belle**   et   **longue** table   /   une table **belle**   et   **longue**
       a   beautiful and long   table   /   a   table beautiful and long
       "a long and beautiful table"

However, 94.6% of coordinated adjectival occurrences (i.e. 758 occurrences) are postposed in our data. Usage-based data thus indicate that coordination is a factor that strongly favours postposition.

Presence of a Pre-adjectival Adverb (ADV). The constraint is the same as for coordination if one considers the adverbial category on a general level: the presence of a pre-adjectival modifier does not restrict the position of the modified adjective (example (5)).

(5)   une très **longue** table / une table très **longue**
        a   very long   table / a   table very long
        "a very long table"

On a more specific level, [6] point out that adjectives can be postposed with any adverb whereas only a small set of adverbs allows anteposition. This is confirmed in our datatable: 11 types of adverb[8] are observed with anteposed adjectives, while 119 different types appear with adjectives in postposition. Furthermore, the adverbs found with adjectives in anteposition are not specific to this position, they also appear with postposed occurrences. From a general quantitative point of view, 74.9% of the premodified adjectival occurrences are in postposition.

3.2   Cognitive Processing Variables

Length and frequency of occurrence are constraints that have cross-linguistically been observed to play a role in different types of phenomena, amongst which the adjective alternation. These constraints are usually related to processing ease (see for instance [16], [17] and [18]). We present the functioning of the constraints in what follows and leave the interpretation in terms of cognition to the discussion of the models performance.

Length. Numerous works on word order use the notion of length: for attributive adjectives in French [2], [3], for word [19], [20] and constituent [21], [16], [9], [10] alternation in other languages. The main idea is expressed by the principle *short comes first*, i.e. short elements tend to appear first. Here, we consider length in terms of number of syllables and we introduce two variables: length of the adjective (ADJ-LENGTH) and length of the adjectival phrase (AP) (AP-LENGTH)[9].

Lemma Frequency (FREQ). In his corpus study, [3] observes that frequency is correlated with the position of the adjective: pre-nominal adjectives tend to be frequent whereas post-nominal adjectives tend to be rare. According to the author, this distribution has historical grounds. In Old French, the general pattern was the reverse of that of Modern French: adjectives were generally placed before the noun, as in English. The evolution to the preference for postposition in Modern French did not affect the most frequent adjectives because their association to anteposition was too robust to reverse the pattern. Note that this hypothesis is not particular to French, nor to the adjective alternation, see for instance the summary in [23, ch.11] of several studies that make the same observation of conservatism linked to frequency.

---

[8] The 11 adverbs are: 'encore' *again*, 'désormais' *from now on*, 'moins' *less*, 'peu' *not much*, 'plus' *more*, 'si' *so*, 'tout' *very*, 'très' *very*, 'trop' *too*, 'bien' *well*, 'aussi' *also*.

[9] We obtain the number of syllables using the speech synthesis software ELITE [22]. It counts the number of syllables for every token, taking into account the actual form of the adjective (feminine versus masculine, for instance) as well as the possible effects of sandhi phenomena, like the *liaison* phenomenon. The length associated to each adjectival type corresponds to the mean of all its tokens length. For both variables, we use the log transformed value of the length in order to reduce the effect of outliers.

3.3   Lexical Variables

Most reference grammars state that adjectives are mainly placed according to their lexical properties. These properties can concern different aspects of language. We propose to examine the relevance of lexical information with the example of three classes, each based on one particular aspect: morphology (DERIVED), semantics (NATIO), and syntactic behaviour (INDEF).

Derived Adjectives (DERIVED). Adjectives may be derived from other parts-of-speech: for instance, certain verbal forms can be used as adjectives (past participles, present participle) or the adjective is obtained by suffixation, to a verbal basis: -*ible* 'faillible' (*faillible*) / -*able* 'faisable' (*doable*) /*if* 'attractif' (*attractive*), or to a noun ('métallique' (*made of metal*), 'scolaire' (*academic*), 'présidentiel' (*presidential*)). These adjectives are described as prefering postposition but anteposition is also possible as shown in example (6).

(6)   notre **charmante** voisine   est beaucoup trop bavarde
       our   charming   neighbour is lot   too talkative
       'our charming neighbour is too talkative'

In our datatable, the adjectives derived from another part-of-speech (noun or verb) are collected using the software of derivational morphological analysis DE-RIF [24]. Our data confirms the strong preference for postposition within this class (91.3%).

Semantic Classes. It is usually said that objective adjectives, i.e. adjectives for which the semantic content is perceptible or can be infered from direct observation, are postposed. Objective adjectives are classified into sub-groups like form, colour, physical property, nationality, technical terms... In order to estimate the relevance of lexical classes according to semantic properties, we test the predictive capacity of adjectives denoting nationality[10] (NATIO). In theory, these adjectives strongly tend to be postposed, but they may also occur in anteposition (example (7)):

(7)   cette très **italienne** invasion de l'Albanie
       this very Italian   invasion of Albania
       "this very Italian invasion of Albania" (in a typical Italian fashion way)[26, p. 142]

The strong preference for postposition of these adjectives is confirmed by our data: only one pre-nominal occurrence is observed (example (8)).

(8)   la   très **britannique** banque d' affaires et   de marché
       the very British   bank   of affairs and of market
       "the very British merchant bank"

---

[10] Using the dictionnary PROLEXBASE [25].

Indefinite Adjectives (INDEF). A relatively closed set of adjectives are special in the fact that their syntacitc properties show a hybrid behaviour between determiners and adjectives. On the one hand, indefinite adjectives may introduce and actualise the noun, like determiners. On the other hand, they may co-occur with a determiner and can be placed in post-nominal position, even though they favour anteposition (89% in our data). These latter properties are specific to attributive adjectives. The adjectives identified as indefinite in the datatable are: 'tel' (*such*), 'autre' (*other*), 'certain' (*some/sure*), 'quelques' (*few*), 'divers' (*various*), 'différent' (*different*), 'maint' (*numerous*), 'nul' (*null/lousy*), 'quelconque' (*any/ordinary*), 'même' (*same/itself*).

3.4   Collocation Variables

It is well known that the nature of some Adjective-Noun combinations is strongly collocational in French [27]. This implies that the position of attributive adjectives in French should also be influenced by collocational effects. Collocations are here defined according to [28, p. 151]. Adjective-Noun collocations may be non-compositional sequences as well as more compositional ones. The sequence 'libre échange' (lit. *free exchange*) is an example of the former: it refers to a specific economical system, not to exchange in general. As an illustration of the latter case, the meaning of 'majeure partie' (*major part*) is predictable from the meaning of the two components. It is nevertheless a collocation because the order between the elements is fixed by convention of use. As mentioned in section 2, the collocation score in our datatable is based on the frequency of Adjective-Noun (COLLOCANT) and Noun-Adjective (COLLOCPOST) bigrams in the ER corpus.

4   Prediction Model of Attributive Adjective Position

The prediction model is built with all the variables described in part 3 and maximized with a backward elimination procedure based on the AIC criterion [29][11]. The ADJ-LENGTH constraint's contribution to the model is not significant according to the procedure. It was thus eliminated. The model is presented in figure 1[12].

The coefficients combined with each variable are estimated from the distribution of the variables in our datatable. In the case of boolean variables, these coefficients are multiplied by 1 when the predictor is true, and by 0 when it is

---

[11] Forward selection procedure gives the same results for this particular model.

[12] The condition number of the model is $\kappa = 13.35$. It indicates that the collinearity of the model is moderate [30]. When the predictors of a regression model are collinear, the interpretation of the contribution of each predictor can rise problems. Given that we do not interpret the values of the coefficients, but only to the sign of these coefficients, the moderate collinearity of our data does not affect the validity of our results.

$$\pi_{\text{ante}} = \frac{e^{\mathbf{X}\beta}}{1+e^{\mathbf{X}\beta}}, \text{ where}$$

$$
\begin{aligned}
\mathbf{X}\beta = \ &-2.14 & *** \\
&-1.07 \ \text{COORD} = 1 & *** \\
&-1.30 \ \text{AP-LENGTH} & *** \\
&+0.29 \ \text{FREQ} & *** \\
&-0.50 \ \text{DERIVED} = 1 & *** \\
&+0.91 \ \text{INDEF} = 1 & *** \\
&-4.58 \ \text{NATIO} = 1 & *** \\
&-0.75 \ \text{ADV} = 1 & *** \\
&+1.28 \ \text{COLLOCANT} & *** \\
&-1.24 \ \text{COLLOCPOST} & *** \\
\end{aligned}
$$

Fig. 1. Formula of prediction model, significant effects are coded *** p<0.001, ** p<0.01, * p<0.1

false. As for the numerical variables (AP-LENGTH, FREQ, COLLOCANT, COL-LOCPOST), their participation to the models consists in the multiplication of the coefficient by the numerical value of the variable itself. In this model, all the variables have positive values, so we can straightforwardly interpret the sign of the coefficients: positive coefficients indicate that the variables prefer anteposition, whereas negative coefficients show that the variables favour postposition. As we expected, the variables COORD, AP-LENGTH, DERIVED, NATIO, ADV and COL-LOCPOST tend to favour postposition, whereas FREQ, INDEF and COLLOCANT vote for anteposition

Compared to the *baseline model* performances (accuracy of 71.4% and AUC = 0.5), this model has significantly better predictive capacities. The prediction performances associated with the procedure of decision are presented in table 3. One can see that the *global model* correctly predicts the position of 92.6% of the datatable. Moreover, the concordance probability is AUC = 0.969 (σ = 0.003), which indicates that the model predictions are very accurate. To have a graphical idea of the goodness of fit of the model, the plot in figure 2 gives the relation between the observed proportions and the corresponding mean expected probability for the model[13]. It shows that the fit is very good for probabilities under 0.5, and not quite as good for higher probabilities.

Table 3. Classification table for *prediction model*

		Predicted position		% Correct
		P	A	
observed	P	10222	355	96.6%
position	A	748	3479	82.3%

Overall accuracy: 92.6% (σ = 0.008)

---

[13] We compute the mean probability of success of ten equally sized bins of probabilities $(0 - 0.1, 0.1 - 0.2, 0.2 - 0.3 \ldots)$ and we compare this mean with the proportion of observed success in the data.

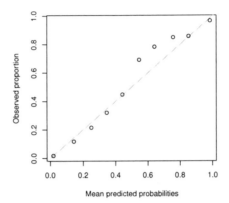

Fig. 2. Observed proportions of anteposition and the corresponding mean predicted probabilities for the prediction model (the line represents a perfect fit)

4.1 Comparison of Models with Different Sets of Constraints

In order to compare the effect of different constraint clusters, we propose 4 prediction models based on different groups of variables: a *Syntactic model* containing COORD and ADV; a *Lexical property model* with NATIO, INDEF and DERIVED; a *Frequency-Length model* containing the variables AP-LENGTH and FREQ and a *Collocation model* containing COLLOCANT and COLLOCPOST.

Syntactic Model (COORD and ADV). The comparison based on accuracy shows that the effect of the syntactic constraints is insignificant when they are not combined with other constraints. The *Syntactic model* accuracy is 71.4% ($\sigma = 0.02$), and the classification table in 4 shows that this model cannot predict anteposition. The value of the concordance probability (AUC = 0.534, $\sigma = 0.008$) confirms that the predictive power of these variables is very poor. This lack of predictive power can be partly explained by the fact that these two variables are relevant for a very small set of data: ADV and COORD represent respectively 5.2% and 5.4% of all the data. In addition, both constraints favour postposition, which is already the default position predicted by the baseline model. This means that these constraints can only be relevant when other constraints are also taken into account.

Table 4. Classification table for *Syntactic model*

		Predicted position		% Correct
		P	A	
observed	P	10574	3	99.9%
position	A	4227	0	0%

Overall accuracy: 71.4% ($\sigma = 0.02$)

Table 5. Classification table for *Lexical properties model*

		Predicted position		% Correct
		P	A	
observed	P	10506	71	99.3%
position	A	3681	546	12.9%

Overall accuracy: 74.7% ($\sigma = 0.02$)

Table 6. Classification table for *Frequency-Length model*

		Predicted position		% Correct
		P	A	
observed	P	9334	1243	88.2%
position	A	1475	2752	65.1%

Overall accuracy: 81.7% ($\sigma = 0.009$)

Lexical Properties Model (NATIO, INDEF and DERIVED). Lexical properties are relevant when they are not combined with the other constraints (*Lexical properties model* accuracy = 74.7% and AUC = 0.717). However, the table in 5 indicates that the lexical properties that we used do not predict satisfactorily anteposition: only 12.9% of anteposed adjectives are correctly accounted for. This is mainly due to the fact that only one of the variables (INDEF) favours the prenominal position. Nevertheless, one can see that these three constraints alone enable the model to consider anteposition, which was not the case with syntactic constraints. This observation suggests that speakers may be sensitive to this type of information and encourages us to extend the lexical classification for all the adjectives of the datatable, in particular those that favour anteposition, in order to improve our modelling.

Frequency-Length Model (AP-LENGTH and FREQ). The variables of length and frequency have an important predictive power (accuracy 81.7% ($\sigma = 0.009$), AUC = 0.869 ($\sigma = 0.010$)). In particular, the predictions for anteposition are much higher than observed with the two preceding models (65%). These two constraints may thus play an important role in the placement of adjectives. As expected, the model tends to predicts anteposition for short and frequent adjectives, and postposition when the adjective is longer and/or less frequent[14].

Collocation Model (COLLOCANT and COLLOCPOST). The *Collocation model* shows that the frequency of bigrams represents the best predictor. The *Collocation model* accuracy is of 89.9% ($\sigma = 0.013$) and the AUC value increases up to 0.940 ($\sigma = 0.006$). This result suggests that the order of the adjective-noun sequence depends highly on the nature of both the noun and the adjective,

---

[14] Note that frequencies are biased by the journalistic nature of corpora: adjectives of nationality are frequent despite the fact that they are postposed in most cases. Nevertheless, the variable NATIO of the global prediction model votes for postposition, which neutralizes the frequency effect.

Table 7. Classification table for *Collocations model*

		Predicted position		% Correct
		P	A	
observed	P	10327	250	97.6%
position	A	1249	2978	70.5%

Overall accuracy: 89.9% ($\sigma = 0.007$)

and on the frequency with which these elements appear in a specific order. It thus appears here again that frequency is a good predictor for the placement of adjectives. However, the fact that this model is more performant than the previous one seems to show that frequency is a better predictor when it takes into account more information than the adjective isolated from its context of appearance.

4.2   Discussion

The models presented above show that the constraints playing a significant role in the adjective alternation are information specific to the adjectival item and to its context of use, rather than constraints based on a more general and abstract level. These specific informations relate to different aspects of language. On the one hand, the constraints tested in the lexical model (NATIO, INDEF and DERIVED) concern inherent linguistic properties. On the other hand, length of the AP, frequency of the adjective, and collocational effects are more related to the way language is processed and used: how speakers place the AP according to its linear constitution during discourse, and how they retrieve the units (or sequences) in accordance with their past experience of these elements. The importance of the predictive power of the second set of specific constraints suggests that adjective alternation may be best accounted for in terms of cognitive approaches to language.

As mentioned in the description of the length variable (sec. 3.2), the tendency to place short elements first is not specific to adnominal adjectives in French. It is also observed in other works for various phenomena in other languages. The general preference for such a placement is explained by the fact that it eases the on-line processing of the structure within which the element occurs: for example, [21], [16], [9], [10] , who study different constituent to constituent ordering phenomena, state that anteposition of the short element helps to faster plan/recognise the overall structure of the immediately dominating constituent. This idea can be applied to the Adjective-Noun combination. A short AP in anteposition leads to a faster production/reception of the Head-Noun in comparison with a longer one, and hence to a faster access to 1) the complete internal constitution of the AP, 2) more information concerning the structure of the NP. The significant contribution of length in the prediction of adjective alternation may thus be viewed as another support for an explanation in terms of processing ease.

In a similar perspective, Usage-based models (see for example [31], [32], [33]) consider that frequency plays an important role in the constitution of the speaker's linguistic knowledge. These approaches view linguistic knowdledge as mental representations based on the storage of instances of language encountered by the speaker. This means that speakers store isolated words like it is traditionally assumed for the constitution of the lexicon, but also that they memorize information about specificities related to their context of appearance. In our study, the assumption is that speakers would have mental representations corresponding to the adjective, and representations of specific ordered Adjective-Noun sequences in which it appears. Furthermore, these models consider that every occurrence of an instance affects the corresponding mental representations. Of particular interest here, [18] notes that the repetition of a language instance strengthens its representation and makes its execution more fluent. The instance also becomes more entrenched in the morpho-syntactic structure in which it usually appears, which leads to more resistance for a change of structure. Applied to adjectives, this means that a highly frequent item (or sequence) is highly accessible, and thus easy to process. When the item is tested in isolation (FREQ), if processing ease plays an important role in the placement of adjectives as it was suggested for length, one would expect highly frequent adjectives to favour anteposition. Concerning collocationnal effects (COLLOCANT and COLLOCPOST), the prediction of this approach is that a collocationnal sequence would be reproduced in the same morpho-syntactic configuration, i.e the order between the Adjective and the Noun should be maintained as it is usually encountered. As it was observed for length, the good results of the models involving frequency constraints are in accordance with theses assumptions and can be seen as a support for this type of approach.

5   Conclusion

We examined in this article the question of the alternation of attributive adjectives in French using quantitative methods applied to corpora. One can draw several conclusions from the logistic regression models that we proposed. First the satisfactory results of the general model show that a good part of the modelling can be done on the basis of the form without considering the semantics due to position. The importance of the form is also outlined by the fact that the constraints identified as having some relevance when isolated from the others are all based on a knowledge linked to the specificities of the item, or to the specific context in which it appears. Nevertheless, the prediction performances may be improved by taking more semantics into account: adding information for other lexical classes, including semantics, should naturally enhance the model. Furthermore, the importance of collocational effects suggests that semantics should also be considered on a specific relational level between the noun and the adjective. It thus raises the question on how to capture and formalise semantic relations in a quantitative study. Finally, the results of our study show that the best models are based on length and frequency, and collocational effects. This confirms the role of the nature of the items involved. It also suggests that usage may have an important role in the construction of linguistic knowledge, and hence in the placement of adjectives.

To conclude, the model proposed in this article is restricted to the journalistic genre. A future perspective in our work would be to extend this study to other genres, in particular spoken data, in order to test the relevance of our conclusions for French more generally. Furthermore, a comparison between the probabilities given by our model and speakers' preferences on the basis of experiments would enable us to see if future psycholinguistic work will confirm our hypothesis that the effects of usage statistics on adjective position in French is mediated by cognitive processes whereby linguistic representations are directly sensitive to the statistics of language use experienced by language users.

Acknowledgements. We would like to express our gratitude to Benoît Crabbé for his support and advise in the work that lead to this paper, and to the anonymous reviewers for their valuable comments.

References

1. Waugh, L.R.: A semantic analysis of word order: Position of the Adjective in French. E. J. Brill, Leiden (1977)
2. Forsgren, M.: La place de l'adjectif épithète en français contemporain, étude quantitative et sémantique. Almqvist & Wilksell, Stockholm (1978)
3. Wilmet, M.: La place de l'épithète qualificative en français contemporain: étude grammaticale et stylistique. Revue de Linguistique Romane 45, 17–73 (1981)
4. Delbecque, N.: Word order as a reflexion of alternate conceptual construals in french and spanish. Similarities and divergences in adjective position. Cognitive Linguistics 1, 349–416 (1990)
5. Nølke, H.: Où placer l'adjectif épithète? focalisation et modularité. Langue Française 111, 38–57 (1996)
6. Abeillé, A., Godard, D.: La position de l'adjectif èpithète en français: le poids des mots. Recherches Linguistiques de Vincennes 28, 9–32 (1999)
7. Noailly, M.: L'adjectif en français. Ophrys (1999)
8. Arnold, J.E., Wasow, T., Losongco, A., Ginstrom, R.: Heaviness vs. newness: the effects of structural complexity and discourse status on constituent ordering. Language 76(1), 28–55 (2000)
9. Rosenbach, A.: Animacy versus weight as determinants of grammatical variation in english. Language 81(3), 613–644 (2005)
10. Bresnan, J., Cueni, A., Nikitina, T., Baayen, H.: Predicting the dative alternation. In: Boume, G., Kraemer, I., Zwarts, J. (eds.) Cognitive Foundations of Interpretation. Royal Netherlands Academy of Science, Amsterdam (2007)
11. Abeillé, A., Barrier, N.: Enriching a french treebank. In: Proceedings of Language Ressources and Evaluation Conference (LREC), Lisbon (2004)
12. Grzegorz Chrupala, G.D., van Genabith, J.: Learning morphology with morfette. In: Calzolari, N., et al. (eds.) Proceedings of LREC 2008, Morocco. ELRA (2008)
13. Agresti, A.: An introduction to categorical data analysis. Wiley interscience (2007)
14. Harrell, F.E.: Regression modeling strategies: with applications to linear models, logistic regression, and survival analysis. Springer series in statistics. Springer (2001)

15. Bresnan, J., Ford, M.: Predicting syntax: Processing dative constructions in american and australian varieties of english. Language 86(1), 186–213 (2010)
16. Wasow, T.: Postverbal behavior. CSLI Publications (2002)
17. Hawkins, J.: Efficiency and Complexity in Grammars. Oxford University Press (2004)
18. Bybee, J., Mcclelland, J.L.: Alternatives to the combinatorial paradigm of linguistic theory based on domain general principles of human cognition. The Linguistic Review 22, 381–410 (2005)
19. Cooper, W.E., Ross, J.R.: World order. Papers from the Parasession on Functionalism, pp. 63–111. Chicago Linguistic Society (1975)
20. Benor, S.B., Levy, R.: The chicken or the egg? a probabilistic analysis of english binomials. Language 82(2), 28–55 (2006)
21. Hawkins, J.: The relative order of prepositional phrases in english: Going beyond manner-place-time. Language Variation and Change 11, 231–266 (2000)
22. Beaufort, R., Ruelle, A.: Elite: système de synthèse de la parole à orientation linguistique. In: Actes des XXVI Journées d'études sur la Parole, Dinard (2006)
23. Croft, W., Cruse, D.A.: Cognitive Linguistics. Cambridge University Press (2004)
24. Namer, F.: Acquisition automatique de sens à partir d'opérations morphologiques en français: étude de cas. In: Traitement Automatique de la Langue Naturelle, TALN (2002)
25. Tran, M., Maurel, D.: Prolexbase: Un dictionnaire relationnel multilingue de noms propres. Traitement Automatique des Langues 47(3), 115–139 (2006)
26. Bouchard, D.: The distribution and interpretation of adjectives in french: a consequence of bare phrase structure. Probus 10(2), 139–183 (1998)
27. Gross, G.: Les expressions figées en français: noms composés et autres locutions. Ophrys, Paris (1996)
28. Manning, C.D., Schütze, H.: Foundations of statistical natural language processing. MIT Press, Cambridge (1999)
29. Akaike, H.: A new look at the statistical model identification. IEEE Transactions on Automatic Control 19(6), 716–723 (1974)
30. Belsley, D.A., Kuh, E., Welsch, R.E.: Regression diagnostics: identifying influential data and sources of collinearity. Wiley, New-York (1980)
31. Bybee, J.: The emergent lexicon. In: Gruber, M.C., Higgins, D., Olson, K.S., Wysocki, T. (eds.) CLS 34: The Panels, University of Chicago, Chicago Linguistic Society (1998)
32. Croft, W.: Radical Construction Grammar. Oxford University Press (2001)
33. Goldberg, A.: Constructions at Work: the nature of generalization in language. Oxford University Press (2006)

Abductive Reasoning for Continual Dialogue Understanding

Miroslav Janíček

German Research Center for Artificial Intelligence (DFKI)
Stuhlsatzenhausweg 3, D-66123 Saarbrücken, Germany
miroslav.janicek@dfki.de

Abstract. In this paper we present a continual context-sensitive abductive framework for understanding situated spoken natural dialogue. The framework builds up and refines a set of partial defeasible explanations of the spoken input, trying to infer the speaker's intention. These partial explanations are conditioned on the eventual verification of the knowledge gaps they contain. This verification is done by executing test actions, thereby going beyond the initial context. The approach is illustrated by an example set in the context of human-robot interaction.

Keywords: Intention recognition, natural language understanding, abduction, context-sensitivity.

1 Introduction

In task-oriented dialogues between two agents, such as between two humans or a human and a robot, there is more to dialogue than just understanding words. The robot needs to understand what is being talked about, but it also needs to understand why it was told something. In other words, what the human *intends* the robot to do with the information in the larger context of their joint activity.

Therefore, understanding language can be phrased as an *intention recognition* problem: given an utterance from the human, how do we find the intention behind it?

In this paper, we explore an idea inspired by the field of continual planning [8], by explicitly capturing the possible knowledge gaps in such an interpretation. The idea is based on the notion of *assertion*, an explicit test for the validity of a certain fact, going beyond the current context.

The structure of the paper is as follows. After briefly introducing the notion of intention recognition, abduction and situatedness in the next section, we introduce the continual abductive reasoning mechanism in §3, and discuss it on an example in §4, before concluding with a short summary.

2 Background

The idea of expressing *understanding* in terms of intention recognition has been introduced by H. P. Grice [12,20]. In this paper, we build on Stone and Thomason's approach to the problem [23] who in turn extend the work done by Hobbs

D. Lassiter and M. Slavkovik (Eds.): ESSLLI Student Sessions, LNCS 7415, pp. 16–31, 2012.

and others [13], and base their approach to intention recognition on *abductive reasoning*.

2.1 Abduction

Abduction is a method of explanatory logical reasoning introduced into modern logic by Charles Sanders Peirce [11]. Given a theory T, a rule $T \vdash A \rightarrow B$ and a fact B, abduction allows inferring A as an explanation of B. B can be deductively inferred from $A \cup T$. If $T \not\vdash A$, then we say that A is an *assumption*.

There may be many possible causes of B besides A. Abduction amounts to *guessing*; assuming that the premise is true, the conclusion holds too. To give a well-known example:

> Suppose we are given two rules saying "if the sprinkler is on, then the lawn is wet" and "if it rained, then the lawn is wet". Abductively inferring the causes for the fact that the lawn is wet then yields two possible explanations: the sprinkler is on, or it rained.

Obviously, as there may be many possible explanations for a fact, in practical applications there needs to be a mechanism for selecting the best one. This may be done by purely syntactic means (e.g. lengths of proofs), or semantically by assigning *weights* to abductive proofs and selecting either the least or most costly proof [22], or by assigning probabilities to proofs [18]. In that case, the most probable proof is also assumed to be the best explanation. Our approach combines both aspects.

2.2 Intention Recognition

Abduction is a suitable mechanism to perform inferences on the pragmatic (discourse) level. For understanding, abduction can be used to infer the explanation *why* an agent said something, in other words the *intention* behind the utterance.

An intention is usually modelled as a goal-oriented cognitive state distinct from *desires* in that there is an explicit commitment to acting towards the goal and refraining from actions that may render it impossible to achieve [7,10].

For the purposes of this paper, we shall treat intentions as intended actions that have pre- and post-conditions, similar to planning operators in automated planning. Pre-conditions express the necessary conditions *before* the action is executed (and sufficient for its execution), and post-conditions express the necessary conditions *after* the action is executed.

Note that reasoning with intentions allows us to reverse the task, and search for appropriate (surface) presentation of a given intention [24]. Intentions can therefore serve as a middle representational layer and abduction as the inference mechanism by using which we either turn a realisation into an intention, or the other way around.

2.3 Situated Understanding

Suppose that a human user is dealing with a household robot capable of manipulating objects (finding them, picking them up, putting them down). The human wants the robot to bring him the mug from the kitchen, so he instructs the robot by saying:

> "Bring me the mug from the kitchen."

Now, what should the robot do? In the beginning, the utterance is just a stream of audio. The robot has to detect voice in the audio data, and if the speech recognition works well enough, it will be able to obtain the surface form of the utterance, i.e. the words that were spoken by the human.

Once the word sequence is recognised, the robot needs to assign linguistic structure to it so that it can reason about its logical structure. The logical structure of the utterance is typically not in any way related to the actual *situated* experience of the robot. The noun phrases "the mug" and "the kitchen" are just referring expressions *standing for* some entities in the real world, and can be manipulated as expressions using logical rules without the need to be concerned about value of the standing-for relation.

However, this relation is absolutely crucial to understanding what the human said and why. Without being able to reduce the referring expressions to the corresponding real-world entities there is no true understanding, and – more importantly – there can be no appropriate reaction, which presumably is one of the reasons why the human uttered the sentence in the first place (i.e. to elicit such a reaction).

Grounding the relation in reality is therefore a crucial task that any cognitive agent has to tackle. However, since all sensory perception is necessarily partial and subject to uncertainty, there is no guarantee that the "knowledge base", a formalisation of the current snapshot of the knowledge about the world, contains the information necessary for such a grounding. In other words, a situated agent cannot afford the luxury of reasoning under closed-world assumption, and has to venture beyond that.

This means that the robot must be able identify its knowledge gaps, and verify or falsify them *while* trying to understand the human's utterance. This implies that the processes of understanding an input and acting on it are interleaved and that there is a bi-directional interface between them.

3 Approach

This paper extends the work of Stone and Thomason on context-sensitive language understanding by explicitly modelling the knowledge gaps that inevitably arise in such an effort due to uncertainty and partial observability. The approach is based on generating partial hypotheses for the explanation of the observed behaviour of other agents, under the assumption that the observed behaviour is intentional. These partial hypotheses are defeasible and conditioned on the validity (and eventual verification) of their assumptions.

In this section, we examine the abductive reasoning system capable of representing knowledge gaps in the form of partial proofs, how such partial proofs can be generated and verified or falsified, and the semantic framework used in our system to capture linguistic meaning that the system then grounds in reality.

3.1   Partial Abductive Proofs

Our abductive inference mechanism is essentially Hobbs and Stickel's logic programming approach to weighted abduction [13,22] enhanced by a contextual aspect [3] with the weights in the system being assigned a probabilistic interpretation following Charniak and Shimony [9].

Abduction Context. Inference in our system makes use of four ingredients: *facts* (denoted $\mathcal{F}$), *rules* ($\mathcal{R}$), *disjoint declarations* ($\mathcal{D}$) and *assumability functions* ($\mathcal{S}$), collectively called the *abduction context*. The proof procedure uses these iteratively in order to derive proofs of an initial *goal*.

- *Facts* are modalised formulas of the form

$$\mu : A$$

  where μ is a (possibly empty) sequence of modal contexts, and A is an atomic formula, possibly containing variables.
- *Rules* are modalised Horn clauses, i.e. formulas of the form

$$(\mu_1 : A_1/t_1) \wedge \ldots \wedge (\mu_n : A_n/t_n) \to (\mu_H : H)$$

  where each of the $\mu_i : A_i$ and $\mu_H : H$ are modalised formulas. Each antecedent is annotated by t_i, which determines the way the antecedent is manipulated and is one of the following:
    - *assumable(f)* – the antecedent is assumable under function f;
    - *assertion* – the antecedent is asserted, i.e. identifies a knowledge gap, conditioning the validity of the proof on it being proved in a subsequent reinterpretation (see below).
- *Assumability functions* are partial functions f, $f : \mathcal{P}(\mathcal{F}) \to \mathbb{R}_0^+$, where $\mathcal{P}(\mathcal{F})$ is the set of modalised formulas, with the additional monotonicity property that if $F \in \mathrm{dom}(f)$, then for all more specific (in terms of variable substitution) facts F', $F' \in \mathrm{dom}(f)$ and $f(F) \leq f(F')$. We also define an empty ("truth") assumability function $\bot$ such that $\mathrm{dom}(\bot) = \emptyset$.

  Since they are partial functions, assumability functions determine both whether a modalised formula may be assumed and the cost of such an assumption. As a special case, the empty assumability function $\bot$ can be used to prevent the formula from being assumed altogether.
- A *disjoint declaration* is a statement of the form

$$\mathrm{disjoint}(\mu : A_1, \ldots, \mu : A_n)$$

  which specifies that at most one of the modalised formulas $\mu : A_i$ may be used in the proof. A_i and A_j cannot be unified for all $i \neq j$.

Proof Procedure. The proof procedure is an iterative rewriting process starting from some initial *goal* state. A *proof state* is a sequence of marked modalised formulas (called *queries* in this context)

$$Q_1[n_1], \ldots, Q_m[n_m]$$

The markings n_i are one of the following:

- *unsolved(f)* – the query is yet to be proved and can be assumed if it is in the domain of the assumability function f;
- *proved* – the query is proved in the proof state;
- *assumed(f)* – the query is assumed under assumability function f;
- *asserted* – the query is asserted – its validity is not to be determined in the current context.

Algorithm 1 defines the proof procedure in detail. The top-level function ABDUCE takes an abduction context c and a proof state Π, and returns a set of proof states that

    (1) are transformations of Π,
    (2) are consistent with c, and
    (3) do not contain any *unsolved* queries.

First, the input proof state is checked for validity with respect to the disjoint declarations $\mathcal{D}$ in the function IS-DISJOINT-VALID. If the check turns out to be negative, the proof state is discarded, and ABDUCE returns an empty set.

If Π satisfies the disjointness constraints, the function TF-DUP turns it into a set of proof states where unsolved queries that have already been proved, assumed or asserted are removed. The transformation returns a non-empty set of proof states. This step ensures that no query is examined more than once.

Next, each proof state resulting from TF-DUP is again checked whether it contains an unsolved query. If it does not, then the conditions (1)–(3) above are already fulfilled, and the proof state ends up in the result.

If it does, the proof procedure resolves the proof state against the facts, rules and assumability functions, collecting the results, and recursively calling ABDUCE on them so as to satisfy the above conditions.

Formally, given a proof state

$$\Pi = Q_1[n_1], \ldots, Q_m[n_m]$$

where Q_i is the leftmost query marked (guaranteed to exist at this point) as *unsolved(f)* where f is an assumability function, the transformation rules TF-FACT, TF-RULE and TF-ASSUME each return a (possibly empty) set of transformed proof states, and are defined as follows:

- TF-FACT (resolution with a fact): For all $Q \in \mathcal{F}$ such that the Q and Q_i are unifiable with a most general unifier σ (denoted $\sigma = \text{unify}(Q, Q_i)$), add a new state Π' to the result of the transformation:

$$\Pi' = Q_1\sigma[n_1], \ldots, Q_i\sigma[proved], \ldots Q_m\sigma[n_m]$$

- TF-RULE (resolution with a rule): For each rule $r \in \mathcal{R}$ of the form

$$G_1/t_1, \ldots, G_k/t_k \to H$$

(with variables renamed so that it has no variables in common with Π) such that there is a $\sigma = \text{unify}(H, Q_i)$, i.e. the rule head is unifiable with the unsolved query, add a new state Π' to the transformation result:

$$\begin{aligned}
\Pi' = \ &Q_1\sigma[n_1], \ldots, Q_{i-1}\sigma[n_{i-1}], \\
&G_1\sigma[p_1], \ldots, G_k\sigma[p_k], Q_i\sigma[proved], \\
&Q_{i+1}\sigma[n_{i+1}], \ldots, Q_m\sigma[n_m]
\end{aligned}$$

The query markings p_i are derived from t_i for all $i \in \{1, \ldots, k\}$ as follows:

$$\begin{aligned}
&\text{if } t_i = assumable(f), \text{ then } p_i = unsolved(f) \\
&\text{if } t_i = assertion, \qquad \text{then } p_i = asserted
\end{aligned}$$

- TF-ASSUME (assumption): If $Q \in \text{dom}(f)$ such that there is a most general unifier $\sigma = \text{unify}(Q, Q_i)$, add a new state Π' to result of the transformation:

$$\Pi' = Q_1\sigma[n_1], \ldots, Q_i\sigma[assumed(f)], \ldots, Q_n\sigma[n_m]$$

Note that the proof procedure along with the definition of assumability functions ensures that the cost of the proofs are monotonic with respect to unification and rule application, allowing for the use of efficient search strategies.

Knowledge Gaps and Assertions. Our extension of the "classical" logic-programming-based weighted abduction as proposed by Stickel and Hobbs lies in the extension of the proof procedure with the notion of *assertion* based on the work in continual automated planning [8], allowing the system to reason about information not present in the knowledge base, thereby addressing the need for reasoning under the open-world assumption.

In continual automated planning, assertions allow a planner to reason about information that is not known at the time of planning (for instance, planning for information gathering), an assertion is a construct specifying a "promise" that the information in question will be resolved eventually. Such a statement requires planning to be a step in a continual loop of interleaved planning and acting.

By using a logic programming approach, we can use unbound variables in the asserted facts in order to reason not only about the fact that the given assertion will be a fact, but also under-specify its eventual arguments.

The proposed notion of *assertion* for our abductive system is based on *test actions* $\langle F \rangle$ [4]. Baldoni et al. specify a test as a proof rule. In this rule, a goal F follows from a state $a_1, \ldots, a_n$ after steps $\langle F \rangle, p_1, \ldots, p_m$ if we can establish F on $a_1, \ldots, a_n$ with answer σ and this (also) holds in the final state resulting from executing $p_1, \ldots, p_m$.

An assertion is the transformation of a test into a partial proof which assumes the verification of the test, while at the same time conditioning the obtainability of the proof goal on the tested statements. $\mu : \langle D \rangle$ within a proof $\Pi[\langle D \rangle]$ to a goal C turns into $\Pi[D] \to C \wedge \mu : D$. Should $\mu : D$ not be verifiable, Π is invalidated.

Algorithm 1. Weighted abduction

$\textsc{abduce}(c = (\mathcal{F}, \mathcal{R}, \mathcal{D}, \mathcal{S}), \Pi = Q_1[n_1], \ldots, Q_m[n_m])$:

  if $\textsc{is-disjoint-valid}(\mathcal{D}, \Pi)$ **then**

    $R \leftarrow \emptyset$

    for all $\Pi' \in \textsc{tf-dup}(\Pi)$ **do**

      if Π' contains a query marked as *unsolved* **then**

        $H \leftarrow \textsc{tf-fact}(\mathcal{F}, \Pi') \cup \textsc{tf-rule}(\mathcal{R}, \Pi') \cup \textsc{tf-assume}(\mathcal{S}, \Pi')$

        $R \leftarrow R \cup \bigcup_{P \in H} \textsc{abduce}(c, P)$

      else

        $R \leftarrow R \cup \{\Pi'\}$

      end if

    end for

    return R

  else

    return $\emptyset$

  end if

$\textsc{is-disjoint-valid}(\mathcal{D}, \Pi = Q_1[n_1], \ldots, Q_m[n_m])$:

  for all $d = \text{disjoint}(D_1, \ldots, D_q) \in \mathcal{D}$ **do**

    if $\exists i \neq j \neq k \neq l$ s.t. $\exists \sigma, \sigma'$: $\sigma = \text{unify}(D_i, Q_k)$ and $\sigma' = \text{unify}(D_j, Q_l)$ **then**

      return false

    end if

  end for

  return true

$\textsc{tf-dup}(\Pi = Q_1[n_1], \ldots, Q_m[n_m])$:

  if Π contains a query marked as *unsolved* **then**

    $i \leftarrow \arg\min_{j \in \{1, \ldots, m-1\}}(\exists f \text{ s.t. } n_j = unsolved(f))$

    $H \leftarrow \emptyset$

    for all $s \in \{i+1, \ldots, m\}$ s.t. $\text{unify}(Q_i, Q_s) = \sigma$ **do**

      $H \leftarrow H \cup \textsc{tf-dup}(Q_1\sigma[n_1], \ldots, Q_{i-1}\sigma[n_{i-1}], Q_{i+1}\sigma[n_{i+1}] \ldots, Q_m\sigma[n_m])$

    end for

    if $H \neq \emptyset$ **then return** H **else return** $\{\Pi\}$ **end if**

  else

    return $\{\Pi\}$

  end if

Probabilistic Interpretation. In weighted abduction, weights assigned to assumed queries are used to calculate the overall proof cost. The proof with the lowest cost is the best explanation. However, weights are usually not assigned any semantics, and often a significant effort by the writer of the rule set is required to achieve expected results [13].

However, Charniak and Shimony [9] showed that by setting weights to $-\log$ of the prior probability of the query, the resulting proofs can be given probabilistic semantics.

Suppose that query Q_k can be assumed true with some probability $P(Q_k$ is true$)$. Then if Q_k is assumable under assumability function f such that $f(Q_k) = -\log(P(Q_k$ is true$))$, and under the independence assumption, we can represent the overall probability of the proof $\Pi = Q_1[n_1], ..., Q_n[n_m]$ as

$$P(\Pi) = e^{\sum_{k=1}^{m} cost(Q_k)}$$

where

$$cost(Q_k) = \begin{cases} f(Q_k) & \text{if } n_k = assumed(f) \\ 0 & \text{otherwise} \end{cases}$$

The best explanation Π_{best} of a the goal state G is then

$$\Pi_{best} = \underset{\Pi \text{ proof of } G}{\arg\min} \; P(\Pi)$$

Exact inference in such a system is NP-complete, and so is approximate inference given a threshold [9]. However, it is straightforward to give an anytime version of the algorithm – simply by performing iterative deepening depth-first search [19] and memorising a list of most probable proofs found so far.

Comparison with Other Approaches. Our system is similar to Poole's Probabilistic Horn abduction [18]. The main difference, apart from the proof procedure which is cost-based in our case, is that we do not include probabilities in our formulation of disjoint declarations. Since we avoid duplicate assumptions, we are able to model the semantics of disjoint declarations with probabilities.

On the other hand, having a general disjoint declaration allows us to define exclusivity rules such as

$$\text{disjoint}([\text{p}(X, \text{yes}), \text{p}(X, \text{no})])$$

without having to specify the prior probabilities of the disjuncts.

Moreover, in our rule sets for natural language understanding and generation, we need to be able to manipulate logical structure (e.g. logical forms of utterances) efficiently. We have found that the logic-programming-based approach is quite satisfactory in this aspect, since it permits the use of standard Prolog programming techniques. In approaches to probabilistic abduction that are *not* based on logic programming, such as Kate and Mooney's abduction in Markov Logic Networks [15], these techniques are not applicable, which crucially limits their applicability to our domain.

Algorithm 2. (Nondeterministic) continual abduction

CONTINUAL-ABDUCTION(c, Π):
    $c = $ context
    $\Pi = $ proof

    while Π contains assertion A **do**
        $c' \leftarrow$ TEST-ACTION(c, A)
        $H \leftarrow$ ABDUCE(c', A)
        for all $\Pi' \in H$ **do**
            CONTINUAL-ABDUCTION(c', Π')
        end for
    end while
    return Π

3.2 Generating Partial Hypotheses

For each goal G, a the function ABDUCE returns a set of proofs H, with a total ordering on this set. Due to the use of assertions, some of these proofs may be partial, and their validity has to be verified. The presence of assertions in the proofs means that there is a knowledge gap, namely the truth value of the assertion. Each assertion thus specifies the need for performing a (test) action. This action might require the access to other knowledge bases than the abductive context, as in the case of resolving referring expressions, or an execution of a physical action.

Formally, given an initial goal G and context c, the abduction procedure produces a set H of hypotheses $c : \Pi \to C \wedge c_i : A_i$, where c_i is a sub-context in which where an assertion $A_i \in \Pi$ may be evaluated. Such proofs are thus both *partial* and *defeasible* — they may be both extended and discarded, depending on the evaluation of the assertions.

The set of possible hypotheses is continuously expanded until the best full proof is found. This process is defined in Algorithm 2.

The algorithm defines the search space in which it is possible to find the most probable proof of the initial goal G. The important point is, however, that it is just that — a definition. The actual implementation may keep track of the partial hypotheses it defines, and take the appropriate test actions when necessary, or postpone them indefinitely. The cost of *performing* an action is not factored into the overall proof cost.

The partial hypotheses therefore serve as an interface layer between the language understanding and external decision-making processes (such as planning in a robotic architecture).

3.3 Representing Linguistic Meaning

For representing linguistic meaning in our system we use the *Hybrid Logic Dependency Semantics* (HLDS), a hybrid logic framework that provides the means for encoding a wide range of semantic information, including dependency relations between heads and dependents [21], tense and aspect [17], spatio-temporal structure, contextual reference, and information structure [16].

Hybrid Logic. Classical modal logic suffers from a surprising "asymmetry". Although the concept of states ("worlds") is at the heart of model theory, there is no way to directly reference specific states in the object language. This asymmetry is at the root of several theoretical and practical problems facing modal logic [6,1].

Hybrid logic provides an elegant solution to many of these problems. It extends standard modal logic with *nominals*, another sort of basic formulas that explicitly name worlds in the object language. Next to propositions, nominals—and, by extension, possible worlds—therefore become first-class citizens in the object language. The resulting logical framework retains decidability and favourable complexity [2].

Each nominal names a unique state. To get to that state, a new operator is added, the *satisfaction operator*. The satisfaction operator that enables us to "jump" to the state named by a nominal. The satisfaction operator is written $@_i$, where i is a nominal.

Formally, let $\text{PROP} = \{p, q, ...\}$ be a set of propositional symbols, $\text{MOD} = \{\pi, \pi', ...\}$ a set of modality labels, and $\text{NOM} = \{i, j, ...\}$ a non-empty set disjoint from PROP and MOD. We define the well-formed formulas of the basic hybrid multimodal language $\mathcal{L}_@$ over PROP, MOD and NOM as such:

$$\phi ::= i \mid p \mid \neg\phi \mid \phi \to \varphi \mid \langle\pi\rangle\phi \mid [\pi]\phi \mid @_i\phi$$

A formula $@_i\phi$ states that the formula ϕ holds at the unique state named by i. In more operational terms, the formula $@_i\phi$ could be translated in the following way: "go to the (unique!) state named by i, and check whether ϕ is true at that state".

Hybrid Logic Dependency Semantics. HLDS uses hybrid logic to capture dependency complexity in a model-theoretic relational structure, using ontological sorting to capture categorial aspects of linguistic meaning, and naturally capture (co-)reference by explicitly using *nominals* in the representation. The dependency structures can be derived from CCG [5], which is the setup used in our system, but other approaches are possible.

Generally speaking, HLDS represents an expression's linguistic meaning as a conjunction of modalised terms, anchored by the nominal that identifies the head's proposition:

$$@_{h:\text{sort}_h} (\mathbf{prop}_h \wedge \langle\mathsf{R}_i\rangle \, (d_i : \text{sort}_{d_i} \wedge \mathbf{dep}_i))$$

Here, the head proposition nominal is h. $\mathbf{prop}_h$ represents the *elementary predication* of the nominal h. The dependency relations (such as Agent, Patient, Subject, etc.) are modelled as modal relations $\langle R_i \rangle$, with the dependent being identified by a nominal d_i. Features attached to a nominal (e.g. $\langle\mathsf{Num}\rangle$ $\langle\mathsf{Quantification}\rangle$, etc.) are specified in the same way.

Figure 1 gives an example of HLDS representation (logical form) of the sentence "Bring me the mug from the kitchen". The logical form has six nominals, $event_1$, $agent_1$, $person_1$, $thing_1$, $from_1$ and $thing_1$, that form a dependency structure: $event_1$ is the the head of dependency relations Actor (the dependent being $agent_1$), Patient ($thing_1$), Recipient ($person_1$), Modifier ($from_1$), and Subject (the sentence subject, $agent_1$).

Each nominal has an ontological sort (illustrated on $event_1$, the sort is action-non-motion) a proposition (**bring**), and may have features (Mood).

$$@_{event_1 : \text{action-non-motion}}(\textbf{bring} \wedge$$
$$\langle \text{Mood} \rangle \ \textbf{imp} \wedge$$
$$\langle \text{Actor} \rangle \ (agent_1 : \text{entity} \wedge \textbf{addressee})$$
$$\langle \text{Patient} \rangle \ (thing_1 : \text{thing} \wedge \textbf{mug} \wedge$$
$$\langle \text{Delimitation} \rangle \ \textbf{unique} \wedge$$
$$\langle \text{Num} \rangle \ \textbf{sg} \wedge$$
$$\langle \text{Quantification} \rangle \ \textbf{specific}) \wedge$$
$$\langle \text{Recipient} \rangle \ (person_1 : \text{person} \wedge \textbf{I} \wedge$$
$$\langle \text{Num} \rangle \ \textbf{sg}) \wedge$$
$$\langle \text{Modifier} \rangle \ (from_1 : \text{m-wherefrom} \wedge \textbf{from} \wedge$$
$$\langle \text{Anchor} \rangle \ (place_1 : \text{e-place} \wedge \textbf{kitchen} \wedge$$
$$\langle \text{Delimitation} \rangle \ \textbf{unique} \wedge$$
$$\langle \text{Num} \rangle \ \textbf{sg} \wedge$$
$$\langle \text{Quantification} \rangle \ \textbf{specific})) \wedge$$
$$\langle \text{Subject} \rangle \ agent_1 : \text{entity})$$

Fig. 1. HLDS semantics for the utterance "Bring me the mug from the kitchen"

Every logical form in HLDS, being a formula in hybrid logic, can be decomposed into a set of facts in the abductive context corresponding to its minimal Kripke model. The resulting set of abduction facts obtained by decomposing the logical form in Figure 1 is shown by Figure 3.

HLDS only represents the meaning as derived from the linguistic realisation of the utterance and does not evaluate the state of affairs denoted by it. This sets the framework apart from semantic formalisms such as DRT [14]. The grounding in reality is partly provided by the continual abductive framework by generating and validating (or ruling out) partial abductive hypotheses as more information is added to the system.

4   Example

Let us examine the mechanism in an example introduced in §2.3.

The human's utterance,

"Bring me the mug from the kitchen."

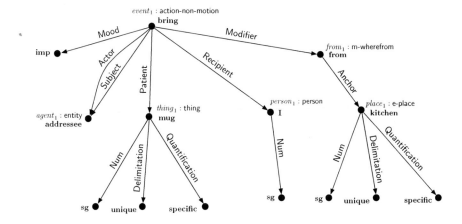

Fig. 2. Minimal model for the hybrid logic formula in Figure 1

is analysed in terms of HLDS (see Figure 1), and its translation (see Figure 3) is made part of the abduction context c.

The robot tries to make sense of the utterance by proving the goal

$$\text{uttered}(\text{human}, \text{robot}, \text{event}_1)$$

in the abduction context c. Suppose that the best proof state returned by AB-DUCE is the following:

$\text{uttered}(\text{human}, \text{robot}, \text{event}_1)\ [proved]$	(1)
$\text{prop}(\text{event}_1, \text{bring})\ [proved]$	(2)
$\text{intends}(\text{event}_1, \text{human}, I)\ [assumed(engagement)]$	(3)
$\text{rel}(\text{event}_1, \text{patient}, \text{thing}_1)\ [proved]$	(4)
$\text{refers-to}(\text{thing}_1, X)\ [asserted]$	(5)
$\text{refers-to}(\text{place}_1, P)\ [asserted]$	(6)
$\text{pre}(I, \text{object}(X)\ [asserted]$	(7)
$\text{pre}(I, \text{is-in}(X, P))\ [asserted]$	(8)
$\text{refers-to}(\text{person}_1, \text{human})\ [proved]$	(9)
$\text{prop}(\text{person}_1, i)\ [proved]$	(10)
$\text{rel}(\text{event}_1, \text{recipient}, \text{person}_1)\ [proved]$	(11)
$\text{post}(I, \text{has}(\text{human}, X))\ [proved]$	(12)

The proof is an explanation of the event (1) in terms of a partially specified intention I (3), defined by its pre- and post-conditions. The pre-conditions are the existence of an entity X (7) and that X is located *in* another entity P (8). The post-condition (12) is the resulting state in which the human has X (12).

The proof appeals to the logical form of the utterance in atoms (2), (4), (10), (11). Also, atom (9) is proved from (1) and (10) (whoever uses "I" refers to themselves), and (12) is a consequence of (2), (9) and (11) (bringing x to a person p means ending up in a state in which p has x).

$$\text{sort}(\text{event}_1, \text{action-non-motion}),$$
$$\text{prop}(\text{event}_1, \text{bring}),$$
$$\text{feat}(\text{event}_1, \text{mood}, \text{imp}),$$
$$\text{rel}(\text{event}_1, \text{actor}, \text{agent}_1),$$
$$\text{sort}(\text{agent}_1, \text{entity}),$$
$$\text{prop}(\text{agent}_1, \text{addressee}),$$
$$\text{rel}(\text{event}_1, \text{patient}, \text{thing}_1),$$
$$\text{sort}(\text{thing}_1, \text{thing}),$$
$$\text{prop}(\text{thing}_1, \text{mug}),$$
$$\text{feat}(\text{thing}_1, \text{delimitation}, \text{unique}),$$
$$\text{feat}(\text{thing}_1, \text{num}, \text{sg}),$$
$$\text{feat}(\text{thing}_1, \text{quantification}, \text{specific}),$$
$$\text{rel}(\text{event}_1, \text{recipient}, \text{person}_1),$$
$$\text{sort}(\text{person}_1, \text{person}),$$
$$\text{prop}(\text{person}_1, \text{i}),$$
$$\text{feat}(\text{person}_1, \text{num}, \text{sg}),$$
$$\text{rel}(\text{event}_1, \text{modifier}, \text{from}_1),$$
$$\text{sort}(\text{from}_1, \text{m-wherefrom}),$$
$$\text{prop}(\text{from}_1, \text{from}),$$
$$\text{rel}(\text{from}_1, \text{anchor}, \text{place}_1),$$
$$\text{sort}(\text{place}_1, \text{e-place}),$$
$$\text{prop}(\text{place}_1, \text{kitchen}),$$
$$\text{feat}(\text{place}_1, \text{delimitation}, \text{unique}),$$
$$\text{feat}(\text{place}_1, \text{num}, \text{sg}),$$
$$\text{feat}(\text{place}_1, \text{quantification}, \text{specific}),$$
$$\text{rel}(\text{event}_1, \text{subject}, \text{agent}_1)$$

Fig. 3. The translation of the hybrid logic formula in Figure 1 into abduction facts

Atom (3) is assumed under the assumability function *engagement*, which is supplied in the abduction context before calling ABDUCE and specifies the robot's subjective probability of being engaged in a conversation with the particular human at the time the utterance was observed.

Note that the proof state contains four atoms marked as assertions: (5), (6), (7) and (8). These are the explicit gaps in the proof that make it a partial interpretation. They are chosen by the domain engineer, and since they need to be verified (or falsified) by an external process, they form the interface to external knowledge bases and decision-making. Since for now those atoms are marked as asserted, there is nothing more that ABDUCE can do.

The initiative then shifts to an external decision-making process. It selects some of the assertions, and tries to verify them.

A sensible strategy[1] might be to first establish the referent of *place*$_1$. This could be resolved against the internal knowledge base (in case the robot has been given a tour of the household), or it could trigger the exploration behaviour – in order to resolve *place*$_1$, the robot could try finding it first. Again, choosing which

---

[1] Note that the problem of what determing good verification strategies and choosing them is beyond the scope of this paper.

behaviour is more appropriate depends on the application, and on the planning method that is invoked by the decision-maker in order to verify the assertion.

Once the assertion is verified, the proof is updated accordingly, in our case by replacing all occurrences by replacing the unbound variable P by a unique symbol, for instance by the identifier $id_{kitchen}$ of the topological region in the robot's topological map:

$$\frac{\text{refers-to}(\text{place}_1, id_{kitchen}) \; [proved] \qquad (6')}{\text{resolves-to-toporegion}(\text{place}_1, id_{kitchen}) \; [assumed(topo)] \; (6'')}$$

The atom (6) in the original proof state is expanded by a proof state consisting of queries (6') and (6''), thereby replacing P in the entire proof by $id_{kitchen}$, and adding the cost of assuming (6'') to the overall proof cost. This atom is assumed under an assumability function $topo$, supplied as part of the abduction context in which the proof is expanded – i.e. by the external knowledge source. An assumption is added instead of a fact so that the external knowledge base performing this operation can express uncertainty about the resolution result.

The proof is therefore expanded into the following:

$$\frac{\text{uttered}(\text{human}, \text{robot}, \text{event}_1) \; [proved] \qquad\qquad\qquad (1)}{\begin{array}{ll} \text{prop}(\text{event}_1, \text{bring}) \; [proved] & (2) \\ \text{intends}(\text{event}_1, \text{human}, I) \; [assumed(engagement)] & (3) \\ \text{rel}(\text{event}_1, \text{patient}, \text{thing}_1) \; [proved] & (4) \\ \text{refers-to}(\text{thing}_1, X) \; [asserted] & (5) \\ \text{refers-to}(\text{place}_1, id_{kitchen}) \; [proved] & (6') \\ \text{resolves-to-toporegion}(\text{place}_1, id_{kitchen}) \; [assumed(topo)] & (6'') \\ \text{pre}(I, \text{object}(X)) \; [asserted] & (7) \\ \text{pre}(I, \text{is-in}(X, id_{kitchen})) \; [asserted] & (8) \\ \text{refers-to}(\text{person}_1, \text{human}) \; [proved] & (9) \\ \text{prop}(\text{person}_1, i) \; [proved] & (10) \\ \text{rel}(\text{event}_1, \text{recipient}, \text{person}_1) \; [proved] & (11) \\ \text{post}(I, \text{has}(\text{human}, X)) \; [proved] & (12) \end{array}}$$

Now there are just three assertions left: (5), (7) and (8). These express the knowledge gaps about the referent of "the mug", the existence of the object, and its location, respectively.

There are, as before, several possible ways of verifying these. The most sensible one would probably be going to the kitchen (i.e. the topological region $id_{kitchen}$) and searching for objects there, which would verify both (8) and (7) and expand them with all objects it finds. There would be many parallel proof states resulting from such an expansion, and the robot would have to prune them down by verifying the remaining assertion (5).

One way of doing that would be to bring all objects one by one to the human, asking "did you mean this one?" Alternatively, the robot might simply bring the most likely object. The human's acceptance of the choice would then verify the assertion. This is, again, a matter for consideration in the higher level of planning and goal management.

5 Conclusion

This paper presents an abductive framework for natural language understanding that is based on abductive reasoning over partial hypotheses. The framework is set within the process of intention recognition.

The abductive framework is contextually-enhanced version of a logic programming approach to weighted abduction with a probabilistic semantics assigned to the weights. Our extension of this framework is in the introduction of the notion of *assertion*, which is essentially a requirement for a future test to verify or falsify the proposition, i.e. to fill a knowledge gap about the validity of the proposition. The hypotheses are therefore defeasible in the sense that the falsification of their assertions leads to a retraction and adoption of an initially less likely alternative.

By explicitly reasoning about these knowledge gaps, the system is able to go beyond the current context and knowledge base, addressing the need for reasoning under the open-world assumption. The responsibility for filling those knowledge gaps then falls to external decision-making processes. These processes can then use probabilities to express their confidence in the solutions they provide, thereby addressing the need for capturing the ubiquitous uncertainty stemming from unreliable sensory perception and partial observability of the world.

Acknowledgments. The work reported in this paper has been supported by the EU ICT FP7 projects CogX, "Cognitive Systems that Self-Understand and Self-Extend" (project no. 215181) and NIFTi, "Natural Human-Robot Collaboration in Dynamic Environments" (project no. 247870).

The author would like to thank Geert-Jan Kruijff for insightful and inspiring discussions, and the anonymous reviewers for their detailed and very helpful comments.

References

1. Areces, C.: Logic Engineering: The Case of Description and Hybrid Logics. Ph.D. thesis, University of Amsterdam, The Netherlands (2000)
2. Areces, C., Blackburn, P.: Bringing them all together. Journal of Logic and Computation 11(5), 657–669 (2001)
3. Baldoni, M., Giordano, L., Martelli, A.: A modal extension of logic programming: Modularity, beliefs and hypothetical reasoning. J. Log. Comp. 8(5), 597–635 (1998)
4. Baldoni, M., Giordano, L., Martelli, A., Patti, V.: A modal programming language for representing complex actions. In: Proc. of DYNAMICS 1998, pp. 1–15 (1998)
5. Baldridge, J., Kruijff, G.J.M.: Coupling CCG and Hybrid Logic Dependency Semantics. In: Proceedings of the 40th Annual Meeting of the Association for Computational Linguistics, ACL (2002)
6. Blackburn, P.: Representation, reasoning, and relational structures: a hybrid logic manifesto. Logic Journal of the IGPL 8(3), 339–625 (2000)
7. Bratman, M.: Intentions, Plans, and Practical Reason. Harvard University Press, Cambridge (1987)
8. Brenner, M., Nebel, B.: Continual planning and acting in dynamic multiagent environments. Journal of Autonomous Agents and Multiagent Systems (2008)

9. Charniak, E., Shimony, S.E.: Probabilistic semantics for cost based abduction. In: AAAI 1990 Proceedings (1990)
10. Cohen, P.R., Levesque, H.J.: Intention is choice with commitment. Artificial Intelligence 42, 213–261 (1990)
11. Fann, K.T.: Peirce's Theory of Abduction. Mouton, The Hague (1970)
12. Grice, H.P.: Meaning. The Philosophical Review 66(3), 377–388 (1957)
13. Hobbs, J.R., Stickel, M.E., Appelt, D.E., Martin, P.A.: Interpretation as abduction. Artificial Intelligence 63(1-2), 69–142 (1993)
14. Kamp, H., Reyle, U.: From Discourse to Logic. Kluwer, Dordrecht (1993)
15. Kate, R.J., Mooney, R.J.: Probabilistic abduction using Markov logic networks. In: Proceedings of the IJCAI 2009 Workshop on Plan, Activity, and Intent Recognition (PAIR 2009), Pasadena, CA, USA (2009)
16. Kruijff, G.J.M.: A Categorial-Modal Logical Architecture of Informativity: Dependency Grammar Logic & Information Structure. Ph.D. thesis, Faculty of Mathematics and Physics, Charles University, Prague, Czech Republic (2001)
17. Moens, M., Steedman, M.: Temporal ontology and temporal reference. Computational Linguistics 14(2), 15–28 (1988)
18. Poole, D.: Probabilistic Horn abduction and Bayesian networks. Artificial Intelligence 64(1), 81–129 (1993)
19. Russell, S.J., Norvig, P.: Artificial Intelligence: A Modern Approach, 2nd edn. Prentice Hall, Upper Saddle River (2003)
20. Schiffer, S.R.: Meaning. Clarendon Press, Oxford (1972)
21. Sgall, P., Hajičová, E., Panevová, J.: The Meaning of the Sentence in Its Semantic and Pragmatic Aspects. Reidel Publishing Company, Academia, Dordrecht, Prague (1986)
22. Stickel, M.E.: A Prolog-like inference system for computing minimum-cost abductive explanations in natural-language interpretation. Annals of Mathematics and Artificial Intelligence 4, 89–105 (1991)
23. Stone, M., Thomason, R.H.: Context in abductive interpretation. In: Proceedings of EDILOG 2002: 6th Workshop on the Semantics and Pragmatics of Dialogue (2002)
24. Stone, M., Thomason, R.H.: Coordinating understanding and generation in an abductive approach to interpretation. In: Proceedings of DIABRUCK 2003: 7th Workshop on the Semantics and Pragmatics of Dialogue (2003)

SCA: Phonetic Alignment Based on Sound Classes

Johann-Mattis List

Heinrich Heine University Düsseldorf
`listm@phil.uni-duesseldorf.de`

Abstract. In this paper I present the most recent version of the SCA method for pairwise and multiple alignment analyses. In contrast to previously proposed alignment methods, SCA is based on a novel framework of sequence alignment which combines new approaches to sequence modeling in historical linguistics with recent developments in computational biology. In contrast to earlier versions of SCA [1, 2] the new version comes along with a couple of modifications that significantly improve the performance and the application range of the algorithm: A new sound class model was defined which works well on highly divergent sequences, the algorithm for pairwise alignment was modified to be sensitive to secondary sequence structures such as syllable boundaries, and an algorithm for the pre-processing of the data in multiple alignment analyses [3] was included to cope for the bias resulting from progressive alignment analyses. In order to test the method, a new gold standard for pairwise and multiple alignment analyses was created which consists of 45 947 sequences covering a total of 435 different taxa belonging to six different language families.

1 Introduction

During the last two decades there has been an increasing interest in automatic approaches to historical linguistics which is reflected in a large amount of literature on phylogenetic reconstruction [4, 5], statistical aspects of genetic relationship [6, 7], and automatic approaches to sequence comparison [8–10]. In this context phonetic alignment plays a crucial role since it constitutes the first step of the traditional comparative method which seeks to detect regular sound correspondences in the lexical material of the languages of the world in order to determine cognate words and to prove their genetic relationship.

The SCA (**S**ound-**C**lass-Based Phonetic **A**lignment) method for pairwise and multiple phonetic alignment, whose most recent version shall be presented in the following, differs from previously proposed alignment methods [8, 9, 11] in so far as it is based on a new framework of sequence modeling which closely mimics traditional manual approaches. SCA is implemented as part of the LingPy library[1], a suite of open source Python modules with C++ extensions for time-consuming

---

[1] Online available under `http://lingulist.de/lingpy`.

D. Lassiter and M. Slavkovik (Eds.): ESSLLI Student Sessions, LNCS 7415, pp. 32–51, 2012.
© Springer-Verlag Berlin Heidelberg 2012

and memory-intensive operations which provides solutions for different quantitative tasks in historical linguistics, and can be invoked from the Python prompt or in Python scripts.

2   Sequence Comparison in Historical Linguistics

Comparison plays a crucial role in historical linguistics. It constitutes the basis of the *comparative method* which takes similarities in the lexical material of different languages as evidence to prove their genetic relationship and to uncover unattested ancestor languages by means of linguistic reconstruction [12]. The basis of the reconstruction of proto-languages within the framework of the comparative method is the identification of *cognates* within languages which are assumed to be genetically related. Cognates are words or morphemes which are descendants of a common ancestor word or morpheme [13, pp. 62f]. The identification of cognates is based on a recursive procedure which starts from a small sample of presumed cognate words taken from different language varieties. These words are then compared for *sound correspondences*, i.e. sound pairs which recurrently occur in similar positions of the presumed cognate words [13, pp. 336f]. Once a preliminary sample of such sound correspondences is identified, the initial samples of presumed cognate words and sound correspondences are repeatedly modified by adding and removing words or correspondence pairs from the samples depending on whether they are consistent with the rest of the data or not.

The specific strength of this procedure is its underlying similarity measure. The similarity between words is determined on the basis of *functionally corresponding phonetic segments* as opposed to similarity based on *surface resemblances*. Comparing, for example, English *token* [təʊkən] and German *Zeichen* [tsaɪçən] "sign", the comparative method may prove that these words are cognates, despite the fact that they do not sound quite similar, since their sound segments can be shown to correspond regularly regarding their distinctive function within other cognates of both languages.[2] In the literature, this notion of similarity has been called *genotypic* as opposed to a *phenotypic* notion of similarity [14, p. 130].

The main comparanda in historical linguistics are *phonetic sequences* (words, morphemes). Generally spoken, sequences are ordered collections of objects whose identity is a product of both their *order* and their *content*. The objects of sequences, the *segments*, receive distinctivity only due to their specific composition. The comparison of sequences requires the comparison of both the structure and the substance of the segments constituting a sequence. This comparison is usually carried out within the framework of *alignment analyses*. In alignment analyses two or more sequences are arranged in a matrix in such a way that all corresponding segments appear in the same column, while empty cells of the matrix, resulting from non-corresponding segments, are filled with gap symbols [15,

---

[2] Compare, for example, English *weak* [ʋiːk] vs. German *weich* [vaɪç] "soft" for the correspondence of [k] with [ç], and English *tongue* [tʌŋ] vs. German *Zunge* [tsʊŋə] "tongue" for the correspondence of [t] with [ts].

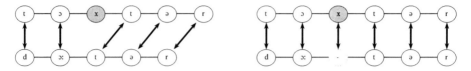

Fig. 1. Alignment analysis of German *Tochter* and English *daughter*

p. 216]. Basically, an alignment analysis consists of two steps. In the first step, corresponding segments are identified, and in the second step, gap symbols (usually a dash -) are introduced as placeholders for non-corresponding segments, as illustrated in Fig. 1 for the sequences German *Tochter* [tɔxtər] "daughter" and English *daughter* [dɔːtər].

Although the term "alignment" has never been explicitly used in historical linguistics, it is obvious that the identification of sound correspondences inevitably relies on sequence alignment, since functionally corresponding sound segments could otherwise not be identified. The traditional analysis in the framework of the comparative method, however, is mostly restricted to a qualitative comparison that leaves it to the researcher to decide which segments are matched and which are not.

3   Automatic Alignment Analyses

The algorithmic basis of automatic alignment analyses was developed quite early. In the begin of the seventies, independent scholarly teams proposed the first algorithms for pairwise sequence alignment [16, 17]. Although up to today – especially in such disciplines as computational biology – many modifications and refinements to the basic algorithm have been proposed, and new improved methods are being constantly developed, it was only recently that historical linguists became interested in automatizing their traditional manual methods.

3.1   The Basic Algorithm for Pairwise Sequence Alignment

The basic algorithm for pairwise sequence alignment (PSA) belongs to the family of *dynamic programming algorithms* (DPA) [18]. The main idea of dynamic programming is to find an approach for the solution of complicated problems 'that essentially works the problem backwards' [19, p. 4]. Thus, instead of calculating all possible alignments between two sequences, the DPA for pairwise sequence alignment '[builds] up an optimal alignment using previous solutions for optimal alignments of smaller subsequences' [20, p. 19]. This is done by creating a matrix which confronts all segments of the sequences under comparison either with each other or with alternative null-sequences (gaps). In a further step, the algorithm recursively calculates the total scores for the optimal alignment of all subsequences by filling the matrix from top to bottom and from left to right. Once the score for one subsequence has been determined, the score for a larger subsequence can also be calculated. In each step of the recursion, a specific

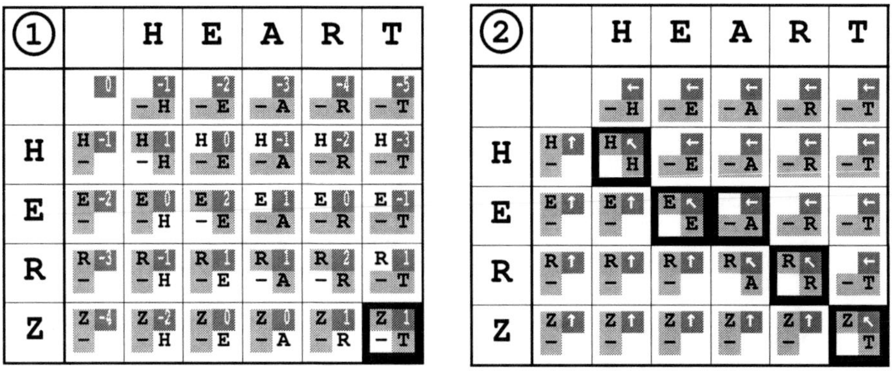

Fig. 2. The DPA matrix for the alignment of the strings `"HEART"` and `"HERZ"`

scoring function evaluates whether the segments in the respective cell of the matrix should be matched with themselves or with one of the gap characters. Once the matrix is filled, the value in the last cell of the matrix yields the general score of the alignment of the sequences. The alignment is then obtained by applying a *traceback function* which finds the 'path of choices [...] which led to this final value' [20, p. 19].

The alignment of the strings `"HEART"` and `"HERZ"` is illustrated in Fig. 2. ① shows the completed alignment matrix for a scoring function which penalizes mismatches and gaps with −1 and matches with 1. ② illustrates the traceback procedure.

3.2 Common Extensions of the Basic Algorithm

Many modifications of the basic algorithm have been proposed in order to address specific alignment problems. Among these modifications one can distinguish those which deal with the structure of sequences (*structural extensions*), and those which deal with their substance (*substantial extensions*). The former are based on the modification of the main recursion part of the algorithm, while the latter deal with the scoring function.

From a structural perspective, the basic algorithm aligns two sequences *globally*. All segments of the sequences are treated equally. Possible prefixes, infixes, and postfixes contribute equally to the alignment score. A *global alignment* may, however, not be what one wants to achieve with an alignment analysis. Often, only specific domains of two sequences are comparable, while others are not. This problem is addressed in *local alignment analyses* where 'subsections of the sequences are aligned without reference to global patterns' [19, p. 12]. The most common solution for local alignment, the Smith-Waterman algorithm [21], seeks for the best alignment between subsequences of the sequences. While in this approach, only the most similar subsequences are aligned and the rest of the sequences is ignored, other approaches proceed globally while at the same time being more sensitive to local similarities. Thus, the algorithm for *semi-global alignment* (or *alignment with overlap matches* [20, p. 26f]) is especially

Table 1. Comparing the output of different alignment modes

Mode	Alignment
global	G R E E N . C A T F I S H . H U N T E R A . F A T . C A T - - - - . H U N T E R
local	green catfish H U N T E R a fat cat H U N T E R
semi-global	G R E E N - . C A T F I S H . H U N T E R - - - - - A . F A T . C A T . H U N T E R
diagonal	- - - - - G R E E N . C A T F I S H . H U N T E R A . F A T - - - - - . C A T - - - - . H U N T E R

useful for the alignment of sequences containing different prefixes or suffixes, since it doesn't penalize gaps which are introduced in the beginning or the end of the sequences. The DIALIGN algorithm [22] for *diagonal alignment* proceeds globally while at the same time trying to find the best-scoring ungapped alignments of two subsequences (*diagonals*). The differences between global, local, semi-global, and diagonal alignment are illustrated in Tab. 1, where the strings `"GREEN.CATFISH.HUNTER"` and `"A.FAT.CAT.HUNTER"` are aligned according to the different modes.

The structural extensions can help to enhance alignment analyses significantly, depending on the respective goal of the alignment analysis. The most important aspect of all alignment analyses, however, is the comparison on the segment level. This comparison is handled by the scoring function which penalizes the matching of segments and the introduction of gaps. A very simple scoring function which penalizes gaps and mismatches with -1 and matches with 1 is employed in the illustration of the basic algorithm in Fig. 2. This scoring function works well in certain applications, such as spelling correction or database searches. In linguistic or biological applications, however, it will often fail to find a satisfying alignment, since the segments usually exhibit different *degrees of similarity*. It is therefore important to modify the scoring function to yield individual scores depending on the segments which are being matched. In biology scoring functions for the alignment of protein alignments are usually derived from an empirical basis [23]. In linguistics it is common to derive scoring functions from phonetic features [8].

3.3   Multiple Sequence Alignment

While it is guaranteed that the basic methods for pairwise alignment find the optimal alignment for two sequences depending on the respective criteria, multiple sequence alignment (MSA) is usually based on certain heuristics which do not guarantee that the optimal alignment for a set of sequences has been found, since the computational effort increases enormously with the number of sequences being analyzed [15, p. 345]. The most common way to address this problem in computational biology is to base the calculation on a *guide-tree* along which the sequences are successively aligned, moving from the leaves of the tree to its root. The guide-tree itself is reconstructed from the pairwise alignment scores, using traditional cluster algorithms such as UPGMA [24] or Neighbor-Joining [25]. This strategy is usually called *progressive alignment* [26].

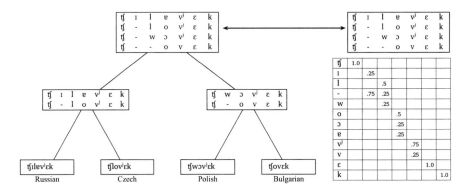

Fig. 3. Multiple sequence alignment based on a guide tree and profiles

Having the advantage of being fast to compute, progressive alignment bears, however, certain shortcomings. Due to the greediness of the procedure, 'any mistakes that are made in early steps of the procedure cannot be corrected by later steps' [19, p. 17]. The accuracy of progressive alignment can be enhanced in different ways. One common modification is the application of *profiles*. A profile represents the relative frequency of all segments of an MSA in all its positions and can therefore be seen as a sequence of vectors [20, p. 146f]. In profile-based approaches, sequences which have been joined during the alignment process are further represented as profiles and the traditional DPA is used for the alignment of profiles with profiles and profiles with sequences. The advantage of this approach is that position-specific information of already aligned sequences can be taken into account when joining more sequences along the guide tree. Fig. 3 gives an illustration for the profile-based progressive alignment of the sequences Russian *čelovek* [ʧɪlɐvʲɛk], Czech *člověk* [ʧlovʲɛk], Polish *człowiek* [ʧwɔvʲɛk], and Bulgarian *čovek* [ʧovɛk] "person".

Further enhancements which make progressive alignment less greedy consist of *pre-* and *post-processing* the data before and after the progressive analysis is carried out. *Library*-based alignment methods, such as the T-Coffee algorithm [3], for example, use the information given in sets (*libraries*) of pairwise global and local alignments of the sequences to derive an alignment-specific scoring function which is later used in the progressive phase. In a similar manner, a post-processing of a given alignment can be carried out with the help of *iterative refinement methods*. In these analyses one or more sequences are repeatedly selected from the completed alignment and realigned [20, p. 148f]. If the overall alignment score increases, the new alignment is retained, otherwise it is discarded.

4   Sequence Modeling in SCA

When dealing with automatic alignment analyses in historical linguistics, it is important to be clear about the underlying sequence model. Apparently, phonetic sequences differ crucially from biological sequences in several respects. The segmentation of sequences into phonetic segments, for example, poses a problem of itself which is addressed in the fields of phonology and phonetics. Another specific characteristic of phonetic sequences which is difficult to model is that they exhibit great *substantial differences* in the languages of the world. While all alignment approaches are based on the assumption that the sequences being compared are drawn from the same alphabet, this does not hold for languages whose sound systems may differ crucially despite the fact that they are genetically related. SCA is based on new approaches to sequence modeling in historical linguistics which shall be presented in the following.

4.1 Paradigmatic Aspects

Sound Classes. The concept of *sound classes* in historical linguistics goes back to A. B. Dolgopolsky [27, 28]. His main idea was to group sounds into different types such that 'phonetic correspondences inside a "type" are more regular than those between different "types"' [28, p. 35]. In his original study, Dolgopolsky proposed ten fundamental sound classes, based on partially empirical observations of sound correspondence frequencies in the languages of the world which are – unfortunately – not further specified by the author. [3]

In a recent study, Dolgopolsky's sound class model has been used as a heuristic device for automatic cognate identification [10]. According to this method, semantically identical basic words are judged to be cognate if their first two consonant classes match, otherwise, no cognacy is assumed. The advantage of this approach is that the number of false positives is usually considerably low, the apparent disadvantage lies in the fact that many true positives are missed, since no true alignment analysis is carried out. Thus, the cognate words German *Tochter* [tɔxtər] "daughter" and English *daughter* [dɔːtər] do not match in their first two consonant classes ("TKTR" vs. "TTR"). An alignment analysis, however, can easily show, that three of four consonant classes match perfectly.

The advantage of sound class representations of phonetic segments compared to pure phonetic representations lies in the specific probabilistic notion of segment similarity inherent in the sound class approach. Since sound classes constitute a model of sound correspondence probabilities, they can be seen as an intermediate solution between the strict language-specific genotypic notion of segment similarity and the language-independent general notion of phenotypic similarity which were discussed in Sec. 2. Another advantage of sound classes is that this meta-phonological way to represent phonetic sequences helps us to get around the specific linguistic problem of aligning sequences drawn from two different alphabets: Ignoring minor phonetic differences enables us to stick to the "one alphabet paradigm" and make use of the traditional alignment algorithms.

---

[3] The sound classes are: P (labial obstruents), T (dental obstruents), S (sibilants), K (velar obstruents and dental affricates), M (labial nasal), N (remaining nasals), R (liquids), W (labial approximant), J (palatal approximant) and Ø (laryngeals and initial velar nasal).

Scoring Functions. Dolgopolsky's original sound class approach defined sound classes as absolute entities. Transitions between sound classes were not allowed, although they are surely desirable, since transitions between classes are well-known to every historical linguist. Transition probabilities between sound classes can be easily modeled in the scoring functions of alignment algorithms. Scoring functions can be based on an *empirical* or a *theoretical* approach. Within an empirical approach scoring functions can be derived from studies on sound correspondence frequencies in the languages of the world. The SCA approach makes use of the data in [29] to derive such a scoring scheme for the sound class model employed by the ASJP project [30].

When deriving scoring functions from a theoretical basis, it is important to find a way to model the nature of sound change and sound correspondences. One crucial characteristic of certain well-known sound changes is their directionality, i.e. if certain sounds change, this change will go into a certain direction and the reverse change can rarely be attested. Other processes of sound change are bidirectional and it cannot be decided which direction occurs more frequently. Thus, regarding velar plosives ([k, g]), we know that they easily can be palatalized, and that the palatalization consists of certain steps, where the velares first become affricates and then turn into sibilants (e.g. [k, g] > [ʧ, ts, ʤ, ʣ] > [ʃ, ʒ, z, s]). The same process of palatalization may happen with dental plosives (e.g. [t, d] > [ʧ, ts, ʤ, ʣ] > [ʃ, ʒ, z, s]). The opposite direction of these changes, however, is rarely attested, and this is the reason, why we often find velar plosives and sibilants or dental plosives and sibilants corresponding regularly in genetically related languages, but rarely velar and dental plosives.

In order to reflect the directionality of certain sound changes, the SCA method applies the following approach: The scoring function is derived from a directed weighted graph. All sound classes which are known to be in very close connection to each other are connected by directed edges which reflect the direction of the respective sound changes. The assumed probability of the sound changes is defined by the edge weights. The higher the assumed probability of sound change, the smaller the weight. If sound change processes are not directional, both directions are reflected in the graph. The similarity score for two segments in the directed graph is calculated by subtracting the similarity score of one segment to itself from the length of the shortest path connecting two segments. Fig. 4 gives an example on how the similarity scores can be calculated for the above-mentioned cases of palatalization of dentals and velars: The resulting similarity score for dentals and fricatives is calculated by subtracting the length of the shortest path (4) from the similarity score for a segment to itself (10). If no shortest path can be found, the similarity score is automatically set to 0.

4.2 Syntagmatic Aspects

Prosodic Profiles. In biological alignment algorithms it is common to treat specific positions of certain sequences differently by modifying the penalties for the introduction of gaps in the alignment [31]. That certain types of sound change (including the loss of segments) are more likely to occur in specific

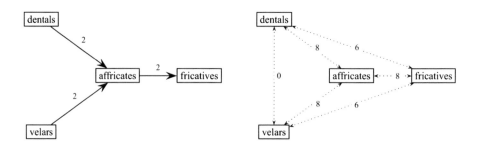

Fig. 4. Modelling the directionality of sound change patterns in scoring schemes

environments is also a well-known fact in historical linguistics. In alignment analyses this can be modeled by constructing *prosodic profiles* from phonetic sequences which were first introduced in [2]. A prosodic profile is hereby understood as a vector representation of sequences which assigns a specific score to each segment depending on its sonority. The sonority score is derived from the sonority hierarchy of [32, p. 30].[4] Once a prosodic profile is constructed, the sound segments can be assigned to different *prosodic environments*. The SCA approach currently distinguishes seven different prosodic environments: # (word-initial consonant), V (word-initial vowel), C (ascending sonority), v (sonority peak), c (descending sonority), $ (word-final consonant), and w (word-final vowel). Following [32, p. 31-34] these environments are ordered in a *hierarchy of strength*.[5] Relative weights for the modification of gap penalties and substitution scores are derived from this hierarchy in such way that it is easier to introduce gaps in weak positions than in strong ones, and that the score for the matching of segments is increased when they belong to the same prosodic environment. How relative weights are derived is illustrated in Tab. 2 for Bulgarian *jabǎlko* [jabəlka] "apple".

Table 2. Prosodic profiles, prosodic environments, and relative weights

Phonetic Sequence	j	a	b	ə	l	k	a
Prosodic Profile	6	7	1	7	5	1	7
Prosodic Environments	#	v	C	v	c	C	>
Relative Weight	7	3	5	3	4	5	1

Secondary Sequence Structures. A specific characteristic of sequences in general is that they may exhibit a *secondary structure* in addition to their *primary structure*. Primary structure is hereby understood as the order of segments, i.e. the smallest units of sequences. Apart from the primary structure, however, sequences can also have a secondary structure where the primary units

---

[4] The hierarchy along with relative scores for sonority, is: *plosives* (1), *affricates* (2), *fricatives* (3), *nasals* (4), *liquids* (5), *glides* (6), and *vowels* (7).

[5] The current hierarchy is: # > V > C > c > v > $ > w.

Table 3. Primary vs. Secondary Alignment analyses

Primary Alignment					
Haikou	z	i	-	t	-	^{3}
Beijing	ʐ̩	ɿ	^{51}	tʰ	ou	^{1}

Secondary Alignment					
Haikou	z	i	t	^{3}	-	-	-
Beijing	ʐ̩	ɿ	-	^{51}	tʰ	ou	^{1}

are grouped into higher ones. The criteria for the secondary segmentation of sequences may vary, depending on the objects one is dealing with, or the specific goal of a certain analysis. Thus, in linguistic applications it may be reasonable to segment a word not only into sound units but also into syllables. Such a secondary segmentation is especially useful when dealing with South-East Asian tone languages like Chinese, since we know that the morphemes in these languages are almost exclusively monosyllabic, while the words usually are not. An alignment analysis of these languages should be able to keep track of the syllable boundaries and avoid matching the sounds of one syllable in one word with sounds in two syllables of the other. Traditional alignment analyses will usually fail to do so. A comparison of Haikou Chinese [zit^3] "sun" with Beijing Chinese [ʐ̩^{51}tʰou^1] "sun" usually wrongly matches the dental plosives of both words, ignoring that one word has only one morpheme while the other one has two (see Tab. 3).[6]

Fortunately, it is possible to modify the traditional DPA algorithm to be sensitive to secondary sequence structures. I shall call such alignment analyses *secondary alignments* as opposed to traditional *primary alignments*. The SCA approach for secondary sequence alignment employs the following strategy: Given a specific boundary marker which marks the end of a secondary segment (such as a tone letter in the phonetic transcription of Sinitic languages, or a whitespace in sentences), additional penalties are introduced into the main recursion. Whenever the recursion comes to a point where the boundary marker of one sequence could be matched with a character that is no boundary marker in the other sequence, or with a gap which is introduced *inside* a secondary segment, this matching is prohibited.

5   Phonetic Alignment in SCA

5.1   Working Procedure

The basic working procedure of SCA consists of four stages: (1) tokenization, (2) class conversion, (3) alignment analysis, and (4) IPA conversion. In stage (1) the input sequences (which should be given in IPA) are tokenized into phonetic segments. In stage (2) the segments are converted into their internal representation format, whereas each sequence is further represented by its corresponding sound class sequence and its prosodic profile. The pairwise or multiple alignment analysis is carried out in stage (3). After the alignment analysis has been

---

[6] The Chinese dialect data is based on [33].

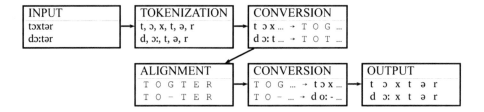

Fig. 5. The working procedure of SCA

carried out, the aligned sequences are converted back to original format in stage (4). This procedure is illustrated in Fig. 5.1 for the sequences German *Tochter* [tɔxtər] "daughter" and English *daughter* [dɔːtər].

5.2 Sequence Models

LingPy comes along with three predefined sequence models and offers support for the import of user-defined models via specific input files. All models consist of two parts, one *class model* which handles the conversion of phonetic transcriptions into sound classes, and one *scoring scheme* which handles the transition probabilities between the sound classes. The three basic models are: the DOLGO model, the SCA model, and the ASJP model. The DOLGO model is based on Dolgopolsky's original proposal extended by a specific class for all vowels along with a simplified scoring function which prohibits the matching of vowels with consonants. The SCA model which is based on an extension of the DOLGO model, consisting of 28 sound classes and a refined scoring scheme that reflects common sound change processes which are often discussed in the literature. The scoring scheme was created by means of the procedure described in Sec. 4.1. The ASJP model is based on the sound class model used by the ASJP project [30] and a scoring scheme which was derived from a study on sound correspondence frequencies in the languages of the world as they are reflected in the ASJP database [29].

5.3 Pairwise Sequence Alignment

SCA supports all extensions to the basic algorithm for pairwise sequence alignment which are mentioned in Sec. 3.2. Additionally, all alignment modes are sensitive to secondary sequence structures, following the extension of the main recursion of the basic algorithm described in Sec. 4.2. When carrying out secondary alignment analyses, the boundary marker has to be defined by the user. By default the boundary marker is a tone letter as they are used in phonetic transcriptions of Sinitic languages. Gap penalties and substitution scores are modified with respect to prosodic context as described above. The relative weights of the different prosodic environments can be defined by the user.

Table 4. The SCA sound class model

No.	Cl.	Description	Examples	No.	Cl.	Description	Examples
1	A	unrounded back vowels	a, ɑ	15	P	labial plosives	p, b
2	B	labial fricatives	f, β	16	R	trills, taps, flaps	r
3	C	dental / alveolar affricates	ts, dz, tʃ, dʒ	17	S	sibilant fricatives	s, z, ʃ, ʒ
4	D	dental fricatives	θ , ð	18	T	dental / alveolar plosives	t, d
5	E	unrounded mid vowels	e, ɛ	19	U	rounded mid vowels	ɔ , o
6	G	velar and uvual fricatives	ɣ , x	20	W	labial approx. / fricative	v, w
7	H	laryngeals	h, ʔ	21	Y	rounded front vowels	u, ʊ, y
8	I	unrounded close vowels	i, ɪ	22	0	low even tones	11, 22
9	J	palatal approximant	j	23	1	rising tones	13, 35
10	K	velare and uvular plosives	k, g	24	2	falling tones	51, 53
11	L	lateral approximants	l	25	3	mid even tones	33
12	M	labial nasal	m	26	4	high even tones	44, 55
13	N	nasals	n, ŋ	27	5	short tones	1, 2
14	0	rounded back vowels	œ, ɒ	28	6	complex tones	214

5.4   Multiple Sequence Alignment

SCA's algorithm for multiple sequence alignment is based on the progressive alignment paradigm. Based on pairwise alignment analyses of all sequence pairs, a distance matrix is computed using the formula of [34] for the conversion of similarity into distance scores. With help of the Neighbor-Joining algorithm [25], a guide tree is reconstructed from the distance matrix and the sequences are successively aligned. In order to cope for the shortcomings of progressive alignment analyses, SCA employs profiles and offers the possibility to carry out a pre- and post-processing of the data. Furthermore, SCA includes a method for the detection of swapped sites in multiple alignments which is described in detail in [2].

The pre-processing in SCA follows the T-Coffee algorithm for multiple sequence alignment in biology [3]. The basic idea of the algorithm is to use the information given in pairwise alignment analyses of the data to derive an alignment-specific scoring matrix. The algorithm starts by computing a set of pairwise alignments of all input sequences, using different alignment approaches, such as, e.g., global, local, and diagonal alignments. Based on this set of pairwise alignments (the *primary library*) an alignment-specific scoring matrix is created. In the initial stage, the substitution scores for all residue pairs in the scoring matrix are set to 0. After the pairwise alignments have been carried out, the scoring matrix is extended by increasing the score for each residue pair which occurs in the primary library by a certain weight. While the original T-Coffee algorithm derives the weight from sequence identity, SCA employs a different strategy. Given the sequences A and B, the weight W_{xy} for the residues x and y being matched in an alignment of A and B is derived by the formula

$$\frac{1}{2} \left(\frac{S_{AB}}{L_{AB}} + M_{xy} \right), \tag{1}$$

where S_{AB} is the similarity score of the alignment of A and B, L_{AB} is the length of the alignment, and M_{xy} is the original substitution score for the residues.

Gongxing	x w ɛ $_{22}$ ɕ y $_{55}$ ʁ w a $_{12}$	Gongxing	x w ɛ $_{22}$ - - - ɕ y $_{55}$ ʁ w a $_{12}$
Jinman	kʰ w a $_{55}$ l a $_{21}$ - ɕ u $_{55}$	Jinman	kʰ w a $_{55}$ l a $_{21}$ ɕ u $_{55}$ - - - -
Enqi	x w i $_{22}$ - - - - ɕ u $_{24}$	Enqi	x w i $_{22}$ - - - ɕ u $_{24}$ - - - -

Fig. 6. Simple (left) and library-based (right) progressive alignment

If a given residue pair occurs more than once in the primary library, the sum of all weights is taken. In a second stage, the primary library is extended by means of a *triplet approach* where two sequences are aligned via a third sequence (see [3, p. 208f] for details), and the resulting weights are again added to the new scoring matrix. The specific strength of this approach is its sensitivity to both global as well as local similarities between sequences. This is illustrated in Fig. 6 where the words for "ashes" in three different dialects of Bai are aligned using simple (left) and library-based (right) progressive alignment.[7]

The post-processing is based on iterative refinement analyses, where a given MSA is split into two parts, one containing a set of probably misaligned sequences, and one containing the rest of all sequences. If realigning the two parts yields a new alignment with an improved score, the new alignment is retained, if not, it is discarded. In order to find probably misaligned sequences in a given MSA, SCA employs three different heuristics: (1) the *similar-gap-sites* heuristic which splits an MSA into sequences in which the same gaps have been introduced in the same positions; (2) the *flat-cluster* heuristic which splits an MSA into sets of sequences whose average distance is beyond a certain threshold, and (3) the *orphan*[8] heuristic which extracts those sequences from an MSA whose distance to all other sequences is greater than the average distance between all sequences.

6   Evaluation

6.1   Gold Standard

In previous analyses, it could be shown that sound class based alignment analyses perform equally well or even better than alternative proposals for pairwise [8] and multiple sequence alignment [9]. A drawback of these analyses was, however, that the testsets underlying the studies were either considerably small [1], or only covered a low range of genetically very close language varieties [2]. In order to test the method more closely, two new gold standards were compiled, one for MSA and one for PSA analyses. The sources of the data and further information are given in Tab. 5.

The MSA gold standard (Online Resource 2) was designed to reflect a large range of different language varieties taken from different language families which show quite different kinds and degrees of variation. It consists of 600 manually edited multiple alignments, covering six different language families, 435 different

---

[7] The dialect data is taken from [35].

[8] In evolutionary biology, the term 'orphan' is commonly used to refer to 'distant members of a family' [36, p. 2684].

Table 5. The gold standard for pairwise and multiple sequence alignments

Dataset	Languages	PSA	MSA	Words	Taxa	Source
Sindial	Chinese dialects	200	20	341	40	[33]
Andean	Andean dialects (Aymara, Quechua)	597	94	983	20	[38]
BulDial	Bulgarian dialects	1504	152	32418	198	[9]
BaiDial	Bai dialects	892	90	1416	17	[35, 39]
NorDial	Norwegian dialects	496	51	2183	53	[40]
TPPSR	French dialects	707	82	3830	62	[41]
GerDial	Germanic languages and dialects	1110	111	4776	45	[42]

taxa, and a total of 45 947 sequences. A large part of the gold standard (the sub-set of Bulgarian dialects) was compiled for the study of [9] and kindly provided by the authors. The rest of the gold standard was edited by the author himself.

The PSA gold standard (Online Resource 1) was created by automatically extracting up to ten of the most divergent unique sequence pairs from each file of the MSA gold standard. Following the practice in computational biology, the diversity of the sequences was measured in terms of the Percentage Identity (PID) of the aligned sequences. The PID is calculated by dividing the number of identical positions in an alignment by the sum of aligned positions and internal gap positions [37].[9] This procedure yielded a set of 5 506 sequence pairs with an average PID of 17.14 %.

6.2   Evaluation Measures

The simplest way to test how well an alignment algorithm performs is to calcu-late the perfect-alignments score (PAS), i.e. the proportion of alignments which are identical with the gold standard. Since this score only reveals very strong tendencies, a couple of different methods have been proposed to test how well an alignment algorithm performs in comparison with a benchmark dataset [9, 36]. In computational biology, the most common evaluation measures are the column score (CS) and the sum-of-pairs score (SPS)[36]. The column score is calculated by dividing the number of identical columns in test and reference alignment by the total number of columns in the reference alignment. The sum-of-pairs score is defined as the size of the intersection of aligned segment pairs in test and reference alignment divided by the number of segment pairs in the reference alignment.

In [2], the advantages and disadvantages of different evaluation scores were discussed in detail, and certain shortcomings of both the CS and the SPS were pointed out. In practice, however, these problems rarely show up, and all eval-uation measures discussed in [2] reflected the same tendencies in this study. Therefore, only the PAS, the CS and the SPS will be reported in the following.

---

[9] Although this score has been criticized for certain obvious shortcomings [37], it provides an easy way to check the diversity of a given alignment independent of any further assumptions.

6.3   Results

Pairwise Sequence Alignment. The PSA gold standard was analyzed using the three different sound-class models provided by LingPy. For each model, analyses in four different modes were carried out: (1) a simple global alignment analysis (BASIC), (2) a global alignment analysis in which gap costs and substitution scores were scaled in dependence of prosodic environments (SCALE), (3) a simple global alignment analysis which was sensitive to secondary sequence structures (SEC), and (4) a global alignment analysis which was sensitive to both prosodic environments and secondary sequence structures (SEC/SCALE). These different modes were chosen in order to test to what degree the syntagmatic modifications described in Sec. 4.2 might influence the performance of SCA.

As can be seen from the results shown in Tab. 6 (see also Online Resource 1), the SCA sound-class model performs best throughout all modes, while DOLGO performs worst. Furthermore, the accuracy of the scores increases as the modes become more complex, with SEC/SCALE showing the best performance. Given that the differences in CS and SPS between BASIC and SEC/SCALE are significant for all sound-class models,[10] a clear improvement of secondary alignment analyses in combination with prosodic profiles can be attested. The benefits of secondary alignment analyses become even more evident when considering only the 1 092 sequence pairs belonging to dialects of the tonal languages Bai and Chinese, where a drastic increase in alignment accuracy can be reported for all models (see Fig. 7).

Table 6. Comparing the results for the four different modes on the PSA gold standard

Model	BASIC			SCALE			SEC			SEC/SCALE		
	PAS	CS	SPS	PAS	CS	SPS	PAS	CS	SPS	PAS	CS	SPS
SCA	85.72	92.32	95.93	86.12	92.38	96.01	87.21	93.37	96.57	87.67	93.47	96.67
ASJP	83.62	91.17	95.43	85.05	91.91	95.76	84.87	92.00	95.90	86.63	92.89	96.34
DOLGO	82.02	89.47	94.29	83.73	90.65	94.96	83.33	90.42	94.86	85.09	91.63	95.53

Multiple Sequence Alignment. In a way similar to the analysis of the PSA gold standard, the MSA gold standard was analyzed using the three different sound-class models provided by LingPy. Again, analyses in four different modes were carried out for each model: (1) a progressive alignment analysis (PROG), (2) a progressive alignment analysis with iterative refinement (ITER), (3) a library-based alignment analysis (LIB), and (4) a library-based alignment analysis in combination with iterative refinement (LIB/ITER). The iterative

---

[10] Assuming equal variances, a two sample t-test yielded: t=-2.20, p=0.03 for SCA (CS); t=-2.28, p=0.02 for SCA (SPS); t=-3.93, p<0.01 for ASJP (CS); t=-2.94, p<0.01 for ASJP (SPS); t=-3.91, p<0.01 for DOLGO (CS); t=-3.48, p<0.01 for DOLGO (SPS).

refinement analysis was based on the three heuristics described in Sec. 5.4. The library was created from pairwise global, local, and diagonal alignment analyses of all sequence pairs. All alignment analyses were based on the extensions for secondary alignment and prosodic profiles described in Sec. 4.2.

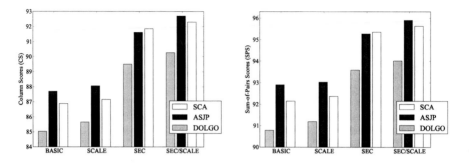

Fig. 7. CS and SPS in the tonal partition of the PSA gold standard

The results for the analyses are given in Tab. 7 (see also Online Resource 2). As can be seen from the table, the analyses using the SCA model again outperformed the other models, while the analyses using the DOLGO model again performed worst. The pre- and post-processing of the data also results in clear improvements of the analyses regardless of the underlying sound-class model, whereas the combination of library-based alignment and iterative refinement seems to be the best approach, showing significant improvements for CS and SPS in almost all models.[11]

In order to check where the specific strengths of the different sound-class models lie, the results for the analyses were divided into four partitions based on the PID of the gold standard alignments: PID-100 (100 – 75), PID-75 (75 – 50), PID-50 (50 – 25), and PID-25 (25 – 0). The results for LIB/ITER on these partitions are plotted in Fig. 8. As one may expect, the accuracy of all methods decreases the more divergent the sequences become. Yet while there are only minor differences in the accuracy of the SCA model compared to the ASJP model in the first three partitions, the SCA model performs considerably better in the PID-25 partition of highly divergent MSAs. This shows that the SCA model is specifically apt for the task of sequence comparison in greater time depths.

Identification of Swapped Sites. Of the 600 files in the MSA gold standard, 50 MSAs were identified to contain swapped sites. Along with the LIB/ITER analyses, the algorithm for swap detection in multiple sequence alignments

---

[11] Assuming equal variances, a two sample t-test yielded: t=-2.91, p<0.01 for SCA (CS); t=-4.28, p<0.01 for SCA (SPS), t=-2.81, p<0.01 for ASJP (CS); t=-4.41, p<0.01 for ASJP (SPS), t=-1.75, p=0.08 for DOLGO (CS); t=-2.15, p=0.03 for DOLGO (SPS).

Table 7. Comparing the results for the four different modes on the MSA gold standard

Model	PROG			ITER			LIB			LIB/ITER		
	PAS	CS	SPS	PAS	CS	SPS	PAS	CS	SPS	PAS	CS	SPS
SCA	79.83	89.74	98.00	83.83	91.98	98.72	81.50	90.42	98.64	86.17	93.19	99.26
ASJP	78.00	88.73	97.88	84.17	92.26	98.70	80.83	89.99	98.76	84.83	92.25	99.17
DOLGO	76.33	87.73	97.68	78.67	89.10	98.13	79.67	89.62	98.33	80.83	90.05	98.42

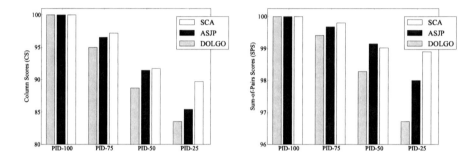

Fig. 8. CS and SPS in the different partitions of the MSA gold standard

Table 8. Identification of swaps

	SCA	ASJP	DOLGO
True Positives	46	41	44
False Positives	2	1	9
False Negatives	4	9	6

described in [2] was tested. The results are given in Tab. 8. As can be seen from the table, the SCA model again performed best. It correctly identified 46 of 50 swaps while at the same time only 2 swaps were wrongly proposed.

7   Conclusion

In this paper, I presented the most recent version of the SCA method for pairwise and multiple phonetic alignments. As could be shown in extensive tests, the current state of the method has many advantages compared to both alternative approaches and older versions of sound-class-based alignments. The specific strength of the SCA method lies in the specific way traditional linguistic concepts are modeled and combined with recent computational approaches. The research on automatic methods for phonetic alignment is still in its infancy, and the results of pairwise and multiple alignment analyses lack far behind the intuitive judgments of trained historical linguists. This should, however, not discourage us from trying to improve our automatic methods, but rather motivate us to put more effort into the development of new models which bring traditional and automatic approaches closer to each other.

References

1. List, J.M.: Phonetic alignment based on sound classes. In: Slavkovik, M. (ed.) Proceedings of the 15th Student Session of the European Summer School for Logic, Language and Information, Kopenhagen, pp. 192–202 (2010)
2. List, J.M.: Multiple sequence alignment in historical linguistics. A sound class based approach. In: Proceedings of ConSOLE XIX (2011) (forthcoming)
3. Notredame, C., Higgins, D.G., Heringa, J.: T-Coffee. A novel method for fast and accurate multiple sequence alignment. Journal of Molecular Biology 302, 205–217 (2000)
4. Gray, R.D., Atkinson, Q.D.: Language-tree divergence times support the Anatolian theory of Indo-European origin. Nature 426(6965), 435–439 (2003)
5. Holman, E.W., Brown, C.H., Wichmann, S., Müller, A., Velupillai, V., Hammarström, H., Sauppe, S., Jung, H., Bakker, D., Brown, P., Belyaev, O., Urban, M., Mailhammer, R., List, J.M., Egorov, D.: Automated dating of the world's language families based on lexical similarity. Current Anthropology 52(6), 841–875 (2011)
6. Baxter, W.H., Manaster Ramer, A.: Beyond lumping and splitting. Probabilistic issues in historical linguistics. In: Renfrew, C., McMahon, A., Trask, L. (eds.) Time Depth in Historical Linguistics, pp. 167–188. McDonald Institute for Archaeological Research, Cambridge (2000)
7. Kessler, B.: The significance of word lists. Statistical tests for investigating historical connections between languages. CSLI Publications, Stanford (2001)
8. Kondrak, G.: Algorithms for language reconstruction. Dissertation. University of Toronto, Toronto (2002)
9. Prokić, J., Wieling, M., Nerbonne, J.: Multiple sequence alignments in linguistics. In: Proceedings of the EACL 2009 Workshop on Language Technology and Resources for Cultural Heritage, Social Sciences, Humanities, and Education, pp. 18–25. Association for Computational Linguistics, Stroudsburg (2009)
10. Turchin, P., Peiros, I., Gell-Mann, M.: Analyzing genetic connections between languages by matching consonant classes. Journal of Language Relationship 3, 117–126 (2010)
11. Covington, M.A.: An algorithm to align words for historical comparison. Computational Linguistics 22(4), 481–496 (1996)
12. Ross, M., Durie, M.: Introduction. In: Durie, M. (ed.) The Comparative Method Reviewed. Regularity and Irregularity in Language Change, pp. 3–38. Oxford University Press, New York (1996)
13. Trask, R.L. (ed.): The dictionary of historical and comparative linguistics. Edinburgh University Press, Edinburgh (2000)
14. Lass, R.: Historical linguistics and language change. Cambridge University Press, Cambridge (1997)
15. Gusfield, D.: Algorithms on strings, trees and sequences. Cambridge University Press, Cambridge (1997)
16. Needleman, S.B., Wunsch, C.D.: A gene method applicable to the search for similarities in the amino acid sequence of two proteins. Journal of Molecular Biology 48, 443–453 (1970)

17. Wagner, R.A., Fischer, M.J.: The string-to-string correction problem. Journal of the Association for Computing Machinery 21(1), 168–173 (1974)
18. Eddy, S.R.: Where did the BLOSUM62 alignment score matrix come from? Nature Biotechnology 22(8), 1035–1036 (2004)
19. Rosenberg, M.S.: Sequence alignment. Concepts and history. In: Rosenberg, M.S. (ed.) Sequence Alignment. Methods, Models, Concepts, and Strategies, pp. 1–22. University of California Press, Berkeley and Los Angeles and London (2009)
20. Durbin, R., Eddy, S.R., Krogh, A., Mitchinson, G.: Biological sequence analysis. Probabilistic models of proteins and nucleic acids, 7th edn. Cambridge University Press, Cambridge (2002)
21. Smith, T.F., Waterman, M.S.: Identification of common molecular subsequences. Journal of Molecular Biology 1, 195–197 (1981)
22. Morgenstern, B., Dress, A., Werner, T.D.: Multiple DNA and protein sequence alignment based on segment-to-segment comparison. Proceedings of the National Acadamy of Science, USA 93, 12098–12103 (1996)
23. Henikoff, S., Henikoff, J.G.: Amino acid substitution matrices from protein blocks. PNAS 89(22), 10915–10919 (1992)
24. Sokal, R.R., Michener, C.D.: A statistical method for evaluating systematic relationships. University of Kansas Scientific Bulletin 28, 1409–1438 (1958)
25. Saitou, N., Nei, M.: The neighbor-joining method: A new method for reconstructing phylogenetic trees. Molecular Biology and Evolution 4(4), 406–425 (1987)
26. Feng, D.F., Doolittle, R.F.: Progressive sequence alignment as a prerequisite to correct phylogenetic trees. Journal of Molecular Evolution 25(4), 351–360 (1987)
27. Dolgopolsky, A.B.: Gipoteza drevnejšego rodstva jazykovych semej Severnoj Evrazii s verojatnostej točky zrenija (A probabilistic hypothesis concerning the oldest relationships among the language families of Northern Eurasia). Voprosy Jazykoznanija 2, 53–63 (1964)
28. Dolgopolsky, A.B.: A probabilistic hypothesis concerning the oldest relationships among the language families of northern Eurasia. In: Shevoroshkin, V.V. (ed.) Typology, Relationship and Time, pp. 27–50. Karoma Publisher, Ann Arbor (1986)
29. Brown, C.H., Holman, E.W., Wichmann, S.: Sound correspondences in the world's languages (2011), Online manuscript, PDF,
    http://wwwstaff.eva.mpg.de/~wichmann/wwcPaper23.pdf
30. Brown, C.H., Holman, E.W., Wichmann, S., Velupillai, V., Cysouw, M.: Automated classification of the world's languages. Sprachtypologie und Universalienforschung 61(4), 285–308 (2008)
31. Thompson, J.D., Higgins, D.G., Gibson, T.J.: CLUSTAL W. Nucleic Acids Research 22(22), 4673–4680 (1994)
32. Geisler, H.: Akzent und Lautwandel in der Romania. Narr, Tübingen (1992)
33. Hóu, J. (ed.): Xiàndài Hànyǔ fāngyán yīnkù (Phonological database of Chinese dialects). Shànghǎi Jiàoyù, Shanghai (2004)
34. Downey, S.S., Hallmark, B., Cox, M.P., Norquest, P., Lansing, S.: Computational feature-sensitive reconstruction of language relationships: Developing the ALINE distance for comparative historical linguistic reconstruction. Journal of Quantitative Linguistics 15(4), 340–369 (2008)
35. Wang, F.: Comparison of languages in contact. Institute of Linguistics Academia Sinica, Taipei (2006)
36. Thompson, J.D., Plewniak, F., Poch, O.: A comprehensive comparison of multiple sequence alignment programs. Nucleic Acids Research 27(13), 2682–2690 (1999)
37. Raghava, G.P.S., Barton, G.J.: Quantification of the variation in percentage identity for protein sequence alignments. BMC Bioinformatics 7(415) (2006)

38. Heggarty, P.: Sounds of the Andean languages. Online resource,
    http://www.quechua.org.uk/
39. Allen, B.: Bai Dialect Survey. SIL International (2007)
40. Almberg, J., Skarbø, K.: Nordavinden og sola. En norsk dialektprøvedatabase på
    nettet (The North Wind and the Sun. A Norwegian dialect database on the web)
    (2011), Online resource, http://www.ling.hf.ntnu.no/nos/
41. Gauchat, L., Jeanjaquet, J., Tappolet, E.: Tableaux phonétiques des patois suisses
    romands. Attinger, Neuchâtel (1925)
42. Renfrew, C., Heggarty, P.: Languages and origins in europe. Online resource,
    http://www.languagesandpeoples.com/

Embodied Quantifiers

Simon Pauw[1] and Michael Spranger[2,3]

[1] Institute for Logic, Language and Computation, University of Amsterdam,
Amsterdam, The Netherlands
`simonpauw@gmail.com`
[2] Sony Computer Science Laboratory, Paris, France
`spranger@csl.sony.fr`
[3] Systems Technology Laboratory, Sony Corporation, Tokyo, Japan

Abstract. This paper studies how quantificational expressions such as
few, *three* and *all* can be grounded in real-world perception. Based on
findings from psycholinguistics, we propose a computational model designed for use in robot-robot interaction scenarios which involve discrimination tasks for objects in the real world. We test the performance of our
model and contrast it with a type theory based model. We show that our
design choices make our model more suitable for real-world applications.

Keywords: semantics, quantifiers, noun phrases, embodied interaction,
generalized quantifiers, montague grammar, fuzzy quantifiers, language
games.

1 Introduction

The experiments reported in this paper are part of a greater research effort that
studies human language-like communication using (artificial) robotic agents [1].
Central to these studies is the question: How can the meaning of language be
grounded in real-world perception? Answers to this problem are given for different aspects of human language such as color [2], space [3], temporal language
[4] and action language [5–7]. All of these models operationalize basic insights
from prototype theory [8] about how people conceptualize objects and relations
between them and propose a degree-based semantics. In this paper we describe
a fully operational model for natural language quantifiers such as *many*, *all* and
three that builds further on these findings. The model, termed *clustering quantification* [9], employs a combination of prototype theory and standard clustering
algorithms and has been successfully used to study the acquisition and evolution
of quantificational terms [10, 11].

Inspired by existing psycholinguistic research on quantification [12–14], the
model presented in this paper focusses on the role of quantifiers in determining
a referent of a quantified noun phrase. The quantificational information of a
noun phrase imposes constraints on the cardinality of its possible referents. For
example, the quantifier *three* in the utterance "the three blocks" signals that the
extension of *blocks* in the context contains three elements.

D. Lassiter and M. Slavkovik (Eds.): ESSLLI Student Sessions, LNCS 7415, pp. 52–66, 2012.

(a) Example scene

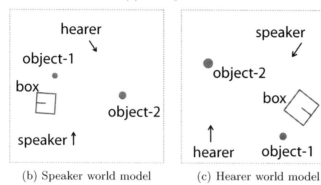

(b) Speaker world model   (c) Hearer world model

Fig. 1. (a): Example scene consisting of various objects, e.g., robots, blocks and boxes. (b) and (c): Top-down view of the world models as perceived by respectively the speaker and the hearer.

We test the adequacy of the clustering quantification model for real-world perception through a series of experiments. In these experiments we contrast the performance of our model with a model that is more in line with type theoretic accounts of quantification which assume that nouns can be modeled as predicates. Accounts falling into this class are Generalized Quantifier Theory (GQ) [15] and Fuzzy Quantifier Theory [16, 17]. This paper proceeds by introducing the embodied interaction paradigm. The section to follow introduces our model for quantification. After that, we introduce an the type theory based model. Finally, we compare both models and show that the clustering quantification performs significantly better.

2 Embodied Interaction

The model presented in this paper is designed for use in real-world situated interaction. Figure 1 shows an example scene with two Sony humanoid robots [18] interacting in a shared environment. Each robot perceives the world through its own onboard sensors, e.g., the camera and proprioceptive sensors. The vision system [19] gathers information from the sensors into a *world model*, that reflects the current belief of a robot about the state of the environment. One of the robots is randomly chosen as the speaker and he will choose a referent, which can be any object or subsets of objects in the environment. The goal of the speaker is to draw the attention of the interlocutor to the referent and make him point to it or to each of the objects that are the referent.

We call these interactions *language games* [20]. The type of language game the agents play depends on the particular research question. For this paper, the two interacting agents use the following script:

1. Both agents establish a joint attentional frame [21] and a world model using their visual and proprioceptive sensors.
2. The speaker chooses an object or a set of objects as referent R. He conceptualizes a meaning for discriminating R and tries to verbalize his conceptualization into a string of words.
3. This utterance is passed to the hearer.
4. The hearer parses and interprets the utterances and tries to find the object or the set of objects he thinks the speaker is trying to discriminate.
5. The hearer points to the object or the set of objects.
6. The speaker checks whether the objects pointed to by the hearer where indeed the ones he had in mind.

This language game can have two different outcomes. If the hearer points to the correct set of objects the game is a success. Otherwise it is a failure.

Such interactions require a mapping of continuous perceptual data to discrete symbols (language). To this end, we use the computational semantics systems *Incremental Recruitment Language* (IRL) [22, 23]. Since the communicative goal is to identify some referent, the semantics of a particular phrase is modeled in IRL as a series of operations, i.e. a program, that the hearer has to go through in order to single out the objects that are the referent.

Figure 2 shows the IRL-program underlying the utterance *the left block*. The program is represented as a network containing *semantic entities* (e.g., `block` and `left`) and *cognitive operations* (e.g., `apply-class`). The semantics entities represent concepts and categories. The cognitive operations instruct the agents what to do with the semantic entities. For example, `apply-class` takes the concept `block` and applies this to the objects in the context. The result of this application is fed to the operation `apply-spatial-category`, which processes the data using the spatial category `left`, and finally, `apply-selector` computes the referent using the selector `unique` for more information.

IRL provides a general framework for the automatic interpretation and composition of such programs, but the concrete implementation of each operation, e.g. `apply-selector` is outside of IRL. IRL makes no assumptions about the inner workings of these operations. Consequently, IRL is an ideal formalism for studying different models of categorization and quantification.

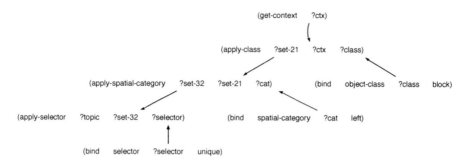

Fig. 2. Semantic structure representing the meaning of the utterance *the left block*. The network contains bind-statements that introduce semantic entities (e.g., the object class `block`), as well as operations that define what to do with these semantic entities. Links in the network are defined by variables (starting with a ?), e.g., the output of operation `apply-class` is linked to `apply-spatial-category` through the variable `?set-21`.

3   Clustering Quantification

There is been substantial research in the past 10 years on grounding basic categories and relations in real world perception. We build upon an existing system for spatial language which has been proposed for the grounding of spatial categories and quantifiers such as "the" [24] and has been shown to be very successful in real world interactions [9]. This system is based on two psycholinguistic processing principles.

acceptability [25], also called *prototypicality* [26, 27], means that categories such as *left* apply to a certain degree. An object can be more or less to the left of a landmark.

contrast requires speakers which are trying to discriminate objects to choose the relation or category which maximizes acceptability of the object and minimizes acceptability of all other objects [28]. The phrase "the left block" refers to the leftmost block in a scene.

Starting from this model the main question is how notions of acceptability and contrast can be extended to quantifiers which might introduce additional constraints such as cardinality (e.g. "three"). In this section we propose to operationalize these ideas for quantifiers using mechanisms from machine learning and clustering. Before we jump to the quantifier model we briefly outline how prototype-based processing is implemented for categories.

3.1   Acceptability

The acceptability of a concept for an object depends on a similarity function that assigns a score to the combination of concept and object. For example a spatial relation such as *left* is represented by a prototypical vector in euclidean space. The degree to which an object is left depends on the angle between the object and the prototypical vector for *left*. The similarity function maps this angle difference to a score between 0 and 1. The following gives an example of a parameterized similarity function used for modeling projective categories such as *front* and *left*.

$$s = e^{\frac{0.5d(a_p.a_o)}{\sigma_p}} \tag{1}$$

With s being the resulting similarity, a_p the prototype distance, a_o the distance of the object, d an angle distance function and σ_p a parameter that determines the rate at which the distance influences the similarity. Similarly, functions for other concepts such as `block` are constructed, except that the similarity/distance space might be the set of features of an object.

For semantic structure such as the one in Figure 2 this means that operations that apply categories such as `apply-spatial-category` and object classes such as `apply-class` assign scores to the objects in the context. Scores for the spatial category and the object class are multiplied so that in the end a single accept-ability rating in the form of a similarity score is computed for each object in the context. In short, this is a model for spatial language which establishes the acceptability of a noun phrase such as "block in front of me" for every object in a given context (See Figure 3).

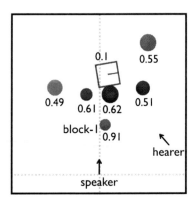

Fig. 3. This figure shows the results of the interpretation of the utterance "block(s) in front". Every object is assigned a score that is the result of multiplying the respective score for the categories *front* and *block*.

3.2   Contrast

But, how do agents use these scores to distill concrete referents? This is where the notion of contrast comes into play. For instance, if an agent wants to discriminate an object from the context then he is likely to try and maximize the applicability contrast between the object he wants to discriminate and all other objects in the context. Hearers choose the object that best fits the description. Speakers choose the categories that maximize the contrast.

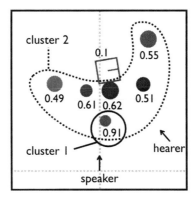

Fig. 4. This figure shows the results of applying agglomerative clustering. The algorithm finds two possible referents for the utterance "block(s) in front" (cluster-1 and cluster-2). The quantificational information of the noun phrase can be used to further constrain the possible referents of the noun. The noun phrase "the block in front of me" signals that there is one unique referent, making cluster-1 the most likely referent. For the noun phrase "all blocks in front of me", the most likely referent is cluster-2.

Similarly, if the referent is a set of objects (as for the utterance *three blocks*) we require a procedure that decides for every entity whether it is part of the referent set or not. Quantificational information constraints this process. For example, the quantifier *three* signals that the referent set contains (at least) three element, and the quantifier *many* signals that the referent set contains more elements than a certain norm. To operationalize these ideas we use standard clustering algorithms from machine learning. In particular, we apply variants of *agglomerative clustering* [29] and *k-means* [30, 31].

The algorithms are used to implement the operation of `apply-selector`. The task of this operation is to decide for every entity in the context if it is part of the referent or not, based on the scores that were assigned by the previous operations. In essence it has to divide the input set into two sets of objects, the objects that are part of the referent (REFSET) and the objects that are not (COMPSET). Finding such a partitioning is precisely what clustering algorithms are designed for. However, there are many ways to partition an input set. The particular partition that is chosen depends on a combination of factors. First of all, the clustering algorithms use heuristics to find good partitioning. Good partitionings are those that maximize *inter-cluster variance* and minimize *intra-cluster variance*. The first is a measure of how far clusters are apart (contrast). The second is a measure how much cohesion there is in each cluster. Both k-means and agglomerative clustering are algorithms that optimize for these two indicators and we apply them here to similarity scores computed for the spatial relation and the object classes.

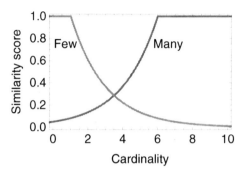

Fig. 5. Plot of the similarity functions of *many* and *few*. The prototypical value for *few* and *many* are 1 and 6 respectively. They intersect at 3.5, meaning that for any cardinality above 3.5 the quantifier *many* is more acceptable, and for any cardinality under 3.5 the quantifier *few* is more acceptable. In practice, the similarity function is modulated by a context parameter which shifts the exact point where *few* becomes more acceptable than *many*. For the purpose of this paper, the parameter is left fixed.

Another factor that is taken into account in determining a good partitioning is the quantificational information. The quantificational information provides information on the cardinality of the REFSET. Consider for example Figure 4. For the utterance "all blocks in front of me", the plural marker and the quantifier *all* enforce that the REFSET should at least contain two (and preferably more) elements. The REFSET for the utterance "the block in front of me" should contain precisely one element. Thus depending on the quantificational information, a different partitioning is chosen.

The result is a flexible algorithm which allows agents to choose a partitioning of data based on whatever quantifying criteria they want to convey. Conversely, it allows them to find the best interpretation upon hearing a quantified noun phrase. The precise nature of the constraints depends on the type of quantifier. The examples above show how this works for crisp quantifiers such as *all* or *three*. It is also possible to define constraints for gradable quantifiers such *many* and *few*. In this case, the quantifiers are not binarily constraining the cardinality of the referent, but rather, they assign a score to every possible partitioning and work as a heuristic value in the same way as the inter- and intra-cluster variance. For example in Figure 4 the REFSET of the utterance "many blocks in front" refers to *cluster-2*, not because the *many* excludes *cluster-1* entirely, but because the constraint imposed by many assigns a higher score to a set of cardinality 6 than a set of cardinality 1.

For the sake of simplicity we implemented quantifiers in the same way as the spatial prototypes, using a prototypical value and a similarity function. The distance function in this case is defined as the difference between the cardinality of the REFSET and some prototypical cardinality ($\mathrm{d}(c_p, c_{\mathrm{REF}}) = |c_p - c_{\mathrm{REF}}|$). For the current experiment the average cardinality of the REFSET is around 3.5. We have chosen the prototypical values for *few* ($c_p = 1$) and *many* ($c_p = 6$) such that any cardinality above 3.5 is will be more similar to *many* and anything under 3.5 will be more similar to *few*. Figure 5 shows a plot of the similarity functions of *few* and *many*.

In sum, this approach regards quantifiers as constraints. They help with identifying the referent of a noun phrase. We use existing clustering methods, that model the reification of the referent as a partitioning process that is partly steered by pragmatic heuristics (e.g., inter- and intra-cluster variance) and partly by semantic heuristics (quantificational expressions).

4 Generalized Quantifiers

To measure the performance of our approach we compare it with an implementation of a common type theoretic way of dealing with quantification [32]. These approaches commonly consider the noun (e.g., *ball*) as a predicate that together with a quantifying expression forms a (quantified) noun phrases (e.g. *all balls*). Such a noun phrase is modeled as a *generalized quantifier* (GQ) [15].

For those not familiar with generalized quantifiers, we provide a brief explanation: A noun or verb phrase denotes a property that can be represented as a function from entities to truth values, in other words, as the set of entities for which the property holds. Consequently, the interpretation of *ball* is the set of all balls B in a context, and *are red* is the set of all things that are red R. Quantifying expressions then are understood as set relations. For instance, the sentence *all blocks are red* can be modeled as $B \subseteq R$. The determined noun phrase is therefore modeled as a function from a set to truth values, in other words, a generalized quantifier. For example, the determined noun phrase *all blocks* is interpreted as a function $f(Q)$ that is true iff $B \subseteq Q$. The functional role of the quantifier under this analysis is to transform the noun predicate into such a generalized quantifier. For example, the meaning of the quantifier *all* is a function $f(P, Q)$ that is true iff $P \subseteq Q$. Where P s the predicate of the noun and Q the predicate of the verb-phrase.

The essential restriction imposed by this approach is the fact that the noun is considered to be a predicate. In light of the previous model, this means that before applying the quantifier, we require some procedure that turns the set of scored items into a predicate (i.e., a procedure that decides for every element if it is part of the noun or not).

In accordance with this observation, we implement a model we will henceforth refer to as the *Generalized Quantifier approach*. The main difference between the Generalized Quantifier approach and our model as described earlier in this paper lies in the operation `apply-selector` (as seen in Figure 2). Before applying the quantificational information, the operation establishes the set of objects that forms the extension of the noun. Just as in the previous model, the interpretation of the noun "block(s) in front of me" establishes a similarity score for every object in the context. The operation `apply-selector` determines for every object if its score is high enough to be part of the noun. In order to make a fair comparison between the two models, we employ the exact same clustering methods for the reification of the noun as above. The main (and essential) difference with the previous model is that the reification is done *before* considering the quantificational information. This difference might seem insignificant, but it is needed to stay in line with the type theoretic approaches and, as we are about to show, has a very important impact on the performance of the model.

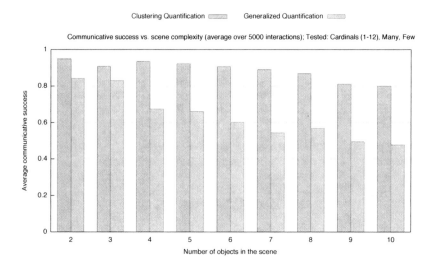

Fig. 6. Average communicative success for 5000 interactions on different sets of spatial scenes (grouped according to number of objects in each scene)

Generalized Quantifiers is fundamentally a theoretical proposal which does not propose any specific form of implementation. Therefore, one might be tempted to question how general our modeling is. For the concrete reification operation, other mechanisms are possible, but the main point from this section is that no matter what the particular implementation is, type theoretic approaches rely on the assumption that we can unambiguously establish the cardinality of the interpretation of the noun *without* regarding the quantificational information. The fact that there is no easy fix for this problem can be seen in the model of Fuzzy Quantifiers. This model is an fuzzy extension of GQ. Here, all set relations and predicates can be degree-based, but nonetheless, the model requires a mechanism to establish the cardinality of the fuzzy set representing the noun. This crisp intermezzo in the analysis of quantified noun phrases is needed to save the GQ representation of nouns, but makes Fuzzy Quantifiers prone to the same problem as GQ.

In sum, although type theoretic approaches do not propose a concrete operationalization, they do impose particular constraints on the way the referent is determined. The reliance on a defined cardinality for the extension of the noun is incompatible with our model as proposed in the previous section. And, as we will see in the next section, it is precisely this reliance on a defined cardinality that makes Generalized Quantifier approach a much less suitable model for real-world application.

5   Experimental Setup and Results

Since we have operational models of the two approaches we can compare their performance in real world interactions. A population of agents play thousands of language games. Each agent is equipped with English spatial categories such as *front, back, left, right, near* and *far* and with the quantifiers *many, few* and the cardinals *one* to *twelve*[1]. We consider two different populations of agents: in one population all agents use our model; the other population uses the generalized quantifier model. Each interaction is either successful (the hearer points to the correct set of objects) or unsuccessful (any of the steps in the language game script fails). The performance of the respective models is reflected by the average communicative success over all language games.

Scene Complexity. Figure 6 shows how the two approaches perform. We test performance in different scenes. Some contain only two objects, others up to ten. The results show two important points: 1) the clustering approach performs significantly better than the generalized quantifier approach in all experimental conditions; and 2) increasing the complexity of the scene the difference in performance grows.

Already in the first condition, where there are only two objects in each scene, our approach reaches ca. 95% success whereas the GQ-based model reaches only ca. 85%. More strikingly though when the number of objects increases this difference grows even more. In the condition where ten objects success of GQ drops to below 50% – only every second interaction is a success. Our approach reaches 80% success even in difficult conditions.

Cardinal vs Vague. To discern the exact performance of cardinal and vague quantifiers we tested each of them separately. Figure 7 shows the result for the quantifiers *few* and *many*. The results show a worse performance overall for our and the GQ model when agents can not use cardinals. Also, the difference between the two models is smaller. Only for four objects or more, the clustering approach is performing better than GQ. And, only for 9 or more objects the difference starts to be more than 10%. This contrasts with populations in which agents can only use cardinal quantifiers (see Figure 8). The overall average communicative success is much higher than vague-only and slightly lower than with all quantifiers. but essentially the same result is obtained. This means that cardinals are responsible for most of the communicative success when agents are given also vague quantifiers. The reason cardinals perform better than just vague quantifiers is that they communicate hard constraints. If the speaker signals he is talking about three objects this is a very clear constraint on the referent set much more so than signalling *few* or *many*.

Perceptual Deviation. To understand why our approach performs consistently better than GQ we have to consider another condition. Figure 9 shows a

---

[1] Syntactic processing is implemented in Fluid Construction Grammar (FCG) [33]. FCG maps IRL-programs to natural phrases and back given a particular lexicon and grammar. Here we implemented lexical and grammatical. Here, we equipped agents with lexical items for spatial categories (e.g., *left, back, front, right*), object classes (e.g., *block, box, robot, thing*) [3] and quantifiers (e.g., *many, few, one, nine*). Moreover, rules for quantified adjective noun phrases, quantified noun phrases, and quantified noun phrases like "three blocks left of the box" are provided [34].

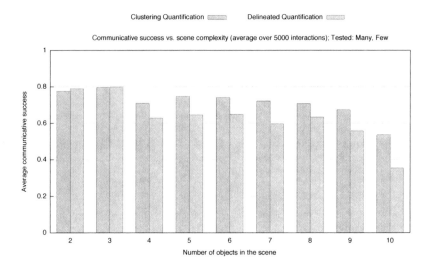

Fig. 7. Average communicative success for populations with vague quantifiers quantifiers such as *many* and *few*

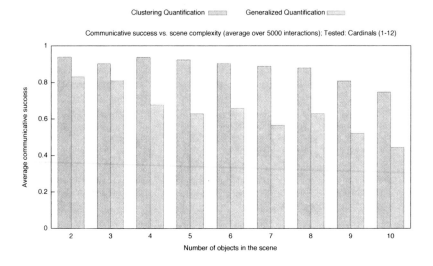

Fig. 8. Average communicative success for cardinal only populations

case where the each two agents interacting in a language game are perceiving the scene through the same robot body. (This manipulation is possible because software agents can access the same hardware.) In this case both approaches perform perfectly.

In embodied interactions, each agent perceives the scene through his own body. Often two agents estimate properties of the world differently. For instance, the agents in Figure 1 each estimate the distance and angle of objects in the scene

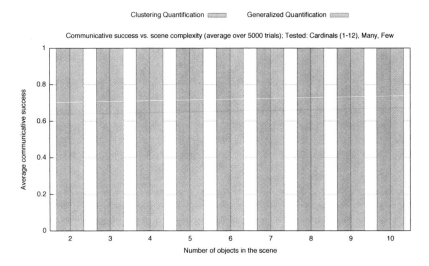

Fig. 9. Average communicative success for populations with all quantifiers. Here both agents perceive the scene through the same camera. I.e., both agents have identical world models.

differently. For instance, for the speaker `object-1` lies at a distance of 31.6cm and an angle of -107 degrees from the box. For the hearer the same object is 22.4cm away from the box at an angle of 81 degrees. We call this the problem of *perceptual deviation* (see [9] for more details). This problem is one of the defining characteristics of interactions in the real world. Importantly, these differences in perception affect the performance of different semantic modeling approaches.

6   Conclusion

In this paper, we have proposed a model for the processing of quantifiers that is intended for use in real world situations. We have extended contrast and acceptability principles known from the psycholinguistics of spatial language and showed how they can be incorporated into a semantics of quantifiers that further adds cardinality constraints. We contrasted our model with a type theory based model and showed that our model 1) is more robust against the effects of perceptual deviation, and 2) scales better with respect to the complexity of scenes.

Cardinality is not the only constraint important for understanding quantifiers. Model theoretic accounts, for instance, strongly focus on the role of quantifiers for inference – a tradition that dates back as far as Aristotle's syllogisms – by considering quantifiers as a functional relation between noun and verb phrase. Our model does not deal with these aspects of quantification. It does however provide an important first step in grounding quantified noun phrases.

An important next step could be to investigate how our model of quantification holds up when used in full sentences. This would undoubtedly raise issues of reasoning and scope resolution [35] and eventually its role in more complex discourse situations [36, 37]. In principle it is fairly straightforward to extend the current model to be used with entire sentences. IRL-networks can easily be extended to verify if a specific property (such as "is red" or "rolls") holds for (a subset of) the referent set. This way IRL-networks can be used to assign truth-values to sentences.

When it comes to inference and scope resolution, a grounded semantics approach like ours can provide important advantages. While on the one hand, grounding introduces complications, such as the problem of perceptual deviation [9], grounding does allow to resolve ambiguities by verifying different possible interpretations in the context [38]. This significantly reduces the need for syntactic resolution. When it comes to dealing with these concerns, the most obvious vantage point is to look at results in Discourse Representation Theory (DRT) [36, 37]. All semantic entities that IRL introduces, become available as free variables throughout the entire discourse. So any referent that is being introduced can freely be used for reference later in the discourse — a treatment of referents that is quite similar to DRT.

Of course, an in depth analysis of quantification in all its complexity is well beyond the scope of this paper. In spite of these reservations, the model does what it was designed for: It models the semantics of natural language quantifiers as expressions of quantity, grounded in real-world perception.

Acknowledgements. We thank Masahiro Fujita, Hideki Shimomura and their team at Sony Corporation Japan for their help with the robotic setups used in the experiments. Funding for the research reported in this paper was provided by Sony CSL Paris and the EU projects ECAgents (FP6) and ALEAR (FP7).

References

1. Steels, L.: Grounding Language through Evolutionary Language Games. In: Steels, L., Hild, M. (eds.) Language Grounding in Robots. Springer, New York (2012)
2. Bleys, J., Loetzsch, M., Spranger, M., Steels, L.: The Grounded Color Naming Game. In: Proceedings of the 18th IEEE International Symposium on Robot and Human Interactive Communication, Ro-man 2009 (2009)
3. Spranger, M.: The co-evolution of basic spatial terms and categories. In: Steels, L. (ed.) Experiments in Cultural Language Evolution. John Benjamins, Amsterdam (2012)
4. Gerasymova, K., Spranger, M.: Handling temporal language: a case study for Russian aspect. In: Steels, L., Hild, M. (eds.) A Whole Systems Approach to Grounding Language in Robots. Springer (2012)
5. Steels, L., Spranger, M., van Trijp, R., Höfer, S., Hild, M.: Emergent action language on real robots. In: Steels, L., Hild, M. (eds.) Language Grounding in Robots. Springer, New York (2012)
6. Steels, L., Spranger, M.: Emergent mirror systems for body language. In: Steels, L. (ed.) Experiments in Cultural Language Evolution, pp. 87–109. John Benjamins (2012)

7. Spranger, M., Loetzsch, M.: The semantics of sit, stand, and lie embodied in robots. In: Taatgen, N.A., van Rijn, H. (eds.) Proceedings of the 31st Annual Conference of the Cognitive Science Society (Cogsci 2009), pp. 2546–2552. Cognitive Science Society, Austin (2009)
8. Rosch, E., Mervis, C., Gray, W., Johnson, D., Boyes-Braem, P.: Basic objects in natural categories. Cognitive Psychology: Key Readings, 448 (2004)
9. Spranger, M., Pauw, S.: Dealing with Perceptual Deviation - Vague Semantics for Spatial Language and Quantification. In: Steels, L., Hild, M. (eds.) Language Grounding in Robots. Springer, Berlin (2012)
10. Pauw, S., Hilfery, J.: The emergence of quantifiers. In: Steels, L. (ed.) Experiments in Cultural Language Evolution. John Benjamins (2012)
11. Pauw, S.: Size matters: A cognitive semantics for quantity (submitted)
12. Hormann, H.: The calculating listener or how many are einige, mehrere, and ein paar (some, several, and a few). In: Meaning, Use, and Interpretation of Language, pp. 221–234 (1983)
13. Newstead, S., Coventry, K.: The role of context and functionality in the interpretation of quantifiers. European Journal of Cognitive Psychology 12(2), 243–259 (2000)
14. Coventry, K., Cangelosi, A., Newstead, S., Bugmann, D.: Talking about quantities in space: Vague quantifiers, context and similarity. Language and Cognition 2(2), 221–241 (2010)
15. Barwise, J., Cooper, R.: Generalized quantifiers and natural language. Linguistics and Philosophy 4(2), 159–219 (1981)
16. Zadeh, L.: Fuzzy sets. Information and Control 8(3), 338–353 (1965)
17. Zadeh, L.: A computational approach to fuzzy quantifiers in natural languages. Computers & Mathematics with Applications 9(1), 149–184 (1983)
18. Fujita, M., Kuroki, Y., Ishida, T.: A small humanoid robot sdr-4x for entertainment applications. In: Proceedings of 2003 IEEE/ASME International Conference on Advanced Intelligent Mechatronics, AIM 2003, vol. 2, pp. 938–943 (2003)
19. Spranger, M., Loetzsch, M., Steels, L.: A Perceptual System for Language Game Experiments. In: Steels, L., Hild, M. (eds.) Language Grounding in Robots. Springer, Berlin (2012)
20. Steels, L.: Language games for autonomous robots. IEEE Intelligent Systems, 16–22 (2001)
21. Tomasello, M.: Constructing a Language: A Usage-Based Theory of Language Acquisition. Harvard University Press (2003)
22. Spranger, M., Loetzsch, M., Pauw, S.: Open-ended Grounded Semantics. In: Coelho, H., Studer, R., Woolridge, M. (eds.) Proceedings of the 19th European Conference on Artificial Intelligence (ECAI 2010). Frontiers in Artificial Intelligence and Applications, pp. 929–934. IOS Press (2010)
23. Spranger, M., Pauw, S., Loetzsch, M., Steels, L.: Open-ended Procedural Semantics. In: Steels, L., Hild, M. (eds.) Language Grounding in Robots. Springer, Berlin (2012)
24. Spranger, M.: The Evolution of Grounded Spatial Language. PhD thesis, Vrije Universiteit Brussels (VUB), Brussels, Belgium (2011)
25. Herskovits, A.: Language and spatial cognition. Studies in Natural Language Processing. Cambridge University Press (1986)
26. Rosch, E., Lloyd, B. (eds.): Cognition and categorization. Lawrence Erlbaum Associates, Hillsdale (1978)
27. Lakoff, G.: Women, Fire, and Dangerous Things: What Categories Reveal about the Mind. University of Chicago Press (1987)

28. Tenbrink, T.: Identifying Objects on the Basis of Spatial Contrast: An Empirical Study. In: Freksa, C., Knauff, M., Krieg-Brückner, B., Nebel, B., Barkowsky, T. (eds.) Spatial Cognition IV. LNCS (LNAI), vol. 3343, pp. 124–146. Springer, Heidelberg (2005)
29. Mitchell, T.M.: Machine learning. McGraw Hill (1997)
30. Lloyd, S.: Least squares quantization in PCM. IEEE Transactions on Information Theory 28(2), 129–137 (1982)
31. Manning, C., Raghavan, P., Schütze, H.: Introduction to information retrieval. Cambridge University Press (2008)
32. Montague, R.: The proper treatment of quantification in ordinary English. Formal Semantics: The Essential Readings (1974)
33. Steels, L., De Beule, J.: Unify and Merge in Fluid Construction Grammar. In: Vogt, P., Sugita, Y., Tuci, E., Nehaniv, C. (eds.) EELC 2006. LNCS (LNAI), vol. 4211, pp. 197–223. Springer, Heidelberg (2006)
34. Spranger, M., Steels, L.: Emergent Functional Grammar for Space. In: Steels, L. (ed.) Experiments in Cultural Language Evolution. John Benjamins, Amsterdam (2012)
35. Kurtzman, H., MacDonald, M.: Resolution of quantifier scope ambiguities. Cognition 48(3), 243–279 (1993)
36. Kamp, H.: A theory of truth and semantic representation. Formal Semantics, 189–222 (1981)
37. van Eijck, J.: Discourse representation theory. Centrum voor Wiskunde en Informatica (1990)
38. Spranger, M., Loetzsch, M.: Syntactic Indeterminacy and Semantic Ambiguity: A Case Study for German Spatial Phrases. In: Steels, L. (ed.) Design Patterns in Fluid Construction Grammar. Constructional Approaches to Language, vol. 11, pp. 265–298. John Benjamins (2011)

Ranked Multidimensional Dialogue Act Annotation

Marcin Włodarczak

Universität Bielefeld, Bielefeld, Germany
mwlodarczak@uni-bielefeld.de

Abstract. In this paper we propose a dialogue act annotation system allowing ranking of communicative functions of utterances in terms of their perceived importance. It is argued that multidimensional dialogue act annotation schemes, while allowing more than one tag per utterance, implicitly treat all functions as equally important. Consequently, they fail to capture the fact that in a given context some of the functions of an utterance may have a higher priority than its other functions. The present approach tries to improve on this deficiency. The results of an annotation experiment suggest that ranking communicative functions accurately reflects the communicative competence of language users.

1 Introduction

Multifunctionality of utterances is often acknowledged in modern dialogue studies [1,2,3]. It is argued that participants simultaneously address several aspects of communication such as providing feedback, managing the turn-taking process and repairing faulty utterances. Various kinds of implicit functions, such as entailed or implicated functions, are an additional source of multifunctionality [4]. The requirement for accounting for multifunctionality of utterances is, of course, also valid for dialogue act annotation schemes. There the notion of multifunctionality is usually introduced explicitly in the form of multidimensional annotation schemes, which allow an utterance to be labelled with more than one function tag. However, since such schemes represent an utterance as an unstructured set of tags, they do not reflect the hierarchical organisation of utterance functions determined by speakers' communicative goals. The approach presented here tries to enrich the existing frameworks with a notion of ranking of communicative functions. Importantly, it allows more than one highest-ranking function and more than two different ranks.

The paper has the following structure. In the following section the notion of multidimensional tagsets is introduced. In Sec. 3 existing annotation frameworks are presented alongside the alternative approach proposed here. The design and the results of an annotation task conducted to validate this framework are presented in Sec. 4, and are followed by conclusions in Sec. 5.

D. Lassiter and M. Slavkovik (Eds.): ESSLLI Student Sessions, LNCS 7415, pp. 67–77, 2012.

2   Multidimensional Tagsets

Unlike in one-dimensional tagsets, which only allow one tag per utterance, in multidimensional tagsets an utterance can be labelled with multiple tags, each representing a different communicative function. We adopt here the formal definitions of both kinds of tagsets given in [2]:

Definition 1. *A one-dimensional tagset is a set $A = \{a_1, a_2, \ldots, a_N\}$, each utterance being tagged with exactly one elementary tag $a_n \in A$.*

Definition 2. *A multi-dimensional tagset is a collection of dimensions (or classes, categories, etc.) $\mathcal{T} = \{A, B, \ldots\}$ where each dimension is in turn a list of tags, say $A = \{a_1, a_2, \ldots, a_M\}, B = \{b_1, b_2, \ldots, b_N\}$. When a multi-dimensional tagset is used, each utterance is tagged with a composite label or tuple of tags $(a_i, b_j, \ldots)$.*

Importantly, the definition requires that a tag be specified in each dimension. If, as is most often the case [4], this requirement is not met and tags are specified only in some dimensions, the empty tag $\emptyset$ must be added to each of the dimensions In such cases, the empty label $(\emptyset, \emptyset, \ldots, \emptyset)$ must be ruled out. The set of possible labels is then $(A \times B \times C \times \ldots) - (\emptyset, \emptyset, \ldots, \emptyset)$.

Alternatively, rather than introduce the empty tag, only those dimensions can be considered in which a non-empty tag is applicable. This is the approach adopted in [5]:

Definition 3. *A multidimensional dialogue act assignment system is a 4-tuple $A = (D, f, C, T)$ where $D = D_1, D_2, \ldots, D_m$ is a dialogue act taxonomy with 'dimensions' $D_1, D_2, \ldots. D_m$, f is a function assigning tags to utterances, C is a set of constraints on admissible combination of tags, which additionally allow a dialogue utterance to be assigned a tag in each of the dimensions, but never more than one tag per dimension, and T is a set of additional labels that f may assign to utterances—T contains such labels as* inaudible *or* abandoned[1].

Notably, the set C should be kept relatively small to make *orthogonality* of dimensions as high as possible. This ensures that any combination of tags from different dimensions is admissible [6].

3   Ranked Annotation System

As mentioned above, multifunctionality of utterances is a result of the fact that speakers simultaneously address several aspects of communication. Furthermore, it could be argued that, depending on the context, specific functions might correspond to speakers' main communicative intentions. Such functions could be perceived as more important than others, thereby forming a hierarchical ordering, a possibility hinted at already in [7]. However, it should be clear that

---

[1] It could be argued that a 5-tuple should be used instead. The additional element should define the domain of the function f—a set of utterances.

multidimensional dialogue act schemes are not capable of capturing this notion. Instead, they (implicitly) treat all functions as equally important.

However, quite apart from their theoretical implications, ranking systems could inform automatic generation of multifunctional utterances by formulating additional constraints on dialogue act combinations. These constraints could the be used by dialogue act managers such as [8] to select the optimal dialogue act candidates in a given context (see also below).

Surprisingly, the problem has received relatively little attention in literature. Geertzen and Bunt [9], while discussing their modifications to the kappa statistic, remark that utterances may be argued to have a *primary function* and possibly several *secondary functions*, and note that disagreement about the former is usually more serious than about the latter.

Popescu-Belis observes that although multidimensional tagsets better reflect the multifunctionality of utterances, one-dimensional tagsets offer an advantage of having a much smaller search space, which leads to higher human and automatic annotation accuracy [10]. One of the ways of overcoming the trade-off between a rich pragmatic representation and a smaller search space is only considering the observed tag combinations. For example, the SWDB-DAMSL tagset [11] was developed by clustering 220 DAMSL [12] tag combinations which occurred in 205,000 utterances of the Switchboard corpus into 42 final mutually exclusive tags.

Instead, [10] proposes an alternative strategy. *Dominant Function Approximation* (DFA) assumes that a tagset specifies default values in every dimension based on linguistic and pragmatic grounds or on frequency counts, and states that at most one communicative function of an utterance is non-default (it is then called a *dominant function*). The author notes that while the DFA might be acceptable for current technological applications, it might not be sufficient for detailed linguistic analyses.

The DFA was verified by checking the number of utterances with more than one non-default functions in existing annotations. Since the number was found to be relatively small (between 3 and 8%), the DFA seems to be correct. However, it could be argued that such findings might be a result of specific annotation guidelines, which often instruct annotators to only mark the most significant function. Indeed, it seems that the possibility of an utterance having several dominant functions cannot be ruled out *a priori*. Moreover, the binary distinction into dominant and default functions may turn out to be too restrictive.

Alternative Approach. The present approach proposes to model the relative prominence of communicative functions by means of *greater or equal prominence* relation. The term *prominence* will be henceforth used to denote the significance of a communicative function relative to other functions of the same utterance in terms of achieving the underlying communicative intentions of the speaker. It is assumed that prominences of every two functions of the same utterance are comparable, i.e. it is possible to decide whether one of the functions is more prominent than the other or whether they are equally prominent. Consequently, the relation in question imposes a *non-strict linear order* on the set of functions of an utterance. Importantly, the ordering of functions is viewed here from the speaker's point of view, i.e. it is assumed that in a given context accomplishing some of the speaker's goals is of greater importance than accomplishing some other goals. For example, in task oriented dialogues functions related to managing the task should be felt to be more prominent than other functions. By contrast, regulating turn-taking should as a rule have low prominence, except when it is communicated explicitly. The lower-ranking functions may either accomplish ancillary goals or be a means of accomplishing higher-ranking goals. This approach is similar to that of Allen and Perrault's plan-based model of speech acts, in which agents' subgoals are formed from unsatisfied conditions of higher-order goals, resulting in partial ordering of the set of goals [13].

A set of functions of an utterance with equal prominences will be referred to as a *level of prominence*. It should be clear that each level of prominence is an equivalence class given an equivalence relation of *equal prominence*. Levels of prominence can be also ordered with respect to the prominence of their elements, i.e. one level of prominence precedes another level of prominence if the prominence of functions in the first is greater than the prominence of functions in the second (relation of *strict linear order*).

This approach might be thought of as a generalisation of the approaches outlined above by imposing fewer constraints on the number of levels of prominence. Specifically, multiple functions are allowed to have the same prominence, i.e. every level of prominence may have more than one element. One of the consequences of this is that many dominant (highest-ranking) functions are permissible, allowing for more flexibility.

It should be also noted that, unlike in the DFA, the notion of default values is not employed here. Moreover, while the DFA was proposed to *simplify* the pragmatic representation of an utterance in order to improve the accuracy of automatic and manual tagging, the present approach aims at *enriching* the pragmatic representation for the needs of linguistic analysis.

Lastly, the concept of the ordering of communicative functions can be easily incorporated into the definition of Multidimensional Dialogue Act Assignment System (Def. 3) to capture the notion of the *Multidimensional Ranked Dialogue Act Assignment System*:

Definition 4. *A Multidimensional Ranked Dialogue Act Assignment System is a 5-tuple $A = (D, f, R, C, T)$ where D, f, C and T are as before, and R is a relation of greater of equal prominence holding between functions represented as tags which f assigns to an utterance.*

This framework was employed in [14] to investigate prominence of feedback functions entailed by backward-looking functions such as *Confirm*, *Answer* or *Accept*, which "indicate how the current utterance relates to the previous discourse" [12]. Such entailed functions were found to be consistently marked as less prominent than the entailing functions. The finding suggests that entailment relations between communicative functions are a major factor influencing their relative prominence.

This was confirmed by results reported in [15, 176-180], in which implicated and side-effect functions were considered in addition to entailed function. Moreover, importance judgements for specific *function combinations* were investigated with a view to improving automatic dialogue act generation. In general, task-management acts were perceived as more important than other acts they co-occured with. It was also found that negative feedback as well as dialogue acts related to maintaining contact, dialogue structuring and resolving problems with speech production are assigned high prominence. Finally, time- and turn-management acts were predominantly judged as equally important.

In this paper we investigate how many dominant functions and how many levels of prominence are identified by annotators.

4 Experiment

Following an analogous experiment proposed by Popescu-Belis [10], participants were asked to order functions assigned to segments with respect to their relative prominence. However, unlike in the original design, minimal constraints were imposed on the ordering of functions of utterances. Since approaches like the DFA impose much stricter constraints on an annotation scheme, they would be supported if under these conditions the proportion of utterances with more than one dominant function and more than two levels of prominence was relatively low. Otherwise, the alternative approach proposed here would be more appropriate.

4.1 Experimental Settings

The HCRC Map Task Corpus [16] was used. Map task dialogues are task related dialogues in which participants cooperate to reproduce a route drawn in one participant's map on the other participant's map. Differences between the maps are introduced to make the task more difficult. A total of 4 minutes and 43 seconds of dialogues were selected for the experiment.

The tagset chosen for the experiment was the DIT^{++} dialogue act taxonomy [17]. It consists of ten dimensions related to managing the task domain (*Task/Activity*), feedback (*Allo-* and *Auto-feedback*), time requirements (*Time Structuring*), problems connected with production of utterances (*Own* and *Partner Communication Management*), attention (*Contact Management*), discourse structure (*Discourse Structuring*) and social conventions (*Social Obligations Management*).

Functional segments, defined as a "minimal stretch of communicative behaviour that has one or more communicative functions" [18], were used as the unit of analysis. The data were segmented in accordance with [19], allowing different segmentations for different dimensions. Communicative functions of the resulting 136 functional segments were annotated by two experts. The differences between annotations were discussed and resolved. Feedback functions entailed by backward-looking functions were included in the annotations.

Four undergraduate students at Tilburg University participated in the experiment. They had been introduced to the annotation scheme and the underlying theory as part of a pragmatics course comprising about three hours of lectures and a few small annotation exercises on data other than map task dialogues. To encourage high quality of annotations the students were motivated by an award of 10% of the total grade for the pragmatic course.

The participants were instructed to order the pre-annotated utterance functions with respect to their relative importance. The ordering was done by assigning each function a numerical value from the set of *consecutive* natural numbers, starting from "1" as the most prominent function. The lowest possible rank was, therefore, equal to the number of utterance functions. However, the same value could be assigned to more then one function. The task was not time-limited.

4.2   Results and Discussion

Since participants failed to rank functions of some segments, the total number of analysed rankings was equal to 294 (243 and 51 for segments with two and three functions respectively). Cohen's kappa [20] was calculated for 53 segments (44 and 9 with two and three functions respectively) ranked properly by all four participants.

Inter-rater agreement values for functions assigned specific ranks are given in Tab. 1 and 2. Mean kappa values indicate fair to moderate agreement [21]. It should be borne in mind, however, that while the participants had some experience using the DIT^{++} tagset, they were completely naïve with respect to ranked annotation. It could be, therefore, hoped that more experienced annotators should achieve much higher agreement.

Proportions of utterances with different numbers of identified levels of prominence are presented in Fig. 1. Overall, in 97% of segments the number of identified levels of prominence was equal to the number of segment functions. Only in three out of 243 two-functional segments, and five out of 51 three-functional segments was it otherwise. Since minimally two levels of prominence were identified in three-functional segments, at most two functions were assigned the same rank. However, all these cases came from the same annotator and might be highly idiosyncratic.

Table 1. Kappa coefficient values for functions assigned specific ranks in two-functional segments

Annotators	Rank 1	Rank 2
1 & 2	0.46	0.35
1 & 3	0.64	0.67
1 & 4	0.34	0.32
2 & 3	0.27	0.21
2 & 4	0.41	0.37
3 & 4	0.47	0.49
Mean	0.43	0.40

Table 2. Kappa coefficient values for functions assigned specific ranks in three-functional segments

Annotators	Rank 1	Rank 2	Rank 3
1 & 2	0.74	0.34	0.35
1 & 3	0.25	0.34	0.50
1 & 4	0.46	0.18	0.50
2 & 3	0.27	0.19	0.06
2 & 4	0.48	0.05	0.38
3 & 4	0.48	0.54	0.38
Mean	0.45	0.27	0.36

The DFA predicts that the proportion of utterances with more than two levels of prominence should be small. Obviously, since utterances with two functions can be assigned the maximum of two distinct ranks, only three-functional segments are of interest in this respect. Although there were relatively few such segments, as much 90% of them would not be represented correctly if more restrictive annotation guidelines, such as the DFA, were adopted.

Fig. 2 presents proportions of utterances with different numbers of identified dominant functions (i.e. functions assigned the rank of one). Here the overwhelming tendency is for a segment to have exactly one such function. This was the case for 99% of two-functional segments and 92% of three-functional segments. The remaining cases again came from the same annotator.

Taken together, the numbers of dominant functions and levels of prominence indicate that there is a very strong tendency for each function to be assigned a

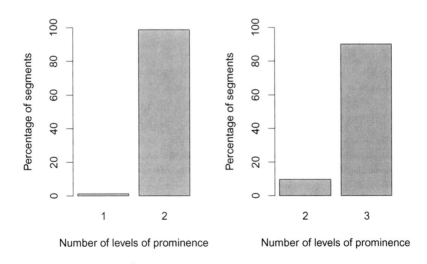

Fig. 1. Proportions of two- (left) and three-functional (right) segments with different numbers of levels of prominence

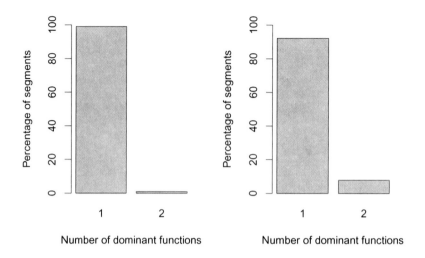

Fig. 2. Proportions of two- (left) and three-functional (right) segments with different numbers of dominant functions

different rank. The relation of *greater or equal prominence* is, therefore, in most cases a relation of *greater prominence*, i.e. it is a relation of *strict* linear order. Consequently, the DFA is only partially adequate. It is right in predicting one dominant function per segment but does not differentiate between the prominences of non-dominant functions. However, it is interesting to note that whenever the same rank was assigned to two functions, it was in fact the first rank in all but one case, which is again a possibility not accounted for by the DFA.

Figure 3 presents distributions of functions of two-functional segments belonging to specific dimensions across the ranks. Although functions from most dimensions are assigned the ranks of one and two with comparable frequencies, there is a noticeable difference between frequencies of *Turn Management* and *Feedback*[2] functions. Specifically, while *Feedback* functions are more frequently assigned the rank of one than the rank of two, the opposite is true for *Turn Management*—these functions are more frequently judged as less prominent when combined with another function. As expected, *Task Management* functions have a higher frequency among the functions ranked first than among those ranked second.

Analogous results for segments with three functions are presented in Fig. 4. However, due to the low number of these segments, it is difficult to draw definite conclusions. More can be said about the relatively more frequent *Feedback* and *Turn Management* functions. Nevertheless, even those tendencies might be specific to the analysed sample. For example, the somewhat surprising high proportion of *Turn Management* functions with the rank of one can be attributed to segments such as "and..." or "well", in which these functions are indeed quite prominent.

---

[2] The *Feedback* category comprises the DIT[++] *Auto-* and *Allo-feedback* dimensions.

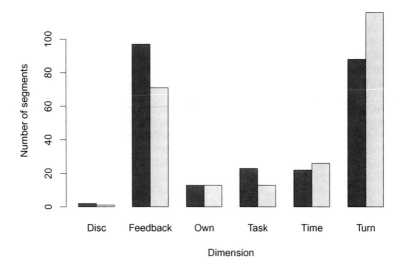

Fig. 3. Distribution of functions from different dimensions between the ranks of one (black bar) and two (grey bar) in two-functional segments. The dimension names were abbreviated as follows: *Feedback–Auto-* and *Allo-feedback* clustered together, *Turn–Turn Management, Task–Task Management, Time–Time Management, Own–Own Communication Management, Disc–Discourse Management.*

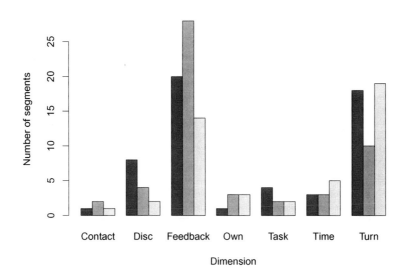

Fig. 4. Distribution of functions from different dimensions between the ranks of one (black bars), two (dark gray bars) and three (light gray bars) in three-functional segments. For the explanation of the dimensions names abbreviations see Fig. 3.

5 Conclusions

The results reported above indicate that in a great majority of cases the number of identified levels of prominence tends to be equal to the number of segment functions. In other words, each function is usually assigned a different rank. Therefore, the relation proposed in Sec. 3 was in most cases a relation of *strict linear order*.

In the light of these findings it must be said that the DFA is right in predicting that most segments have just one highest-ranking function but it fails to account for distinctions among lower-prominence functions. It is, of course, a question of specific research goals whether the resulting underspecification is considered acceptable. Regarding the notion of default values assumed in the DFA, the fact that each function was assigned a different rank in most of the three-functional segments seems to suggest that the usefulness of this notion is limited.

In addition, certain dependencies between dimensions and ranks were discovered. However, since the analysed dataset (and, in particular, the number of segments with three functions) was relatively small, these results require validation with more experimental data.

Notably, the ordinal scale used in the experiment does not reflect the distances between ranks. Consequently, in a three-functional segment the difference in prominence between the function ranked first and the function ranked second could be smaller (or greater) than between the function ranked second and the function ranked third. To address this issue another experiment using a different (e.g. interval) scale would be necessary.

Acknowledgements. I would like to thank Harry Bunt and Volha Petukhova (Tilburg University) for granting me access to their data and for many stimulating discussions. I'd also like to thank the anonymous reviewer for valuable comments.

References

1. Bunt, H.: Dialogue pragmatics and context specification. In: Bunt, H., Black, W. (eds.) Abduction, Belief and Context in Dialogue, pp. 81–150. John Benjamins, Amsterdam (2000)
2. Popescu-Belis, A.: Dialogue acts: One or more dimensions? ISSCO Working Paper, ser. 62. University of Geneva (2005)
3. Allwood, J.: An activity based approach to pragmatics. In: Bunt, H., Black, W. (eds.) Abduction, Belief and Context in Dialogue: Studies in Computational Pragmatics, pp. 47–80. John Benjamins, Amsterdam (2000)
4. Bunt, H.: Multifunctionality in dialogue. Computer Speech and Language 25(2), 225–245 (2011)
5. Bunt, H., Girard, Y.: Designing an open, multidimensional dialogue act taxonomy. In: Gardent, C., Gaiffe, B. (eds.) Proceedings of the Ninth International Workshop on the Semantics and Pragmatics of Dialogue, DIALOR 2005, Nancy (2005)

6. Petukhova, V., Bunt, H.: The independence of dimensions in multidimensional dialogue act annotation. In: Proceedings of Human Language Technologies: The 2009 Annual Conference of the North American Chapter of the Association for Computational Linguistics, Boulder, Colorado, pp. 197–200 (2009)
7. Jakobson, R.: Linguistics and poetics. In: Sebeok, T.A. (ed.) Style in Language, pp. 350–377. MIT Press, Cambridge (1960)
8. Keizer, S., Bunt, H.: Multidimensional dialogue management. In: Proceedings of SIGDIAL 2006, Sydney, pp. 37–45 (2006)
9. Geertzen, J., Bunt, H.: Measuring annotator agreement in a complex hierarchical dialogue act scheme. In: Proceedings of SIGDIAL 2006, Sydney, pp. 126–133 (2006)
10. Popescu-Belis, A.: Dimensionality of dialogue act tagsets: An empirical analysis of large corpora. Language Resources and Evaluation 42(1), 99–107 (2008)
11. Jurafsky, D., Shriberg, E., Biasca, D.: Switchboard SWBD-DAMSL labelling project coder's manual. Draft 13. University of Colorado, Institute of Congnitive Science, Tech. Rep. 97-02 (1997)
12. Allen, J., Core, M.: Draft of Damsl: Dialogue Act Markup in Several Layers (1997), ftp://ftp.cs.rochester.edu/pub/packages/dialog-annotation/manual.ps.gz
13. Allen, J.F., Perrault, C.R.: Analyzing intentions in utterances. Artificial Intelligence 3(15), 143–178 (1980)
14. Włodarczak, M., Bunt, H., Petukhova, V.: Entailed feedback: evidence from a ranking experiment. In: Łupkowski, P., Purver, M. (eds.) Aspects of Semantic and Pragmatics of Dialogue, Poznań, pp. 159–162 (2010)
15. Petukhova, V.V.: Multidimensional dialogue modelling. Ph.D. dissertation. Tilburg University, Tilburg (2011)
16. Anderson, A.H., Bader, M., Gurman Bard, E., Boyle, E., Doherty, G., Garrod, S., Isard, S., Kowtko, J., McAllister, J., Miller, J., Sotillo, C., Thompson, H.S., Weinert, R.: The HCRC map task corpus. Language and Speech 34(4), 351–366 (1991)
17. Bunt, H.: The DIT^{++} taxonomy for functional dialogue markup. In: Proceedings of 8th Int. Conf. on Autonomous Agents and Multiagent Systems (AAMAS 2009), Budapest, pp. 13–24 (2009)
18. ISO, Semantic annotation framework (semaf), part 2: Dialogue acts. ISO, Geneva, Tech. Rep. ISO 24617-2 (2012)
19. Geertzen, J., Petukhova, V., Bunt, H.: A multidimensional approach to utterance segmentation and dialogue act classification. In: Proceedings of the 8th SIGdial Workshop on Discourse and Dialogue, Antwerp, pp. 140–149 (2007)
20. Cohen, J.: A coefficient of agreement for nominal scales. Educational and Psychological Measurement 20(1), 37–46 (1960)
21. Landis, J.R., Koch, G.G.: The measurement of observer agreement for categorical data. Biometrics 33, 159–174 (1977)

The Good, the Bad, and the Odd: Cycles in Answer-Set Programs

Johannes Klaus Fichte

Institute of Information Systems
Vienna University of Technology, Vienna, Austria
`fichte@kr.tuwien.ac.at`

Abstract. Backdoors of answer-set programs are sets of atoms that represent "clever reasoning shortcuts" through the search space. Assignments to backdoor atoms reduce the given program to several programs that belong to a tractable target class. Previous research has considered target classes based on notions of acyclicity where various types of cycles (good and bad cycles) are excluded from graph representations of programs. We generalize the target classes by taking the parity of the number of negative edges on bad cycles into account and consider backdoors for such classes. We establish new hardness results and non-uniform polynomial-time tractability relative to directed or undirected cycles.

Keywords: Answer-Set Programming, Non-monotonic Reasoning.

1   Introduction

Answer-set programming (ASP) is a popular framework to describe concisely search and combinatorial problems [14,16]. It has been successfully applied in crypto-analysis, code optimization, the semantic web, and several other fields [18]. Problems are encoded by rules and constraints into disjunctive logic programs whose solutions are answer-sets (stable models). The problem of deciding answer-set existence for a disjunctive logic program is Σ_2^P-complete. [4]. However, this hardness result does not exclude quick solutions for large instances if we can exploit structural properties that might be present in real-world instances.

Recently, Fichte and Szeider [5] have established a new approach to ASP based on the idea of backdoors, a concept that originates from the area of satisfiability [20]. Backdoors exploit the structure of instances by identifying sets of atoms that are important for reasoning. A *backdoor* of a disjunctive logic program is a set of variables such that any instantiation of the variables yields a simplified logic program that lies in a class of programs where the decision problem we are interested in is tractable. By means of a backdoor of size k for a disjunctive logic program we can solve the program by solving all the 2^k tractable programs that correspond to the truth assignments of the atoms in the backdoor. For every answer-set of each of the 2^k tractable programs we need to check whether it gives rise to an answer-set of the given program. In order to do this efficiently,

D. Lassiter and M. Slavkovik (Eds.): ESSLLI Student Sessions, LNCS 7415, pp. 78–90, 2012.

we consider tractable programs that have a small number of answer-sets (e.g., stratified programs [9]).

We consider target classes based on various notions of acyclicity on the *directed/undirected dependency graph* of the disjunctive logic program. A cycle is *bad* if it contains an edge that represents an atom from a negative body of a rule. Since larger target classes facilitate smaller backdoors, we are interested in large target classes that allow small backdoors and efficient algorithms for finding the backdoors.

Contribution

In this paper, we extend the backdoor approach of [5] using ideas from Zhao [23]. We enlarge the target classes by taking the parity of the number of negative edges or vertices on bad cycles into account and consider backdoors with respect to such classes. This allows us to consider larger classes that also contain non-stratified programs. Our main results are as follows:

1. For target classes based on directed bad even cycles, the detection of backdoors of bounded size is co-NP-hard (Theorem 2).
2. For target classes based on undirected bad even cycles, the detection of backdoors is non-uniform polynomial-time tractable (Theorem 4).

The result (2) is a *non-uniform* polynomial-time result since the order of the polynomial depends on the backdoor size. The class of all non-uniform polynomial-time tractable problems is also known as XP [3]. An algorithm is *uniform* polynomial-time tractable if it runs in time $\mathcal{O}(f(k) \cdot n^c)$ where f is an arbitrary function and c is a constant independent from the *parameter* k. Uniform polynomial-time tractable problems are also known as *fixed-parameter tractable* problems [3]. We provide strong theoretical evidence in Proposition 2 that result (2) cannot be extended to uniform polynomial-time tractability. Furthermore, we establish in Proposition 4 that result (2) generalizes a result of Lin and Zhao [13].

2 Formal Background

We consider a universe U of propositional *atoms*. A *literal* is an atom $a \in U$ or its negation $\neg a$. A *disjunctive logic program* (or simply a *program*) P is a set of *rules* of the following form

$$x_1 \vee \ldots \vee x_l \quad \leftarrow \quad y_1, \ldots, y_m, \neg z_1, \ldots, \neg z_n \qquad (1)$$

where $x_1, \ldots, x_l, y_1, \ldots, y_m, z_1, \ldots, z_n$ are atoms and l, m, n are non-negative integers. Let r be a rule. We write $\{x_1, \ldots, x_l\} = H(r)$ (the *head* of r), $\{y_1, \ldots, y_m\} = B^+(r)$ (the *positive body* of r) and $\{z_1, \ldots, z_n\} = B^-(r)$ (the *negative body* of r). We denote the sets of atoms occurring in a rule r or in a program P by $\mathrm{at}(r) = H(r) \cup B^+(r) \cup B^-(r)$ and $\mathrm{at}(P) = \bigcup_{r \in P} \mathrm{at}(r)$, respectively. A rule r is *normal* if $|H(r)| = 1$. A rule is *Horn* (or definite) if normal and $B^-(r) = \emptyset$. We say that a program has a certain property if all its rules have the property. **Horn** refers to the class of all Horn programs.

A set M of atoms *satisfies* a rule r if $(H(r) \cup B^-(r)) \cap M \neq \emptyset$ or $B^+(r) \backslash M \neq \emptyset$. M is a *model* of P if it satisfies all rules of P. The *Gelfond-Lifschitz (GL) reduct* of a program P under a set M of atoms is the program P^M obtained from P by first removing all rules r with $B^-(r) \cap M \neq \emptyset$ and second removing all $\neg z$ where $z \in B^-(r)$ from the remaining rules r [10]. M is an *answer-set* (or *stable model*) of a program P if M is a minimal model of P^M. We denote by $\mathrm{AS}(P)$ the set of all answer-sets of P. The main computational problems in ASP are:

- CONSISTENCY: given a program P, does P have an answer-set?
- CREDULOUS/SKEPTICAL REASONING: given a program P and an atom $a \in \mathrm{at}(P)$, is a contained in some/all answer-set(s) of P?
- AS COUNTING: how many answer-sets does P have?
- AS ENUMERATION: list all answer-sets of P.

2.1 Strong Backdoors

Backdoors are small sets of atoms which can be used to simplify the considered computational problems in ASP. They have originally been introduced by Williams, Gomes, and Selman [20,21] as a concept for the analysis of decision heuristics in propositional satisfiability [6]. Fichte and Szeider [5] have recently adapted backdoors to the field of ASP. First, we define a reduct of a program with respect to a given set of atoms. Subsequently, we give the notion of strong backdoors. In the following we refer to $\mathcal{C}$ as the *target class* of the backdoor.

A *truth assignment* is a mapping $\tau : X \to \{0,1\}$ defined for a set $X \subseteq U$ of atoms. For $x \in X$ we let $\tau(\neg x) = 1 - \tau(x)$. By $\mathrm{ta}(X)$ we denote the set of all truth assignments $\tau : X \to \{0,1\}$.

Definition 1. *Let P be a program, X a set of atoms, and $\tau \in \mathrm{ta}(X)$. The* truth assignment reduct *of P under τ is the logic program P_τ obtained by*

1. *removing all rules r with $H(r) \cap \tau^{-1}(1) \neq \emptyset$ or $H(r) \subseteq X$;*
2. *removing all rules r with $B^+(r) \cap \tau^{-1}(0) \neq \emptyset$;*
3. *removing all rules r with $B^-(r) \cap \tau^{-1}(1) \neq \emptyset$;*
4. *removing from the heads and bodies of the remaining rules all literals $v, \neg v$ with $v \in X$.*

Definition 2. *A set X of atoms is a strong $\mathcal{C}$-backdoor of a program P if $P_\tau \in \mathcal{C}$ for all truth assignments $\tau \in \mathrm{ta}(X)$. We define the problem of finding strong backdoors as follows: k-STRONG $\mathcal{C}$-BACKDOOR DETECTION: given a program P, find a strong $\mathcal{C}$-backdoor X of P of size at most k, or report that such X does not exist.*

Example 1. Consider the program

$$P = \{b \leftarrow a; \ d \leftarrow a; \ b \leftarrow \neg c; \ a \leftarrow d, \neg c; \ a \vee c \leftarrow d, \neg b; \ d\}.$$

The set $X = \{b, c\}$ is a strong **Horn**-backdoor since the truth assignment reducts $P_{b=0,c=0} = P_{00} = \{d \leftarrow a; \ a \leftarrow d; \ d\}$, $P_{01} = \{d \leftarrow a; \ d\}$, $P_{10} = \{d \leftarrow a; \ a \leftarrow d; \ d\}$, and $P_{11} = \{d \leftarrow a; \ d\}$ are in the target class **Horn**.

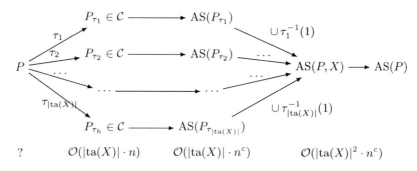

Fig. 1. Exploit pattern of ASP backdoors if the target class $\mathcal{C}$ is normal and enumerable where n denotes the input size of P

Definition 3. *A class $\mathcal{C}$ of programs is* enumerable *if for each $P \in \mathcal{C}$ we can compute* $\mathrm{AS}(P)$ *in polynomial time.*

Fichte and Szeider [5] have shown that backdoors to normal programs can be used to determine answer-sets. The result is stated subsequently.

Theorem 1 ([5]). *Let $\mathcal{C}$ be an enumerable class of normal programs. The computation of $\mathrm{AS}(P)$ is uniform polynomial-time tractable for programs with a strong $\mathcal{C}$-backdoor of bounded size, assuming that the backdoor is given as an input (fixed-parameter-tractable for the parameter size of a strong $\mathcal{C}$-backdoor).*

Figure 1 illustrates the structure of the proof. For a given program P and a strong $\mathcal{C}$-backdoor X of P we have to consider $|\mathrm{ta}(X)|$ truth assignments to the atoms in the backdoor X. For each truth assignment $\tau \in \mathrm{ta}(X)$ we reduce the program P to a program P_τ and compute the answer-sets $\mathrm{AS}(P_\tau)$. Finally, we obtain the answer-sets $\mathrm{AS}(P)$ by checking for each $M \in \mathrm{AS}(P_\tau)$ in uniform polynomial time whether it gives rise to an answer-set of P.

Example 2. We consider the program of Example 1. The answer-sets of P_τ are $\mathrm{AS}(P_{00}) = \{\{a, d\}\}$, $\mathrm{AS}(P_{01}) = \{\{d\}\}$, $\mathrm{AS}(P_{10}) = \{\{a, d\}\}$, and $\mathrm{AS}(P_{11}) = \{\{d\}\}$. Thus $\mathrm{AS}(P, X) = \{\{a, d\}, \{c, d\}, \{a, b, d\}, \{b, c, d\}\}$, and since $\{c, d\}$ and $\{a, b, d\}$ are answer-sets of P, we obtain $\mathrm{AS}(P) = \{\{a, b, d\}, \{c, d\}\}$.

2.2 Deletion Backdoors

For a program P and a set X of atoms we define $P - X$ as the program obtained from P by deleting all atoms contained in X and their negations from the heads and bodies of all the rules of P. The definition gives rise to deletion backdoors and the problem of finding deletion backdoors, which is in some cases easier to solve than the problem of finding strong backdoors.

Definition 4 (Deletion C-backdoor). *Let C be a class of programs. A set X of atoms is a deletion C-backdoor of a program P if $P - X \in C$. We define the problem k-DELETION C-BACKDOOR DETECTION as follows: given a program P, find a deletion C-backdoor X of P of size at most k, or report that such X does not exist.*

2.3   Target Classes

As explained above, we need to consider target classes of programs that only have a small number of answer-sets. There are two causes for a program to have a large number of answer-sets: (i) disjunctions in the heads of rules, and (ii) certain cyclic dependencies between rules. Disallowing both causes yields so-called *stratified* programs [9]. In order to define acyclicity we associate with each program P its *directed dependency graph* D_P and its *undirected dependency graph* U_P where D_P is an extended version of the dependency graph in [1] and U_P of the undirected dependency graph in [11]. D_P has as vertices the atoms of P, a directed edge (x, y) between any two atoms x, y for which there is a rule $r \in P$ with $x \in H(r)$ and $y \in B(r)$ or a rule $r \in P$ with $x, y \in H(r)$; if there is a rule $r \in P$ with $x \in H(r)$ and $y \in B^-(r)$ or there is a rule $r \in P$ with $x, y \in H(r)$, then the edge (x, y) is called a *negative edge*. U_P is obtained from D_P by replacing each negative edge $e = (x, y)$ with two undirected edges $\{x, v_e\}, \{v_e, y\}$ where v_e is a new *negative vertex*, and by replacing each remaining directed edge (x, y) with an undirected edge $\{x, y\}$. By an *(un)directed cycle of P* we mean an (un)directed simple cycle in D_P (U_P). An (un)directed cycle is *bad* if it contains a negative edge (a negative vertex), otherwise it is *good*.

In recent research, Fichte and Szeider [5] have considered target classes that consist of normal programs without directed bad cycles (**no-DBC**), without undirected bad cycles (**no-BC**), without directed cycles (**no-DC**), and without undirected cycles (**no-C**). **no-DBC** is exactly the class that contains all stratified programs [1]. Fichte and Szeider have examined the problems k-STRONG C-BACKDOOR DETECTION and k-DELETION C-BACKDOOR DETECTION on the target classes $C \in \{\text{no-C}, \text{no-BC}, \text{no-DC}, \text{no-DBC}\}$.

Example 3. The set $X = \{a, b\}$ is a deletion **no-BC**-backdoor of the program P of Example 1, since the simplification $P - X = \{d; \leftarrow \neg c; \leftarrow d, \neg c; c \leftarrow d\}$ is in the target class **no-BC**. There is no deletion **no-BC**-backdoor of size 1 as $P - \{a\}$ and $P - \{d\}$ contain the cycle $(b, v_{(b,c)}, c, v_{(c,b)}, b)$, $P - \{b\}$ contains the cycle $(a, v_{(a,c)}, c, d, a)$, and $P - \{c\}$ contains the cycle $(a, b, v_{(a,b)}, a)$.

3   Parity Cycles

In this section, we generalize the acyclicity based target classes by taking the parity of the number of negative edges (vertices) into account and consider

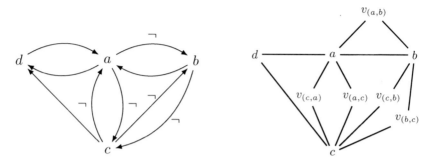

Fig. 2. Directed dependency graph D_P (left) and undirected dependency graph U_P (right) of the program P of Example 1

backdoors for such classes. We say that an (un)directed cycle in a given program P is *even* if the cycle has an even number of negative edges (vertices). The definition gives rise to the new target classes of all *normal* programs without directed bad even cycles (**no-DBEC**), without undirected bad even cycles (**no-BEC**), without directed even cycles (**no-DEC**), and without even cycles (**no-EC**).

Example 4. For instance in the program P of Example 1 the sequence (a, b, c, a) is a directed bad even cycle, $(a, b, v_{(b,c)}, c, v_{(c,a)}, a)$ is an undirected bad even cycle, (a, d, a) is a directed even cycle, and $(a, b, v_{(b,c)}, c, v_{(c,a)}, a)$ is an undirected even cycle (see Figure 2). The set $X = \{c\}$ is a strong **no-DBEC**-backdoor since the truth assignment reducts $P_{c=0} = P_0 = \{b \leftarrow a;\ d \leftarrow a;\ b;\ a \leftarrow d;\ a \leftarrow d, \neg b;\ d\}$ and $P_1 = \{b \leftarrow a;\ d \leftarrow a;\ d\}$ are in the target class **no-DBEC**. X is also a strong **no-BEC**-backdoor, since $P_0 \in$ **no-BEC** and $P_1 \in$ **no-BEC**. The answer-sets of P_τ are $\mathrm{AS}(P_0) = \{\{a, b, d\}\}$ and $\mathrm{AS}(P_1) = \{\{d\}\}$. Thus $\mathrm{AS}(P, X) = \{\{a, b, d\}, \{c, d\}\}$, and since $\{a, b, d\}$ and $\{c, d\}$ are answer-sets of P, we obtain $\mathrm{AS}(P) = \{\{a, b, d\}, \{c, d\}\}$.

3.1   Computing Answer-Sets

First, we discuss the connection between the problem of finding bad even cycles in signed graphs and even cycles in graphs. A *signed (directed) graph* is a graph whose edges are either positive (unlabeled) or negative. We construct the *unlabeled directed graph* G' of a signed directed graph $G = (V, E)$ as follows: we replace in G each positive edge $e = (u, v) \in E$ by two edges $(u, v_e), (v_e, v)$ where v_e is a new vertex. Then we remove the labels from the negative edges. Analogously, we construct the *unlabeled undirected graph* where we ignore the direction of the edges. The following connection was already observed by Aracena, Gajardo, and Montalva [15].

Lemma 1 ([15]). *A signed (un)directed graph G has an even cycle if and only if its unlabeled (un)directed graph G' has a cycle of even length.*

Proof. Let $G = (V, E)$ be the signed directed graph and $G' = (V', E')$ its unlabeled directed graph. Since every positive edge $e \in E$ corresponds to two edges $e_1, e_2 \in E'$ and every negative edge $e \in E$ corresponds to one edge $e \in E'$, a cycle in G with an even number of negative edges gives a cycle of even length in G'. Conversely, let $G' = (V', E')$ be an unlabeled directed graph that contains a cycle of even length. Then G contains an even cycle since every two edges $e_1, e_2 \in E'$ correspond either to two negative edges or no negative edge. The proof works analogously for undirected graphs.   □

The *well-founded model* introduced by Van Gelder, Ross, and Schlipf [8] represents a three valued model where truth assignments additionally map to the value "undefined". We follow the definition by Lin and Zhao [13]. Let P be a normal program and $M \subseteq \mathrm{at}(P)$. Then $\mathrm{W}_P(M)$ consists of the minimal model of P^M. Let L be the least fixed point of $\mathrm{W}_P(\mathrm{W}_P(M))$ and K the greatest fixed point of $\mathrm{W}_P(\mathrm{W}_P(M))$. The well-founded model WFM(P) consists of the set L of atoms that are mapped to 1, the set $\mathrm{at}(P) \setminus K$ of atoms that are mapped to 0, and the set $\mathrm{at}(P) \setminus (L \cup (\mathrm{at}(P) \setminus K))$ that are undefined.

Lemma 2. *The target classes* **no-DBEC, no-BEC, no-DEC, no-EC** *are enumerable.*

Proof. Zhao [23] has shown that a program without a bad even cycle has either no answer-set or the well-founded model is its answer-set. Since $\mathrm{W}_P(\mathrm{W}_P(M))$ is monotone for a normal program, there is a least fixed point and it can be computed in polynomial time [7,8]. Thus the answer-sets can be computed in polynomial time. By definition **no-DEC** $\subsetneq$ **no-DBEC** and **no-EC** $\subsetneq$ **no-BEC** $\subsetneq$ **no-DBEC**, thus it prevails for the remaining target classes.   □

The following statement is a direct consequence of Theorem 1.

Proposition 1. *The problems* CONSISTENCY, CREDULOUS *and* SKEPTICAL REASONING, AS COUNTING *and* AS ENUMERATION *are all polynomial-time solvable for programs with strong $\mathcal{C}$-backdoor of bounded size, $\mathcal{C} \in \{$***no-DBEC, no-BEC, no-DEC, no-EC***$\}$, assuming that the backdoor is given as an input.*

Proof (Sketch). Since the (un)directed dependency graph of a program P contains an even cycle on distinct atoms $x, y \in H(r)$ for some $r \in P$, every target class $\mathcal{C} \in \{$ **no-DBEC, no-BEC, no-DEC, no-EC** $\}$ contains only programs that are normal. Hence we obtain the proposition.

If the problem of determining backdoors is also polynomial-time solvable with respect to the fixed size of a smallest strong $\mathcal{C}$-backdoor, then the ASP problems are polynomial-time solvable.

Lemma 3. *For all target classes* $\mathcal{C} \in \{$**no-DBEC, no-BEC, no-DEC, no-EC**$\}$ *every deletion $\mathcal{C}$-backdoor is also a strong $\mathcal{C}$-backdoor.*

Proof. We show the statement by proving that $P_\tau \subseteq P - X$ for every $\tau \in \mathrm{ta}(X)$ and for every program $P \in \mathcal{C}$. Let P be a program and $X \subseteq \mathrm{at}(P)$. We choose arbitrarily a truth assignment $\tau \in \mathrm{ta}(X)$. For a rule $r \in P$ if the conditions (1), (2), and (3) of Definition 1 do not apply, then all literals $x, \neg x$ with $x \in X$ are removed from the heads $H(r)$ and bodies $B^+(r) \cup B^-(r)$ by the truth assignment reduct of P under τ. This is also done by $P - X$. If at least one of the conditions (1), (2), or (3) applies, then $r \notin P_\tau$. Hence $P_\tau \subseteq P - X$.   □

3.2   Backdoor Detection for Directed Target Classes

In order to apply backdoors, we need to find them first. In this section we consider the problems k-STRONG $\mathcal{C}$-BACKDOOR DETECTION and k-DELETION $\mathcal{C}$-BACKDOOR DETECTION for the target classes $\mathcal{C} \in \{\mathbf{no\text{-}DEC}, \mathbf{no\text{-}DBEC}\}$.

Theorem 2. *The problems k-STRONG $\mathbf{no\text{-}DBEC}$-BACKDOOR DETECTION and k-DELETION $\mathbf{no\text{-}DBEC}$-BACKDOOR DETECTION are co-NP-hard for every constant $k \geq 0$.*

Proof. Let $G = (V, E)$ be an unlabeled directed graph and $s, m, t \in V$ distinct vertices. We prove the theorem by reducing the decision problem whether G contains a simple path from s to t via m to the complement of k-STRONG (DELETION) $\mathbf{no\text{-}DBEC}$-BACKDOOR DETECTION. Lapaugh and Papadimitriou [12] have shown that deciding whether G contains a simple path from s to t via m is NP-complete.

We define the *program* $P_{s,m,t}(G)$ as follows: For each edge $e = (v, w) \in E$ where $v, w \in V$ and $w \neq m$ we construct a rule r_e: $v \leftarrow w$. For the edges $e = (v, m)$ where $v \in V$ we construct a rule r_e: $v \leftarrow \neg m$. Then we add the rule $r_{s,t}$: $t \leftarrow \neg s$. We show that G has a simple path from s to t via m if and only if $P_{s,m,t}(G) \notin \mathbf{no\text{-}DBEC}$.

Let $p = (s, s_1, \ldots, s_k, m, t_1, \ldots, t_l, t)$ be a path in G where s, m, and t are distinct. The construction $P_{s,m,t}$ gives rules $\{s \leftarrow s_1; s_1 \leftarrow s_2; \ldots; s_k \leftarrow \neg m; m \leftarrow t_1; t_1 \leftarrow t_2; \ldots; t_l \leftarrow t; t \leftarrow \neg s\} \in P_{s,m,t}(G)$. Since D_P contains the cycle $c = (s, s_1, \ldots, s_k, m, t_1, \ldots, t_l, t, s)$ and c contains an even number of negative edges, the program $P_{s,m,t}(G) \notin \mathbf{no\text{-}DBEC}$.

Conversely, let $P_{s,m,t}(G) \in \mathbf{no\text{-}DBEC}$, then $P_{s,m,t}(G)$ contains a bad even cycle c. Since the construction of $P_{s,m,t}(G)$ gives only negative edges $(t, s) \in D_{P_{s,m,t}(G)}$ and $(v, m) \in D_{P_{s,m,t}(G)}$ where $v \in \mathrm{at}(P_{s,m,t}(G))$, the cycle c must have the vertices s, m, and t. Further every rule $r_e \in P_{s,m,t}(G)$ corresponds to an edge $e \in E$. It follows that there is a simple path $s, \ldots, m, \ldots, t$.

The reduction shows that k-STRONG $\mathbf{no\text{-}DBEC}$-BACKDOOR DETECTION and k-DELETION $\mathbf{no\text{-}DBEC}$-BACKDOOR DETECTION are co-NP-hard for $k = 0$. Next, we describe how this can be generalized to arbitrary k. Let $P_{s,m,t}^k$ denote the program obtained from $P_{s,m,t}$ by adding rules $s_i \leftarrow m_i$, $m_i \leftarrow t_i$, and $t_i \leftarrow \neg s_i$ where s_i, m_i, t_i are new atoms, for $1 \leq i \leq k$. Clearly $P_{s,m,t}^k$ has a deletion $\mathbf{no\text{-}DBEC}$-backdoor of size $\leq k$ if and only if $P_{s,m,t}^k(G) \in \mathbf{no\text{-}DBEC}$, hence k-DELETION $\mathbf{no\text{-}DBEC}$-BACKDOOR DETECTION is co-NP-hard. Similarly, $P_{s,m,t}^k$ has a strong $\mathbf{no\text{-}DBEC}$-backdoor of size $\leq k$ if and only if

$P^k_{s,m,t}(G) \in$ **no-DBEC**, and so k-STRONG **no-DBEC**-BACKDOOR DETECTION is co-NP-hard as well. Hence the theorem follows.   □

Theorem 3. *The problems* k-DELETION **no-DEC**-BACKDOOR DETECTION *and* k-STRONG **no-DEC**-BACKDOOR DETECTION *are non-uniform polynomial-time tractable.*

Proof. By Lemma 1, we can reduce to the problem of finding a cycle of even length in the unlabeled dependency graph. Vazirani and Yannakakis [19] have shown that finding a cycle of even length in a directed graph is equivalent to finding a Pfaffian orientation of a graph. Since Robertson, Seymour, and Thomas [17] have shown that a Pfaffian orientation can be found in polynomial time, for each possible backdoor size k we need to test for $\binom{n}{k} \leq n^k$ subsets $S \subseteq V$ of size k whether $D_P - S$ contains a cycle of even length, respectively D_{P_τ} for $\tau \in \mathrm{ta}(S)$. Since we can do this in polynomial time for each fixed k, the theorem follows.   □

In Theorem 3 we consider k as a constant. In the following proposition we show that if k is considered as part of the input, then the problem k-STRONG **no-DEC**-BACKDOOR DETECTION is polynomial-time equivalent to the problem k-HITTING SET which is $W[2]$-hard. An instance of this problem is a pair (S, k) where $\mathsf{S} = \{S_1, \ldots, S_m\}$ is a family of sets and k is an integer. The question is whether there exists a set H of size at most k which intersects with all the S_i; such H is a hitting set. Note that there is strong theoretical evidence that the problem k-HITTING SET does not admit uniform polynomial-time tractability [3].

Proposition 2. *The problem* k-STRONG **no-DEC**-BACKDOOR DETECTION *is polynomial-time equivalent to the problem* k-HITTING SET.

Proof. The proof is very similar to the proof for target classes without respecting the parity by Fichte and Szeider [5]. We construct a program P as follows. As atoms we take the elements of $\mathcal{S} = \bigcup_{i=1}^m S_i$ and new atoms a_i^j and b_i^j for $1 \leq i \leq m$, $1 \leq j \leq k+1$. For each $1 \leq i \leq m$ and $1 \leq j \leq k+1$ we take two rules r_i^j, s_i^j where $H(r_i^j) = \{a_i^j\}$, $B^-(r_i^j) = S_i \cup \{b_i^j\}$, $B^+(r_i^j) = \emptyset$; $H(s_i^j) = \{b_i^j\}$, $B^-(s_i^j) = \{a_i^j\}$, $B^+(s_i^j) = \mathcal{S}$.

We show that S has a hitting set of size at most k if and only if P has a strong **no-DEC**-backdoor of size at most k. Let S be a family of sets and H an hitting set of S of size at most k. Choose arbitrarily an atom $s_i \in H$ and a truth assignment $\tau \in \mathrm{ta}(H)$. If $s_i \in \tau^{-1}(0)$, then $B^+(s_i^j) \cap \tau^{-1}(0) \neq \emptyset$ for $1 \leq j \leq k+1$. Thus $s_i^j \notin P_\tau$. If $s_i \in \tau^{-1}(1)$, then $B^-(r_i^j) \cap \tau^{-1}(1) \neq \emptyset$ for $1 \leq j \leq k+1$. Thus $r_i^j \notin P_\tau$. Since H contains at least one element $e \in S$ from each set $S \in \mathcal{S}$, the truth assignment reduct $P_\tau \in$ **no-DEC**. We conclude that H is a strong **no-DEC**-backdoor of P of size at most k.

Conversely, let X be a strong **no-DEC**-backdoor of P of size at most k. Since the directed dependency graph D_P contains $k+1$ directed even cycles (a_i^j, b_i^j, a_i^j) and a_i^j (respectively b_i^j) is contained in exactly one rule r_i^j (respectively s_i^j), we have to select atoms from S_i. Since $S_i \subseteq B^-(r_i^j)$ for $1 \leq i \leq m$ and $1 \leq j \leq k+1$, we have to select at least one element from each S_i into the backdoor X. Thus we have established that X is a hitting set of S of size at most k, and so the theorem follows.   □

3.3   Backdoor Detection for Undirected Target Classes

The results of Theorem 2 suggest to consider the backdoor detection on the weaker target classes based on undirected even acyclicity.

Lemma 4. *Let P be a program. $P \in$ **no-EC** can be decided in polynomial time.*

Proof. Let P be a program and D_P its directed dependency graph. Lemma 1 allows to consider the problem of finding an even cycle in the unlabeled, undirected version of D_P. Since Yuster and Zwick [22] have shown that finding an even cycle in an undirected graph is polynomial-time solvable, the lemma holds.   □

Lemma 5. *Let P be a program. $P \in$ **no-BEC** can be decided in polynomial time.*

Proof. Let P be a program and G its directed dependency graph D_P. For a negative edge e of G we define G_e to be the unlabeled undirected graph of $G - e$. Now G contains a bad even cycle if and only if G has an edge $e = \{s, t\}$ such that G_e contains an odd path from s to t. Since Arikati and Peled [2] have shown that finding an odd path in an undirected graph is polynomial-time solvable, the lemma follows.   □

Theorem 4. *For the target classes $\mathcal{C} \in \{$**no-EC**, **no-BEC**$\}$ the problems k-DELETION $\mathcal{C}$-BACKDOOR DETECTION and k-STRONG $\mathcal{C}$-BACKDOOR DETECTION are non-uniform polynomial-time tractable.*

Proof. Let P be a program and $U_P = (V, E)$ its undirected dependency graph. Let n be the size of V. For each possible backdoor of size k we need to test $\binom{n}{k} \leq n^k$ subsets $S \subseteq V$ of size k whether $U_P - S$ contains a (bad) cycle of even length, respectively U_{P_τ} for $\tau \in \mathrm{ta}(S)$. Since we can do this in polynomial time for each fixed k, the problems k-DELETION $\mathcal{C}$-BACKDOOR and k-STRONG $\mathcal{C}$-BACKDOOR DETECTION are non-uniform polynomial-time tractable.   □

In Theorem 4 we consider k as a constant. If k is considered as part of the input we can show that for each class $\mathcal{C} \in \{$**no-EC**, **no-BEC**$\}$ the problem k-STRONG $\mathcal{C}$-BACKDOOR DETECTION is polynomial-time equivalent to k-HITTING SET [5]. As mentioned before for **no-DEC** there is strong theoretical evidence that k-STRONG $\mathcal{C}$-BACKDOOR DETECTION does not admit a uniform polynomial-time tractability result.

Proposition 3. *The problem k-STRONG $\mathcal{C}$-BACKDOOR DETECTION is polynomial-time equivalent to the problem k-HITTING SET for each class $\mathcal{C} \in \{$**no-EC**, **no-BEC**$\}$.*

Proof. We modify the above reduction from k-HITTING SET by redefining the rules r_i^j, s_i^j. We put $H(r_i^j) = \{a_i^j\}$, $B^-(r_i^j) = S_i \cup \{b_i^j\}$, $B^+(r_i^j) = S_i$; $H(s_i^j) = \{b_i^j\}$, $B^-(s_i^j) = \{a_i^j\}$, $B^+(s_i^j) = \emptyset$. $\qquad\square$

4   Relationship between Target Classes

In this section, we compare ASP parameters in terms of their *generality*. We have already observed that every deletion $\mathcal{C}$-backdoor is a strong $\mathcal{C}$-backdoor for a target class $\mathcal{C} \in \{\textbf{no-EC}, \textbf{no-DEC}, \textbf{no-BEC}, \textbf{no-DBEC}\}$. For the considered target classes it is easy to see that if $\mathcal{C} \subseteq \mathcal{C}'$, then every $\mathcal{C}'$-backdoor of a program P is also a $\mathcal{C}$-backdoor, but there might exist smaller $\mathcal{C}'$-backdoors. Thus we compare the target classes among each other instead of the backdoors. By definition we have $\textbf{no-DBC} \subsetneq \textbf{no-DBEC}$, $\textbf{no-DEC} \subsetneq \textbf{no-DBEC}$, $\textbf{no-EC} \subsetneq \textbf{no-BEC}$, $\textbf{no-C} \subsetneq \textbf{no-EC}$, and $\textbf{no-DC} \subsetneq \textbf{no-DEC}$. The diagram in Fig. 3 shows the relationship between the various classes, an arrow from $\mathcal{C}$ to $\mathcal{C}'$ indicates that $\mathcal{C}$ is a proper subset of $\mathcal{C}'$. If there is no arrow between two classes (or the arrow does not follow by transitivity of set inclusion), then the two classes are incomparable.

Lin and Zhao [13] have studied even cycles as a parameter to ASP. They have shown that for fixed l the main reasoning problems are polynomial-time solvable if the number of even cycles is bounded. The following proposition states that the size k of **no-DBEC**-backdoors is a more general parameter than the number of even cycles. In particular, it follows that the reduction that maps a program to itself and replaces the parameter l with k provides a trivial fpt-reduction with respect to any decision problem on programs (fpt-reductions are extensions

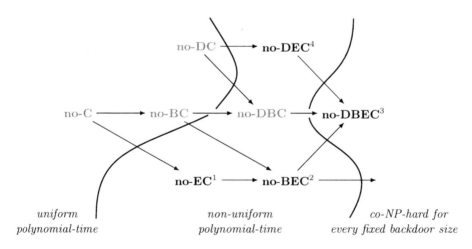

Fig. 3. Relationship between classes of programs and known complexity of the problem DELETION $\mathcal{C}$-BACKDOOR DETECTION. The new results are colored in black. (1) and (2) are established in Theorem 4, (3) is established in Theorem 2, (4) is established in Theorem 3.

of polynomial-time reductions that ensure a parameter of one problem maps into a parameter of another problem [3]). The reverse mapping that replaces k with l, however, is not a fpt-reduction. Consequently, whenever a problem is fixed-parameter tractable for parameter k, it is fixed-parameter tractable for parameter l, but the converse is not necessarily always true.

Proposition 4. *There is a function f such that $k \leq f(l)$ and no function g such that $l < g(k)$ for all programs P where k is the size of the smallest deletion-* **no-DBEC***-backdoor of P and l is the number of even cycles in D_P.*

Proof. Let P be some program. If P has at most k bad even cycles, we can construct a **no-DBEC**-backdoor X for P by taking one element from each bad even cycle into X. Thus there is a function f such that $k \leq f(l)$. If a program P has a **no-DBEC**-backdoor of size 1, it can have arbitrarily many even cycles that run through the atom in the backdoor. It follows that there is no function g such that $l < g(k)$ and the proposition holds.   □

5   Conclusion

We have extended the backdoor approach of [5] by taking the parity of the number of negative edges on bad cycles into account. In particular, this allowed us to consider target classes that contain non-stratified programs. We have established new hardness results and non-uniform polynomial-time tractability depending on whether we consider directed or undirected even cycles. We have shown that the backdoor approach with parity target classes generalizes a result of Lin and Zhao [13]. Since Theorem 2 states that target classes based on directed even cycles are intractable, we think these target classes are of limited practical interest. The results of this paper give rise to research questions that are of theoretical interest. For instance, it would be stimulating to find out whether the problem k-DELETION $\mathcal{C}$-BACKDOOR DETECTION is uniform polynomial-time solvable (fixed-parameter tractable) for the classes **no-BC** and **no-BEC**, which is related to the problems parity feedback vertex set and parity subset feedback vertex set.

Acknowledgement. The author would like to thank Stefan Szeider for suggesting the new target class that takes the parity of the number of negative edges into account, for many helpful comments, and his valuable advice. The author is thankful to Serge Gaspers for pointing out the result of Arikati and Peled on finding odd paths in polynomial time and many helpful comments and to the anonymous referees for their very detailed and very helpful comments. The author was supported by the European Research Council (ERC), Grant COMPLEX REASON 239962.

References

1. Apt, K.R., Blair, H.A., Walker, A.: Towards a theory of declarative knowledge. In: Foundations of Deductive Databases and Logic Programming, pp. 89–148. Morgan Kaufmann (1988)

2. Arikati, S.R., Peled, U.N.: A polynomial algorithm for the parity path problem on perfectly orientable graphs. Discrete Applied Mathematics 65(1-3), 5–20 (1996)
3. Downey, R.G., Fellows, M.R.: Parameterized Complexity. Monographs in Computer Science. Springer (1999)
4. Eiter, T., Gottlob, G.: On the computational cost of disjunctive logic programming: Propositional case. Annals of Mathematics and AI 15(3-4), 289–323 (1995)
5. Fichte, J.K., Szeider, S.: Backdoors to tractable answer-set programming. Extended and updated version of a paper that appeared in IJCAI 2011, CoRR abs/1104.2788 (2012)
6. Gaspers, S., Szeider, S.: Backdoors to Satisfaction. CoRR abs/1110.6387 (2011)
7. Van Gelder, A.: The alternating fixpoint of logic programs with negation. In: Proceedings of the Ninth ACM SIGACT-SIGMOD-SIGART Symposium on Principles of Database Systems, pp. 1–10. ACM (1989)
8. Van Gelder, A., Ross, K.A., Schlipf, J.S.: The well-founded semantics for general logic programs. Journal of the ACM 38(3), 620–650 (1991)
9. Gelfond, M., Lifschitz, V.: The stable model semantics for logic programming. In: Proceedings of the Fifth International Conference and Symposium on Logic Programming (ICLP/SLP), vol. 2, pp. 1070–1080. MIT Press (1988)
10. Gelfond, M., Lifschitz, V.: Classical negation in logic programs and disjunctive databases. New Generation Computing 9(3/4), 365–386 (1991)
11. Gottlob, G., Scarcello, F., Sideri, M.: Fixed-parameter complexity in AI and non-monotonic reasoning. AI 138(1-2), 55–86 (2002)
12. Lapaugh, A.S., Papadimitriou, C.H.: The even-path problem for graphs and digraphs. Networks 14(4), 507–513 (1984)
13. Lin, F., Zhao, X.: On odd and even cycles in normal logic programs. In: Proceedings of the Nineteenth National Conference on AI (AAAI), pp. 80–85. AAAI Press (2004)
14. Marek, V.W., Truszczynski, M.: Stable models and an alternative logic programming paradigm: a 25-Year Perspective. In: The Logic Programming Paradigm, pp. 375–398 (1999)
15. Montalva, M., Aracena, J., Gajardo, A.: On the complexity of feedback set problems in signed digraphs. Electronic Notes in Discrete Mathematics 30, 249–254 (2008)
16. Niemelä, I.: Logic programs with stable model semantics as a constraint programming paradigm. Annals of Mathematics and AI 25(3), 241–273 (1999)
17. Robertson, N., Seymour, P., Thomas, R.: Permanents, Pfaffian orientations, and even directed circuits. Annals of Mathematics 150(3), 929–975 (1999)
18. Schaub, T.: Collection on answer set programming (ASP) and more. Tech. rep., University of Potsdam (2008), http://www.cs.uni-potsdam.de/~torsten/asp
19. Vazirani, V., Yannakakis, M.: Pfaffian Orientations, 0/1 Permanents, and Even Cycles in Directed Graphs. In: Lepistö, T., Salomaa, A. (eds.) ICALP 1988. LNCS, vol. 317, pp. 667–681. Springer, Heidelberg (1988)
20. Williams, R., Gomes, C., Selman, B.: Backdoors to typical case complexity. In: Proceedings of the Eighteenth International Joint Conference on AI (IJCAI), pp. 1173–1178. Morgan Kaufmann (2003)
21. Williams, R., Gomes, C., Selman, B.: On the connections between backdoors, restarts, and heavy-tailedness in combinatorial search. In: Proceedings of the Sixth International Conference on Theory and Applications of Satisfiability Testing (SAT), pp. 222–230. Morgan Kaufmann (2003)
22. Yuster, R., Zwick, U.: Finding Even Cycles Even Faster. In: Shamir, E., Abiteboul, S. (eds.) ICALP 1994. LNCS, vol. 820, pp. 532–543. Springer, Heidelberg (1994)
23. Zhao, J.: A Study of Answer Set Programming. MPhil thesis, The Hong Kong University of Science and Technology, Dept. of Computer Science (2002)

Distributed Knowledge with Justifications

Meghdad Ghari

Department of Mathematical Sciences, Isfahan University of Technology
Isfahan, 84156-83111, Iran
mghari@math.iut.ac.ir

Abstract. In this paper, we introduce justification counterparts of distributed knowledge logics. Our justification logics include explicit knowledge operators of the form $[[t]]_i F$ and $[[t]]_\mathcal{D} F$, which are interpreted respectively as "t is a justification that agent i accepts for F", and "t is a justification that all agents implicitly accept for F". We present Kripke style models and prove the completeness theorem. Finally, we give a semantical proof of the realization theorem.

1 Introduction

Justification logics (cf. [2]) are a new generation of epistemic logics in which the knowledge operators $\mathcal{K}_i F$ (agent i knows F) are replaced with evidence-based knowledge operators $[[t]]_i F$ (agent i accepts t as an evidence for F), where t is a justification term. The first justification logic, Logic of Proofs **LP**, was introduced by Artemov in [1] as an one-agent justification counterpart of the epistemic modal logic **S4**. The exact correspondence between **LP** and **S4** is given by the *Realization Theorem*: all occurrences of knowledge operator $\mathcal{K}$ in a theorem of **S4** can be replaced by suitable terms to obtain a theorem of **LP**, and vise versa. Artemov used a cut-free sequent calculus of **S4** to give a syntactic proof of the realization theorem ([1]). A semantical proof of the realization theorem is presented by Fitting in [9].

Logic of proofs is a justification logic with a new operator $[[\cdot]]$ for one agent. In [15] Yavorskaya (Sidon) studied two-agent justification logics that have interactions, e.g., evidences of one agent can be verified by the other agent, or evidences of one agent can be converted to evidences of the other agent. Renne introduced dynamic epistemic logics with justification, systems for multi-agent communication (see e.g. [13, 14]). Bucheli, Kuznets and Studer in [5] suggested an explicit evidence system with common knowledge, an attempt to find a justification counterpart of epistemic logics with common knowledge (although proving the realization theorem for this system is still an open problem). Dynamic justification logic of public announcements also studied in [4, 6]. None of the aforementioned papers deal with the notion of distributed knowledge.

In this paper, we study multi-agent evidence-based systems in a distributed environment. Distributed knowledge is the knowledge that is implicitly available in a group, and can be discovered through communication (cf. [8, 12]). We introduce an evidence-based knowledge operator for distributed knowledge $[[t]]_\mathcal{D} F$,

D. Lassiter and M. Slavkovik (Eds.): ESSLLI Student Sessions, LNCS 7415, pp. 91–108, 2012.

with the intuitive meaning "t is an evidence that all agents implicitly accept for F". In other words, $[\![t]\!]_{\mathcal{D}}F$ states that t is an evidence (or justification) that could be obtained for F if all agents pooled their knowledge (or justifications) together. To capture this notion, we present distributed knowledge logics with justifications $\mathbf{JK_n^D}$, $\mathbf{JT_n^D}$, $\mathbf{JS4_n^D}$, and $\mathbf{JS5_n^D}$. We establish basic properties of justification logics for our logics, and give two examples to show how these logics can be used to track evidences of distributed knowledge (more information on tracking evidences and its applications can be found in [3, 16, 17]).

We also present possible world semantics for these logics. In the present paper, we consider $[\![\cdot]\!]_{\mathcal{D}}$ as an agent, and give pseudo-Fitting models with additional accessibility relation $\mathcal{R}_{\mathcal{D}}$ and evidence function $\mathcal{E}_{\mathcal{D}}$ for distributed knowledge.

Finally, by proving the *Realization Theorem*, we show that our logics are the justification counterparts of the known distributed knowledge logics $\mathbf{K_n^D}$, $\mathbf{T_n^D}$, $\mathbf{S4_n^D}$, and $\mathbf{S5_n^D}$. There are several methods for proving the realization theorem, see e.g. [1, 9, 11]. We employ the technique of Fitting ([9]) to present a semantical proof of the realization theorem.[1]

2   Distributed Knowledge Logics

In this paper, we fix a set of n agents $G = \{1, 2, \ldots, n\}$. The language of distributed knowledge logics is obtained by adding the modal operators $\mathcal{K}_1, \ldots, \mathcal{K}_n, \mathcal{D}$ to propositional logic. Hence, if A is a formula then $\mathcal{K}_i A$, for $i = 1, \ldots, n$, and $\mathcal{D}A$ are also formulas. The intended meaning of $\mathcal{K}_i A$ is "agent i knows A", and of $\mathcal{D}A$ is "A is distributed knowledge". Now, we recall the well known distributed knowledge logics (for more expositions see [8, 12]).

Definition 1. *The axioms of* $\mathbf{K_n^D}$ *are (where $i = 1, \ldots, n$):*

Taut. *Finite set of axioms for propositional logic,*
K. $\mathcal{K}_i(A \to B) \to (\mathcal{K}_i A \to \mathcal{K}_i B)$,
KD. $\mathcal{D}(A \to B) \to (\mathcal{D}A \to \mathcal{D}B)$,
K$_i$D. $\mathcal{K}_i A \to \mathcal{D}A$.

The rules of inference are:

Modus Ponens: *from A and $A \to B$, infer B,*
Necessitation: *from A infer $\mathcal{K}_i A$.*

If the number of agents $n = 1$, then we add the additional axiom:

$\mathcal{D}A \to \mathcal{K}_1 A$.

Extensions of $\mathbf{K_n^D}$ *obtain by adding some axioms as follows:*

- $\mathbf{T_n^D} = \mathbf{K_n^D} + (\mathcal{K}_i A \to A) + (\mathcal{D}A \to A)$,
- $\mathbf{S4_n^D} = \mathbf{T_n^D} + (\mathcal{K}_i A \to \mathcal{K}_i \mathcal{K}_i A) + (\mathcal{D}A \to \mathcal{D}\mathcal{D}A)$,
- $\mathbf{S5_n^D} = \mathbf{S4_n^D} + (\neg \mathcal{K}_i A \to \mathcal{K}_i \neg \mathcal{K}_i A) + (\neg \mathcal{D}A \to \mathcal{D}\neg \mathcal{D}A)$.

---

[1] Since it seems the method used in the proof of the realization theorem in [10] is not correct, we use a different method in Section 5 to prove the realization theorem.

Note that the axioms $\mathcal{K}_i A \to A$ in $\mathbf{T_n^D}$ are redundant, since they follow from axioms $\mathcal{K}_i A \to \mathcal{D}A$ and $\mathcal{D}A \to A$.

In what follows, $\mathbf{L^D}$ is any of the logics $\mathbf{K_n^D}$, $\mathbf{T_n^D}$, $\mathbf{S4_n^D}$, or $\mathbf{S5_n^D}$. Next we recall Kripke models for the logics $\mathbf{L^D}$.

Definition 2. *A Kripke model $\mathcal{M}$ for $\mathbf{K_n^D}$ is a tuple $\mathcal{M} = (\mathcal{W}, \mathcal{R}_1, \ldots, \mathcal{R}_n, \Vdash)$ where $\mathcal{W}$ is a non-empty set of worlds (or states), each $\mathcal{R}_i$ is a binary accessibility relation between worlds, and the forcing relation $\Vdash$ is a relation between pairs $(\mathcal{M}, w)$ and propositional letters, that can be extended to all formulas as follows:*

1. *$\Vdash$ respects classical Boolean connectives,*
2. *$(\mathcal{M}, w) \Vdash \mathcal{K}_i A$ iff for every $v \in \mathcal{W}$ with $w\mathcal{R}_i v$, $(\mathcal{M}, v) \Vdash A$,*
3. *$(\mathcal{M}, w) \Vdash \mathcal{D}A$ iff for every $v \in \mathcal{W}$ with $w\mathcal{R}_{\mathcal{D}} v$, $(\mathcal{M}, v) \Vdash A$, where $\mathcal{R}_{\mathcal{D}} = \cap_{i=1}^n \mathcal{R}_i$.*

For Kripke models of $\mathbf{T_n^D}$, $\mathbf{S4_n^D}$ and $\mathbf{S5_n^D}$ each $\mathcal{R}_i$ should be reflexive, reflexive and transitive and an equivalence relation, respectively.

Theorem 1. *([7]) $\mathbf{K_n^D}$, $\mathbf{T_n^D}$, $\mathbf{S4_n^D}$ and $\mathbf{S5_n^D}$ are sound and complete with respect to their models.*

3   Distributed Knowledge Logics with Justifications

In this section, we introduce distributed knowledge logics with justifications $\mathbf{JK_n^D}$, $\mathbf{JT_n^D}$, $\mathbf{JS4_n^D}$, and $\mathbf{JS5_n^D}$. In the rest of the paper, we extend our set of agents by the distributed knowledge operator $\mathcal{D}$, and denote by $*$ one of the agents in G or $\mathcal{D}$ (i.e. $* \in \{1, \ldots, n, \mathcal{D}\}$). Similar to the language used in [5] and [15], we define a set of terms as justifications for each $* \in \{1, \ldots, n, \mathcal{D}\}$. We start by defining the set of justification variables and constants:

$$Var^* = \{x_1^*, x_2^*, \ldots\} \qquad Cons^i = \{c_1^i, c_2^i, \ldots\}.$$

Now define the set of admissible terms Tm_* (for each $*$) as follows

1. $Var^* \subseteq Tm_*$,
2. $Cons^i \subseteq Tm_i$,
3. if $s, t \in Tm_*$, then $s +_* t$, $s \cdot_* t \in Tm_*$,
   for $\mathbf{JS4_n^D}$ and $\mathbf{JS5_n^D}$: if $t \in Tm_*$, then $!_* t \in Tm_*$,
   for $\mathbf{JS5_n^D}$: if $t \in Tm_*$, then $?_* t \in Tm_*$,
4. $Tm_i \subseteq Tm_{\mathcal{D}}$, for each $i \in G$.

Indeed, each distributed justification logic includes those clauses in the construction of terms that contains the corresponding operator in its language. Note that by clause 4 there is no need to define variables $Var^{\mathcal{D}}$ for operator $\mathcal{D}$. However, since using variables in $Var^{\mathcal{D}}$ simplifies some arguments (see for instance Lemma 3) we keep it. In addition, as we will see from the formulation of our logics (see Definition 3), there is no need to define a set of justification constants $Cons^{\mathcal{D}}$ for $\mathcal{D}$.

Another different alternative is to define only one set of terms Tm that is admissible for all agents as well as for distributed knowledge operator (see e.g. [13, 14], in which Renne considers a set of terms for all agents' evidences). Nevertheless, using labels for justification variables and constants for each agent enables us to tracking evidences (see Example 1, and the discussion after it).

Formulas of the distributed knowledge logics with justifications are constructed as follows:

$$F := P \mid \bot \mid F \to F \mid [\![t]\!]_* F,$$

where P is a propositional variable and $t \in Tm_*$. The intended meaning of $[\![t]\!]_i F$ is "t is a justification that agent i accepts for F", and of $[\![t]\!]_{\mathcal{D}} F$ is "t is a justification that all agents implicitly accept for F". We begin by defining the language and axioms of the basic distributed knowledge logic with justifications.

Definition 3. *The language of* $\mathbf{JK_n^D}$ *contains only the operators* $\cdot_*$ *and* $+_*$. *The axioms of* $\mathbf{JK_n^D}$ *are:*

A0. *Finite set of axioms for propositional logic,*
A1. $[\![s]\!]_* A \vee [\![t]\!]_* A \to [\![s +_* t]\!]_* A$,
A2. $[\![s]\!]_* (A \to B) \to ([\![t]\!]_* A \to [\![s \cdot_* t]\!]_* B)$,
A3. $[\![t]\!]_i A \to [\![t]\!]_{\mathcal{D}} A$, *where* $t \in Tm_i$.

The rules of inference are:

R1. *Modus Ponens: from* A *and* $A \to B$, *infer* B,
R2. *Iterated Axiom Necessitation:* $\vdash [\![c_{j_m}^{i_m}]\!]_{i_m} \ldots [\![c_{j_1}^{i_1}]\!]_{i_1} A$, *where* A *is an axiom,* $c_{j_l}^{i_k}$*'s are justification constants and* $i_1, \ldots, i_m$ *are in* G.

If the number of agents $n = 1$, *then we add the additional axiom:*

A4. $[\![t]\!]_{\mathcal{D}} A \to [\![t]\!]_1 A$, *where* $t \in Tm_1$.

The justification system $\mathbf{JT_n^D}$ *is obtained from* $\mathbf{JK_n^D}$ *by adding the following axioms:*

A5. $[\![t]\!]_* A \to A$.

The justification system $\mathbf{JS4_n^D}$ *is obtained from* $\mathbf{JT_n^D}$ *by first extending the language with operators* $!_*$ *and then adding the following axioms:*

A6. $[\![t]\!]_* A \to [\![!_* t]\!]_* [\![t]\!]_* A$.

and replacing the rule **R2** *by the following simple one:*

R3. *Axiom Necessitation:* $\vdash [\![c^i]\!]_i A$, *where* A *is an axiom,* c^i *is a justification constant and* $i \in G$.

The justification system $\mathbf{JS5_n^D}$ *is obtained from* $\mathbf{JS4_n^D}$ *by first extending the language with operators* $?_*$ *and then adding the following axioms:*

A7. $\neg [\![t]\!]_* A \to [\![?_* t]\!]_* \neg [\![t]\!]_* A$.

Notice that, in the axioms **A1**, **A2**, **A6** and **A7** all occurrences of $*$ are the same agent. Moreover, axioms $[\![t]\!]_i A \to A$ in $\mathbf{JT_n^D}$ are redundant, since they can be obtained from axioms $[\![t]\!]_i A \to [\![t]\!]_{\mathcal{D}} A$ and $[\![t]\!]_{\mathcal{D}} A \to A$.

By $\mathbf{JL^D}$ we denote one of the logics $\mathbf{JK_n^D}$, $\mathbf{JT_n^D}$, $\mathbf{JS4_n^D}$, and $\mathbf{JS5_n^D}$. Following [15], we define constant specifications as follows:

Definition 4. *A Constant Specification* $\mathcal{CS}$ *for* $\mathbf{JK_n^D}$ *(or* $\mathbf{JT_n^D}$*) is a set of formulas of the form* $[\![c_{j_m}^{i_m}]\!]_{i_m} \ldots [\![c_{j_1}^{i_1}]\!]_{i_1} A$*, where* A *is an axiom of* $\mathbf{JK_n^D}$ *(or* $\mathbf{JT_n^D}$*),* $c_{j_l}^{i_l}$*'s are justification constants and* $i_1, \ldots, i_m$ *are in* G*, and moreover it is downward closed:*

$$\text{if } [\![c_{j_m}^{i_m}]\!]_{i_m} [\![c_{j_{m-1}}^{i_{m-1}}]\!]_{i_{m-1}} \ldots [\![c_{j_1}^{i_1}]\!]_{i_1} A \in \mathcal{CS}, \text{ then } [\![c_{j_{m-1}}^{i_{m-1}}]\!]_{i_{m-1}} \ldots [\![c_{j_1}^{i_1}]\!]_{i_1} A \in \mathcal{CS}.$$

A constant specification $\mathcal{CS}$ *is axiomatically appropriate if for each axiom* A *and* $i \in G$ *there is a constant* $c^i \in Tm_i$ *such that* $[\![c^i]\!]_i A \in \mathcal{CS}$ *and also* $\mathcal{CS}$ *is upward closed:*

$$\text{if } [\![c_{j_m}^{i_m}]\!]_{i_m} \ldots [\![c_{j_1}^{i_1}]\!]_{i_1} A \in \mathcal{CS}, \text{ then } [\![c_{j_{m+1}}^{i_{m+1}}]\!]_{i_{m+1}} [\![c_{j_m}^{i_m}]\!]_{i_m} \ldots [\![c_{j_1}^{i_1}]\!]_{i_1} A \in \mathcal{CS},$$

for some $i_{m+1} \in G$ *and constant* $c_{j_{m+1}}^{i_{m+1}} \in Tm_{m+1}$*.*

Definition 5. *A Constant Specification* $\mathcal{CS}$ *for* $\mathbf{JS4_n^D}$ *(or* $\mathbf{JS5_n^D}$*) is a set of formulas of the form* $[\![c^i]\!]_i A$*, such that* c^i *is a justification constant in* $Cons^i$*,* A *is an axiom of* $\mathbf{JS4_n^D}$ *(or* $\mathbf{JS5_n^D}$*) and* $i \in G$*. A constant specification* $\mathcal{CS}$ *is axiomatically appropriate if for each axiom* A *and* $i \in G$ *there is a constant* $c^i \in Tm_i$ *such that* $[\![c^i]\!]_i A \in \mathcal{CS}$*.*

Let $\mathbf{JL^D}(\mathcal{CS})$ be the fragment of $\mathbf{JL^D}$ where the (Iterated) Axiom Necessitation rule only produces formulas from the given $\mathcal{CS}$. Thus $\mathbf{JL^D}(\emptyset)$ is the fragment of $\mathbf{JL^D}$ without (Iterated) Axiom Necessitation rule. By $\mathbf{JL^D} \vdash F$ we mean $\mathbf{JL^D}(\mathcal{CS}) \vdash F$ for some constant specification $\mathcal{CS}$.

Definition 6. *A substitution* σ *is a mapping from* $\bigcup_* Var^*$ *to* $\bigcup_* Tm_*$ *such that each justification variable in* Var^* *maps to a term in* Tm_**. The domain of* σ *is* $dom(\sigma) := \{x \mid \sigma(x) \neq x\}$*. The result of substitution* σ *on the term* t *and formula* A *is denoted by* $t\sigma$ *and* $A\sigma$ *respectively.*

Distributed knowledge logics with justifications $\mathbf{JL^D}$ enjoy the deduction theorem and substitution lemma (the proofs are standard and are omitted here).

Lemma 1. *Let* $\mathcal{CS}$ *be a constant specification.*

1. *Deduction Theorem for* $\mathbf{JL^D}(\mathcal{CS})$*:* $\Gamma, A \vdash B$ *if and only if* $\Gamma \vdash A \to B$*.*
2. *Substitution Lemma: (i) If* $\Gamma \vdash A$ *in* $\mathbf{JL^D}(\mathcal{CS})$*, then* $\Gamma\sigma \vdash A\sigma$ *in* $\mathbf{JL^D}(\mathcal{CS}\sigma)$*.* *(ii) If* $\Gamma \vdash A$ *in* $\mathbf{JL^D}(\mathcal{CS})$*, then* $\Gamma(F/P) \vdash A(F/P)$ *in* $\mathbf{JL^D}(\mathcal{CS}')$*, where* $\mathcal{CS}' = \mathcal{CS}(F/P)$ *and* $A(F/P)$ *denotes the result of simultaneously replacing all occurrences of propositional variable* P *by formula* F *in* A*.*

Distributed knowledge logics with justifications can internalize their own proofs. This is one of the fundamental properties of justification logics.

Lemma 2 (Internalization Lemma). *For each* $* \in \{1, \ldots, n, \mathcal{D}\}$, *the following statements hold:*

1. *If* $\mathbf{JL^D}(\mathcal{CS}) \vdash F$, *then* $\mathbf{JL^D}(\mathcal{CS'}) \vdash [\![p]\!]_* F$, *for some term* p *in* Tm_* *and some* $\mathcal{CS'} \supseteq \mathcal{CS}$.
2. *Suppose* $\mathcal{CS}$ *is axiomatically appropriate. If* $\mathbf{JL^D}(\mathcal{CS}) \vdash F$, *then* $\mathbf{JL^D}(\mathcal{CS}) \vdash [\![p]\!]_* F$, *for some term* p *in* Tm_*.

Proof. By induction on the derivation of F. If F is an axiom, then using (Iterated) Axiom Necessitation rule $[\![c^i]\!]_i F$ is derivable in $\mathbf{JL^D}(\mathcal{CS'})$ for some $c^i \in Const^i$ and $\mathcal{CS'} = \mathcal{CS} \cup \{[\![c^i]\!]_i F\}$. If $\mathcal{CS}$ is axiomatically appropriate then there is a constant $c^i \in Tm_i$ such that $[\![c^i]\!]_i F \in \mathcal{CS}$, for each $i \in G$. Hence, $[\![c^i]\!]_i F$ is derivable in $\mathbf{JL_n^D}(\mathcal{CS})$, for each $i \in G$. Moreover, using axiom instance $[\![c^i]\!]_i F \rightarrow [\![c^i]\!]_{\mathcal{D}} F$, we can derive $[\![c^i]\!]_{\mathcal{D}} F$. If F is obtained by Modus Ponens from G and $G \rightarrow F$, then by the induction hypothesis, there are terms $t, s \in Tm_*$ such that $[\![t]\!]_* G$ and $[\![s]\!]_* (G \rightarrow F)$ are provable. By axiom **A2**, we derive $[\![s \cdot_* t]\!]_* F$.

If $F = [\![c_{j_m}^{i_m}]\!]_{i_m} \ldots [\![c_{j_1}^{i_1}]\!]_{i_1} A \in \mathcal{CS}$, is obtained by the Iterated Axiom Necessitation rule **IAN** in $\mathbf{JK_n^D}$ or $\mathbf{JT_n^D}$, then using **IAN** we obtain $[\![c^i]\!]_i [\![c_{j_m}^{i_m}]\!]_{i_m} \ldots [\![c_{j_1}^{i_1}]\!]_{i_1} A$. If $\mathcal{CS}$ is axiomatically appropriate then it is upward closed, and therefore there is a constant $c^i \in Tm_i$ such that $[\![c^i]\!]_i [\![c_{j_m}^{i_m}]\!]_{i_m} \ldots [\![c_{j_1}^{i_1}]\!]_{i_1} A$ is in $\mathcal{CS}$, and hence is derivable in $\mathbf{JK_n^D}(\mathcal{CS})$ or $\mathbf{JT_n^D}(\mathcal{CS})$. Moreover, using axiom **A3**, we can derive $[\![c^i]\!]_{\mathcal{D}} [\![c_{j_m}^{i_m}]\!]_{i_m} \ldots [\![c_{j_1}^{i_1}]\!]_{i_1} A$.

If $F = [\![c^i]\!]_i A \in \mathcal{CS}$ is obtained by the Axiom Necessitation rule **AN** in $\mathbf{JS4_n^D}$ or $\mathbf{JS5_n^D}$, then use axiom **A6** to derive $[\![!_i c^i]\!]_i A$ in $\mathbf{JL_n^D}(\mathcal{CS})$. Moreover, using axiom **A3**, we can derive $[\![!_i c^i]\!]_{\mathcal{D}} A$. $\qquad \square$

Lemma 3 (Lifting Lemma). *For each* $* \in \{1, \ldots, n, \mathcal{D}\}$, *the following statements are provable:*

1. *If* $[\![t_1]\!]_* A_1, \ldots, [\![t_m]\!]_* A_m, B_1, \ldots, B_l \vdash F$ *in* $\mathbf{JS4_n^D}(\mathcal{CS})$, *then*

$$[\![t_1]\!]_* A_1, \ldots, [\![t_m]\!]_* A_m, [\![x_1^*]\!]_* B_1, \ldots, [\![x_l^*]\!]_* B_l \vdash [\![p(\vec{t}, \vec{x})]\!]_* F \quad (\dagger)$$

in $\mathbf{JS4_n^D}(\mathcal{CS'})$, *for some justification variables* x_i^* *(in* Var^*), *term* $p(\vec{t}, \vec{x})$ *in* Tm_* *and* $\mathcal{CS'} \supseteq \mathcal{CS}$ *(all* $*$'s *in* $(\dagger)$ *stand for the same agent).*
2. *In part (1), if* $\mathcal{CS}$ *is axiomatically appropriate, then* $(\dagger)$ *is provable in* $\mathbf{JS4_n^D}(\mathcal{CS})$.

Proof. The proof is similar to the proof of Lemma 2, with two new cases. If $F = [\![t_i]\!]_* A_i$, for some $1 \leq i \leq m$, then put $p(\vec{t}, \vec{x}) =!_* t_i$. If $F = B_i$, for some $1 \leq i \leq l$, then put $p(\vec{t}, \vec{x}) = x_i^*$. $\qquad \square$

It is worth noting that the terms p and $p(\vec{t}, \vec{x})$ constructed, respectively, in the proof of lifting and internalization lemmas depends on the agent $*$.

Example 1. We prove that $\mathbf{JK_n^D}(\emptyset) \vdash [\![s]\!]_i(A \to B) \wedge [\![t]\!]_j A \to [\![s \cdot_{\mathcal{D}} t]\!]_{\mathcal{D}} B$, where $s \in Tm_i$ and $t \in Tm_j$. The proof is as follows:

1. $[\![s]\!]_i(A \to B) \wedge [\![t]\!]_j A \to [\![s]\!]_i(A \to B)$, tautology in propositional logic
2. $[\![s]\!]_i(A \to B) \wedge [\![t]\!]_j A \to [\![t]\!]_j A$, tautology in propositional logic
3. $[\![s]\!]_i(A \to B) \wedge [\![t]\!]_j A \to [\![s]\!]_{\mathcal{D}}(A \to B)$, from 1 by reasoning in propositional logic and axiom **A3**
4. $[\![s]\!]_i(A \to B) \wedge [\![t]\!]_j A \to [\![t]\!]_{\mathcal{D}} A$, from 2 by reasoning in propositional logic and axiom **A3**
5. $[\![s]\!]_i(A \to B) \wedge [\![t]\!]_j A \to [\![s]\!]_{\mathcal{D}}(A \to B) \wedge [\![t]\!]_{\mathcal{D}} A$, from 3 and 4 by reasoning in propositional logic
6. $[\![s]\!]_i(A \to B) \wedge [\![t]\!]_j A \to [\![s \cdot_{\mathcal{D}} t]\!]_{\mathcal{D}} B$, from 5 by reasoning in propositional logic and axiom **A2**.

This is similar to the fact that $\mathbf{K_n^D} \vdash \mathcal{K}_i(A \to B) \wedge \mathcal{K}_j A \to \mathcal{D}B$. This theorem of $\mathbf{K_n^D}$ states that if agent i knows $A \to B$ and agent j knows A, then B is distributed knowledge, which means if all agents combine their knowledge together, they can infer B. But, in fact, to obtain knowledge of B we do not need the information of all agents other than agents i and j.

Distributed knowledge logics with justifications allow us to track evidences occur in $[\![\cdot]\!]_{\mathcal{D}}$. For instance, Example 1 shows that if s is an agent i's evidence for $A \to B$ and t is an agent j's evidence for A, then $s \cdot_{\mathcal{D}} t$ is an evidence for B that all agents can obtain whenever they combine their knowledge. Since $s \in Tm_i$ and $t \in Tm_j$, the term $s \cdot_{\mathcal{D}} t$ shows that in order to get knowledge of B and make a justification for it, we only require information of agents i and j, and particularly it determines which part of their knowledge is required.

Example 2. The rule

$$\frac{A_1 \wedge \ldots \wedge A_n \to B}{\mathcal{K}_1 A_1 \wedge \ldots \wedge \mathcal{K}_n A_n \to \mathcal{D}B}$$

is admissible in $\mathbf{L^D}$ (see, e.g., [12]). Likewise, we prove that the following rule is admissible in $\mathbf{JL_n^D}$:

$$\frac{A_1 \wedge \ldots \wedge A_n \to B}{[\![t_1]\!]_1 A_1 \wedge \ldots \wedge [\![t_n]\!]_n A_n \to [\![t]\!]_{\mathcal{D}} B}$$

for some term t in $Tm_{\mathcal{D}}$, where $t_i \in Tm_i$ for $i = 1, \ldots, n$. The proof is as follows:

1 . $A_1 \wedge \ldots \wedge A_n \to B$, hypothesis
2. $[\![t_1]\!]_1 A_1 \wedge \ldots \wedge [\![t_n]\!]_n A_n$, hypothesis
3.1. $[\![t_1]\!]_1 A_1$, from 2 by reasoning in propositional logic
3.2. $[\![t_2]\!]_2 A_2$, from 2 by reasoning in propositional logic

$\vdots$

3.n. $[\![t_n]\!]_n A_n$, from 2 by reasoning in propositional logic
4.1. $[\![t_1]\!]_{\mathcal{D}} A_1$, from 3.1 by axiom **A3**

4.2. $[\![t_2]\!]_{\mathcal{D}}A_2$, from 3.2 by axiom **A3**

$$\vdots$$

4.n. $[\![t_n]\!]_{\mathcal{D}}A_n$, from 3.n by axiom **A3**

5. $A_1 \to (A_2 \to \ldots \to (A_n \to B)\ldots)$, from 1 by reasoning in propositional logic

6. $[\![p]\!]_{\mathcal{D}}[A_1 \to (A_2 \to \ldots \to (A_n \to B)\ldots)]$, from 5 by Lemma 2

7.1. $[\![p \cdot_{\mathcal{D}} t_1]\!]_{\mathcal{D}}[A_2 \to (A_3 \to \ldots \to (A_n \to B)\ldots)]$, from 4.1 and 6 by axiom **A2**

7.2. $[\![p \cdot_{\mathcal{D}} t_1 \cdot_{\mathcal{D}} t_2]\!]_{\mathcal{D}}[A_3 \to (A_4 \to \ldots \to (A_n \to B)\ldots)]$, from 4.2 and 7.1 by axiom **A2**

$$\vdots$$

7.n. $[\![p \cdot_{\mathcal{D}} t_1 \cdot_{\mathcal{D}} \ldots \cdot_{\mathcal{D}} t_n]\!]_{\mathcal{D}}B$, from 4.n and 7.(n-1) by axiom **A2**

8. $[\![t_1]\!]_1 A_1 \wedge \ldots \wedge [\![t_n]\!]_n A_n \to [\![t]\!]_{\mathcal{D}}B$, from 2 and 8 by the Deduction Theorem (Lemma 1), where $t = p \cdot_{\mathcal{D}} t_1 \cdot_{\mathcal{D}} \ldots \cdot_{\mathcal{D}} t_n$.

These two examples show that evidence-based distributed knowledge could be viewed as the knowledge the agents would have by pooling their individual justifications together.

4   Semantics

In this section, we consider $[\![\cdot]\!]_{\mathcal{D}}$ as an agent, rather than as explicit distributed knowledge, and give pseudo-Fitting models for all systems $\mathbf{JL^D}$. Fitting models first introduced by Fitting in [9] for **LP**.

Definition 7. *A pseudo-Fitting model $\mathcal{M}$ for $\mathbf{JK_n^D}$ is a tuple*

$$\mathcal{M} = (\mathcal{W}, \mathcal{R}_1, \ldots, \mathcal{R}_n, \mathcal{R}_{\mathcal{D}}, \mathcal{E}_1, \ldots, \mathcal{E}_n, \mathcal{E}_{\mathcal{D}}, \Vdash_p)$$

(or $\mathcal{M} = (\mathcal{W}, \mathcal{R}_*, \mathcal{E}_*, \Vdash_p)$ for short) where $(\mathcal{W}, \mathcal{R}_1, \ldots, \mathcal{R}_n, \mathcal{R}_{\mathcal{D}}, \Vdash_p)$ is a Kripke model, in which $\mathcal{R}_{\mathcal{D}}$ is also a binary accessibility relation between worlds such that $\mathcal{R}_{\mathcal{D}} \subseteq \cap_{i=1}^n \mathcal{R}_i$. Admissible evidence functions $\mathcal{E}_*$ are mappings from the set of terms and formulas to the set of all worlds, i.e., $\mathcal{E}_*(t, A) \subseteq \mathcal{W}$, for any justification term t in Tm_* and formula A, and satisfying the following conditions. For all justification terms s and t and for all formulas A and B:

$\mathcal{E}1.$ $\mathcal{E}_*(s, A) \cup \mathcal{E}_*(t, A) \subseteq \mathcal{E}_*(s +_* t, A)$,

$\mathcal{E}2.$ $\mathcal{E}_*(s, A \to B) \cap \mathcal{E}_*(t, A) \subseteq \mathcal{E}_*(s \cdot_* t, B)$,

$\mathcal{E}3.$ $\mathcal{E}_i(t, A) \subseteq \mathcal{E}_{\mathcal{D}}(t, A)$, *for each $i \in G$ and $t \in Tm_i$.*

If $n = 1$, then $\mathcal{R}_1 = \mathcal{R}_{\mathcal{D}}$ and evidence functions should also satisfy:

$\mathcal{E}4.$ $\mathcal{E}_{\mathcal{D}}(t, A) \subseteq \mathcal{E}_1(t, A)$, *for each $t \in Tm_1$.*

The forcing relation $\Vdash_p$ is a relation between pairs $(\mathcal{M}, w)$ and propositional letters, that can be extended to all formulas as follows:

1. *$\Vdash_p$ respects classical Boolean connectives,*
2. *$(\mathcal{M}, w) \Vdash_p [\![t]\!]_*A$ iff $w \in \mathcal{E}_*(t, A)$ and for every $v \in \mathcal{W}$ with $w\mathcal{R}_*v$, $(\mathcal{M}, v) \Vdash_p A$.*

We say that A is true in a model $\mathcal{M}$ ($\mathcal{M} \Vdash_p A$) if it is true at each world of the model. For a set S of formulas, $\mathcal{M} \Vdash_p S$ if $\mathcal{M} \Vdash_p F$ for all formulas F in S. Given a constant specification $\mathcal{CS}$, a model $\mathcal{M}$ respects $\mathcal{CS}$ (or meets $\mathcal{CS}$) if $\mathcal{M} \Vdash_p \mathcal{CS}$. A set S of $\mathbf{JL^D}$-formulas is $\mathbf{JL^D}(\mathcal{CS})$-satisfiable if there is a model $\mathcal{M}$ for $\mathbf{JL^D}$ respecting $\mathcal{CS}$ and a world w in $\mathcal{M}$ such that $(\mathcal{M}, w) \Vdash A$ for all $A \in S$.

Pseudo–Fitting models for the other distributed justification logics have more restrictions on accessibility relations and evidence functions. For $\mathbf{JT_n^D}$ each $\mathcal{R}_*$ is reflexive. For $\mathbf{JS4_n^D}$ each $\mathcal{R}_*$ is reflexive and transitive and evidence functions should satisfy:

$\mathcal{E}5.$ If $w \in \mathcal{E}_*(t, A)$ and $w\mathcal{R}_*v$, then $v \in \mathcal{E}_*(t, A)$,
$\mathcal{E}6.$ $\mathcal{E}_*(t, A) \subseteq \mathcal{E}_*(!_* t, [\![t]\!]_* A)$,

For $\mathbf{JS5_n^D}$ each $\mathcal{R}_*$ is an equivalence relation and evidence functions should satisfy:

$\mathcal{E}7.$ If $[\mathcal{E}_*(t, A)]^c \subseteq \mathcal{E}_*(?_* t, \neg [\![t]\!]_* A)$, where the superscript operation "c" on sets is the complement relative to the set of worlds $\mathcal{W}$,
$\mathcal{E}8.$ If $w \in \mathcal{E}_*(t, A)$, then $(\mathcal{M}, w) \Vdash_p [\![t]\!]_* A$.

Next, we prove the completeness theorem for $\mathbf{JL^D}$. Since the proof is similar to the proof of the completeness theorem of justification logics in [2, 9], we omit the details.

Theorem 2 (Completeness). *For a given constant specification $\mathcal{CS}$, distributed justification logics $\mathbf{JL^D}(\mathcal{CS})$ are sound and complete with respect to their pseudo-Fitting models that respect $\mathcal{CS}$.*

Proof. Soundness is straightforward, as usual, by induction on derivations in $\mathbf{JL^D}(\mathcal{CS})$. Let us only check the validity of axiom **A7**, $\neg [\![t]\!]_* A \rightarrow [\![?_* t]\!]_* \neg [\![t]\!]_* A$, in a model of $\mathbf{JS5_n^D}$. Let $(\mathcal{M}, w) \Vdash_p \neg [\![t]\!]_* A$. By $\mathcal{E}8$, $w \notin \mathcal{E}_*(t, A)$. By $\mathcal{E}7$, $w \in \mathcal{E}_*(?_* t, \neg [\![t]\!]_* A)$, and by $\mathcal{E}8$ we have $(\mathcal{M}, w) \Vdash_p [\![?_* t]\!]_* \neg [\![t]\!]_* A$.

For completeness we first construct a canonical model $\mathcal{M} = (\mathcal{W}, \mathcal{R}_*, \mathcal{E}_*, \Vdash_p)$ as follows:

- $\mathcal{W}$ is the set of all maximally consistent sets in $\mathbf{JL^D}(\mathcal{CS})$,
- $\Gamma \mathcal{R}_* \Delta$ iff $\Gamma^{\sharp_*} \subseteq \Delta$, for $\Gamma, \Delta \in \mathcal{W}$,
- $\mathcal{E}_*(t, F) = \{\Gamma \in \mathcal{W} \mid [\![t]\!]_* F \in \Gamma\}$
- for each propositional letter P: $(\mathcal{M}, \Gamma) \Vdash_p P$ iff $P \in \Gamma$.

where P is a propositional variable and

$$\Gamma^{\sharp_*} = \{A \mid [\![t]\!]_* A \in \Gamma, \text{ for some term } t \in Tm_*\}.$$

Forcing relation $\Vdash_p$ on arbitrary formulas is defined as in Definition 7.

Specially, for each $\mathbf{JL^D}$ the evidence function $\mathcal{E}_*$ in the canonical model $\mathcal{M}$ satisfies the corresponding properties $\mathcal{E}1 - \mathcal{E}8$ in the definition of pseudo–Fitting model. We only show the new property $\mathcal{E}3$ ($\mathcal{E}4$ is similar). Let $\Gamma \in \mathcal{E}_i(t, A)$.

Then $[\![t]\!]_i A \in \Gamma$. Since $[\![t]\!]_i A \to [\![t]\!]_\mathcal{D} A \in \Gamma$, we have $[\![t]\!]_\mathcal{D} A \in \Gamma$, and therefore $\Gamma \in \mathcal{E}_\mathcal{D}(t, A)$.

Let us now prove that $\mathcal{R}_\mathcal{D} \subseteq \cap_{i=1}^n \mathcal{R}_i$. Suppose $\Gamma \mathcal{R}_\mathcal{D} \Delta$ and $[\![t]\!]_i A \in \Gamma$, for an arbitrary $i \in G$. We have to show that $A \in \Delta$. Since $[\![t]\!]_i A \to [\![t]\!]_\mathcal{D} A \in \Gamma$, we have $[\![t]\!]_\mathcal{D} A \in \Gamma$, and therefore $A \in \Delta$. It is not difficult to verify that for $n = 1$ we have $\mathcal{R}_\mathcal{D} = \mathcal{R}_1$.

We now prove the Truth Lemma: for all formulas F we have

$$F \in \Gamma \quad \text{iff} \quad (\mathcal{M}, \Gamma) \Vdash_p F.$$

The proof is by induction on the complexity of F and is similar to that for justification logics in [2]. We only show the case when F is $[\![t]\!]_* G$.

If $[\![t]\!]_* G \in \Gamma$, then $\Gamma \in \mathcal{E}_*(t, G)$ by the definition of $\mathcal{E}_*$. In addition, for all $\Delta \in \mathcal{W}$ such that $\Gamma \mathcal{R}_* \Delta$, by the definition of $\mathcal{R}_*$, we have $G \in \Delta$. Hence, by the induction hypothesis, we obtain $(\mathcal{M}, \Delta) \Vdash_p G$. Thus $(\mathcal{M}, \Gamma) \Vdash_p [\![t]\!]_* G$.

If $[\![t]\!]_* G \notin \Gamma$, then $\Gamma \notin \mathcal{E}_*(t, G)$. Thus $(\mathcal{M}, \Gamma) \nVdash_p [\![t]\!]_* G$.

Now suppose $\mathbf{JL^D}(\mathcal{CS}) \nvdash A$, then $\{\neg A\}$ is a $\mathbf{JL^D}(\mathcal{CS})$-consistent set. Extend it to a maximal consistent set Γ by standard Lindenbaum construction, then by truth lemma we have $(\mathcal{M}, \Gamma) \nVdash_p A$. □

Note that in the canonical model $\mathcal{M}$ we have $\cup_{i=0}^n \mathcal{E}_i(t, A) \subseteq \mathcal{E}_\mathcal{D}(t, A)$, for every term t and formula A.

Theorem 3 (Compactness). *For a given $\mathcal{CS}$ for $\mathbf{JL^D}$, a set of formulas S is $\mathbf{JL^D}(\mathcal{CS})$-satisfiable iff any finite subset of S is $\mathbf{JL^D}(\mathcal{CS})$-satisfiable.*

Proof. Suppose every finite subset of S is $\mathbf{JL^D}(\mathcal{CS})$-satisfiable. Clearly S is $\mathbf{JL^D}(\mathcal{CS})$-consistent. Extend S to a maximal consistent set Γ. Thus Γ is a world in the canonical model $\mathcal{M}$ of $\mathbf{JL^D}(\mathcal{CS})$. Since $S \subseteq \Gamma$, by the Truth Lemma, $(\mathcal{M}, \Gamma) \Vdash A$ for all $A \in S$. Therefore, S is satisfiable. □

One of the important properties of Fitting models is the fully explanatory property, which first proved by Fitting in [9] for models of the logic of proofs.

Definition 8. *A $\mathbf{JL^D}$-model $\mathcal{M}$ is a strong model if it has the* fully explanatory *property:*

1. *if for every v such that $w \mathcal{R}_* v$ we have $(\mathcal{M}, v) \Vdash_p A$, then for some term $t \in Tm_*$ we have $(\mathcal{M}, w) \Vdash_p [\![t]\!]_* A$, and*
2. *if for every v such that $w \mathcal{R}_1 v, \ldots, w \mathcal{R}_n v$ we have $(\mathcal{M}, v) \Vdash_p A$, then for some term $t \in Tm_\mathcal{D}$ we have $(\mathcal{M}, w) \Vdash_p [\![t]\!]_\mathcal{D} A$.*

It is worth noting that the term t introduced in the above definition depends on the formula A and world w. Moreover, the definition of the fully explanatory property of $\mathbf{JL^D}$-models is slightly different from that for one agent justification logics (see [2,9]). In contrast to the one agent case, in Definition 8 we extended the fully explanatory property of models to multi-agent case in statement 1, and add the statement 2.

Theorem 4 (Strong Completeness). *For any axiomatically appropriate constant specification $\mathcal{CS}$, $\mathbf{JL^D}(\mathcal{CS})$ is sound and complete with respect to their strong models that respect $\mathcal{CS}$.*

Proof. It suffices to prove that, for any axiomatically appropriate constant specification $\mathcal{CS}$, the canonical model of $\mathbf{JL^D}(\mathcal{CS})$ satisfies the fully explanatory property. Let $\mathcal{M} = (\mathcal{W}, \mathcal{R}_*, \mathcal{E}_*, \Vdash_p)$ be the canonical model of $\mathbf{JL^D}(\mathcal{CS})$, and $\Gamma \in \mathcal{W}$.

(1) Suppose $* \in \{1, \ldots, n, \mathcal{D}\}$ and $(\mathcal{M}, \Delta) \Vdash_p A$ for every Δ such that $\Gamma \mathcal{R}_* \Delta$. Suppose towards a contradiction that there is no justification term $t \in Tm_*$ such that $(\mathcal{M}, \Gamma) \Vdash_p [\![t]\!]_* A$. Then, the set $\Gamma^{\sharp_*} \cup \{\neg A\}$ would have to be $\mathbf{JL^D}(\mathcal{CS})$-consistent. Indeed, otherwise

$$\mathbf{JL^D}(\mathcal{CS}) \vdash X_1 \to (X_2 \to \ldots \to (X_m \to A)\ldots),$$

for some $[\![t_1]\!]_* X_1, \ldots, [\![t_m]\!]_* X_m \in \Gamma$. Since the constant specification $\mathcal{CS}$ is axiomatically appropriate, by Lemma 2, we would obtain a term s in Tm_* such that

$$\mathbf{JL^D}(\mathcal{CS}) \vdash [\![s]\!]_* (X_1 \to (X_2 \to \ldots \to (X_m \to A)\ldots)).$$

By axiom **A2**,

$$\mathbf{JL^D}(\mathcal{CS}) \vdash [\![t_1]\!]_* X_1 \to ([\![t_2]\!]_* X_2 \to \ldots \to ([\![t_m]\!]_* X_m \to [\![t]\!]_* A)\ldots).$$

where $t = s \cdot_* t_1 \cdot_* \ldots \cdot_* t_m$. Hence $[\![t]\!]_* A \in \Gamma$. Thus, by the Truth Lemma, $(\mathcal{M}, \Gamma) \Vdash_p [\![t]\!]_* A$, a contradiction. Now since $\Gamma^{\sharp_*} \cup \{\neg A\}$ is $\mathbf{JL^D}(\mathcal{CS})$-consistent, it could be extended to a maximal $\mathbf{JL^D}(\mathcal{CS})$-consistent set Δ. Since $\Gamma^{\sharp_*} \subseteq \Delta$, we have $\Gamma \mathcal{R}_* \Delta$. But since $A \notin \Delta$, by the Truth Lemma, $(\mathcal{M}, \Delta) \not\Vdash_p A$, which contradicts the assumption.

(2) Suppose for every $\Delta \in \mathcal{W}$ such that $\Gamma \mathcal{R}_1 \Delta, \ldots, \Gamma \mathcal{R}_n \Delta$ we have $(\mathcal{M}, \Delta) \Vdash_p A$, and $(\mathcal{M}, \Gamma) \not\Vdash_p [\![t]\!]_\mathcal{D} A$, for each $t \in Tm_\mathcal{D}$. We show that there is $\Delta \in \mathcal{W}$ with $\Gamma \mathcal{R}_\mathcal{D} \Delta$ such that $(\mathcal{M}, \Delta) \not\Vdash_p A$. We prove that $\Gamma^{\sharp_\mathcal{D}} \cup \{\neg A\}$ is consistent. Otherwise, for some $[\![t_1]\!]_\mathcal{D} X_1, \ldots, [\![t_m]\!]_\mathcal{D} X_m$ in Γ we have

$$\mathbf{JL^D}(\mathcal{CS}) \vdash X_1 \to (X_2 \to \cdots \to (X_m \to A)\cdots).$$

Since the constant specification $\mathcal{CS}$ is axiomatically appropriate, by Lemma 2, there is a term s in $Tm_\mathcal{D}$ such that

$$\mathbf{JL^D}(\mathcal{CS}) \vdash [\![s]\!]_\mathcal{D} (X_1 \to (X_2 \to \cdots \to (X_m \to A)\cdots)).$$

By axiom **A2**, we conclude that

$$\mathbf{JL^D}(\mathcal{CS}) \vdash [\![t_1]\!]_\mathcal{D} X_1 \to ([\![t_2]\!]_\mathcal{D} X_2 \to \cdots \to ([\![t_m]\!]_\mathcal{D} X_m \to [\![t]\!]_\mathcal{D} A)\cdots)$$

where $t = s \cdot_\mathcal{D} t_1 \cdot_\mathcal{D} \cdots \cdot_\mathcal{D} t_m$. Hence, $[\![t]\!]_\mathcal{D} A \in \Gamma$, and by the Truth Lemma, $(\mathcal{M}, \Gamma) \Vdash_p [\![t]\!]_\mathcal{D} A$, which is a contradiction. Thus $\Gamma^{\sharp_\mathcal{D}} \cup \{\neg A\}$ is a consistent set. Now extend it to a maximal consistent set Δ. By the truth lemma $(\mathcal{M}, \Delta) \not\Vdash_p A$. On the other hand, it is obvious that $\Gamma \mathcal{R}_\mathcal{D} \Delta$, and since $\mathcal{R}_\mathcal{D} \subseteq \cap_{i=0}^n \mathcal{R}_i$, we have $\Gamma \mathcal{R}_i \Delta$, for each $i \in G$, which contradicts the assumption. $\square$

5   Realization Theorem

In this section, we prove that each theorem of $\mathbf{JL^D}$ can be translated into a theorem of $\mathbf{L^D}$, and vise versa. First, we define a translation, called the forgetful projection, from formulas of $\mathbf{JL^D}$ to formulas of $\mathbf{L^D}$.

Definition 9. *For a $\mathbf{JL^D}$-formula F, the forgetful projection of F, denoted by F°, is defined inductively as follows:*

1. *For propositional letter P, $P^\circ = P$, and $\perp^\circ = \perp$,*
2. *$(A \to B)^\circ = A^\circ \to B^\circ$,*
3. *$(\llbracket t \rrbracket_i A)^\circ = \mathcal{K}_i A^\circ$,*
4. *$(\llbracket t \rrbracket_\mathcal{D} A)^\circ = \mathcal{D} A^\circ$.*

For a set S of justification formulas we let $S^\circ = \{F^\circ \mid F \in S\}$.

Lemma 4. *For any formula F of $\mathbf{JL^D}$, if $\mathbf{JL^D} \vdash F$ then $\mathbf{L^D} \vdash F^\circ$.*

Proof. By induction on a derivation of F in $\mathbf{JL^D}$. If F is an axiom of $\mathbf{JL^D}$, then it is easy to verify that F° is provable in $\mathbf{L^D}$. For instance, $(\llbracket t \rrbracket_i A \to \llbracket t \rrbracket_\mathcal{D} A)^\circ = \mathcal{K}_i A^\circ \to \mathcal{D} A^\circ$, which is an instance of $\mathbf{K_i D}$ axiom. If F is obtained by Modus Ponens from G and $G \to F$, then by the induction hypothesis G° and $G^\circ \to F^\circ$ are provable in $\mathbf{L^D}$. Thus, F° is provable in $\mathbf{L^D}$. If $F = \llbracket c_{j_m}^{i_m} \rrbracket_{i_m} \cdots \llbracket c_{j_1}^{i_1} \rrbracket_{i_1} A \in \mathcal{CS}$ is obtained by the Iterated Axiom Necessitation rule, then A° is provable in $\mathbf{L^D}$, since A is an axiom of $\mathbf{JL_n^D}$. Hence, by iterated applications of the Necessitation rule, we can derive $\mathcal{K}_{i_m} \cdots \mathcal{K}_{i_1} A^\circ$. Likewise, If $F = \llbracket c^i \rrbracket_i A \in \mathcal{CS}$ is obtained by the Axiom Necessitation rule, then use the Necessitation rule to derive $\mathcal{K}_i A^\circ$. $\square$

Definition 10. *Let A be a formula in the language of $\mathbf{L^D}$. A realization of the formula A is a $\mathbf{JL^D}$-formula A^r such that $(A^r)^\circ = A$.*

More precisely, a realization A^r is obtained by replacing each modality $\mathcal{K}_i$ in A by a term in Tm_i, and each modality $\mathcal{D}$ in A by a term in $Tm_\mathcal{D}$. A realization is called *normal* if all negative occurrences of modalities are replaced by distinct variables. In the rest of this section we will prove the following results:

$$\mathbf{JK_n^{D^\circ}} = \mathbf{K_n^D}, \qquad \mathbf{JT_n^{D^\circ}} = \mathbf{T_n^D},$$
$$\mathbf{JS4_n^{D^\circ}} = \mathbf{S4_n^D}, \qquad \mathbf{JS5_n^{D^\circ}} = \mathbf{S5_n^D}. \tag{1}$$

The existence of an $\mathbf{JL^D}$-realization of any theorems of $\mathbf{L^D}$ can be established semantically by a method developed in [9].

Definition 11. *By $\mathbf{JL^{D-}}$ we mean the system $\mathbf{JL^D}$ in a language without operations $+_*$ and without axioms $\mathbf{A1}$. Models of $\mathbf{JL^{D-}}$ are the same as for those of $\mathbf{JL^D}$ except that the evidence function is not required to satisfy the condition $\mathcal{E}1$.*

It is easy to verify that the internalization lemma holds for $\mathbf{JL^{D-}}$ and the fully explanatory property of the canonical model holds for $\mathbf{JL^{D-}}$-models (the canonical models of $\mathbf{JL^{D-}}$ are defined similar to the canonical models of $\mathbf{JL^D}$).

Let φ be a formula in the language of $\mathbf{L^D}$, fixed for the rest of this section. By subformula we mean subformula occurrence. The set of all subformulas, positive subformulas and negative subformulas of φ are denoted, respectively, by $Sub(\varphi)$, $Sub^+(\varphi)$ and $Sub^-(\varphi)$.

Definition 12. *Let $\mathcal{A}$ be any assignment of justification variables*

$$\bigcup_{*\in\{1,\dots,n,\mathcal{D}\}} Var^*$$

to negative subformulas of φ of the form $\mathcal{K}_i X$ or $\mathcal{D}X$ such that

- *If $\mathcal{A}(\mathcal{K}_i X) = x$, then $x \in Var^i$.*
- *If $\mathcal{A}(\mathcal{D}X) = x$, then $x \in Var^{\mathcal{D}}$.*

We define two mappings $w_{\mathcal{A}}$ and $v_{\mathcal{A}}$ of subformulas of φ to sets of formulas of $\mathbf{JL^D}$ and $\mathbf{JL^{D^-}}$, respectively, as follows:

1. *$w_{\mathcal{A}}(P) = v_{\mathcal{A}}(P) = \{P\}$, where P is a propositional variable;*
   $w_{\mathcal{A}}(\bot) = v_{\mathcal{A}}(\bot) = \{\bot\}$.
2. *$w_{\mathcal{A}}(X \to Y) = \{X' \to Y' \,|\, X' \in w_{\mathcal{A}}(X), Y' \in w_{\mathcal{A}}(Y)\}$,*
   $v_{\mathcal{A}}(X \to Y) = \{X' \to Y' \,|\, X' \in v_{\mathcal{A}}(X), Y' \in v_{\mathcal{A}}(Y)\}$.
3. *If $\mathcal{K}_i X \in Sub^-(\varphi)$, then*
   $w_{\mathcal{A}}(\mathcal{K}_i X) = \{[\![x]\!]_i X' \,|\, \mathcal{A}(\mathcal{K}_i X) = x, x \in Var^i, X' \in w_{\mathcal{A}}(X)\}$,
   $v_{\mathcal{A}}(\mathcal{K}_i X) = \{[\![x]\!]_i X' \,|\, \mathcal{A}(\mathcal{K}_i X) = x, x \in Var^i, X' \in v_{\mathcal{A}}(X)\}$.
4. *If $\mathcal{K}_i X \in Sub^+(\varphi)$, then*
   $w_{\mathcal{A}}(\mathcal{K}_i X) = \{[\![t]\!]_i X' \,|\, t \in Tm_i, X' \in w_{\mathcal{A}}(X)\}$,
   $v_{\mathcal{A}}(\mathcal{K}_i X) = \{[\![t]\!]_i (X_1 \vee \dots \vee X_m) \,|\, t \in Tm_i, X_1, \dots, X_m \in v_{\mathcal{A}}(X)\}$.
5. *If $\mathcal{D}X \in Sub^-(\varphi)$, then*
   $w_{\mathcal{A}}(\mathcal{D}X) = \{[\![x]\!]_i X' \,|\, \mathcal{A}(\mathcal{D}X) = x, x \in Var^{\mathcal{D}}, X' \in w_{\mathcal{A}}(X)\}$,
   $v_{\mathcal{A}}(\mathcal{D}X) = \{[\![x]\!]_i X' \,|\, \mathcal{A}(\mathcal{D}X) = x, x \in Var^{\mathcal{D}}, X' \in v_{\mathcal{A}}(X)\}$.
6. *If $\mathcal{D}X \in Sub^+(\varphi)$, then*
   $w_{\mathcal{A}}(\mathcal{D}X) = \{[\![t]\!]_{\mathcal{D}} X' \,|\, t \in Tm_{\mathcal{D}}, X' \in w_{\mathcal{A}}(X)\}$,
   $v_{\mathcal{A}}(\mathcal{D}X) = \{[\![t]\!]_{\mathcal{D}} (X_1 \vee \dots \vee X_m) \,|\, t \in Tm_{\mathcal{D}}, X_1, \dots, X_m \in v_{\mathcal{A}}(X)\}$.

By $\neg v_{\mathcal{A}}(X)$ we mean $\{\neg X' \,|\, X' \in v_{\mathcal{A}}(X)\}$. It is assumed that $\mathcal{A}$ assigns different variables to different subformulas (this assumption is required in the proof of Lemma 6).

Let $\mathcal{M} = (\mathcal{W}, \mathcal{R}_*, \mathcal{E}_*, \Vdash_p)$ be the canonical model of $\mathbf{JL^{D^-}}$. We may consider $\mathcal{M}$ as a model for $\mathbf{L^D}$, in which the accessibility relation $\mathcal{R}_{\mathcal{D}}$ and evidence functions $\mathcal{E}_*$ play no role and $\Vdash_p$ is defined as in Definition 2. In this case we write $(\mathcal{M}, \Gamma) \Vdash_{\mathbf{L^D}} A$ to denote that $\mathcal{M}$ is considered as a model of $\mathbf{L^D}$.

Lemma 5. *Let CS be an axiomatically appropriate constant specification for $\mathbf{JL^{D^-}}$, and $\mathcal{M}$ be a canonical model for $\mathbf{JL^{D^-}}$ that respects CS. Then for each world Γ of the model:*

1. *If $\psi \in Sub^+(\varphi)$ and $(\mathcal{M}, \Gamma) \Vdash_p \neg v_{\mathcal{A}}(\psi)$, then $(\mathcal{M}, \Gamma) \Vdash_{\mathbf{L^D}} \neg\psi$.*
2. *If $\psi \in Sub^-(\varphi)$ and $(\mathcal{M}, \Gamma) \Vdash_p v_{\mathcal{A}}(\psi)$, then $(\mathcal{M}, \Gamma) \Vdash_{\mathbf{L^D}} \psi$.*

Proof. The proof is by induction on the complexity of ψ. The proof for propositional variables and the case for implication is similar to the proof of Proposition 7.7 in [9].

Suppose $\psi = \mathcal{K}_i X \in Sub^+(\varphi)$ and $(\mathcal{M}, \Gamma) \Vdash_p \neg v_{\mathcal{A}}(\psi)$. First we show that $\Gamma^{\sharp_i} \cup \neg v_{\mathcal{A}}(X)$ is $\mathbf{JL^{D^-}}(\mathcal{CS})$-consistent. Indeed, otherwise

$$\mathbf{JL^{D^-}}(\mathcal{CS}) \vdash Y_1 \to (Y_2 \to \ldots (Y_m \to X_1 \vee \ldots \vee X_k)\ldots)$$

for some $[\![t_1]\!]_i Y_1, \ldots, [\![t_m]\!]_i Y_m \in \Gamma$ and $X_1, \ldots, X_k \in v_{\mathcal{A}}(X)$. By the internalization lemma, since $\mathcal{CS}$ is axiomatically appropriate, there is a term $s \in Tm_i$ such that

$$\mathbf{JL^{D^-}}(\mathcal{CS}) \vdash [\![s]\!]_i[Y_1 \to (Y_2 \to \ldots (Y_m \to X_1 \vee \ldots \vee X_k)\ldots)]$$

By axiom **A2** and propositional reasoning, we have

$$\mathbf{JL^{D^-}}(\mathcal{CS}) \vdash [\![t_1]\!]_i Y_1 \wedge \ldots \wedge [\![t_m]\!]_i Y_m \to [\![t]\!]_i(X_1 \vee \ldots \vee X_k)$$

where $t = s \cdot_i t_1 \cdot_i \ldots \cdot_i t_m \in Tm_i$. Therefore, $(\mathcal{M}, \Gamma) \Vdash_p [\![t]\!]_i(X_1 \vee \ldots \vee X_k)$, which is impossible since $[\![t]\!]_i(X_1 \vee \ldots \vee X_k) \in v_{\mathcal{A}}(\psi)$. Hence, $\Gamma^{\sharp_i} \cup \neg v_{\mathcal{A}}(X)$ is $\mathbf{JL^{D^-}}(\mathcal{CS})$-consistent, and can be extended to a maximal $\mathbf{JL^{D^-}}(\mathcal{CS})$-consistent set Δ. Thus $\Gamma \mathcal{R}_i \Delta$ and $(\mathcal{M}, \Delta) \Vdash_p \neg v_{\mathcal{A}}(X)$. Since $X \in Sub^+(\varphi)$, by the induction hypothesis, $(\mathcal{M}, \Delta) \Vdash_{\mathbf{L^D}} \neg X$. Hence, $(\mathcal{M}, \Gamma) \Vdash_{\mathbf{L^D}} \neg \psi$.

Suppose $\psi = \mathcal{D}X \in Sub^+(\varphi)$ and $(\mathcal{M}, \Gamma) \Vdash_p \neg v_{\mathcal{A}}(\psi)$. First we show that $\Gamma^{\sharp_{\mathcal{D}}} \cup \neg v_{\mathcal{A}}(X)$ is $\mathbf{JL^{D^-}}(\mathcal{CS})$-consistent. Indeed, otherwise

$$\mathbf{JL^{D^-}}(\mathcal{CS}) \vdash Y_1 \to (Y_2 \to \ldots (Y_m \to X_1 \vee \ldots \vee X_k)\ldots)$$

for some $[\![t_1]\!]_{\mathcal{D}} Y_1, \ldots, [\![t_m]\!]_{\mathcal{D}} Y_m \in \Gamma$ and $X_1, \ldots, X_k \in v_{\mathcal{A}}(X)$. By internalization, there is a term $s \in Tm_{\mathcal{D}}$ such that

$$\mathbf{JL^{D^-}}(\mathcal{CS}) \vdash [\![s]\!]_{\mathcal{D}}[Y_1 \to (Y_2 \to \ldots (Y_m \to X_1 \vee \ldots \vee X_k)\ldots)]$$

By axiom **A2** and propositional reasoning, we have

$$\mathbf{JL^{D^-}}(\mathcal{CS}) \vdash [\![t_1]\!]_{\mathcal{D}} Y_1 \wedge \ldots \wedge [\![t_m]\!]_{\mathcal{D}} Y_m \to [\![t]\!]_{\mathcal{D}}(X_1 \vee \ldots \vee X_k)$$

where $t = s \cdot_{\mathcal{D}} t_1 \cdot_{\mathcal{D}} \ldots \cdot_{\mathcal{D}} t_m \in Tm_{\mathcal{D}}$. Therefore, $(\mathcal{M}, \Gamma) \Vdash_p [\![t]\!]_{\mathcal{D}}(X_1 \vee \ldots \vee X_k)$, which is impossible since $[\![t]\!]_{\mathcal{D}}(X_1 \vee \ldots \vee X_k) \in v_{\mathcal{A}}(\psi)$. Hence, $\Gamma^{\sharp_{\mathcal{D}}} \cup \neg v_{\mathcal{A}}(X)$ is $\mathbf{JL^{D^-}}(\mathcal{CS})$-consistent, and can be extended to a maximal $\mathbf{JL^{D^-}}(\mathcal{CS})$-consistent set Δ. Thus $\Gamma \mathcal{R}_{\mathcal{D}} \Delta$ and $(\mathcal{M}, \Delta) \Vdash_p \neg v_{\mathcal{A}}(X)$. Since $\mathcal{R}_{\mathcal{D}} \subseteq \bigcap_{i=1}^n \mathcal{R}_i$, we have $\Gamma \mathcal{R}_i \Delta$ for any $i \in G$. Since $X \in Sub^+(\varphi)$, by the induction hypothesis, $(\mathcal{M}, \Delta) \Vdash_{\mathbf{L^D}} \neg X$. Hence, $(\mathcal{M}, \Gamma) \Vdash_{\mathbf{L^D}} \neg \psi$.

Suppose $\psi = \mathcal{K}_i X \in Sub^-(\varphi)$ and $(\mathcal{M}, \Gamma) \Vdash_p v_{\mathcal{A}}(\psi)$. Let X' be an arbitrary element of $v_{\mathcal{A}}(X)$. Then $[\![x]\!]_i X' \in v_{\mathcal{A}}(\psi)$, where $\mathcal{A}(\mathcal{K}_i X) = x$, and therefore $(\mathcal{M}, \Gamma) \Vdash_p [\![x]\!]_i X'$. Now for any world Δ such that $\Gamma \mathcal{R}_i \Delta$, $(\mathcal{M}, \Delta) \Vdash_p X'$. Thus $(\mathcal{M}, \Delta) \Vdash_p v_{\mathcal{A}}(X)$. Since $X \in Sub^-(\varphi)$, by the induction hypothesis, $(\mathcal{M}, \Delta) \Vdash_{\mathbf{L^D}} X$. Hence, $(\mathcal{M}, \Gamma) \Vdash_{\mathbf{L^D}} \psi$.

Suppose $\psi = \mathcal{D}X \in Sub^-(\varphi)$ and $(\mathcal{M}, \Gamma) \Vdash_p v_{\mathcal{A}}(\psi)$. Let X' be an arbitrary element of $v_{\mathcal{A}}(X)$. Then $[\![x]\!]_{\mathcal{D}}X' \in v_{\mathcal{A}}(\psi)$, where $\mathcal{A}(\mathcal{D}X) = x$, and therefore $(\mathcal{M}, \Gamma) \Vdash_p [\![x]\!]_{\mathcal{D}}X'$. Now for any world Δ such that $\Gamma \mathcal{R}_{\mathcal{D}} \Delta$, we have $(\mathcal{M}, \Delta) \Vdash_p X'$. Thus $(\mathcal{M}, \Delta) \Vdash_p v_{\mathcal{A}}(X)$. Since $X \in Sub^-(\varphi)$, by the induction hypothesis, $(\mathcal{M}, \Delta) \Vdash_{\mathbf{L}^{\mathbf{D}}} X$. Since $\mathcal{R}_{\mathcal{D}} \subseteq \bigcap_{i=1}^n \mathcal{R}_i$, we have $\Gamma \mathcal{R}_i \Delta$ for any $i \in G$. Hence, $(\mathcal{M}, \Gamma) \Vdash_{\mathbf{L}^{\mathbf{D}}} \psi$.   □

Corollary 1. *Let* $\mathcal{CS}$ *be an axiomatically appropriate constant specification for* $\mathbf{JL}^{\mathbf{D}^-}$. *If* $\mathbf{L}^{\mathbf{D}} \vdash \varphi$ *then there are* $\varphi_1, \ldots, \varphi_m \in v_{\mathcal{A}}(\varphi)$ *such that*

$$\mathbf{JL}^{\mathbf{D}^-}(\mathcal{CS}) \vdash \varphi_1 \vee \ldots \vee \varphi_m.$$

Proof. Suppose towards a contradiction that $\mathbf{JL}^{\mathbf{D}^-}(\mathcal{CS}) \nvdash \varphi_1 \vee \ldots \vee \varphi_m$ for all $\varphi_1, \ldots, \varphi_m \in v_{\mathcal{A}}(\varphi)$. Thus $\neg v_{\mathcal{A}}(\varphi)$ is $\mathbf{JL}^{\mathbf{D}^-}(\mathcal{CS})$-consistent. For otherwise there would be $\varphi_1, \ldots, \varphi_m \in v_{\mathcal{A}}(\varphi)$ such that $\mathbf{JL}^{\mathbf{D}^-}(\mathcal{CS}) \vdash \varphi_1 \vee \ldots \vee \varphi_m$, contrary to assumption. Since $\neg v_{\mathcal{A}}(\varphi)$ is $\mathbf{JL}^{\mathbf{D}^-}(\mathcal{CS})$-consistent, extend it to a maximal consistent set $\Gamma \in \mathcal{W}$. By Truth Lemma, $(\mathcal{M}, \Gamma) \Vdash_p \neg v_{\mathcal{A}}(\varphi)$. Hence, by Lemma 5, $(\mathcal{M}, \Gamma) \Vdash_{\mathbf{L}^{\mathbf{D}}} \neg \varphi$, contra with the assumption $\mathbf{L}^{\mathbf{D}} \vdash \varphi$ and Theorem 1.   □

Lemma 6. *Let* $\mathcal{CS}$ *be an axiomatically appropriate constant specification for* $\mathbf{JL}^{\mathbf{D}}$. *For every subformula* ψ *of* φ *and each* $\psi_1, \ldots, \psi_m \in v_{\mathcal{A}}(\psi)$, *there is a substitution* σ *and a formula* $\psi' \in v_{\mathcal{A}}(\psi)$ *such that:*

1. *If* $\psi \in Sub^+(\varphi)$, *then* $\mathbf{JL}^{\mathbf{D}}(\mathcal{CS}) \vdash (\psi_1 \vee \ldots \vee \psi_m)\sigma \to \psi'$.
2. *If* $\psi \in Sub^-(\varphi)$, *then* $\mathbf{JL}^{\mathbf{D}}(\mathcal{CS}) \vdash \psi' \to (\psi_1 \wedge \ldots \wedge \psi_m)\sigma$.

Proof. The proof is by induction on the complexity of ψ. The proof for propositional variables and the case for implication is similar to the proof of Proposition 7.8 in [9].

Suppose $\psi = \mathcal{K}_i X \in Sub^+(\varphi)$, and the result is known for X (which also occurs positively in φ). Let $\psi_1 = [\![t_1]\!]_i D_1, \ldots, \psi_m = [\![t_m]\!]_i D_m$ be in $v_{\mathcal{A}}(\psi)$, such that $t_1, \ldots, t_m \in Tm_i$ and $D_1, \ldots, D_m$ are disjunctions of formulas from $v_{\mathcal{A}}(X)$. Thus $D_1, \ldots, D_m \in v_{\mathcal{A}}(X)$. By the induction hypothesis, there is a substitution σ and $X' \in v_{\mathcal{A}}(X)$ such that $\mathbf{JL}^{\mathbf{D}}(\mathcal{CS}) \vdash (D_1 \vee \ldots \vee D_m)\sigma \to X'$. Note that $(D_1 \vee \ldots \vee D_m)\sigma = D_1\sigma \vee \ldots \vee D_m\sigma$. Consequently, for each $j = 1, \ldots, m$, we have $\mathbf{JL}^{\mathbf{D}}(\mathcal{CS}) \vdash D_j\sigma \to X'$. By the internalization lemma, there are terms $s_1, \ldots, s_m \in Tm_i$ such that $\mathbf{JL}^{\mathbf{D}}(\mathcal{CS}) \vdash [\![s_j]\!]_i(D_j\sigma \to X')$, for each $j = 1, \ldots, m$. Hence by axiom **A2**

$$\mathbf{JL}^{\mathbf{D}}(\mathcal{CS}) \vdash [\![t_j\sigma]\!]_i D_j\sigma \to [\![s_j \cdot_i t_j\sigma]\!]_i X'.$$

Note that $[\![t_j\sigma]\!]_i D_j\sigma = ([\![t_j]\!]_i D_j)\sigma$. Let $t = s_1 \cdot_i t_1\sigma +_i \ldots +_i s_m \cdot_i t_m\sigma \in Tm_i$. By axiom **A1**,

$$\mathbf{JL}^{\mathbf{D}}(\mathcal{CS}) \vdash ([\![t_j]\!]_i D_j)\sigma \to [\![t]\!]_i X',$$

for each $j = 1, \ldots, m$. Thus,

$$\mathbf{JL}^{\mathbf{D}}(\mathcal{CS}) \vdash \Big(\bigvee_{1 \leq j \leq m} [\![t_j]\!]_i D_j \Big)\sigma \to [\![t]\!]_i X'.$$

Therefore, letting $\psi' = [\![t]\!]_i X'$, we have

$$\mathbf{JL^D}(\mathcal{CS}) \vdash \Big(\bigvee_{1 \le j \le m} \psi_j \Big)\sigma \to \psi'.$$

Suppose $\psi = \mathcal{D}X \in Sub^+(\varphi)$, and the result is known for X (which also occurs positively in φ). Let $\psi_1 = [\![t_1]\!]_{\mathcal{D}}D_1, \ldots, \psi_m = [\![t_m]\!]_{\mathcal{D}}D_m$ be in $v_{\mathcal{A}}(\psi)$, such that $t_1, \ldots, t_m \in Tm_{\mathcal{D}}$ and $D_1, \ldots, D_m$ are disjunctions of formulas from $v_{\mathcal{A}}(X)$. By the induction hypothesis, there is a substitution σ and $X' \in v_{\mathcal{A}}(X)$ such that $\mathbf{JL^D}(\mathcal{CS}) \vdash (D_1 \vee \ldots \vee D_m)\sigma \to X'$. Consequently, for each $j = 1, \ldots, m$, we have $\mathbf{JL^D}(\mathcal{CS}) \vdash D_j\sigma \to X'$. By the internalization lemma, there are terms $s_1, \ldots, s_m \in Tm_{\mathcal{D}}$ such that $\mathbf{JL^D}(\mathcal{CS}) \vdash [\![s_j]\!]_{\mathcal{D}}(D_j\sigma \to X')$, for each $j = 1, \ldots, m$. Hence by axiom **A2**

$$\mathbf{JL^D}(\mathcal{CS}) \vdash [\![t_j\sigma]\!]_i D_j\sigma \to [\![s_j \cdot_{\mathcal{D}} t_j\sigma]\!]_{\mathcal{D}}X'.$$

Let $t = s_1 \cdot_{\mathcal{D}} t_1\sigma +_{\mathcal{D}} \ldots +_{\mathcal{D}} s_m \cdot_{\mathcal{D}} t_m\sigma$. By axiom **A1**,

$$\mathbf{JL^D}(\mathcal{CS}) \vdash ([\![t_j]\!]_{\mathcal{D}}D_j)\sigma \to [\![t]\!]_{\mathcal{D}}X',$$

for each $j = 1, \ldots, m$. Thus,

$$\mathbf{JL^D}(\mathcal{CS}) \vdash \Big(\bigvee_{1 \le j \le m} [\![t_j]\!]_{\mathcal{D}}D_j \Big)\sigma \to [\![t]\!]_{\mathcal{D}}X'.$$

Therefore, letting $\psi' = [\![t]\!]_{\mathcal{D}}X'$, we have

$$\mathbf{JL^D}(\mathcal{CS}) \vdash \Big(\bigvee_{1 \le j \le m} \psi_j \Big)\sigma \to \psi'.$$

Suppose $\psi = \mathcal{K}_i X \in Sub^-(\varphi)$, and the result is known for X (which also occurs negatively in φ). Let $\psi_1 = [\![x]\!]_i X_1, \ldots, \psi_m = [\![x]\!]_i X_m$ be in $v_{\mathcal{A}}(\psi)$, such that $\mathcal{A}(\mathcal{K}_i X) = x$ (where $x \in Var^i$), and $X_1, \ldots, X_m \in v_{\mathcal{A}}(X)$. By the induction hypothesis, there is a substitution σ and $X' \in w_{\mathcal{A}}(X)$ such that $\mathbf{JL^D}(\mathcal{CS}) \vdash X' \to (X_1 \wedge \ldots \wedge X_m)\sigma$. Since $\mathcal{A}$ assigns different variables to different subformulas, x does not occur in $X_1, \ldots, X_m$, and hence $x \notin dom(\sigma)$. It follows that, for each $j = 1, \ldots, m$, $\mathbf{JL^D}(\mathcal{CS}) \vdash X' \to X_j\sigma$. By the internalization lemma, there are terms $t_1, \ldots, t_m \in Tm_i$ such that $\mathbf{JL^D}(\mathcal{CS}) \vdash [\![t_j]\!]_i(X' \to X_j\sigma)$, for each $j = 1, \ldots, m$. Thus $\mathbf{JL^D}(\mathcal{CS}) \vdash [\![s]\!]_i(X' \to X_j\sigma)$ for $s = t_1 +_i \ldots +_i t_m$. Therefore, for each $j = 1, \ldots, m$, $\mathbf{JL^D}(\mathcal{CS}) \vdash [\![x]\!]_i X' \to [\![s \cdot_i x]\!]_i(X_j\sigma)$. Letting $\sigma' = \sigma \cup \{(x, s \cdot_i x)\}$ we have $\mathbf{JL^D}(\mathcal{CS}) \vdash [\![x]\!]_i X' \to ([\![x]\!]_i X_j)\sigma'$, from which we get

$$\mathbf{JL^D}(\mathcal{CS}) \vdash \psi' \to ([\![x]\!]_i X_1 \wedge \ldots \wedge [\![x]\!]_i X_m)\sigma'$$

for $\psi' = [\![x]\!]_i X'$.

Suppose $\psi = \mathcal{D}X \in Sub^-(\varphi)$, and the result is known for X (which also occurs negatively in φ). Let $\psi_1 = [\![x]\!]_{\mathcal{D}} X_1, \ldots, \psi_m = [\![x]\!]_{\mathcal{D}} X_m$ be in $v_{\mathcal{A}}(\psi)$, such that $\mathcal{A}(\mathcal{D}X) = x$ (where $x \in Var^{\mathcal{D}}$), and $X_1, \ldots, X_m \in v_{\mathcal{A}}(X)$. By the induction hypothesis, there is a substitution σ and $X' \in w_{\mathcal{A}}(X)$ such that $\mathbf{JL^D}(\mathcal{CS}) \vdash X' \to (X_1 \wedge \ldots \wedge X_m)\sigma$. Since $\mathcal{A}$ assigns different variables to different subformulas, x does not occur in $X_1, \ldots, X_m$, and hence $x \notin dom(\sigma)$. It follows that $\mathbf{JL^D}(\mathcal{CS}) \vdash X' \to X_j\sigma$, for each $j = 1, \ldots, m$. By the internalization lemma, there are terms $t_1, \ldots, t_m \in Tm_{\mathcal{D}}$ such that $\mathbf{JL^D}(\mathcal{CS}) \vdash [\![\, t_j \,]\!]_{\mathcal{D}}(X' \to X_j\sigma)$, for each $j = 1, \ldots, m$. Thus $\mathbf{JL^D}(\mathcal{CS}) \vdash [\![\, s \,]\!]_{\mathcal{D}}(X' \to X_j\sigma)$ for $s = t_1 +_{\mathcal{D}} \ldots +_{\mathcal{D}} t_m$. Therefore $\mathbf{JL^D}(\mathcal{CS}) \vdash [\![\, x \,]\!]_{\mathcal{D}}X' \to [\![\, s \cdot_{\mathcal{D}} x \,]\!]_{\mathcal{D}}(X_j\sigma)$, for each $j = 1, \ldots, m$. Letting $\sigma' = \sigma \cup \{(x, s \cdot_{\mathcal{D}} x)\}$ we have $\mathbf{JL^D}(\mathcal{CS}) \vdash [\![\, x \,]\!]_{\mathcal{D}}X' \to ([\![\, x \,]\!]_{\mathcal{D}}X_j)\sigma'$, from which we get

$$\mathbf{JL^D}(\mathcal{CS}) \vdash \psi' \to ([\![\, x \,]\!]_{\mathcal{D}}X_1 \wedge \ldots \wedge [\![\, x \,]\!]_{\mathcal{D}}X_m)\sigma'$$

for $\psi' = [\![\, x \,]\!]_{\mathcal{D}}X'$. $\square$

Corollary 2. *Let $\mathcal{CS}$ be an axiomatically appropriate constant specification for $\mathbf{JL^D}$. If $\mathbf{L^D} \vdash \varphi$ then there is a substitution σ and $\varphi' \in w_{\mathcal{A}}(\varphi)$ such that*

$$\mathbf{JL^D}(\mathcal{CS} \cup \mathcal{CS}\sigma) \vdash \varphi'.$$

Proof. Suppose $\mathbf{L^D} \vdash \varphi$. By Corollary 1, there are $\varphi_1, \ldots, \varphi_m \in v_{\mathcal{A}}(\varphi)$ such that $\mathbf{JL^{D^-}}(\mathcal{CS}) \vdash \varphi_1 \vee \ldots \vee \varphi_m$. By Lemma 6, there is a substitution σ and a formula $\varphi' \in v_{\mathcal{A}}(\varphi)$ such that $\mathbf{JL^D}(\mathcal{CS}) \vdash (\varphi_1 \vee \ldots \vee \varphi_m)\sigma \to \varphi'$. By the substitution lemma, $\mathbf{JL^D}(\mathcal{CS}\sigma) \vdash (\varphi_1 \vee \ldots \vee \varphi_m)\sigma$, and therefore $\mathbf{JL^D}(\mathcal{CS} \cup \mathcal{CS}\sigma) \vdash \varphi'$. $\square$

Our main theorem in this section is the realization theorem. In fact, we give a uniform realization theorem for all systems $\mathbf{JL_n^D}$.

Theorem 5 (Realization Theorem). $\mathbf{JL^{D^\circ}} = \mathbf{L^D}$

Proof. One direction of the proof is done by Lemma 4. For the other direction suppose $\mathbf{L^D} \vdash \varphi$. By Corollary 2, there is a formula $\psi \in w_{\mathcal{A}}(\varphi)$ such that $\mathbf{JL^D} \vdash \psi$. Note that, by the definition of $w_{\mathcal{A}}$, ψ is a realization of φ, i.e. $\psi^\circ = \varphi$. $\square$

6 Conclusions

In this paper we study logics of distributed knowledge with justifications. The advantage of this study is to incorporate the notion of evidence (or justification) into the distributed knowledge logics. For future work, it is natural to combine the justified distributed knowledge logic $\mathbf{JS4_n^D}$ with the explicit evidence system with common knowledge $\mathbf{LP_n^C}$ introduced in [5]. There remains also some questions: Are there Fitting models (that are pseudo-Fitting models without accessibility relation $\mathcal{R}_{\mathcal{D}}$) for $\mathbf{JL^D}$? Are $\mathbf{JL^D}$ conservative over multi-agent justification systems $\mathbf{JL_n}$ (the systems $\mathbf{JL^D}$ without distributed knowledge operator)? Are there cut-free tableau or Gentzen systems for $\mathbf{JL^D}$?

Acknowledgements. I would like to thank the anonymous referees for their useful comments and suggestions.

References

1. Artemov, S.: Explicit provability and constructive semantics. Bulletin of Symbolic Logic 7(1), 1–36 (2001)
2. Artemov, S.: The logic of justification. The Review of Symbolic Logic 1(4), 477–513 (2008)

3. Artemov, S.: Tracking Evidence. In: Blass, A., Dershowitz, N., Reisig, W. (eds.) Fields of Logic and Computation. LNCS, vol. 6300, pp. 61–74. Springer, Heidelberg (2010)

4. Bucheli, S., Kuznets, R., Renne, B., Sack, J., Studer, T.: Justified belief change. In: Arrazola, X., Ponte, M. (eds.) Proceedings of the Second ILCLI International Workshop on Logic and Philosophy of Knowledge, Communication and Action, LogKCA 2010, pp. 135–155. University of the Basque Country Press (2010)

5. Bucheli, S., Kuznets, R., Studer, T.: Justifications for common knowledge. Journal of Applied Non-Classical Logics 21(1), 35–60 (2011)

6. Bucheli, S., Kuznets, R., Studer, T.: Partial Realization in Dynamic Justification Logic. In: Beklemishev, L.D., de Queiroz, R. (eds.) WoLLIC 2011. LNCS, vol. 6642, pp. 35–51. Springer, Heidelberg (2011)

7. Fagin, R., Halpern, J.Y., Vardi, M.Y.: What can machines know? on the properties of knowledge in distributed systems. Journal of the ACM 39, 328–376 (1992)

8. Fagin, R., Halpern, J.Y., Moses, Y., Vardi, M.Y.: Reasoning about knowledge. MIT Press (1995)

9. Fitting, M.: The logic of proofs, semantically. Annals of Pure and Applied Logic 132(1), 1–25 (2005)

10. Ghari, M.: Justification counterpart of distributed knowledge systems. In: Slavkovik, M. (ed.) Proceedings of the 15th ESSLLI Student Session, Copenhagen, Denmark, pp. 25–36 (2010)

11. Goetschi, R., Kuznets, R.: Realization for Justification Logics via Nested Sequents: Modularity through Embedding. Annals of Pure and Applied Logic (to appear)

12. Meyer, J.-J.C., van der Hoek, W.: Epistemic logic for AI and computer science. Cambridge University Press (1995)

13. Renne, B.: Public communication in justification logic. Journal of Logic and Computation 21(6), 1005–1034 (2011)

14. Renne, B.: Multi-Agent Justification Logic: Communication and Evidence Elimination. Synthese (Published Online July 5, 2011)

15. Yavorskaya (Sidon), T.: Interacting explicit evidence systems. Theory of Computing Systems 43, 272–293 (2008)

16. Studer, T.: Justification logic, inference tracking, and data privacy. Logic and Logical Philosophy 20(4), 297–306 (2011)

17. Studer, T.: An application of justification logic to protocol verification. In: Proceedings of 2011 Seventh International Conference on Computational Intelligence and Security, CIS 2011, pp. 779–783. IEEE (2011)

Epistemic Logic, Relevant Alternatives, and the Dynamics of Context

Wesley H. Holliday

Department of Philosophy, Stanford University

Abstract. According to the Relevant Alternatives (RA) Theory of knowledge, knowing that something is the case involves *ruling out (only) the relevant alternatives*. The conception of knowledge in epistemic logic also involves the elimination of possibilities, but without an explicit distinction, among the possibilities consistent with an agent's information, between those *relevant* possibilities that an agent must rule out in order to know and those remote, far-fetched or otherwise irrelevant possibilities. In this article, I propose formalizations of two versions of the RA theory. Doing so clarifies a famous debate in epistemology, pitting Fred Dretske against David Lewis, about whether the RA theorist should accept the principle that *knowledge is closed under known implication*, familiar as the K axiom in epistemic logic. Dretske's case against closure under known implication leads to a study of other closure principles, while Lewis's defense of closure by appeal to the claimed *context sensitivity* of knowledge attributions leads to a study of the dynamics of context. Having followed the first lead at length in other work, here I focus more on the second, especially on logical issues associated with developing a dynamic epistemic logic of context change over models for the RA theory.

1 Introduction

Example 1 (Medical Diagnosis). Suppose that two medical students, A and B, are subjected to a test. Their professor introduces them to the same patient, who presents various symptoms, and the students are to make a diagnosis of the patient's condition. After some independent investigation, both students conclude that the patient has a common condition c. In fact, they are both correct. Yet only student A passes the test. For the professor wished to see if the students would check for another common condition c' that causes the same visible symptoms as c. While A ran laboratory tests to rule out c' before making the diagnosis of c, B made the diagnosis of c after only a physical exam.

In evaluating the students, the professor concludes that although both gave the correct diagnosis of c, student B did not know that the patient's condition was c, since B did not rule out the alternative of c'. Had the patient's condition been c', student B might still have made the diagnosis of c, since the physical exam would not have revealed a difference. Student B was *lucky*. The condition B associated with the patient's visible symptoms happened to be the condition the patient had, but if the professor had chosen a patient with c', student B

D. Lassiter and M. Slavkovik (Eds.): ESSLLI Student Sessions, LNCS 7415, pp. 109–129, 2012.

might have made a misdiagnosis. By contrast, student A secured against this possibility of error by running the lab tests. For this reason, the professor judges that student A knew that the patient's condition was c and passed the test.

Of course, A did not secure against *every* possibility of error. Suppose there is an extremely rare disease[1] x such that people with x appear to have c on lab tests given for c and c', even though people with x are *immune* to c, and only extensive further testing can detect x in its early stages. Should we say that A did not know that the patient had c after all, since A did not rule out x?

According to a classic *relevant alternatives* style answer (e.g., [15, p. 775], [13, p. 365]), the requirement that one rule out *all* possibilities of error would make knowledge impossible, since there are always some possibilities of error—however remote and far-fetched—that are not eliminated by one's evidence and experience. Yet if no one had a special reason to think that the patient may have had x instead of c, it should not have been necessary to rule out such a remote possibility in order to know that the patient had the common condition c.[2]

Much could be said about Example 1, but our interest here is in the pressure it appears to put on the claim that knowledge is *closed under known implication*. At its simplest, this is the claim that if an agent knows φ and knows that φ implies ψ, then she knows ψ: $(K\varphi \wedge K(\varphi \to \psi)) \to K\psi$, familiar as the K axiom of standard epistemic logic [19,14]. One obvious objection to K is that an agent with bounded rationality may know φ and know that φ implies ψ, yet not "put two and two together" and draw a conclusion about ψ. Such an agent may not even believe ψ, let alone know it. The challenge of the much-discussed "problem of logical omniscience" [27,16] is to develop a good theoretical model of the knowledge of such agents. However, according to a different objection to K made famous in epistemology by Dretske [12] and Nozick [26] (and applicable to more sophisticated closure claims), knowledge would not be closed under known implication even for "ideally astute logicians" [12, p. 1010], who always put two and two together and come to believe all the consequences of what they know. It is this objection, not the logical omniscience problem, that is our starting point.

If one accepts the analysis at the end of Example 1, then one is close to denying K. For suppose A knows that if her patient has c, then he does not have x (because x confers immunity to c), (i) $K(c \to \neg x)$. Since A did not run any of the tests that could detect the presence or absence of x, arguably she does not know that the patient does not have x, (ii) $\neg K\neg x$. Given the professor's judgment that A knows that the patient has condition c, (iii) Kc, together (i) through (iii) violate the following instance of K: (iv) $(Kc \wedge K(c \to \neg x)) \to K\neg x$. To retain K, one must say either that A does not know that the patient has condition c after all (having not excluded x), or else that A can know that a patient does not have a disease x without running any of the specialized tests for the disease (having learned instead that the patient has c, but from lab results consistent with x). While the second option threatens to commit us to problematic "easy

---

[1] Perhaps it has never been documented, but it is a possibility of medical theory.
[2] Skeptics about medical knowledge may substitute one of the standard cases in the epistemology literature with a similar structure (see, e.g., [12, p. 1015], [13, p. 369]).

knowledge" [8], the first option threatens to commit us to radical skepticism about knowledge, given the inevitability of uneliminated possibilities of error.

Response 1. Dretske [12] and others [26,17] respond to the inconsistency of (i) through (iv), a version of the now standard "skeptical paradox" [7,9], by arguing that K is invalid, for reasons other than bounded rationality. Dretske's explanation of why K is invalid even for ideally astute logicians is in terms of his Relevant Alternatives (RA) Theory of knowledge [13]. According to this theory, to know p is (to truly believe p and) to have *ruled out the relevant alternatives to* p. In coming to know c and $c \rightarrow \neg x$, student A rules out certain relevant alternatives. In order to know $\neg x$, A must rule out certain relevant alternatives. However, the relevant alternatives in the two cases are *not the same*. According to our earlier reasoning, x is not an alternative that must be ruled out in order for Kc (or $K(c \rightarrow \neg x)$) to hold. But x *is* an alternative that must be ruled out in order for $K\neg x$ to hold. It is because the relevant alternatives may be different for what is in the antecedent and consequent of K that K is not valid in general.

Response 2. Against Response 1, Lewis [25] and others [7,9] attempt to explain away apparent closure failures by appeal to *epistemic contextualism*, the thesis that the truth values of knowledge attributions are context sensitive. According to Lewis's contextualist RA theory, in the context C of our conversation before we raised the possibility of the rare disease x, that possibility was irrelevant; so although A had not eliminated the possibility of x, we could truly say in C that A knew (at time t) that the patient's condition was c (Kc). However, by raising the possibility of x in our conversation, we changed the context to a new C' in which the uneliminated possibility of x was relevant. Hence we could truly say in C' that A did *not* know that the patient did not have x $(\neg K\neg x)$, although A knew that x confers immunity to c $(K(c \rightarrow \neg x))$, which did not require ruling out x. Is this a violation of K in context C'? It is not, because in C', unlike C, we could *no longer* truly say that A knew (at t) that the patient's condition was c (Kc), given that A had not eliminated the newly relevant possibility of x. Moreover, Lewis argues that there is no violation of K in context C either:

> Knowledge *is* closed under implication.... Implication preserves truth— that is, it preserves truth in any given, fixed context. But if we switch contexts, all bets are off.... Dretske gets the phenomenon right...it is just that he misclassifies what he sees. He thinks it is a phenomenon of logic, when really it is a phenomenon of pragmatics. Closure, rightly understood, survives the rest. If we evaluate the conclusion for truth not with respect to the context in which it was uttered, but instead with respect to the different context in which the premise was uttered, then truth is preserved. (564)

Lewis claims that if we evaluate the consequent of (iv), $K\neg x$, with respect to the context C of our conversation before we raised the possibility of x, then it should come out *true*—despite the fact that A had not eliminated the possibility of x through any special tests—because the possibility of x was irrelevant in C. If this is correct, then there is no violation of K in either context C' or C.

This article introduces a formal framework to study Responses 1 and 2: in §2, the response of denying K leads to a study of other closure principles; in §3, the response of maintaining K with contextualism leads to a study of context dynamics. Having focused on the first response in detail elsewhere [20], here I focus more on the second, especially on logical issues associated with developing a *dynamic epistemic logic* [11,2] of context change over models for the RA theory.

2 Relevant Alternatives

An important distinction between versions of the RA theory, which our formalization will capture, has to do with logical structure. On the one hand, Dretske [13] states the following definition in developing his RA theory: "call the set of possible alternatives that a person must be in an evidential position to exclude (when he knows P) the *Relevancy Set* (RS)" (371). On the other hand, Heller [17] considers (and rejects) an interpretation of the RA theory in which "there is a certain set of worlds selected as relevant," independently of any proposition, "and S must be able to rule out the not-p worlds within that set" (197).

According to Dretske, for every proposition P, there is a relevancy set for that P. Let us translate this into Heller's talk of worlds. Where $\overline{P}$ is the set of worlds in which P is false, let $r(P)$ be the relevancy set for P, for which Dretske assumes $r(P) \subseteq \overline{P}$. To be more precise, since objective features of an agent's situation in world w may affect what alternatives are relevant (see [13, p. 377] and [10, p. 30f] on "subject factors"), let us write $r(P, w)$ for the relevancy set for P in world w, which may differ from $r(P, v)$ for a distinct world v in which the agent's situation is different. Finally, if we allow (unlike Dretske) that the conversational context $\mathcal{C}$ of those attributing knowledge to the agent can also affect what alternatives are relevant (see [10, p. 30f] on "attributor factors"), then we should write $r_c(P, w)$ to make the relativization to context explicit.

The quote from Dretske suggests the following definition:

> $RS_{\forall\exists}$: for every context $\mathcal{C}$, world w, and for every ($\forall$) proposition P, there is ($\exists$) a set of *relevant (in w) not-P worlds*, $r_c(P, w) \subseteq \overline{P}$, such that in order to know P in w (relative to $\mathcal{C}$) one must rule out the worlds in $r_c(P, w)$.

By contrast, the quote from Heller suggests the following definition:

> $RS_{\exists\forall}$: for every context $\mathcal{C}$ and world w, there is ($\exists$) a set of *relevant (in w) worlds*, $R_c(w)$, such that for every ($\forall$) proposition P, in order to know P in w (relative to $\mathcal{C}$) one must rule out the worlds in $R_c(w) \cap \overline{P}$.

As a simple logical observation, every $RS_{\exists\forall}$ theory is a $RS_{\forall\exists}$ theory (take $r_\mathcal{C}(P, w) = R_\mathcal{C}(w) \cap \overline{P}$), but not necessarily *vice versa*. From now on, when I refer to $RS_{\forall\exists}$ theories, I have in mind theories that are not also $RS_{\exists\forall}$ theories. This distinction is at the heart of the disagreement about epistemic closure between Dretske and Lewis [25], as Lewis clearly adopts an $RS_{\exists\forall}$ theory.

Below we define our first class of models, following Heller's RA picture of "worlds surrounding the actual world ordered according to how realistic they are, so that those worlds that are more realistic are closer to the actual world than the less realistic ones" [18, p. 25] with "those that are too far away from the actual world being irrelevant" [17, p. 199]. These models represent the epistemic state of an agent from a third-person perspective. We should not assume that anything in the model is something that the agent has in mind. Contextualists should think of the model $\mathcal{M}$ as associated with a fixed context of knowledge attribution, so a change in context corresponds to a change in models from $\mathcal{M}$ to $\mathcal{M}'$ (see §3). Just as the model is not something that the agent has in mind, it is not something that particular speakers attributing knowledge to the agent have in mind either. For possibilities may be relevant and hence should be included in our model, even if the attributors are not considering them (see [10, p. 33]).

For simplicity (and in line with [25]) we will not represent in our RA models an agent's beliefs separately from her knowledge. Adding the usual machinery to do so is easy, but if the only point is to add *believing* φ as a necessary condition for knowing φ, it will not change any of our results about RA knowledge.

Definition 1 (RA Model). A *relevant alternatives model* is a tuple $\mathcal{M}$ of the form $\langle W, \twoheadrightarrow, \preceq, V \rangle$ where:

1. W is a non-empty set;
2. $\twoheadrightarrow$ is a reflexive binary relation on W;
3. $\preceq$ assigns to each $w \in W$ a binary relation $\preceq_w$ on some $W_w \subseteq W$;
   (a) $\preceq_w$ is reflexive and transitive;
   (b) for all $v \in W_w$, $w \preceq_w v$;
4. V assigns to each $p \in \mathsf{At}$ a set $V(p) \subseteq W$.

For $w \in W$, the pair $\mathcal{M}, w$ is a *pointed* model.

In addition, I assume the *well-foundedness* of each $\preceq_w$ (always satisfied in finite models) in what follows, since it allows us to state more perspicuous truth definitions. However, this does not affect our results about closure (see [20]).

I refer to elements of W as "worlds" or "possibilities" interchangeably. As usual, the function V maps each atom p to the set of worlds $V(p)$ where it holds.

Take $w \twoheadrightarrow v$ to mean that v is an *uneliminated* possibility for the agent in w. According to Lewis's [25] notion of elimination, $\twoheadrightarrow$ should be an equivalence relation; but for generality I assume only that $\twoheadrightarrow$ is reflexive, reflecting the fact that an agent can never eliminate her actual world as a possibility. Whether we assume transitivity and symmetry in addition to reflexivity does not affect our results about closure, unless we make further assumptions about $\preceq$ (see [20]).

Take $u \preceq_w v$ to mean that u is *at least as relevant* (at w) as v is.[3] A relation satisfying Definition 1.3a is a *preorder*. The family of preorders in an RA model is like one of Lewis's (weakly centered) comparative similarity systems [23, §2.3] or standard γ-models [22], but without his assumption that each $\preceq_w$ is *total* on its field W_w. Condition 3b, that w is at least as relevant at w as any other

---

[3] One might expect $u \preceq_w v$ to mean that v is at least as relevant (at w) as u is, by analogy with $x \leq y$ in arithmetic, but Lewis's [23, §2.3] convention is now standard.

world is, follows Lewis's [25] *Rule of Actuality* that "actuality is always a relevant alternative" (554). Allowing $\preceq_w \neq \preceq_v$ when $w \neq v$ reflects the *world-relativity* of comparative relevance (based on "subject factors") mentioned above. A fixed context may help to determine not only which possibilities are relevant, given the way things actually are, but also which possibilities would be relevant, were things different. Moreover, we allow $\preceq_w \neq \preceq_v$ even when v is an uneliminated possibility for the agent in w, so $w \twoheadrightarrow v$. For we do not assume that in w the agent can eliminate any v for which $\preceq_v \neq \preceq_w$. As Lewis [25] put it, "the subject himself may not be able to tell what is properly ignored" (554).

Notation 1 (Derived Relations, Min). Where $w, v, u \in W$ and $S \subseteq W$,

- $u \prec_w v$ iff $u \preceq_w v$ and not $v \preceq_w u$; and $u \simeq_w v$ iff $u \preceq_w v$ and $v \preceq_w u$;
- $\text{Min}_{\preceq_w}(S) = \{v \in S \cap W_w \mid \text{there is no } u \in S \text{ such that } u \prec_w v\}$.

Hence $u \prec_w v$ means that possibility u is *more relevant* (at w) than possibility v is, while $u \simeq_w v$ means that they are equally relevant. $\text{Min}_{\preceq_w}(S)$ is the set of *most relevant* (at w) possibilities out of those in S that are ordered by $\preceq_w$.

When it comes to choosing a formal language to go with our RA models, we have a number of choices. For our first, we choose the following (cf. §3.2).

Definition 2 (Epistemic Language). Let $\text{At} = \{p, q, r, \dots\}$ be a set of atomic sentences. The *epistemic language* is generated as follows, where $p \in \text{At}$:

$$\varphi ::= p \mid \neg\varphi \mid (\varphi \wedge \varphi) \mid K\varphi.$$

As usual, expressions containing $\vee$, $\rightarrow$, and $\leftrightarrow$ are abbreviations, and by convention $\wedge$ and $\vee$ bind more strongly than $\rightarrow$ or $\leftrightarrow$ in the absence of parentheses.

We now interpret the language of Definition 2 in RA models, considering three semantics for the K operator. I call these C-semantics, for **C**artesian, D-semantics, for **D**retske, and L-semantics, for **L**ewis. C-semantics is not supposed to capture Descartes' view of knowledge. Rather, it is supposed to reflect a high standard for the truth of knowledge claims—knowledge requires ruling out *all* possibilities of error—in the spirit of Descartes' worries about error in the First Meditation. D-semantics is one (but not the only) way of understanding Dretske's [13] RS$_{\forall\exists}$ theory, using Heller's [18,17] picture of relevance orderings of worlds.[4] Finally, L-semantics follows Lewis's [25] RS$_{\exists\forall}$ theory (for a fixed context).

Definition 3 (Truth in an RA Model). Given a well-founded RA model $\mathcal{M} = \langle W, \twoheadrightarrow, \preceq, V \rangle$ with $w \in W$ and a formula φ in the epistemic language, define $\mathcal{M}, w \vDash_x \varphi$ (φ is true at w in $\mathcal{M}$ according to X-semantics) as follows:

$$
\begin{aligned}
\mathcal{M}, w \vDash_x p \quad &\text{iff} \quad w \in V(p); \\
\mathcal{M}, w \vDash_x \neg\varphi \quad &\text{iff} \quad \mathcal{M}, w \nvDash_x \varphi; \\
\mathcal{M}, w \vDash_x \varphi \wedge \psi \quad &\text{iff} \quad \mathcal{M}, w \vDash_x \varphi \text{ and } \mathcal{M}, w \vDash_x \psi.
\end{aligned}
$$

---

[4] Elsewhere [21] I argue for a better way of developing Dretske's [13] RS$_{\forall\exists}$ theory, without the familiar world-ordering picture. Hence I take the 'D' in D-semantics as loosely as the 'C' in C-semantics. Still, it is a helpful mnemonic for remembering that D-semantics formalizes an RA theory that allows closure failure, as Dretske's does, while L-semantics formalizes an RA theory that does not, like Lewis's.

For the K operator, the C-semantics clause is that of standard modal logic:

$$\mathcal{M}, w \vDash_c K\varphi \text{ iff } \forall v \in W : \text{if } w \rightarrow v \text{ then } \mathcal{M}, v \vDash_c \varphi,$$

which states that φ is known at w iff φ is true in all possibilities uneliminated at w. I will write this clause in another, equivalent way below, for comparison with the D- and L-semantics clauses. First, we need two pieces of notation.

Notation 2 (Extension and Complement). Where $\mathcal{M} = \langle W, \rightarrow, \preceq, V \rangle$,

- $[\![\varphi]\!]_x^{\mathcal{M}} = \{v \in W \mid \mathcal{M}, v \vDash_x \varphi\}$ is the set of worlds where φ is true in $\mathcal{M}$ according to X-semantics; if $\mathcal{M}$ and x are clear from context, we write $[\![\varphi]\!]$.
- For $S \subseteq W$, we write $\overline{S} = \{v \in W \mid v \notin S\}$ for the complement of S in W.

Definition 4 (Truth in an RA Model cont.). For C-, D-, and L-semantics, the clauses for the K operator are:

$$\mathcal{M}, w \vDash_c K\varphi \text{ iff } \forall v \in \overline{[\![\varphi]\!]_c} : w \not\rightarrow v;$$
$$\mathcal{M}, w \vDash_d K\varphi \text{ iff } \forall v \in \text{Min}_{\preceq_w}\left(\overline{[\![\varphi]\!]_d}\right) : w \not\rightarrow v;$$
$$\mathcal{M}, w \vDash_l K\varphi \text{ iff } \forall v \in \text{Min}_{\preceq_w}(W) \cap \overline{[\![\varphi]\!]_l} : w \not\rightarrow v.$$

In C-semantics, for an agent to know φ in w, *all* $\neg\varphi$-possibilities must be eliminated by the agent in w. In D-semantics, for any φ there is a set $\text{Min}_{\preceq_w}\left(\overline{[\![\varphi]\!]_d}\right)$ of *most relevant (at w)* $\neg\varphi$-possibilities that the agent must eliminate in order to know φ. Finally, in L-semantics, there is a set of relevant possibilities, $\text{Min}_{\preceq_w}(W)$, such that for any φ, in order to know φ the agent must eliminate the $\neg\varphi$-possibilities *within that set*. Recall the RS$_{\forall\exists}$ vs. RS$_{\exists\forall}$ distinction above. If φ is valid in X-semantics, we say that φ is *X-valid* and write $\vDash_x \varphi$.

Since for L-semantics we think of $\text{Min}_{\preceq_w}(W)$ as the set of simply *relevant* worlds, ignoring the rest of $\preceq_w$, we allow $\text{Min}_{\preceq_w}(W)$ to contain multiple worlds.

It is easy to check that according to C/D/L-semantics, whatever is known is true. For D- and L-semantics, Fact 1 reflects Lewis's [25, p. 554] observation that the veridicality of knowledge follows from his Rule of Actuality, given that an agent can never eliminate her actual world as a possibility. Formally, veridicality follows from the fact that w is minimal in $\preceq_w$ (Definition 1.3b) and $w \rightarrow w$.

Fact 1 (Veridicality). $K\varphi \rightarrow \varphi$ is C/D/L-valid.

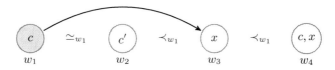

Fig. 1. An RA model for Example 1 (partially drawn, reflexive loops omitted)

Consider the model in Fig. 1, drawn for student A in Example 1. An arrow from w to v indicates that $w \twoheadrightarrow v$. (For all $v \in W$, $v \twoheadrightarrow v$, but we omit all reflexive loops.) The ordering of the worlds by their relevance at w_1, thought of as the actual world, is indicated between worlds.[5] In w_1, the patient has the common condition c, represented by the atomic sentence c true at w_1. Possibility w_2, in which the patient has the other common condition c' instead of c, is just as relevant as w_1. Since the model is for student A, who ran the lab tests to rule out c', A has eliminated w_2 in w_1.[6] A more remote possibility than w_2 is w_3, in which the patient has the rare disease x. Since A has not run any tests to rule out x, A has not eliminated w_3 in w_1. Finally, the most remote possibility of all is w_4, in which the patient has both c and x. We assume that A has learned from textbooks that x confers immunity to c, so A has eliminated w_4 in w_1.

Now consider C-semantics. In discussing Example 1, we held that student A knows that the patient's condition is c, despite the fact that A did not rule out the remote possibility of the patient's having x. C-semantics issues the opposite verdict. According to C-semantics, Kc is true at w_1 iff *all* $\neg c$-worlds, regardless of their relevance, are ruled out by the agent in w_1. However, w_3 is not ruled out by A in w_1, so Kc is false at w_1. Nonetheless, A has some knowledge in w_1. For example, one can check that $K(\neg x \to c)$ is true at w_1 in C-semantics.

Consider D-semantics. First observe that D-semantics issues our original verdict that student A knows the patient's condition is c. Kc is true at w_1 since the most relevant (at w_1) $\neg c$-world, w_2, is ruled out by A in w_1. $K(c \to \neg x)$ is also true at w_1, since the most relevant (at w_1) $\neg(c \to \neg x)$-world, w_4, is ruled out by A in w_1. Not only that, but $K(c \leftrightarrow \neg x)$ is true at w_1, since the most relevant (at w_1) $\neg(c \leftrightarrow \neg x)$-world, w_2, is ruled out by A in w_1. However, the most relevant (at w_1) x-world, w_3, is *not* ruled out by A in w_1, so $K\neg x$ is false at w_1 in D-semantics. Hence A does not know that the patient does not have x.

We have shown the second part of the following fact, which matches Dretske's [12] view. The first part, which is standard, matches Lewis's [25, p. 563n21].

Fact 2 (Known Implication). The principles $K\varphi \land K(\varphi \to \psi) \to K\psi$ and $K\varphi \land K(\varphi \leftrightarrow \psi) \to K\psi$ are C/L-valid, but not D-valid.

Finally, consider the model in Fig. 1 from the perspective of L-semantics. What is noteworthy in this case is that according to L-semantics, student A *does* know that the patient does not have disease x. $K\neg x$ is true at w_1, because $\neg x$ is true in all of the most relevant (at w_1) worlds, namely in w_1 and w_2.

In the terminology of Dretske [12, p. 1007], Fact 2 shows that the knowledge operator K is not *fully penetrating*, since it does not penetrate to all logical consequence of what is known. Yet Dretske claims that K is *semi-penetrating*, since

---

[5] We ignore the relevance orderings for other worlds, as well as which possibilities are ruled out at other worlds, since we are not concerned here with student A's higher-order knowledge at w_1. If we were, we should include other worlds in the model.

[6] We could add new atomic sentences t_c and $t_{c'}$ standing for "the test results favor c over c'" and "the test results favor c' over c," respectively. We would then make t_c true and $t_{c'}$ false at w_1, w_3, and w_4, while making $t_{c'}$ true and t_c false at w_2.

it does penetrate to some logical consequences: "it seems to me fairly obvious that if someone knows that P and Q, he thereby knows that Q" and "If he knows that P is the case, he knows that P or Q is the case" (1009). This is supposed to be the "trivial side" of Dretske's thesis (ibid.). However, if we understand the RA theory according to D-semantics, even these monotonicity principles fail.

Fact 3 (Simplification & Addition). The principles $K(\varphi \wedge \psi) \rightarrow K\varphi \wedge K\psi$ and $K\varphi \rightarrow K(\varphi \vee \psi)$ are C/L-valid, but not D-valid.

Proof : The proof of C/L-validity is standard. For D-semantics, the pointed model $\mathcal{M}, w_1$ in Fig. 1 falsifies both $K(c \wedge \neg x) \rightarrow K\neg x$ and $Kc \rightarrow K(c \vee \neg x)$. These principle are of the form $K\alpha \rightarrow K\beta$. In both cases, the most relevant (at w_1) $\neg\alpha$-world in $\mathcal{M}$ is w_2, which is eliminated by the agent in w_1, so $K\alpha$ is true at w_1. However, in both cases the most relevant (at w_1) $\neg\beta$-world in $\mathcal{M}$ is w_3, which is uneliminated by the agent in w_1, so $K\beta$ is false at w_1. □

Facts 2 and 3 point to a dilemma. On the one hand, if we understand the RA theory according to D-semantics, then the knowledge operator lacks even the basic closure properties that Dretske wanted from a semi-penetrating operator, contrary to the "trivial side" of his thesis. On the other hand, if we understand the RA theory according to L-semantics, then the knowledge operator is a fully-penetrating operator, contrary to the non-trivial side of Dretske's thesis. It is difficult to escape this dilemma while retaining something like Heller's [18,17] world-ordering picture with which we started before Definition 1. In [21], I propose a different way of developing the theory such that the knowledge operator is semi-penetrating in Dretske's sense, thereby avoiding the dilemma above.

Facts 2 and 3 also raise the question: what is the complete logic of knowledge over RA models? Theorem 1, proven in [20,21], gives the answer. Interestingly, the answer depends on whether we assume that each $\preceq_w$ is *total* on its field W_w ($\forall u, v \in W_w$: $u \preceq_w v$ or $v \preceq_w u$), so that $\preceq_w$ is a *ranking* of worlds in W_w by their relevance. (In this case, we call the RA model itself "total.") Following the nomenclature of Chellas [6], **E** is the weakest of the classical modal systems extending propositional logic with the rule RE, and $\mathbf{ES_1 \ldots S_n}$ is the extension of **E** with every instance of schemas $S_1 \ldots S_n$. The X axiom schema is new.

RE. $\dfrac{\varphi \leftrightarrow \psi}{K\varphi \leftrightarrow K\psi}$ T. $K\varphi \rightarrow \varphi$ N. $K\top$

C. $K\varphi \wedge K\psi \rightarrow K(\varphi \wedge \psi)$ M. $K(\varphi \wedge \psi) \rightarrow K\varphi \wedge K\psi$ X. $K(\varphi \wedge \psi) \rightarrow K\varphi \vee K\psi$

Theorem 1 (Completeness).

1. *The system **EMCNT (KT)** is sound and complete for C/L-semantics over RA models.*

2. *(The Logic of Ranked Relevant Alternatives) The system **ECNTX** is sound and complete for D-semantics over* total *RA models.*

3. *The system **ECNT** is sound and complete for D-semantics over RA models.*

3   The Dynamics of Context

In this section, we extend our formalization to capture the *contextualist* Response 2 to Example 1 in §1. (It may be helpful to reread Response 2 as a reminder.)

In the framework of Lewis [24], the family $\preceq$ of relevance orderings in an RA model may be thought of as a component of the *conversational score*. Changes in this component of the conversational score, an aspect of what Lewis calls the *kinematics of score*, correspond to transformations of RA models. We begin with an RA model $\mathcal{M}$ representing what an agent counts as knowing relative to an initial conversational context. If some change in the conversation makes the issue of φ relevant, then corresponding to this change the model transforms from $\mathcal{M}$ to $\mathcal{M}^{\uparrow\varphi}$. In the new model, what the agent counts as knowing may be different.

For variety, we will define two types of operations on models, $\uparrow \varphi$ and $\curlywedge \varphi$. Roughly speaking, $\uparrow \varphi$ changes the model so that the *most relevant φ-worlds* in $\mathcal{M}$ become among the *most relevant worlds overall* in $\mathcal{M}^{\uparrow\varphi}$. By contrast, $\curlywedge \varphi$ changes the model so that any worlds *at least as relevant* as the most relevant φ-worlds in $\mathcal{M}$ become among the most relevant worlds overall in $\mathcal{M}^{\curlywedge\varphi}$. The following definition makes these descriptions more precise. For convenience, in this section we assume that each preorder $\preceq_w$ is total on its field W_w, but all of the definitions and results can be modified to apply to the non-total case.

Definition 5 (RA Context Change). Given an RA model $\mathcal{M} = \langle W, \twoheadrightarrow, \preceq, V \rangle$, define the models $\mathcal{M}^{\uparrow\varphi} = \langle W, \twoheadrightarrow, \preceq^{\uparrow\varphi}, V \rangle$ and $\mathcal{M}^{\curlywedge\varphi} = \langle W, \twoheadrightarrow, \preceq^{\curlywedge\varphi}, V \rangle$ such that for all $w, u, v \in W$:

1. if $u \in \mathrm{Min}_{\preceq_w}\left(\llbracket\varphi\rrbracket^{\mathcal{M}}\right) \cup \mathrm{Min}_{\preceq_w}(W)$, then $u \preceq_w^{\uparrow\varphi} v$;
2. if $u, v \notin \mathrm{Min}_{\preceq_w}\left(\llbracket\varphi\rrbracket^{\mathcal{M}}\right) \cup \mathrm{Min}_{\preceq_w}(W)$, then $u \preceq_w^{\uparrow\varphi} v$ iff $u \preceq_w v$;

and

3. if $\exists x \in \mathrm{Min}_{\preceq_w}\left(\llbracket\varphi\rrbracket^{\mathcal{M}}\right)$ such that $u \preceq_w x$, then $u \preceq_w^{\curlywedge\varphi} v$;
4. if $\forall x \in \mathrm{Min}_{\preceq_w}\left(\llbracket\varphi\rrbracket^{\mathcal{M}}\right)$, $u \not\preceq_w x$ and $v \not\preceq_w x$, then $u \preceq_w^{\curlywedge\Phi} v$ iff $u \preceq_w v$.

In other words, for $\uparrow \varphi$, the *most relevant φ-worlds* according to $\preceq_w$ become among the *most relevant worlds* according to $\preceq_w^{\uparrow\varphi}$; the most relevant worlds according to $\preceq_w$ remain among the most relevant worlds according to $\preceq_w^{\uparrow\varphi}$; and for all other worlds, $\preceq_w^{\uparrow\varphi}$ agrees with $\preceq_w$. For $\curlywedge \varphi$, all worlds *at least as relevant* as the most relevant φ-worlds according to $\preceq_w$ become among the most relevant worlds according to $\preceq_w^{\curlywedge\varphi}$; and for all other worlds, $\preceq_w^{\curlywedge\varphi}$ agrees with $\preceq_w$.

Which of these operations is most appropriate for modeling a given context change is an interesting question, which I leave aside here. Other operations could be defined as well, but these will suffice as examples of the general method. Fig. 2 shows the application of either $\uparrow x$ or $\curlywedge x$ (denoted $+x$) to the model $\mathcal{M}$ for Example 1, the result of which is the same for both. Fig. 3 shows $\uparrow x$ and $\curlywedge x$ applied to a different initial model, $\mathcal{N}$, in which case the results are different.

To describe the effect of these context change operations using our formal language, we extend the language of Definition 2 with *dynamic* context change

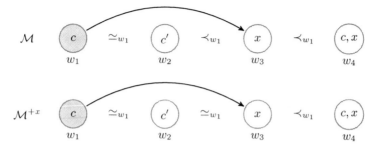

Fig. 2. Result of context change by raising the possibility of x in Example 1

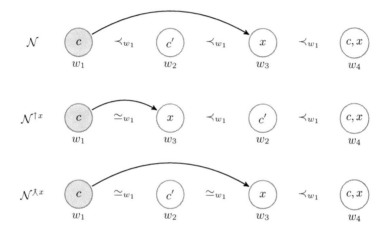

Fig. 3. Different results of context change by $\uparrow x$ and $\curlywedge x$

operators of the form $[+\varphi]$ for $+ \in \{\uparrow, \curlywedge\}$, in the style of dynamic epistemic logic [11,2]. One can read $[+\varphi]\psi$ as "after φ becomes relevant, ψ is the case" or "after φ is raised, ψ is the case" or "after context change by φ, ψ is the case," etc.

Definition 6 (Contextualist Epistemic Language). Let $\mathsf{At} = \{p, q, r, \dots\}$ be a set of atomic sentences. The *contextualist epistemic language* is generated as follows, where $p \in \mathsf{At}$:

$$\varphi ::= p \mid \neg\varphi \mid (\varphi \wedge \varphi) \mid K\varphi \mid [\pi]\varphi$$
$$\pi ::= \uparrow \varphi \mid \curlywedge \varphi.$$

We give the truth clauses for the operators $[\uparrow \varphi]$ and $[\curlywedge \varphi]$ with the help of Definition 5, using $+$ to stand for either $\uparrow$ or $\curlywedge$ in definitions applicable to both.

Definition 7 (Truth). The truth clause for the context change operator is:

$$\mathcal{M}, w \vDash [+\varphi]\psi \text{ iff } \mathcal{M}^{+\varphi}, w \vDash \psi.$$

In other words, "after context change by φ, ψ is the case" is true at w in the initial model $\mathcal{M}$ if and only if ψ is true at w in the new model $\mathcal{M}^{+\varphi}$.

Having set up this contextualist machinery, there are a number of directions to explore. Given the space available here, we will touch on two: first, a brief comparison between (non-contextualist) D-semantics and contextualist L-semantics; second, a technical excursion in search of *reduction axioms* for context change.

3.1   D-Semantics vs. Contextualist L-Semantics

The following fact matches Lewis's [25] view on closure and context from §1.

Fact 4 (Known Implication Cont.). According to D-semantics, closure under known implication can fail. According to L-semantics, closure under known implication always holds for a fixed context, but may fail across context changes:

1. $\nvDash_d K\varphi \wedge K(\varphi \rightarrow \psi) \rightarrow K\psi$
2. $\vDash_l K\varphi \wedge K(\varphi \rightarrow \psi) \rightarrow K\psi$
3. $\nvDash_l K\varphi \wedge K(\varphi \rightarrow \psi) \rightarrow [+\neg\psi]K\psi$
4. $\nvDash_l K\varphi \rightarrow [+\neg\psi](K(\varphi \rightarrow \psi) \rightarrow K\psi)$

Proof: We have already noted part 1 and 2 in §2. For 3, its instance

$$Kc \wedge K(c \rightarrow \neg x) \rightarrow [+x]K\neg x \tag{1}$$

is false at $\mathcal{M}, w_1$ in Fig. 2. As we saw in §2, the antecedent is true at $\mathcal{M}, w_1$. To determine whether $\mathcal{M}, w_1 \vDash_l [+x]K\neg x$, by Definition 7 we must check whether $\mathcal{M}^{+x}, w_1 \vDash_l K\neg x$. Since in $\mathcal{M}^{+x}$ there is a most relevant (at w_1) world, w_3, which satisfies x and is not ruled out at w_1, we have $\mathcal{M}^{+x}, w_1 \nvDash_l K\neg x$. Therefore, $\mathcal{M}, w_1 \nvDash_l [+x]K\neg x$, so (1) is false at $\mathcal{M}, w_1$. It is also easy to check that $\mathcal{M}^{+x}, w_1 \vDash K(c \rightarrow \neg x)$, so the corresponding instance of 4 is false at $\mathcal{M}, w_1$. □

We will use the next fact to generalize Fact 4 to all kinds of closure failure (Fact 6), not only failures of closure under known implication.

Fact 5 (Relation of D- to Contextualist L-semantics). Given an RA model $\mathcal{M} = \langle W, \rightarrowtail, \preceq, V \rangle$ with $w \in W$, for any *propositional* formula φ,

$$\mathcal{M}, w \vDash_d K\varphi \text{ iff } \mathcal{M}, w \vDash_l [+\neg\varphi]K\varphi.$$

Proof: For the case where $+$ is $\uparrow$, by Definition 5,

$$\text{Min}_{\preceq_w^{\uparrow\neg\varphi}}(W) = \text{Min}_{\preceq_w}(W) \cup \text{Min}_{\preceq_w}(\overline{\llbracket \varphi \rrbracket}^{\mathcal{M}}), \tag{2}$$

so

$$\text{Min}_{\preceq_w^{\uparrow\neg\varphi}}(W) \cap \overline{\llbracket \varphi \rrbracket}^{\mathcal{M}^{\uparrow\neg\varphi}} = (\text{Min}_{\preceq_w}(W) \cup \text{Min}_{\preceq_w}(\overline{\llbracket \varphi \rrbracket}^{\mathcal{M}})) \cap \overline{\llbracket \varphi \rrbracket}^{\mathcal{M}^{\uparrow\neg\varphi}}. \tag{3}$$

Since φ is propositional, by an obvious induction we have

$$\overline{\llbracket \varphi \rrbracket}^{\mathcal{M}^{+\neg\varphi}} = \overline{\llbracket \varphi \rrbracket}^{\mathcal{M}}, \tag{4}$$

so from (3) we have

$$\text{Min}_{\preceq^{\uparrow\neg\varphi}_w}(W) \cap \overline{[\![\varphi]\!]}^{\mathcal{M}^{\uparrow\neg\varphi}} = (\text{Min}_{\preceq_w}(W) \cup \text{Min}_{\preceq_w}(\overline{[\![\varphi]\!]}^{\mathcal{M}})) \cap \overline{[\![\varphi]\!]}^{\mathcal{M}}$$

$$= \text{Min}_{\preceq_w}(\overline{[\![\varphi]\!]}^{\mathcal{M}}). \tag{5}$$

It follows from (5) that

$$\forall v \in \text{Min}_{\preceq_w}(\overline{[\![\varphi]\!]}^{\mathcal{M}}): w \not\rightarrow v \tag{6}$$

is equivalent to

$$\forall v \in \text{Min}_{\preceq^{\uparrow\neg\varphi}_w}(W) \cap \overline{[\![\varphi]\!]}^{\mathcal{M}^{\uparrow\neg\varphi}}: w \not\rightarrow v, \tag{7}$$

which by Definition 4 means that $\mathcal{M}, w \vDash_d K\varphi$ is equivalent to $\mathcal{M}^{\uparrow\neg\varphi}, w \vDash_l K\varphi$, which by Definition 7 is equivalent to $\mathcal{M}, w \vDash_l [\uparrow \neg\varphi]K\varphi$.

The proof for the case where $+$ is $\curlywedge$ is similar. $\square$

Using Fact 5, we can now state a generalization of Fact 4 as follows.

Fact 6 (Inter-context Closure Failure). Let $\varphi_1, \dots, \varphi_n$ and ψ be propositional formulas. Given an RA model $\mathcal{M} = \langle W, \dashrightarrow, \preceq, V \rangle$ with $w \in W$, if

$$\mathcal{M}, w \nvDash_d K\varphi_1 \wedge \cdots \wedge K\varphi_n \rightarrow K\psi$$

then

$$\mathcal{M}, w \nvDash_l K\varphi_1 \wedge \cdots \wedge K\varphi_n \rightarrow [+\neg\psi]K\psi.$$

Proof: Assume the first line. Since for any formula φ, $\mathcal{M}, w \vDash_d K\varphi$ implies $\mathcal{M}, w \vDash_l K\varphi$, we have $\mathcal{M}, w \vDash_l K\varphi_1 \wedge \cdots \wedge K\varphi_n$. Since $\mathcal{M}, w \nvDash_d K\psi$, we have $\mathcal{M}, w \nvDash_l [+\neg\psi]K\psi$ by Fact 5, which gives the second line. $\square$

Most contextualists deny that closure fails in any of the ways allowed by D-semantics. But Fact 6 shows that for *every way* in which closure fails for D-semantics, there is a corresponding *inter-context* "closure failure" for L-semantics when the context changes with the negation of the consequent of the closure principle becoming relevant. According to some standard contextualist views, asserting that the agent knows the consequent has just this effect on the context. For example, according to DeRose [9], "When it's asserted that S knows (or doesn't know) that P, then, if necessary, enlarge the sphere of epistemically relevant worlds so that it at least includes the closest worlds in which P is false" (37). According to Lewis [25], "No matter how far-fetched a certain possibility may be, no matter how properly we might have ignored it in some other context, if in this context we are not in fact ignoring it but attending to it, then for us now it is a relevant alternative" (559). If such views of the shiftiness of context are correct, then Fact 6 shows that contextualists who claim to "preserve closure"— with respect to a fixed context—may not vindicate *closure reasoning* (reasoning over time about an agent's knowledge that applies closure principles to draw conclusions) any more than those who allow failures of closure as in D-semantics.

Much more could be said about these conceptual issues (see [21]), but now we will pursue a different line, checking our logical grip on the dynamics of context.

3.2   Reduction Axioms for Context Change

In this section, we turn to a more technical topic. Our goal is to apply one of the main ideas of dynamic epistemic logic, that of *reduction axioms*, to the picture of context change presented in the previous sections. Roughly speaking, reduction axioms are valid equivalences of the form $[+\chi]\psi \leftrightarrow \psi'$, where the left-hand side states that some ψ is true *after* the context change with χ, while the right-hand side gives an *equivalent* ψ' describing what is true *before* the context change. For example, we can ask whether the agent counts as knowing φ after χ becomes relevant, i.e., is $[+\chi]K\varphi$ true? The reduction axioms will answer this question by describing what must be true of the agent's epistemic state *before* the context change in order for the agent to count as knowing φ after the context change.

To obtain reduction axioms for context change that are valid over our RA models, we will use a language more expressive than the epistemic language used in the previous sections. Our new *RA language* will be capable of describing what is relevant at a world and what is ruled out at a world independently. This additional expressive power will allow us to obtain reduction axioms using methods similar to those applied by van Benthem and Liu [4] to *dynamic epistemic preference logic* (also see [3]), but with an important difference.

Van Benthem and Liu work with models with a *single* preorder over worlds (for each agent), representing an agent's preferences between worlds, and their language contains an operator $\Box^{\succ}$ used to quantify over all worlds that are *better* than the current world according to the agent.[7] In our setting, $\Box^{\succ}$ would quantify over all worlds that are *more relevant*. Using another operator $\Box^{\rightarrow}$ to quantify over all worlds that are *uneliminated* at the current world, we can try to write a formula expressing that all of the most relevant $\neg\varphi$-worlds are eliminated at the current world. An equivalent statement is that for all uneliminated worlds v, if v is a $\neg\varphi$-world, then there is another $\neg\varphi$-world that is strictly more relevant than v. This is expressed by $\Box^{\rightarrow}(\neg\varphi \rightarrow \Diamond^{\succ}\neg\varphi)$, where $\Diamond^{\succ}\psi := \neg\Box^{\succ}\neg\psi$.

The problem with the above approach is that unlike the models of van Benthem and Liu (but like models for conditional logic and the general *belief revision structures* of [5]), our RA models include a preorder $\preceq_w$ for *each* world w. Hence if the operator $\Box^{\succ}$ quantifies over all worlds that are more relevant than the current world according to the relevance relation of the current world, then $\Box^{\rightarrow}(\neg\varphi \rightarrow \Diamond^{\succ}\neg\varphi)$ will be true at w just in case for all worlds v uneliminated at w, if v is a $\neg\varphi$-world, then there is another $\neg\varphi$-world that is strictly more relevant than v *according to* $\preceq_v$. Yet this is not the desired truth condition.[8] The desired truth condition is that for all worlds v uneliminated at w, if v is a $\neg\varphi$-world, then there is another $\neg\varphi$-world that is strictly more relevant than

---

[7] Van Benthem et al. [3] write this operator as $\Box^{<}$, since they take $w \prec v$ to mean that v is strictly better than w according to the agent. Since we take $w \prec v$ to mean that w is strictly more relevant than v, we write $\Box^{\succ}$ for the operator that quantifies over more relevant worlds. We will write $\Box^{\preceq}$ for the operator that quantifies over worlds that are of equal or lesser relevance. We use the same $\preceq$ for the superscript of the operator and for the relation in the model, trusting that no confusion will arise.

[8] Since v is assumed to be minimal in $\preceq_v$, the condition would never be met.

v according to $\preceq_w$. To capture this truth condition, we will use an approach inspired by *hybrid logic* [1]. First, different modalities $\Box^{\succ_x}$, $\Box^{\succ_v}$, etc., will be associated in a given model with different relevance relations $\preceq_w$, $\preceq_v$, etc., by an assignment function g. Second, a *binder* $\downarrow$ will be used to bind a world variable x to the current world, so that the formula $\downarrow x.\Box^{\rightarrow}(\neg\varphi \rightarrow \Diamond^{\succ_x}\neg\varphi)$ will capture the desired truth condition described above (cf. [23, §2.8] on the $\dagger$ operator).

In addition to the operator $\Box^{\succ_x}$ that quantifies over all worlds more relevant than the current world according to $\preceq_{g(x)}$, we will use an operator $\Box^{\preceq_x}$ that quantifiers over all worlds whose relevance is equal to or lesser than that of the current world according to $\preceq_{g(x)}$. The second operator is necessary for writing reduction axioms for the context change operation λ. Together the two types of operators will also allow us to quantify over all worlds in the field of $\preceq_{g(x)}$, $W_{g(x)}$, with formulas of the form $\Box^{\succ_x}\varphi \wedge \Box^{\preceq_x}\varphi$, which we will use in writing reduction axioms for both of the context change operations, $\uparrow$ and λ.

Definition 8 (Dynamic & Static RA Languages). Let $\mathsf{At} = \{p, q, r \ldots\}$ be a set of atomic sentences and $\mathsf{Var} = \{x, y, z, \ldots\}$ a set of variables. The *dynamic RA language* is generated as follows, where $p \in \mathsf{At}$ and $x \in \mathsf{Var}$:

$$\varphi ::= p \mid \neg\varphi \mid (\varphi \wedge \varphi) \mid \Box^{\rightarrow}\varphi \mid \Box^{\preceq_x}\varphi \mid \Box^{\succ_x}\varphi \mid \downarrow x.\varphi \mid [\pi]\varphi$$

$$\pi ::= \uparrow \varphi \mid \lambda\,\varphi.$$

Where R is $\preceq_x$, $\succ_x$, or $\rightarrow$, let $\Diamond^R\varphi := \neg\Box^R\neg\varphi$; let R_x stand for either $\preceq_x$ or $\succ_x$ in definitions that apply to both; and let us use $+$ as before. Finally, let the *static RA language* be the fragment of the dynamic RA language consisting of those formulas that do not contain any context change operators $[\pi]$.

The truth clauses are as one would expect from our description above, and the clause for the context change operators is the same as Definition 7.

Definition 9 (Truth). Given an RA model $\mathcal{M} = \langle W, \rightarrow, \preceq, V \rangle$ and an assignment function $g\colon \mathsf{Var} \rightarrow W$, we define $\mathcal{M}, g, w \vDash \varphi$ as follows (with propositional cases as in Definition 3):

$$\mathcal{M}, g, w \vDash \Box^{\rightarrow}\varphi \quad \text{iff} \quad \forall v \in W\colon \text{if } w \rightarrow v \text{ then } \mathcal{M}, g, v \vDash \varphi;$$
$$\mathcal{M}, g, w \vDash \Box^{R_x}\varphi \quad \text{iff} \quad \forall v \in W\colon \text{if } wR_{g(x)}v \text{ then } \mathcal{M}, g, v \vDash \varphi;$$
$$\mathcal{M}, g, w \vDash [+\chi]\varphi \quad \text{iff} \quad \mathcal{M}^{+\chi}, g, w \vDash \varphi;$$
$$\mathcal{M}, g, w \vDash \downarrow x.\varphi \quad \text{iff} \quad \mathcal{M}, g^x_w, w \vDash \varphi,$$

where g^x_w is such that $g^x_w(x) = w$ and $g^x_w(y) = g(y)$ for all $y \neq x$.

Hence the $\downarrow x.\varphi$ clause captures the idea of letting x stand for the current world by changing the assignment g to one that maps x to w but is otherwise the same.

We now show how the epistemic language can be translated into the RA language in two different ways, corresponding to D- and L-semantics.[9] To simplify the translation, let us assume for the moment that all of our RA models $\mathcal{M} = \langle W, \rightarrow, \preceq, V \rangle$ are *universal* in the sense that for all $w \in W$, $W_w = W$.

---

[9] Note that since the translation of Definition 10 only requires a single variable x, for our purposes here it would suffice to define the RA language such that $|\mathsf{Var}| = 1$.

Definition 10 (Translation). Let σ_d be a translation from the epistemic language of Definition 2 to the static RA language of Definition 8 defined by:

$$\sigma_d(p) = p$$
$$\sigma_d(\neg\varphi) = \neg\sigma_d(\varphi)$$
$$\sigma_d(\varphi \wedge \psi) = (\sigma_d(\varphi) \wedge \sigma_d(\psi))$$
$$\sigma_d(K\varphi) = \downarrow x.\Box^{\rightarrow}(\neg\sigma_d(\varphi) \rightarrow \Diamond^{\curlyvee x}\neg\sigma_d(\varphi)).$$

Let σ_l be a translation analogous to σ_d but with

$$\sigma_l(K\varphi) = \downarrow x.\Box^{\rightarrow}(\neg\sigma_l(\varphi) \rightarrow \Diamond^{\curlyvee x}\top).$$

As explained at the beginning of this section, the idea of the σ_d translation is that the truth clause for $K\varphi$ in D-semantics—stating that the most relevant $\neg\varphi$-worlds are eliminated—is equivalent to the statement that for all worlds v unlimited at the current world w, if v is a $\neg\varphi$-world, then there is another $\neg\varphi$-world that is strictly more relevant than v according to $\preceq_w$. This is exactly what $\sigma_d(K\varphi)$ expresses. Similarly, the idea of the σ_l translation is that the truth clause for $K\varphi$ in L-semantics—stating that among the most relevant worlds overall, all $\neg\varphi$-worlds are eliminated—is equivalent to the statement that for all worlds v unlimited at the current world w, if v is a $\neg\varphi$-world, then there is another world that is strictly more relevant than v according to $\preceq_w$, in which case v is not among the most relevant worlds overall according to $\preceq_w$. This is exactly what $\sigma_l(K\varphi)$ expresses. The following proposition confirms these claims.

Proposition 1 (Simulation). For any RA model $\mathcal{M} = \langle W, \twoheadrightarrow, \preceq, V \rangle$, assignment $g: \mathsf{Var} \rightarrow W$, world $w \in W$, and formula φ of the epistemic language:

$$\mathcal{M}, w \vDash_d \varphi \text{ iff } \mathcal{M}, g, w \vDash \sigma_d(\varphi);$$
$$\mathcal{M}, w \vDash_l \varphi \text{ iff } \mathcal{M}, g, w \vDash \sigma_l(\varphi).$$

Proof: By induction on φ. All of the cases are trivial except where φ is of the form $K\psi$. By Definition 10, we are to show

$$\mathcal{M}, w \vDash_d K\psi \text{ iff } \mathcal{M}, g, w \vDash \downarrow x.\Box^{\rightarrow}(\neg\sigma_d(\varphi) \rightarrow \Diamond^{\curlyvee x}\neg\sigma_d(\varphi)). \tag{8}$$

By Definition 9, the rhs of (8) holds iff for all $v \in W$, if $w \twoheadrightarrow v$, then

$$\mathcal{M}, g_w^x, v \vDash \neg\sigma_d(\psi) \rightarrow \Diamond^{\curlyvee x}\neg\sigma_d(\psi). \tag{9}$$

By Definition 9, (9) is equivalent to the disjunction of the following:

$$\mathcal{M}, g_w^x, v \vDash \sigma_d(\psi); \tag{10}$$
$$\exists u \in W: u \prec_{g_w^x(x)} v \text{ and } \mathcal{M}, g_w^x, u \nvDash \sigma_d(\psi). \tag{11}$$

By the inductive hypothesis, (10) and (11) are respectively equivalent to

$$\mathcal{M}, v \vDash_d \psi \text{ and} \tag{12}$$
$$\exists u \in W: u \prec_w v \text{ and } \mathcal{M}, u \nvDash_d \psi. \tag{13}$$

Assuming $\mathcal{M}$ is universal, the disjunction of (12) and (13) is equivalent to

$$v \notin \mathrm{Min}_{\preceq_w}(\overline{\llbracket \psi \rrbracket}). \tag{14}$$

Hence the rhs of (8) holds if and only if for all $v \in W$, if $w \twoheadrightarrow v$, then (14) holds. The rhs of this biconditional is equivalent to the lhs of (8), $\mathcal{M}, w \vDash_d K\psi$, by Definition 3. The proof for the case of L-semantics is similar. □

If we do not assume that RA models are universal, then we must modify the translation of Definition 10 such that

$$\sigma'_d(K\varphi) = {\downarrow}x.\square^{\rightarrow}(\neg\sigma'_d(\varphi) \to (\lozenge^{\succ x}\neg\sigma'_d(\varphi) \vee \square^{\preceq x}\bot));$$
$$\sigma'_l(K\varphi) = {\downarrow}x.\square^{\rightarrow}(\neg\sigma'_l(\varphi) \to (\lozenge^{\succ x}\top \vee \square^{\preceq x}\bot)).$$

We leave it to the reader to verify that given the modified translation, Proposition 1 holds for RA models that are not necessarily universal.

We are now prepared to do what we set out to do at the beginning of this section: give reduction axioms for the context change operations of Definition 5. For the following proposition, let us define $\square^x \varphi := \square^{\succ x}\varphi \wedge \square^{\preceq x}\varphi$.

Proposition 2 (RA Reduction). Given the following valid reduction axioms and the rule of replacement of logical equivalents,[10] any formula of the *dynamic* RA language is equivalent to a formula of the *static* RA language:

$$[+\chi]\, p \quad\leftrightarrow\quad p; \tag{15}$$

$$[+\chi]\, \neg\varphi \quad\leftrightarrow\quad \neg\,[+\chi]\,\varphi; \tag{16}$$

$$[+\chi]\, (\varphi \wedge \psi) \leftrightarrow [+\chi]\,\varphi \wedge [+\chi]\,\psi; \tag{17}$$

$$[+\chi]\, {\downarrow}x.\varphi \quad\leftrightarrow\quad {\downarrow}x.[+\chi]\varphi; \tag{18}$$

$$[+\chi]\, \square^{\rightarrow}\varphi \quad\leftrightarrow\quad \square^{\rightarrow}[+\chi]\,\varphi; \tag{19}$$

$$[\uparrow \chi]\, \square^{\succ x}\varphi \quad\leftrightarrow\quad \square^{\succ x}\bot \vee (\chi \wedge \square^{\succ x}\neg\chi)$$
$$\vee\, (\square^{\succ x}[\uparrow \chi]\varphi \wedge \square^{\preceq x}((\chi \wedge \square^{\succ x}\neg\chi) \to [\uparrow \chi]\varphi)); \tag{20}$$

$$[\uparrow \chi]\, \square^{\preceq x}\varphi \quad\leftrightarrow\quad ((\square^{\succ x}\bot \vee (\chi \wedge \square^{\succ x}\neg\chi)) \wedge \square^x[\uparrow \chi]\varphi)$$
$$\vee\, \square^{\preceq x}((\chi \wedge \square^{\succ x}\neg\chi) \vee [\uparrow \chi]\varphi); \tag{21}$$

$$[\curlywedge \chi]\, \square^{\succ x}\varphi \quad\leftrightarrow\quad \lozenge^{\preceq x}(\chi \wedge \square^{\succ x}\neg\chi)$$
$$\vee\, \left(\neg\lozenge^{\preceq x}(\chi \wedge \square^{\succ x}\neg\chi) \wedge \square^{\succ x}[\curlywedge \chi]\,\varphi\right); \tag{22}$$

$$[\curlywedge \chi]\, \square^{\preceq x}\varphi \quad\leftrightarrow\quad \left(\lozenge^{\preceq x}(\chi \wedge \square^{\succ x}\neg\chi) \wedge \square^x[\curlywedge \chi]\varphi\right)$$
$$\vee\, \left(\neg\lozenge^{\preceq x}(\chi \wedge \square^{\succ x}\neg\chi) \wedge \square^{\preceq x}[\curlywedge \chi]\,\varphi\right). \tag{23}$$

Proof: Assuming the axioms are valid, the argument for the claim of the proposition is straightforward. Each of the axioms drives the context change

---

[10] Semantically, if $\alpha \leftrightarrow \beta$ is valid, so is $\varphi(\alpha/p) \leftrightarrow \varphi(\beta/p)$, where (ψ/p) indicates substitution of ψ for p.

operators $[+\chi]$ inward until eventually these operators apply only to atomic sentences p, at which point they can be eliminated altogether using (15). In case we encounter something of the form $[+\chi_1][+\chi_2]\varphi$, we first reduce $[+\chi_2]\varphi$ to an equivalent static formula φ' and then use the replacement of logical equivalents to obtain $[+\chi_1]\varphi'$, which we then reduce to an equivalent static formula φ'', etc.

Let us now check the validity of (15) - (19) in turn. First, (15) is valid because the context change operations of Definition 5 do not change the valuation V for atomic sentences in the model. For (16), in the left-to-right direction we have the following implications: $\mathcal{M}, w \vDash [+\chi]\neg\varphi \Rightarrow \mathcal{M}^{+\chi}, w \vDash \neg\varphi \Rightarrow \mathcal{M}^{+\chi}, w \nvDash \varphi$ $\Rightarrow \mathcal{M}, w \nvDash [+\chi]\varphi \Rightarrow \mathcal{M}, w \vDash \neg[+\chi]\varphi$. For the right-to-left direction of (16), simply reverse the direction of the implications. It is also immediate from the truth definitions that (17) is valid. For (18) and (19), $[+\chi]$ and $\downarrow x.$ commute and $[+\chi]$ and $\square^{\rightarrow}$ commute because the $+\chi$ operations do not change the assignment function g or the relation $\rightarrow$ from the initial model $\mathcal{M}$ to the new model $\mathcal{M}^{+\chi}$.

For (20), the lhs expresses that after context change by $\uparrow \chi$, all worlds that are more relevant than the current world w according to $\preceq^{\uparrow\chi}_{g(x)}$ satisfy φ:

$$\{v \in W \mid v \prec^{\uparrow\chi}_{g(x)} w\} \subseteq \llbracket\varphi\rrbracket^{\mathcal{M}^{\uparrow\chi}}. \tag{24}$$

Case 1: $\{v \in W \mid v \prec^{\uparrow\chi}_{g(x)} w\} = \emptyset$. This implies (24) and is equivalent to

$$w \in \mathrm{Min}_{\preceq^{\uparrow\chi}_{g(x)}}(W). \tag{25}$$

By Definition 5 for $\uparrow$, (25) holds iff either

$$w \in \mathrm{Min}_{\preceq_{g(x)}}(W), \tag{26}$$

which is equivalent to $\mathcal{M}, g, w \vDash \square^{\succ_x}\bot$, or else

$$w \in \mathrm{Min}_{\preceq_{g(x)}}(\llbracket\chi\rrbracket^{\mathcal{M}}), \tag{27}$$

which is equivalent to $\mathcal{M}, g, w \vDash \chi \wedge \square^{\succ_x}\neg\chi$. This accounts for the first two disjuncts on the rhs of (20).

Case 2: $\{v \in W \mid v \prec^{\uparrow\chi}_{g(x)} w\} \neq \emptyset$. In this case, by Definition 5 for $\uparrow$,

$$\{v \in W \mid v \prec^{\uparrow\chi}_{g(x)} w\} = \{v \in W \mid v \prec_{g(x)} w\} \cup \mathrm{Min}_{\preceq_{g(x)}}(\llbracket\chi\rrbracket^{\mathcal{M}}). \tag{28}$$

Hence (24) requires that

$$\{v \in W \mid v \prec_{g(x)} w\} \subseteq \llbracket\varphi\rrbracket^{\mathcal{M}^{\uparrow\chi}} = \llbracket[\uparrow \chi]\varphi\rrbracket^{\mathcal{M}}, \tag{29}$$

which is equivalent to $\mathcal{M}, g, w \vDash \square^{\succ_x}[\uparrow \chi]\varphi$, and

$$\mathrm{Min}_{\preceq_{g(x)}}(\llbracket\chi\rrbracket^{\mathcal{M}}) \subseteq \llbracket\varphi\rrbracket^{\mathcal{M}^{\uparrow\chi}} = \llbracket[\uparrow \chi]\varphi\rrbracket^{\mathcal{M}}, \tag{30}$$

which is equivalent to $\mathcal{M}, g, w \vDash \Box^x((\chi \wedge \Box^{\succ_x} \neg \chi) \to [\uparrow \chi]\varphi)$. The conjunction of $\Box^{\succ_x}[\uparrow \chi]\varphi$ and $\Box^x((\chi \wedge \Box^{\succ_x} \neg \chi) \to [\uparrow \chi]\varphi)$ is equivalent to

$$\Box^{\succ_x}[\uparrow \chi]\varphi \wedge \Box^{\preceq_x}((\chi \wedge \Box^{\succ_x} \neg \chi) \to [\uparrow \chi]\varphi), \tag{31}$$

which is the last disjunct on the rhs of (20).

For (21), what the lhs expresses about the current world w is

$$\{v \in W \mid w \preceq_{g(x)}^{\uparrow \chi} v\} \subseteq \llbracket \varphi \rrbracket^{\mathcal{M}^{\uparrow \chi}}. \tag{32}$$

Case 1: $\{v \in W \mid w \preceq_{g(x)}^{\uparrow \chi} v\} = W_{g(x)}$. This is equivalent to (25), which explains the first conjunct of the first disjunct on the rhs of (21). In this case, (32) requires that

$$W_{g(x)} \subseteq \llbracket \varphi \rrbracket^{\mathcal{M}^{\uparrow \chi}} = \llbracket [\uparrow \chi]\varphi \rrbracket^{\mathcal{M}}, \tag{33}$$

which is equivalent to $\mathcal{M}, g, w \vDash \Box^x[\uparrow \chi]\varphi$. This accounts for the second conjunct of the first disjunct on the rhs of (21).

Case 2: $\{v \in W \mid w \preceq_{g(x)}^{\uparrow \chi} v\} \neq W_{g(x)}$. In this case, by Definition 5 for $\uparrow$,

$$\{v \in W \mid w \preceq_{g(x)}^{\uparrow \chi} v\} = \{v \in W \mid w \preceq_{g(x)} v\} \setminus \mathrm{Min}_{\preceq_{g(x)}}(\llbracket \chi \rrbracket^{\mathcal{M}}). \tag{34}$$

Hence (32) requires that

$$\{v \in W \mid w \preceq_{g(x)} v\} \setminus \mathrm{Min}_{\preceq_{g(x)}}(\llbracket \chi \rrbracket^{\mathcal{M}}) \subseteq \llbracket \varphi \rrbracket^{\mathcal{M}^{\uparrow \chi}} = \llbracket [\uparrow \chi]\varphi \rrbracket^{\mathcal{M}}, \tag{35}$$

which is equivalent to $\mathcal{M}, g, w \vDash \Box^{\preceq_x}((\chi \wedge \Box^{\succ_x} \neg \chi) \vee [\uparrow \chi]\varphi)$. This explains the second disjunct on the rhs of (21). The arguments for (22) - (23) are similar. □

Given Propositions 1 and 2, if we combine the epistemic and RA languages and interpret $K\varphi$ according to D-semantics (a similar point holds for L), then we can write a reduction axiom for context change and knowledge as follows:

$$[+\chi]K\psi \leftrightarrow \downarrow x.\Box^{\to}(\neg[+\chi]\sigma_d(\psi) \to \neg\alpha), \tag{36}$$

where α is the rhs of (20) if $+$ is $\uparrow$ (resp. of (22) if $+$ is $\curlywedge$) with $\varphi := \sigma_d(\psi)$. Here we have used the fact that $\Diamond^{\succ_x} \neg \sigma_d(\psi)$ is equivalent to $\neg \Box^{\succ_x} \sigma_d(\psi)$, and $[+\chi]\neg \Box^{\succ_x} \sigma_d(\psi)$ reduces to $\neg[+\chi]\Box^{\succ_x} \sigma_d(\psi)$, which in turn reduces to $\neg\alpha$.

An important technical and conceptual issue raised by a result like Proposition 2 concerns the distinction between *valid* and *schematically valid* principles of context change. Where a principle is schematically valid just in case all of its substitution instances are valid [2, §3.12], the valid reduction principle $[+\chi]p \leftrightarrow p$ is clearly not schematically valid. Observe that $[+\chi]Kp \leftrightarrow Kp$ is not valid; if it were, there would be no epistemic dynamics. A more interesting example is the valid principle $\neg Kp \to [+\chi]\neg Kp$, which holds for our operations that make the context more epistemically "demanding." Observe that $\neg K\psi \to [+\chi]\neg K\psi$ is not valid for all ψ; it is possible to count as having some knowledge after the context becomes more demanding that one did not count as having before. How can this be? The answer is that this new knowledge may be knowledge of *ignorance*.[11] This can be seen by substituting $\neg Kp$ for ψ and either trying out model changes or using (36) to reduce $\neg K \neg Kp \rightarrow [+\neg p] \neg K \neg Kp$ to a static principle that can be seen to be invalid. These observations raise the question, which we leave open, of what is the complete set of schematically valid principles of context change.

We leave as another open problem the task of finding an axiomatization of the theory of RA models in the static RA language (or some static extension thereof), which together with the reduction axioms of Proposition 2 would give an axiomatization of the theory of RA models in the dynamic RA language to go alongside the axiomatization in the epistemic language given by Theorem 1.

4   Conclusion

We have touched on two sides of RA theory, static (§2) and dynamic (§3), setting up a formal framework to study both. The range of results obtainable in this framework and its extensions, as well as their philosophical repercussions, are explored in [21]. On the dynamic side, having formally defined context change operations, we can see more clearly the systematic relations between theories that accept closure failures (Response 1 in §1) and theories that try to explain away closure failures in terms of context change (Response 2 in §1). On the static side, by using models like our RA models, we can characterize the epistemic closure properties not only for RA theories, but also for a family of "subjunctivist" theories that posit counterfactual conditions on knowledge, as well as the relations between these theories [20]. Moreover, these formalizations do not only help us to clarify the landscape of standard theories. They can also help us to see beyond the standard theories to new and improved pictures of knowledge.

Acknowledgements. I wish to thank Johan van Benthem, Tomohiro Hoshi, Thomas Icard, Krista Lawlor, and Eric Pacuit for helpful discussions and the anonymous reviewers for helpful comments on this paper.

References

1. Areces, C., ten Cate, B.: Hybrid Logics. In: Blackburn, P., van Benthem, J., Wolter, F. (eds.) Handbook of Modal Logic, pp. 821–868. Elsevier (2007)
2. van Benthem, J.: Logical Dynamics of Information and Interaction. Cambridge University Press (2011)

---

[11] This is easiest to understand in a multi-agent setting. (Note that all of our definitions easily generalize to the multi-agent case where the modal operators in our language and relations in our models are indexed for different agents.) Taking $\psi := \neg K_j p$, suppose agent i believes of agent j that $\neg K_j p$, but i does not know $\neg K_j p$, as i has not eliminated some relevant $K_j p$-worlds. If the context changes in such a way that j no longer counts as knowing p under any circumstances, then relative to this new context, i can count as knowing $\neg K_j p$. We can no longer fault i for not having eliminated some relevant $K_j p$-worlds if there are none relative to the current context.

3. van Benthem, J., Girard, P., Roy, O.: Everything else being equal: A modal logic for *Ceteris Paribus* preferences. Journal of Philosophical Logic 38, 83–125 (2009)
4. van Benthem, J., Liu, F.: Dynamic logic of preference upgrade. Journal of Applied Non-Classical Logics 17(2), 157–182 (2007)
5. Board, O.: Dynamic interactive epistemology. Games and Economic Behavior 49, 49–80 (2004)
6. Chellas, B.F.: Modal Logic: An Introduction. Cambridge University Press (1980)
7. Cohen, S.: How to be a Fallibilist. Philosophical Perspectives 2, 91–123 (1988)
8. Cohen, S.: Basic Knowledge and the Problem of Easy Knowledge. Philosophy and Phenomenological Research 65(2), 309–329 (2002)
9. DeRose, K.: Solving the Skeptical Problem. The Philosophical Review 104(1), 1–52 (1995)
10. DeRose, K.: The Case for Contextualism. Oxford University Press (2009)
11. van Ditmarsch, H., van der Hoek, W., Kooi, B.: Dynamic Epistemic Logic. Springer (2008)
12. Dretske, F.: Epistemic Operators. The Journal of Philosophy 67(24), 1007–1023 (1970)
13. Dretske, F.: The Pragmatic Dimension of Knowledge. Philosophical Studies 40, 363–378 (1981)
14. Fagin, R., Halpern, J.Y., Moses, Y., Vardi, M.Y.: Reasoning about Knowledge. MIT Press (1995)
15. Goldman, A.I.: Discrimination and Perceptual Knowledge. The Journal of Philosophy 73(20), 771–791 (1976)
16. Halpern, J.Y., Pucella, R.: Dealing with Logical Omniscience: Expressiveness and Pragmatics. Artificial Intelligence 175, 220–235 (2011)
17. Heller, M.: Relevant Alternatives and Closure. Australasian Journal of Philosophy 77(2), 196–208 (1999)
18. Heller, M.: Relevant Alternatives. Philosophical Studies 55, 23–40 (1989)
19. Hintikka, J.: Knowledge and Belief: An Introduction to the Logic of the Two Notions. College Publications (2005)
20. Holliday, W.H.: Epistemic Closure and Epistemic Logic I: Relevant Alternatives and Subjunctivism (manuscript, 2012)
21. Holliday, W.H.: Knowing What Follows: Epistemic Closure and Epistemic Logic. PhD thesis. Stanford University (2012)
22. Lewis, D.: Completeness and Decidability of Three Logics of Counterfactual Conditionals. Theoria 37(1), 74–85 (1971)
23. Lewis, D.: Counterfactuals. Blackwell, Oxford (1973)
24. Lewis, D.: Scorekeeping in a Language Game. Journal of Philosophical Logic 8, 339–359 (1979)
25. Lewis, D.: Elusive Knowledge. Australasian Journal of Philosophy 74(4), 549–567 (1996)
26. Nozick, R.: Philosophical Explanations. Harvard University Press (1981)
27. Stalnaker, R.: The Problem of Logical Omniscience I. Synthese 89, 425–440 (1991)

Towards a Generalization of Modal Definability

Tin Perkov

Polytechnic of Zagreb, Croatia
tin.perkov@tvz.hr

Abstract. Known results on global definability in basic modal logic are generalized in the following sense. A class of Kripke models is usually called modally definable if there is a set of modal formulas such that a class consists exactly of models on which every formula of that set is globally true, i. e. universally quantified standard translations of these formulas to the corresponding first order language are true. Here, the notion of definability is extended to existentially quantified translations of modal formulas – a class is called *modally ∃-definable* if there is a set of modal formulas such that a class consists exactly of models in which every formula of that set is *satisfiable*. A characterization result is given in usual form, in terms of closure conditions on such classes of models.

Keywords: modal logic, model theory, modal definability.

1 Introduction

One of the ways to measure the expressivity of a language is to establish conditions of definability, which outline the power of a language to describe properties of models. In modal logic, this can be done in a similar way on different levels of semantics. Only the Kripke semantics is considered in this paper, but even so we can speak about local definability on the level of pointed models, global definability for Kripke models (without designated point), or frame definability on the level of Kripke frames, where we demand that a defining formula is valid on a frame, i. e. globally true regardless of a choice of valuation of propositional variables.

For the sake of simplicity, only the basic propositional modal language, which has one modal operator $\Diamond$, is considered in this paper. As for the semantics, the global level of models is considered, with fixed valuation, but without designated point. Throughout the paper, notation and terminology follows [1], so some of the most basic definitions and results are omitted or only briefly reviewed. A *Kripke frame* for the basic modal language is a pair $\mathfrak{F} = (W, R)$, where W is a non-empty set, and R a binary relation on W. A *Kripke model* based on a frame $\mathfrak{F}$ is $\mathfrak{M} = (W, R, V)$, where V is a function called *valuation*, which maps every propositional variable p to a subset $V(p) \subseteq W$. It is assumed throughout the paper that the set of propositional variables is countable.

The truth of a formula is defined locally and inductively as usual, and denoted $\mathfrak{M}, w \Vdash \varphi$. Namely, for the modal operator we have that a formula of a form

D. Lassiter and M. Slavkovik (Eds.): ESSLLI Student Sessions, LNCS 7415, pp. 130–139, 2012.

$\Diamond\varphi$ is true in $w \in W$ if $\mathfrak{M}, u \Vdash \varphi$ for some u such that wRu. We say that a formula is *globally true* on $\mathfrak{M}$ if it is true in every $w \in W$, and we denote this by $\mathfrak{M} \Vdash \varphi$. On the other hand, a formula is called *satisfiable* in $\mathfrak{M}$ if it is true in some $w \in W$.

A class $\mathcal{K}$ of Kripke models is *modally definable* if there is a set S of formulas such that $\mathcal{K}$ consists exactly of models on which every formula from S is globally true, i. e. $\mathcal{K} = \{\mathfrak{M} : \mathfrak{M} \Vdash S\}$. If this is the case, we say that $\mathcal{K}$ is *defined* by S.

The expressive power of a language can be outlined by model-theoretic closure conditions that are necessary and sufficient for a class of models to be modally definable. On the level of frames such conditions are given by the famous Goldblatt-Thomason Theorem, and for pointed models we have the de Rijke characterization (detailed proofs of both are given in [1]). For the global level of models we have the following characterization, which is really the starting point of this paper.

Theorem (de Rijke-Sturm). *A class $\mathcal{K}$ of models is globally definable by a set of modal formulas if and only if $\mathcal{K}$ is closed under surjective bisimulations, disjoint unions and ultraproducts, and $\overline{\mathcal{K}}$ is closed under ultrapowers.*

A class $\mathcal{K}$ of models is globally definable by means of a single modal formula if and only if $\mathcal{K}$ is closed under surjective bisimulations and disjoint unions, and both $\mathcal{K}$ and $\overline{\mathcal{K}}$ are closed under ultraproducts.

Here, $\overline{\mathcal{K}}$ denotes the complement of $\mathcal{K}$, that is, the class of all Kripke models that are not in $\mathcal{K}$.

The truth-preserving model constructions used in the theorem are briefly presented in Section 2, save for the disjoint union, which is a straightforward set-theoretic notion, so the definition is omitted. All of the constructions are described in full detail in [1], and ultraproducts on even deeper level in [2], since they are fundamental for the first-order model theory. In fact, the de Rijke-Sturm results are proved (in [4]) using correspondence between the basic modal language and the first-order language with one binary relation symbol R and a unary relation symbol P for each propositional variable p of the basic modal language. It is clear that a Kripke model can be considered as a model for this first-order language. Correspondence is naturally established by the *standard translation*, a function that maps every modal formula φ to the first-order formula $ST_x(\varphi)$ (where x is the only variable that can occur freely), which is defined as follows:

$ST_x(p) = Px$, for each propositional variable p,
$ST_x(\bot) = \bot$,
$ST_x(\neg\varphi) = \neg ST_x(\varphi)$,
$ST_x(\varphi \vee \psi) = ST_x(\varphi) \vee ST_x(\psi)$,
$ST_x(\Diamond\varphi) = \exists y(xRy \wedge ST_y(\varphi))$, where y is fresh variable.

The basic property of the standard translation is that $\mathfrak{M} \Vdash \varphi$ if and only if $\mathfrak{M} \models \forall x ST_x(\varphi)$. Therefore it is clear that every modally definable class of Kripke models is elementary, i. e. definable by a set of first-order formulas. These formulas are of the form $\forall x ST_x(\varphi)$. This is the point where the idea of this paper emerges. Why not consider the classes definable by formulas of the form $\exists x ST_x(\varphi)$ also modally definable?

Example 1. The formula $\Diamond\top$ defines the class $\mathcal{K}$ of models such that each point has an R-successor, but its complement, i. e. the class of models such that there is a point which has no successors, is not modally definable, since it is not closed under surjective bisimulations. Indeed, the model $\mathfrak{M} = (\{w, v\}, \{(w, w)\}, V)$, where $V(p) = \emptyset$ for all p, is in $\overline{\mathcal{K}}$, but $\mathfrak{M}' = (\{w'\}, \{(w', w')\}, V')$, where $V'(p) = \emptyset$ for all p, is not. Clearly, $Z = \{(w, w')\}$ is a surjective bisimulation form $\mathfrak{M}$ to $\mathfrak{M}'$. On the other hand, $\overline{\mathcal{K}}$ consists exactly of models in which the formula $\neg\Diamond\top$, i. e. $\Box\bot$, is satisfiable.

Example 2. The class $\mathcal{K}$ of all models $\mathfrak{M} = (W, R, V)$ in which there is a finite R-chain of arbitrary length, i. e. for all $n \in \mathbb{N}$ there exist $w_1, \dots, w_n$ such that $w_1 R w_2 R w_3 \dots R w_n$, is not modally definable: it is not hard to show that it is not closed under surjective bisimulations. But clearly, $\mathcal{K}$ consists exactly of models in which all the formulas $\Diamond\top, \Diamond\Diamond\top, \Diamond\Diamond\Diamond\top \dots$, are satisfiable.

The following definition enables us to consider any such example also modally definable in a broader sense.

Definition. A class $\mathcal{K}$ of Kripke models is called *modally $\exists$-definable* if there is a set S of modal formulas such that $\mathcal{K}$ consists exactly of models in which every formula from S is satisfiable.

Remark 1. Note that it is not required that all formulas of S are satisfied at the same point of a model – it suffices that each formula of S is satisfied at some point. Otherwise, in the finite case it would not make much difference: we would get the notion equivalent to the modal $\exists$-definability by a single formula, since a finite set of modal formulas $\{\varphi_1, \dots, \varphi_k\}$ is satisfiable in a model $\mathfrak{M}$ if and only if $\mathfrak{M} \Vdash \exists x ST_x(\varphi_1 \wedge \dots \wedge \varphi_k)$. But the infinite case would go beyond elementary classes, which might be interesting in its own right, but the intention here is to keep the analogy with modal definability in the usual sense, which always implies elementarity. Namely, the class of all Kripke models such that there is a point which satisfies all propositional variables is not an elementary class (see Example 3 in the next section).

It seems natural to generalize the notion of modal definability on the global level of models such that it includes $\exists$-definable classes, together with modally definable classes in the usual sense. A prospect of further generalization is outlined in the concluding section of this paper.

The following characterization, proof of which is the main result of this paper, holds.

Theorem. *Let $\mathcal{K}$ be a class of Kripke models.*

1. *$\mathcal{K}$ is $\exists$-definable by a single modal formula if and only if $\mathcal{K}$ is closed under total bisimulations and ultraproducts, and $\overline{\mathcal{K}}$ is closed under disjoint unions and ultraproducts.*

2. $\mathcal{K}$ *is* $\exists$-*definable by a finite set of modal formulas if and only if* $\mathcal{K}$ *is closed under total bisimulations and ultraproducts, and* $\overline{\mathcal{K}}$ *is closed under ultraproducts.*

3. $\mathcal{K}$ *is* $\exists$-*definable by a set of modal formulas if and only if* $\mathcal{K}$ *is closed under total bisimulations and ultraproducts, and* $\overline{\mathcal{K}}$ *is closed under ultrapowers.*

Remark 2. The case of $\exists$-definability by a single formula is trivial, since we have obvious duality with usual modal definability by a single formula. But the cases of a set of formulas, both finite and infinite, are not trivial, since notions are not exactly dual anymore. Clearly, a class is globally definable by a set of formulas if and only if its complement consists exactly of models in which the negation of *some* formula from that set is satisfiable. To say that a class is $\exists$-definable, means that *each* formula from a defining set is satisfiable.

2   Model-Theoretic Constructions

This section is just a brief overview of the basic facts about constructions used in the main theorem, so the reader familiar with these constructions could skip it and just use it as a quick reference if needed.

A *bisimulation* between $\mathfrak{M} = (W, R, V)$ and $\mathfrak{M}' = (W', R', V')$ is a relation $Z \subseteq W \times W'$ such that:

(at) if wZw' then we have: $w \in V(p)$ if and only if $w' \in V'(p)$, for all propositional variables p,

(forth) if wZw' and wRv, then there is v' such that vZv' and $w'R'v'$,

(back) if wZw' and $w'R'v'$, then there is v such that vZv' and wRv.

The basic property of bisimulations is that (at) extends to all formulas: if wZw' then $\mathfrak{M}, w \Vdash \varphi$ if and only if $\mathfrak{M}', w' \Vdash \varphi$, i. e. w and w' are modally equivalent.

A bisimulation is called *surjective* if for all $w' \in W'$ there is $w \in W$ such that wZw', and *total* if for all $w \in W$ there is $w' \in W'$ such that wZw'.

To define the ultraproducts, we need the notion of ultrafilters. An *ultrafilter* over a set $I \neq \emptyset$ is a family $U \subseteq \mathcal{P}(I)$ such that:

(1) $I \in U$,

(2) if $A, B \in U$, then $A \cap B \in U$,

(3) if $A \in U$ and $A \subseteq B \subseteq I$, then $B \in U$,

(4) for all $A \subseteq I$ we have: $A \in U$ if and only if $I \setminus A \notin U$.

By (2), any ultrafilter is closed under finite intersections. An ultrafilter that is not closed under countable intersections is called *countably incomplete*. It is not hard to prove that such ultrafilter contains only infinite subsets and all cofinite subsets of I. Together with the fact that any family of subsets which has the finite intersection property (that is, each finite intersection is non-empty) can be extended to an ultrafilter, this provides the existence of countably incomplete ultrafilters (see e. g. [1] for details). For example, the family of all cofinite subsets of $\mathbb{N}$ can be extended to a countably incomplete ultrafilter over $\mathbb{N}$.

Let $\{\mathfrak{M}_i = (W_i, R_i, V_i) : i \in I\}$ be a family of Kripke models and let U be an ultrafilter over I. The *ultraproduct* of this family over U is the model $\prod_U \mathfrak{M}_i = (W, R, V)$ such that:

(1) W is the set of equivalence classes of the following relation defined on the Cartesian product $\prod_{i \in I} W_i = \{f : I \to \bigcup_{i \in I} W_i : f(i) \in W_i \text{ for all } i \in I\}$: put $f \sim g$ if and only if $\{i \in I : f(i) = g(i)\} \in U$. We denote by f^U the equivalence class generated by $f \in \prod_{i \in I} W_i$.

(2) $f^U R g^U$ if and only if $\{i \in I : f(i) R_i g(i)\} \in U$,

(3) $f^U \in V(p)$ if and only if $\{i \in I : f(i) \in V_i(p)\} \in U$, for all p.

It is not hard to verify that the ultraproduct is well defined. The basic property of ultraproducts is that (3) extends to all formulas: $\prod_U \mathfrak{M}_i, f^U \Vdash \varphi$ if and only if $\{i \in I : \mathfrak{M}_i, f(i) \Vdash \varphi\} \in U$. This is an analogue of the Łoś Fundamental Theorem on ultraproducts from the first-order model theory (see [2] for this, and [1] for the proof of the modal analogue).

Another important fact is that an ultraproduct over a countably incomplete ultrafilter is ω-saturated, thus also modally saturated. The definition of saturation is omitted here, since we only need some facts which it implies. Most importantly, saturation implies a converse of the basic property of bisimulations, which generally does not hold. In fact, modal equivalence between points of modally saturated models is a bisimulation. Furthermore, if a set S of modal formulas is finitely satisfiable in an ω-saturated model (that is, if each finite subset of S is satisfied at some point of the model), then S is satisfiable in that model, i. e. there is a point in which all formulas from S are true. This is a simple consequence of the definition of ω-saturation (see [1] for proofs of these facts).

An ultraproduct such that $\mathfrak{M}_i = \mathfrak{M}$ for all $i \in I$ is called an *ultrapower* of $\mathfrak{M}$ and denoted $\prod_U \mathfrak{M}$. The Łoś Theorem implies that any ultrapower of a model is elementarily equivalent to the model, that is, the same first-order sentences are true on $\mathfrak{M}$ and $\prod_U \mathfrak{M}$.

Finally, classical model-theoretic characterization of elementary classes is also needed in the proof of the main theorem: a class of models is elementary if and only if it is closed under isomorphisms and ultraproducts, and its complement is closed under ultrapowers. For a class to be definable by a single first-order sentence, complement also needs to be closed under ultraproducts (see [2] for the proof).

Example 3. Let $\mathcal{K}$ be the class of all Kripke models $\mathfrak{M} = (W, R, V)$ such that there is $w \in W$ in which all propositional variables hold. Then $\mathcal{K}$ is not elementary, since $\overline{\mathcal{K}}$ is not closed under ultrapowers. To see this, let $\{p_i : i \in \mathbb{N}\}$ be the set of all propositional variables and put $\mathfrak{M} = (\mathbb{N}, R, V)$, where R is arbitrary, and $V(p_i) = \mathbb{N} \setminus \{i\}$ for all $i \in \mathbb{N}$. Clearly, $\mathfrak{M} \in \overline{\mathcal{K}}$. Now, let U be a countably incomplete ultrafilter over $\mathbb{N}$. Put $f(i) = i$, $i \in \mathbb{N}$. Since U contains all cofinite subsets of $\mathbb{N}$, the Łoś Theorem implies $\prod_U \mathfrak{M}, f^U \Vdash p_i$ for all $i \in \mathbb{N}$, hence $\prod_U \mathfrak{M} \in \mathcal{K}$.

3   Modal ∃-Definability by a Finite Set of Formulas

To prove the statement (1) of the main theorem, note the obvious fact that any class of models is closed under surjective bisimulations if and only if its complement is closed under total bisimulations.

Proof (of 1). The claim follows from the fact that $\mathcal{K}$ is ∃-definable by a single formula if and only if $\overline{\mathcal{K}}$ is globally definable by a single formula. This is a consequence of the fact that φ is globally true on a model $\mathfrak{M}$ if and only if $\neg\varphi$ is not satisfiable in $\mathfrak{M}$. □

The following observation, given by de Rijke and Sturm in the concluding remarks of [4], is used in the proof of the second statement of the theorem.

Lemma 1. *A class $\mathcal{K}$ of models is $\vee$-definable, i. e. definable by a set of formulas of the form $\forall x ST_x(\varphi_1) \vee \ldots \vee \forall x ST_x(\varphi_n)$ for some modal formulas $\varphi_1, \ldots, \varphi_n$, if and only if $\mathcal{K}$ is closed under surjective bisimulations and ultraproducts, and $\overline{\mathcal{K}}$ is closed under ultrapowers.*

Proof. Let $\mathcal{K}$ be a $\vee$-definable class of models. Then $\mathcal{K}$ is elementary, thus it is closed under ultraproducts and its complement under ultrapowers, so it remains to be proved that $\mathcal{K}$ is closed under surjective bisimulations. For this, it suffices to show that the truth of any formula α of the form $\forall x ST_x(\varphi_1) \vee \ldots \vee \forall x ST_x(\varphi_n)$ is preserved under surjective bisimulations. So, assume $\mathfrak{M} \models \alpha$ and suppose we have a surjective bisimulation from $\mathfrak{M}$ to $\mathfrak{M}'$. Then $\mathfrak{M} \models \forall x ST_x(\varphi_i)$ for some $i \in \{1, 2, \ldots, n\}$. Now, the de Rijke-Sturm theorem clearly implies that $\mathfrak{M}' \models \forall x ST_x(\varphi_i)$, thus $\mathfrak{M}' \models \alpha$, as desired.

For the converse, let $\mathcal{K}$ be a class with these properties. Let S be the set of all formulas of the form $\forall x ST_x(\varphi_1) \vee \ldots \vee \forall x ST_x(\varphi_n)$ that are true on all models from $\mathcal{K}$. Clearly, $\mathcal{K} \subseteq Mod(S)$, where $Mod(S)$ denotes the class defined by S. It remains to show the reverse inclusion.

So, let $\mathfrak{M} \in Mod(S)$, i. e. $\mathfrak{M} \models S$. Let Σ be the set of all modal formulas that are satisfiable in $\mathfrak{M}$. The language is countable, so we can index $\Sigma = \{\sigma_1, \sigma_2, \ldots\}$. For any $k \in \mathbb{N}$, there is $\mathfrak{N}_k \in \mathcal{K}$ in which $\sigma_1, \ldots, \sigma_k$ are all satisfiable. Otherwise we would have that $\forall x ST_x(\neg\varphi_1) \vee \ldots \vee \forall x ST_x(\neg\varphi_k)$ is true in all models from $\mathcal{K}$, so it is in S, thus true on $\mathfrak{M}$. This implies $\mathfrak{M} \Vdash \neg\sigma_i$ for some $i \in \{1, \ldots, k\}$, which contradicts the definition of Σ.

Now, let U be a countably incomplete ultrafilter over $\mathbb{N}$. Since U contains all cofinite subsets of $\mathbb{N}$, it is easy to verify that each formula from Σ is satisfiable in the ultraproduct $\prod_U \mathfrak{N}_k$. By assumption we have $\prod_U \mathfrak{N}_k \in \mathcal{K}$. Furthermore, $\prod_U \mathfrak{N}_k$ is ω-saturated. Assume for the moment that $\mathfrak{M}$ is also saturated. Then the modal equivalence between points of $\prod_U \mathfrak{N}_k$ and $\mathfrak{M}$ is a bisimulation.

To prove that this bisimulation is surjective, let w be any point from $\mathfrak{M}$ and put $\Sigma_w = \{\sigma : \mathfrak{M}, w \Vdash \sigma\}$. Clearly, $\Sigma_w \subseteq \Sigma$, so we already have that each formula from Σ_w is satisfiable in $\prod_U \mathfrak{N}_k$. Now, since Σ_w is closed under conjunctions, it is finitely satisfiable in $\prod_U \mathfrak{N}_k$, which is ω-saturated, thus Σ_w is satisfiable in $\prod_U \mathfrak{N}_k$. This means that there is an element in $\prod_U \mathfrak{N}_k$ modally equivalent with w, as desired. This shows that $\mathfrak{M}$ is also in $\mathcal{K}$, which concludes the proof in case $\mathfrak{M}$ is saturated. It remains to prove that we can assume this without loss of generality.

So, let $\mathfrak{M}$ be any model such that $\mathfrak{M} \models S$. An ultrapower of $\mathfrak{M}$ is elementarily equivalent to $\mathfrak{M}$, so we have $\prod_U \mathfrak{M} \models S$. But, $\prod_U \mathfrak{M}$ is saturated, so we have already proved $\prod_U \mathfrak{M} \in \mathcal{K}$. Now, since $\overline{\mathcal{K}}$ is closed under ultrapowers, we conclude $\mathfrak{M} \in \mathcal{K}$. □

The formulas of the form used in the previous lemma will be referred to as ∨-*formulas*.

Proof (of 2). Let $S = \{\varphi_1, \ldots, \varphi_n\}$ be a set of modal formulas and let $\mathfrak{M}$ be a model. Assume that there is a formula from S that is not satisfiable in $\mathfrak{M}$. Clearly, negation of that formula is globally true on $\mathfrak{M}$, so we have $\mathfrak{M} \models \forall x ST_x(\neg\varphi_1) \vee \ldots \vee \forall x ST_x(\neg\varphi_n)$. It easily follows that a class $\mathcal{K}$ is ∃-definable by a finite set of formulas if and only if $\overline{\mathcal{K}}$ is ∨-definable by a single formula. So, to complete the proof, we need to show that a class $\mathcal{K}$ is ∨-definable by a single formula if and only if $\mathcal{K}$ is closed under surjective bisimulations and ultraproducts, and $\overline{\mathcal{K}}$ is also closed under ultraproducts.

Let $\mathcal{K}$ be ∨-definable by a single formula. This is a first-order formula, so $\overline{\mathcal{K}}$ is closed under ultraproducts. The other conditions follow from the Lemma 1.

For the converse, let $\mathcal{K}$ be closed under surjective bisimulations and ultraproducts, and $\overline{\mathcal{K}}$ closed under ultraproducts. Since isomorphism is clearly a special case of surjective bisimulation, the characterization of elementarity implies that $\mathcal{K}$ definable by a single first-order sentence. On the other hand, $\mathcal{K}$ satisfies all conditions of the Lemma 1, thus $\mathcal{K}$ is ∨-definable. Let Σ be a set of ∨-formulas that defines $\mathcal{K}$. The Compactness Theorem for the first-order logic (see [2]) implies that there is a finite $\Delta \subseteq \Sigma$ such that $\mathcal{K}$ is actually defined by Δ. It is easy to see that a conjunction of ∨-formulas is equivalent to a single ∨-formula, which completes the proof. □

Before turning to the infinite case, note that we have got the following preservation result as a consequence of previously established facts.

Corollary. *A first-order sentence α (over the appropriate vocabulary) is equivalent to a formula of the form $\exists x ST_x(\varphi_1) \wedge \ldots \wedge \exists x ST_x(\varphi_n)$, where $\varphi_1, \ldots, \varphi_n$ are modal formulas, if and only if it is preserved under total bisimulations.*

4   Modal ∃-Definability by an Infinite Set of Formulas

In this section infinite disjunctions are used, hopefully on the intuitively clear level which does not call for the proper introduction to infinitary languages. Results could have been stated and proved without the use of infinite formulas – this usage is just for the purpose of clearer statements and easier observation of analogies to the finite case.

A $\vee_\infty$-*formula* is a countably infinite disjunction of the form $\forall x ST_x(\varphi_1) \vee \forall x ST_x(\varphi_2) \vee \forall x ST_x(\varphi_3) \vee \ldots$, for some modal formulas $\varphi_k, k \in \mathbb{N}$. Of course, such formula is true if and only if there exists $k \in \mathbb{N}$ such that $\forall x ST_x(\varphi_k)$ is true. Saying that a class $\mathcal{K}$ of Kripke models is $\vee_\infty$-*definable* means that there is a set of $\vee_\infty$-formulas such that $\mathcal{K}$ consists exactly of models on which all of the formulas from that set are true.

Since we work in the language with countably many propositional variables, it is clear, by analogy to the finite case, that a class $\mathcal{K}$ of models is $\exists$-definable if and only if its complement is $\vee_\infty$-definable by a single formula.

Lemma 2. *A class $\mathcal{K}$ of models is $\vee_\infty$-definable if and only if $\mathcal{K}$ is closed under surjective bisimulations and ultrapowers, and $\overline{\mathcal{K}}$ is closed under ultrapowers.*

Proof. Let $\mathcal{K}$ be a $\vee_\infty$-definable class. The proof that $\mathcal{K}$ closed under surjective bisimulation is similar as in the proof of the Lemma 1. The closure of $\mathcal{K}$ and $\overline{\mathcal{K}}$ under ultrapowers follows easily from the fact that ultrapower of a model is elementarily equivalent to that model.

For the converse, assume that $\mathcal{K}$ fulfils all of the closure conditions stated above. Let S be the set of all $\vee_\infty$-formulas that are true on all models in $\mathcal{K}$. Clearly, $\mathcal{K}$ lies in the class defined by S, so to prove that S defines $\mathcal{K}$ it remains to show that any model on which all of the formulas from S are true is in fact in $\mathcal{K}$.

So, let $\mathfrak{M}$ be a model such that $\mathfrak{M} \models S$. Let Σ denote the set of all formulas satisfiable in $\mathfrak{M}$. There is a model $\mathfrak{N}$ in $\mathcal{K}$ such that each formula from Σ is satisfiable in $\mathfrak{N}$. For if not, we have that $\vee_\infty$-formula $\vee_{\sigma \in \Sigma}(\forall x ST_x(\neg \sigma))$ is true on all models in $\mathcal{K}$, so it is in S, hence $\mathfrak{M} \Vdash \neg \sigma$ for some $\sigma \in \Sigma$, which is a contradiction.

Since the ultrapower $\prod_U \mathfrak{N}$ over a countably incomplete ultrafilter U is an ω-saturated elementary extension of $\mathfrak{N}$, we have that every formula from Σ is satisfiable in $\prod_U \mathfrak{N}$. By assumption, $\prod_U \mathfrak{N}$ is in $\mathcal{K}$, and we can assume without loss of generality that $\mathfrak{M}$ is also saturated. Thus the modal equivalence between points of $\prod_U \mathfrak{N}$ and $\mathfrak{M}$ is a bisimulation. Surjectivity of this bisimulation is proved similarly as in Lemma 1. This shows that $\mathfrak{M}$ is also in $\mathcal{K}$, which concludes the proof. $\qquad\qquad\square$

Proof (of 3). Due to the previous remarks, it suffices to show that $\mathcal{K}$ is $\vee_\infty$-definable by a single formula if and only if it is closed under surjective bisimulations and ultrapowers, and $\overline{\mathcal{K}}$ is closed under ultraproducts. Again, necessity is easily verified. For the converse, let $\mathcal{K}$ be a class of models such that all of the above closure conditions hold. It follows from Lemma 2 that $\mathcal{K}$ is $\vee_\infty$-definable.

Let S be a set of all $\vee_\infty$-formulas that are true on all models from $\mathcal{K}$. Suppose that there is no single $\vee_\infty$-formula α such that $\mathcal{K}$ is actually defined by α. So, for any $\alpha \in S$ there is a model $\mathfrak{M}_\alpha$ in $\overline{\mathcal{K}}$ such that $\mathfrak{M}_\alpha \models \alpha$.

For each member $\forall x ST_x(\alpha_i)$ of the disjunction α such that $\mathfrak{M}_\alpha \models \forall x ST_x(\alpha_i)$, define $I_{\alpha_i} = \{\sigma \in S : \mathfrak{M}_\sigma \models \forall x ST_x(\alpha_i)\}$. Clearly, the family of all these subsets of S has the finite intersection property. So, it can be extended to an ultrafilter U over S. (This is one of the basic properties of ultrafilters, which can be recalled using [1] or [2].) Since $\overline{\mathcal{K}}$ is closed under ultraproducts by assumption, we have that $\prod_U \mathfrak{M}_\sigma$ is also in $\overline{\mathcal{K}}$.

But, for any I_{α_i} we have $I_{\alpha_i} \in U$, so (by Łoś fundamental theorem on ultraproducts – see [2]) we have $\prod_U \mathfrak{M}_\sigma \models \forall x ST_x(\alpha_i)$, thus $\prod_U \mathfrak{M}_\sigma \models \alpha$ for all $\alpha \in S$. Since S defines $\mathcal{K}$, $\prod_U \mathfrak{M}_\sigma$ is in $\mathcal{K}$, which is a contradiction. $\qquad\square$

5   Concluding Remarks

On the level of Kripke frames, a notion similar to $\exists$-definability is the *negative definability*, defined by Venema in [5], and characterized for some special cases by Hollenberg in [3]. In cited papers, a class of frames is called negatively definable if there is a set of formulas such that the class consists exactly of frames such that any formula of that set is refutable in each point, under some valuation. This notion can be equivalently defined by demanding that for each formula and each point there is a valuation that satisfies the formula at that point. So, a kind of satisfiability is used, but satisfiability *everywhere* (by some valuation), while the notion of satisfiability on the level of models used in this paper requires that a formula is satisfiable *somewhere* (with fixed valuation).

To generalize the perspective of expressivity of modal logic, it may be worthwhile to try to define more analogous notion of satisfiability and $\exists$-definability for the level of frames and to give characterization of such definability.

Also, similarly to the notion of $\pm$-definability in [3], the notion of generalized modal definability could be defined by saying that a class of models is *modally $\forall\exists$-definable* if there is a pair (S_1, S_2) of sets of formulas such that a class consists exactly of models on which every formula from S_1 is globally true and every formula from S_2 is satisfiable.

This is a proper generalization of usual modal definability and $\exists$-definability, as will be clear from the following example.

Example 4. Let p be a propositional variable and let $\mathcal{K}$ be the class of models such that $V(p) \neq \emptyset$ and each point has a successor. Then $\mathcal{K}$ is $\forall\exists$-definable by a pair $(\{\Diamond\top\}, \{p\})$. But $\mathcal{K}$ is not modally definable, since it is not closed under surjective bisimulations. To see this, put $\mathfrak{M} = (\{w, v\}, \{(w, w), (v, v)\}, V)$, where $V(p) = \{v\}$ and $V(q) = \emptyset$ for $q \neq p$, and $\mathfrak{M}' = (\{w'\}, \{(w', w')\}, V'(p))$, where $V'(p) = \emptyset$ and also $V(q) = \emptyset$ for $q \neq p$. Clearly, $\{(w, w')\}$ is a surjective bisimulation and $\mathfrak{M} \in \mathcal{K}$, but $\mathfrak{M}' \notin \mathcal{K}$.

Also, $\mathcal{K}$ is not modally $\exists$-definable, since it is not closed under total bisimulation. Indeed, put $\mathfrak{M} = (\{w\}, \{(w, w)\}, V)$, where $V(p) = \{w\}$, and $\mathfrak{M}' = (\{w', v'\}, \{(w', w')\}, V')$, where $V'(p) = \{w'\}$ and $V(q) = V'(q) = \emptyset$ for $q \neq p$. Again, $\{(w, w')\}$ is a bisimulation, $\mathfrak{M} \in \mathcal{K}$, $\mathfrak{M}' \notin \mathcal{K}$.

A model-theoretic characterization of $\forall\exists$-definability will be presented in a near future paper.

And finally, although the approach of this paper was not to extend the language, it should be noted that modal $\exists$-definability is equivalent to the usual notion of modal definability by the existential fragment of the modal language enriched with the global modality, i. e. by basic modal formulas prefixed with the existential global modality (see [1] for definitions and basic facts about this language). Modal ∀∃-definability also corresponds to a fragment of this language – conjunctions of basic modal formulas prefixed with the universal or existential modality.

References

1. Blackburn, J., de Rijke, M., Venema, Y.: Modal Logic. Cambridge University Press (2001)
2. Chang, C.C., Keisler, H.J.: Model Theory. Elsevier (1990)
3. Hollenberg, M.: Characterizations of Negative Definability in Modal Logic. Studia Logica 60, 357–386 (1998)
4. de Rijke, M., Sturm, H.: Global Definability in Basic Modal Logic. In: Wansing, H. (ed.) Essays on Non-classical Logic, pp. 111–133. World Scientific Publishers (2001)
5. Venema, Y.: Derivation rules as anti-axioms in modal logic. Journal of Symbolic Logic 58, 1003–1034 (1993)

Modeling Semantic Competence: A Critical Review of Frege's Puzzle about Identity

Rasmus K. Rendsvig

Philosophy and Science Studies, Roskilde University
rakrre@ruc.dk

Abstract. The present paper discusses Frege's Puzzle about Identity as an argument against a Millian theory of meaning for proper names. The key notion here is semantic competence. Strict notions of semantic competence are extrapolated from a two-sorted first-order epistemic logical modeling of a cognitive neuropsychological theory of the structure of lexical competence. The model allows for a rigorous analysis of Frege's argument. The theory and model of lexical semantic competence includes a multitude of types of competence, each yielding a different argument, far from all being as decisive against Millianism as has been the mainstream assumption in 20th century philosophy of language.

1   Introduction

In his 1892 paper *On Sense and Reference*, Gottlob Frege developed an argument against so-called *Millian* theories of meaning for proper names, later denoted *Frege's Puzzles about Identity*, cf. [11]. The Millian theory derives from philosopher John Stuart Mill, and equates meaning with reference. The view states that the meaning of a given, unambiguous proper name is constituted solely by the object to which the name refers, i.e. by its referent. On this view, the meaning of the name 'Hesperus' (the Evening Star) is constituted by the planet Venus construed as an existing object, and nothing more. Against this view, Frege's Puzzle can be formulated as follows. Consider the two true identity statements

(a) Hesperus is Hesperus
(b) Hesperus is Phosphorus

Given that the two names co-refer (Phosphorus, the Morning Star, does in fact denote the planet Venus), the two identity statements have the same meaning and must therefore be equally informative to a semantically competent speaker of English. As the first is a trivial validity of self-identity, this does not carry informational content. Opposed to this, the latter is a contingent, empirical fact, and may hence convey information. Hence, (a) and (b) *do* differ in informational content, and the Millian view should be rejected. The argument can be pinned out as follows:

D. Lassiter and M. Slavkovik (Eds.): ESSLLI Student Sessions, LNCS 7415, pp. 140–157, 2012.

(A) (a) and (b) mean the same.

(A→B) If (a) and (b) mean the same, then a semantically competent speaker would know that (a) and (b) mean the same.

(B→C) If a semantically competent speaker would know that (a) and (b) mean the same, then they are equally informative to the speaker.

(¬C) (a) and (b) differ in informativeness to the competent speaker.

∴ Contradiction.

The four premises are jointly inconsistent, and the typical textbook choice[1] is to reject the premise (A). This premise is a consequence of the Millian view, and the conclusion drawn is that there must be more to meaning than mere reference.

In this paper, the above argument will be given a critical evaluation focusing on the notion of *semantic competence*, and doing so in an epistemic light. This is done by constructing a formal theory which includes the fundamental elements of the argument: an agent which has knowledge of the *objects* of the world it inhabits as well as a *basic language* for the agent. Further, the agent's knowledge of the meaning of the terms from its language is explicitly modeled. These things are included in order to gain the expressibility required to express the premises of the argument above wholly within the syntax of the formal language constructed.

The paper is organized as follows: first, a theory of semantic competence based on empirical evidence from cognitive neuropsychology is presented. This theory is then modeled using two-sorted first-order epistemic logic, a formal counterpart to Millian meaning is introduced, and strict notions of semantic competence are identified. In the ensuing section, the above argument will be evaluated using the identified notions of competence. Due to limitations of space, proof theory will not be considered. A complete axiomatization can easily be constructed based on the general completeness result for many-sorted modal logics from [15].

2   Lexical, Semantic Competence

Semantic competence is not in general a well-defined term, and its usage far from normalized. In the present, the notion is used as an objective measure, which allows for comparison of agents with respect to their individual competence. This is in contrast with the view of semantic competence used in e.g. [14], which depends on both subjective status and social context. It should further be noted that it is assumed that a satisfactory notion of semantic competence *simpliciter* cannot be found. Rather, it is assumed that agents will be semantically competent *with respect to* some part of language – be it a language, a sentence or a set of sentences or lexical items.

---

[1] See, for example, [2] or [10].

2.1   The Structure of Semantic Competence

The notion(s) of semantic competence invoked here are adopted from [12]. There, Diego Marconi constructs a conceptual theory of the *structure* of semantic, *lexical* competence (SLC). The focal point is *lexical* competence, understood as competence with respect to words, as opposed to e.g. a truth-theoretic account of semantic competence, where competence consists in knowledge of T-sentence. See [9, ch. 9], [15] and [16] for critique of such theories. In structure, the theory is close to that of [3], but is deemed stronger as it is more precise and has empirical backing from studies in cognitive neuropsychology.[2] Time has not permitted a proper survey of literature from cognitive neuropsychology and related fields, and it is therefore unknown if this theory is inconsistent with newer findings or has been surpassed by later developments.

The elements of the theory consist of three relations defined over four ontologies. Each of the three relations correspond to a competence type. These are *inferential competence* and two types of *referential competence*, being *naming* and *application*. The four ontologies include one of *external objects*, one of *external words* (e.g., spoken or written words) and two mental modules: a *word lexicon* and a *semantic lexicon*. This structure is illustrated in Figure 1.

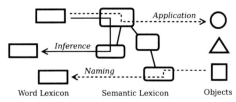

Fig. 1. A simplified illustration of the SLC. Elements in the word lexicon are not connected, only elements in the semantic lexicon are. External words are not pictured.

Ex.: Inferential competence requires connecting two items from the word lexicon *through* the semantic lexicon.

Word Lexicon, Semantic Lexicon and Inferential Competence. *Inferential competence* is the ability to correctly connect lexical items via the semantic lexicon, "underlying such performances as semantic inference, paraphrase, definition, retrieval of a word from its definition, finding a synonym, and so forth" [12, p. 59]. As such, inferential competence with respect to a given word consists "in the knowledge of true sentences in which [the] word is used" [p.58]. Hence, inferential competence is not a matter of logical proficiency and deductive skill, but rather depends on how well-connected the mental structure of the agent is. If the mental structure of the agent connects a given word in a way suitable for the agent to perform tasks like those mentioned, the agent is deemed inferentially competent with respect to that word.

To illustrate the competence form and introduce the modules required, assume an agent was to perform one of the mentioned tasks, namely finding a synonym for some name. On input, the external word (e.g., a name written on a piece of paper) is first analyzed and related to an mental representation from the word

---

[2] For the review of these studies, arguments for the structure and references to relevant literature, the reader is referred to [12].

lexicon. In [12], two word lexica are included for different input, a phonetic and a graphical. Here, attention is restricted to a simplified structure with only one arbitrary such, as illustrated in Figure 1, consisting only of proper names.[3] Using a graphical lexicon as an example, the word lexicon consists of the words an agent is able to recognize in writing. In the second step towards finding a synonym, the mental representation of the word is related to a mental concept in the semantic lexicon (or semantic system, in the terminology of [5]). The semantic lexicon is a collection of non-linguistic, mental concepts possessed by the agent, *distinct* from the word lexicon. The semantic lexicon reflects the agent's mental model of the world, and the items in this lexicon stand in various relations to one another. In contrast, in the word lexicon connections between the various items *do not exist*. Such only exist *via* the semantic lexicon. The third step is exactly a connection between two entries in the semantic lexicon. As the agent is to produce a synonym, this connection is assumed to be the reflexive loop. Finally, the reached note is connected to an entry in the word lexicon distinct from the input name, and output can be performed.[4]

Referential Competence and External Objects. *Referential competence* is "the ability to map lexical items onto the world" [12, p.60]. This is an ability involving all four ontologies, the last being *external objects*. It consists of two distinct subsystems. The first is *naming*. This is the act of retrieving a lexical item from the word lexicon when presented with an object. Naming is a two-step process, where first the external object is connected to a suitable concept in the semantic lexicon, which is then connected to a word lexicon item for output. The ability to name is required for correctly answering questions such as 'what is this called?'

The second subsystem is that of *application*. Application is the act of identifying an object when presented with a word. Again, this is a two-stage process, where first the word lexicon item is connected to a semantic lexicon item, which is then connected to an external object. The ability to apply words is required for correctly carrying out instructions such as 'hand me the orange.'

A naming or application deficit can occur if either stage is affected: if, e.g., either an object is not mapped to a suitable concept due to lack of recognition, or a suitable concept is not mapped to the correct (or any) word, then a naming procedure will not be successfully completed.

Empirical Reasons for Multiple Lexica and Competence Types. Marconi's structure of lexical competence may seem overly complex. It may be questioned, for example, why one should distinguish between word and semantic type modules, or why referential competence is composed of two separate competence types, instead of one bi-directional. These distinctions are made, however, as

---

[3] To only include proper names is technically motivated, as the modeling would otherwise require second-order expressivity. This is returned to below.

[4] For simplicity, a distinction between input and output lexica will not be made. See [17] for discussion.

empirical studies from cognitive neuropsychology indicate that the separation of these systems is mentally real, cf. [12, ch. 3]. In these studies, reviews of subjects with various brain-injuries indicate that these modules and abilities of human cognition are separate, in the sense that an ability may be lost or acutely impaired as a result of brain damage, while the other is left largely unaffected.

The distinction between word lexicon and semantic lexicon is also made in [13,17], and is supported in [5] by cases where patients are able to recognize various objects, but are unable to name them (they cannot access the word lexicon from the semantic lexicon). In the opposite direction, cases are reported where patients are able to reason about objects and their relations when shown objects, yet unable to do the same when prompted by their names (i.e., the patients cannot access the semantic lexicon from the word lexicon). The latter indicates that reasoning is done with elements from the semantic lexicon, rather than with items from the word lexicon.

Regarding competence types, it is stressed in [12] that inferential and referential competence are distinct abilities. Specifically, it is argued that the ability to name an object does not imply inferential competence with the used name, and, *vice versa*, that inferential knowledge about a name does not imply the ability to use it in naming tasks. No conclusions are drawn with respect to the relationship between inferential competence and application. Further, application is dissociated from naming, in the sense that application can be preserved while naming is lost. No evidence is presented for the opposite dissociation, i.e. that application can be lost, but naming maintained.

The model constructed in the ensuing section respects these dissociations. Space does not permit a long validation of the constructed model, but for this purpose, the reader can refer to [15].

3   Modeling the Structure of Lexical Competence

To model the structure from the previous section, a two-sorted first-order epistemic logic will be used. Do to limitations of space, only the absolutely required elements for the analysis of the argument from the introduction are included, though the syntax and semantics could easily be extended to include more agents, sorts, function- and relation symbols, cf. [15].

A two-sorted language is used to ensure that the model respects the dissociation of word lexicon and semantic lexicon. The first sort, σ_{OBJ}, is used to represent external objects and the semantic lexicon entries. As such, these are *non-linguistic* in nature. The second sort, σ_{LEX}, is used to represent the lexical items from the agent's language and entries in the word lexicon. Had terms been used to represent both simultaneously, the model would be in contradiction with empirical evidence.

The choice of quantified epistemic logic fits well with the Marconi's theory, if one assumes the competence types to be (perhaps implicitly) knowledge-based. The notions of object identification required for application is well-understood as modeled in the quantified S5 framework, cf. [4]. The 'knowing who/what' *de re* constructions using quantified epistemic logic from [7] captures nicely the knowledge required for object identification by the subjects reviewed in [12]. These constructions will be returned to below.

3.1   Syntax

Define a language $\mathcal{L}$ with two sorts, σ_{OBJ} and σ_{LEX}. For sort σ_{OBJ}, include

1. $OBJ = \{a, b, c, ...\}$, a countable set of *object constant symbols*
2. $VAR = \{x_1, x_2, ...\}$, a countably infinite set of *object variables*

The set of terms of sort σ_{OBJ} is $TER_{OBJ} = OBJ \cup VAR$. For sort σ_{LEX}, include

1. $LEX = \{n_1, n_2, ...\}$, a countable set of *name constant symbols*
2. $VAR_{LEX} = \{\dot{x}_1, \dot{x}_2, ...\}$, a countably infinite set of *name variables*

The set of terms of sort σ_{LEX} is $TER_{LEX} = LEX \cup VAR_{LEX}$. Include further in $\mathcal{L}$ a unary function symbol, μ, of sort $TER_{LEX} \longrightarrow TER_{OBJ}$. The set of all *terms, TER,* of $\mathcal{L}$ are $OBJ \cup VAR \cup LEX \cup VAR_{LEX} \cup \{\mu(t)\}$, for all $t \in LEX \cup VAR_{LEX}$. Finally, include the binary relations symbol for identity, $=$. The well-formed formulas of $\mathcal{L}$ are given by

$$\varphi ::= (t_1 = t_2) \,|\, \neg\varphi \,|\, \varphi \wedge \psi \,|\, \forall x\varphi \,|\, K_i\varphi$$

The definitions of the remaining boolean connectives, the dual operator of K_i, $\hat{K}_i$, the existential quantifier and free/bound variables and sentences are all defined as usual. Though a mono-agent system, the operators are indexed by i to allow third-person reference to agent i.

3.2   Semantics

Define a model to be a quadruple $M = \langle W, \sim, Dom, \mathcal{I} \rangle$ where

1. $W = \{w, w_1, w_2, ...\}$ is a set of *epistemic alternatives* to actual world w.
2. $\sim$ is an *indistinguishability (equivalence) relation* on $W \times W$.
3. $Dom = Obj \cup Nam$ is the *(constant) domain of quantification*, where $Obj = \{d_1, d_2, ...\}$ is a non-empty set of *objects*, and $Nam = \{\dot{n}_1, \dot{n}_2, ..., \dot{n}_k\}$ is a finite, non-empty set of *names*.[5]
4. $\mathcal{I}$ is an *interpretation function* such that

$$\mathcal{I} : OBJ \times W \longrightarrow Obj \,|\, \mathcal{I} : LEX \longrightarrow Nam \,|\, \mathcal{I} : \{\mu\} \times W \longrightarrow Obj^{Nam}$$

Define a *valuation function, v,* by

$$v : VAR \longrightarrow Obj \,|\, v : VAR_{LEX} \longrightarrow Nam$$

---

[5] The set of names is assumed finite to be, in principle, learnable for a finite agent.

and a *x-variant of v* as a valuation v' such that $v'(y) = v(y)$ for all $y \in VAR_{(LEX)}/\{x\}$.

Based on the such models, define the truth conditions for formulas of $\mathcal{L}$ as follows:

$$M, w \models_v (t_1 = t_2) \quad \text{iff} \quad d_1 = d_2$$
$$\text{where } d_i = \begin{cases} v(t_i) & \text{if } t_i \in VAR \cup VAR_{LEX} \\ \mathcal{I}(w, t_i) & \text{if } t_i \in OBJ \\ \mathcal{I}(t_i) & \text{if } t_i \in LEX \end{cases}$$
$$M, w \models_v \varphi \wedge \psi \quad \text{iff} \quad M, w \models_v \varphi \text{ and } M, w \models_v \psi$$
$$M, w \models_v \neg\varphi \quad \text{iff} \quad \text{not } M, w \models_v \varphi$$
$$M, w \models_v K_i\varphi \quad \text{iff} \quad \text{for all } w' \text{ such that } w \sim w', M, w' \models_v \varphi$$
$$M, w \models_v \forall x \varphi(x) \quad \text{iff} \quad \text{for all } x\text{-variants } v' \text{ of } v, M, w \models_{v'} \varphi(x)$$

Comments on the semantics are postponed to the ensuing section.

Logic. A sound and complete two-sorted logic for the presented semantics can be found in [15]. The logic is here denoted $\mathsf{QS5}_{(\sigma_{LEX}, \sigma_{OBJ})}$. As of now, no arguments have been provided to the effect that $\mathsf{QS5}_{(\sigma_{LEX}, \sigma_{OBJ})}$ reflects the SLC or it's properties. This is focus of the ensuing section.

4 Correlation between Conceptual Theory and Formal Model

We argue that $\mathsf{QS5}_{(\sigma_{LEX}, \sigma_{OBJ})}$ represent the structure and properties of the SLC in two steps. First, it is shown by model-theoretic considerations that the logic, albeit indirectly, represent the ontologies of the SLC. Secondly, it is shown that the model can express the three competence types and that the dissociation properties are preserved in the logic. Before moving on to the latter, the interpretation of the function symbol μ as a *Millian meaning function* is presented.

4.1 Ontologies

The two sets of external objects and external words are easy to identify in the semantic structure. The external objects constitute the sub-domain *Obj*, and are denoted in the syntax by the terms TER_{OBJ}, when these occur outside the scope of an operator. External words (proper names) constitute the sub-domain *Nam* denoted by the terms TER_{LEX}, when occurring outside the scope of an operator.

The word lexicon and the semantic lexicon are harder to identify. The strategy is to extract a suitable notion from the already defined semantic structure. These constructs will not be utilized explicitly later on, but are included in order to validate the correctness of the modeling. To bite the bullet, we commence with the more complicated semantic lexicon.

Semantic Lexicon. No corresponding notion to the semantic lexicon have been defined so far, but it may be extrapolated from the introduced formalism. In order to include a befitting notion, define an *object indistinguishability relation* $\sim_w^a$:

$$d \sim_w^a d' \text{ iff } \exists w' \sim w : \mathcal{I}(a, w) = d \text{ and } \mathcal{I}(a, w') = d'.$$

and from this define the agent's *individual concept class for a at w* by

$$C_w^a(d) = \{d' : d \sim_w^a d'\}.$$

The semantic lexicon of agent i may then be defined as the collection of non-empty concept classes: $\mathsf{SL}_i = \{C_w^a(d) : C_w^a(d) \neq \emptyset\}$.

The set $C_w^a(d)$ consists of the objects indistinguishable to the agent by a from object d in the part of the given model connected to w by $\sim$. As an example, consider a scenario with two cups (d and d' from Obj) upside down on a table, where one cup conceals a ball. Let a denote the cup containing the ball, say d, so $\mathcal{I}(a, w) = d$. If the agent is not informed as to which of the two cups contain the ball, there will be an alternative w' to w such that $\mathcal{I}(a, w') = d'$. Hence, $d \sim_w^a d'$ so $d' \in C_w^a(d)$. The interpretation is that the agent cannot tell cups d and d' apart *with respect to which conceals the ball*.[6]

It is worth noting the object indistinguishability relation is *not* an equivalence relation, though this would fit nicely with the S5 interpretation of knowledge. The lack of equivalence can be seen from the fact that $\sim_w^a$ is not guaranteed to be reflexive as possibly $\mathcal{I}(a, w) \neq d$ for all w.

Properties of such defined individual concepts can be expressed in $\mathcal{L}$. In particular, it is the case that

$$M, w \models_v \hat{K}_i(a = b) \text{ iff } \mathcal{I}(b, w') \in C_w^a(\mathcal{I}(a, w)),$$

i.e. agent i finds it possible that a and b are the same object iff b belongs to i's individual concept for a. Further,

$$M, w \models_v K_i(a = b) \text{ implies } C_w^a(\mathcal{I}(a, w)) = C_w^b(\mathcal{I}(b, w)),$$

i.e. if agent i knows two objects to be the same, then the their individual concept classes are identical. Finally, it is guaranteed that

$$|C_w^a(d)| = 1 \text{ iff } M, w \models_v \exists x K_i(x = a), \tag{1}$$

i.e. the agents has a singleton concept of a in w iff it is the case that the agent *knows which object a is*, in the reading of [4,6,7]. The intuition behind this reading is that the satisfaction of the *de re* formula $\exists x K_i(x = a)$ requires that the interpretation of a is constant across i's epistemic alternatives. Hence, there is no uncertainty for i with respect to which object a is, and i is therefore able to identify a. Using a contingent identity system for objects, i.e. giving these a non-rigid interpretation as done in the semantics above, results in the invalidity

---

[6] Though the agent may be able to tell them apart with respect to their color or position.

of both $(a = b) \rightarrow K_i(a = b)$ and $(a = b) \rightarrow \exists x K_i(x = b)$. Hence, agent i does *not* by default know object identities, and neither is the agent able to *identify* objects by default – as in the example above.

Word Lexicon. A suitable representation of the word lexicon is simpler to extract than for the semantic lexicon. This is due to the non-world relative interpretation of name constants $n \in LEX$, which so far has gone without comment. The interpretation function $\mathcal{I}$ of the name constants is defined constant in order ensure that the agent is *syntactically competent*. From the definition of $\mathcal{I}$, it follows that $(n_1 = n_2) \rightarrow K_i(n_1 = n_2)$ is valid on the defined class of models. This corresponds formally to the incontingent identity system used in [8]. The interpretation is that whenever the agent is presented by two name tokens of the same type of name, the agent knows that these are tokens of the same name type. The assumptions is adopted as the patients reviewed in [12] are able to recognize the words utilized.

Notice that identity statements such as $(n_1 = n_2)$ *do not* convey any information regarding the *meaning* of the names. Rather, they express identity of the two *signs*. Hence, the identity '*London = London*' is true, where as the identity '*London = Londres*' is false – as the two first occurrences of '*London*' are two tokens (e.g. $n_1, n_2 \in LEX$) of the same type (the type being $\dot{n} \in Nam$), whereas '*London*' and '*Londres*' are occurrences of two different name types, albeit with the same meaning.

Due to the simpler definition of $\mathcal{I}$ for name constants, we can define i's *name class* for n directly. Where $\dot{n} \in Nam$ and $n \in LEX$ this is the set $C_i^n(\dot{n}) = \{\dot{n}' : \mathcal{I}(n) = \dot{n}'\}$. The word lexicon of i is then the collection of such sets: $\mathsf{WL}_i = \{C_i^n(\dot{n}) : n \in LEX\}$. Each name class is a singleton equivalence class, and WL_i is a partition of Nam. Further, (1) (if suitably modified) holds also for name classes, and the construction of WL_i therefore fits nicely with the assumption of syntactic competence.

4.2   Interlude: Giving Words Meaning

In order to investigate the theory of Millian meaning, this theory must be embedded in the formal framework. This is simple due to the simplicity of the Millian theory: all it takes is for each name to be assigned a referent. To this effect we have in $\mathcal{L}$ included the function symbol μ. This is interpreted as a Millian meaning function. A function rather than a relation is used as only proper names are included in the agent's language, and for these to have unambiguous meanings, the function requirement is natural. Given it's defined arity, μ assigns a term from TER_{OBJ} to each term in TER_{LEX}. From the viewpoints of the agents, μ hence assigns an object to each name.

On the semantic level, we take $M, w \models_v (\mu(n) = a)$ to state that the meaning/referent of name n is the object a in the actual world w. The reference map is defined *world relatively*, i.e. the value $\mu(n)$ for $n \in LEX$, can change from world to world. This is the result of the world relative interpretation of μ given in the semantics above. Hence, *names are assigned values relative to epistemic alternatives*.

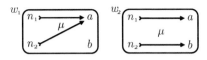

Fig. 2. The meaning function μ is defined world relatively, so meaning of a name may shift across epistemic alternatives

Two points need to be addressed here. One is the rigidity of names thus construed, and the other is knowledge of the reference of a name. With respect to the rigidity of the names in the present model, then they are indeed rigid, for they *do* refer to the same object in *every metaphysically possible world*. Note here, that it may be the case that the only metaphysically possible world included in the model is the actual world w, as all other elements of W are epistemic alternatives to w. All such epistemic alternatives may be metaphysically impossible under the assumption that names are *rigid designators*, cf. [11]. The epistemic alternatives can deviate from the actual world in any *logically possible way*[7]. This implies that *the meaning function is not by default known to the agents*. They may fail to know what object a given name refers to. On the other hand, the present modeling does not preclude such knowledge from being possible.

4.3   Competence Types

Inferential Competence. With respect to inferential competence, the present model is rather limited in the features expressible. This is a direct consequence of the simplifying assumptions. In particular, the limitation to proper names in the word lexicon limits the types of inferential competence to knowing relations between referring names, and thus precludes inferential knowledge regarding names and verbs. As an example, one cannot express that the agent knows the true sentence 'name is planet' as the word lexicon does not contain an entry for the verb 'is' nor for the predicate. As a result, it cannot be expressed, e.g., that an agent has the knowledge appropriate to retrieve a word from it's definition.

We are, however, able to express one feature of inferential competence important for the analysis of the Fregean argument, namely *knowledge of co-reference*:

$$K_i(\mu(n) = \mu(n')). \tag{2}$$

(2) states that i knows that n and n' mean the same, i.e., that the two names are Millian synonyms.

Based on (2), we may define that agent i is *generally inferentially competent with respect to* n by

$$M, w \models_v \forall \dot{x}((\mu(n) = \mu(\dot{x})) \rightarrow K_i(\mu(n) = \mu(\dot{x}))) \tag{3}$$

---

[7] Based on the present axiom system.

where $\dot{x} \in VAR_{LEX}$. If (3) is satisfied for all names n, agent i will have full 'encyclopedic' knowledge of the singular terms of her language. Alone, this will however be 'Chinese room style' knowledge, as it does not imply that the agent can apply any names, nor that the agent can name any objects.

Referential Competence. Regarding referential competence, recall that this compromises two distinct relations between names and objects, relating these through the semantic lexicon. The two relations are *application* and *naming*. An agent can *apply a name* if, when presented with a name, the agent can identify the appropriate referent. This ability can be expressed of the agent with respect to name n in w by

$$M, w \models_v \exists x K_i(\mu(n) = x) \tag{4}$$

i.e. there is an object which the agent can identify as being the referent of n. Given the assumption of syntactical competence, there is no uncertainty regarding which name is presented. Since the existential quantifier has scope over the knowledge operator, the interpretation of $\mu(n)$ is fixed across epistemic alternatives, and i thus knows which object n refers to.

To be able to *name an object*, the agent is required to be able to produce a correct name when presented with an object, say a. For this purpose, the *de re* formula $\exists \dot{x} K_i(\mu(\dot{x}) = a)$ is insufficient as $\mu(\dot{x})$ and a may simply co-vary across states. This means that i will be guessing *about which object is to be named*, and may therefore answer incorrectly. Since there may in this way be uncertainty regarding the presented object, naming must include a requirement that i can identify a, as well as know a name for a. This is captured by

$$M, w \models_v \exists x \exists \dot{x} K_i((x = a) \wedge (\mu(\dot{x}) = a)). \tag{5}$$

Here, the object quantification and first conjunction ensures that i can identify the presented object a and the second conjunct ensures that the name refers to a in all epistemic alternatives.

Dissociations. As mentioned, inferential competence and naming are dissociated. This is preserved in the model in that neither (2) nor (3) alone imply (5). Nor does (5) alone imply either of the two. The dissociation of application from naming is also preserved, as (4) does not alone entail (5). That application does not imply naming is illustrated in Figure 3.

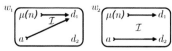

Fig. 3. Application and naming are not correlated. In actual world w_1, n refers to a and i can correctly apply n, but cannot name a using n: $w_1 \models_v (\mu(n) = a) \wedge \exists x K_i(\mu(n) = x)$, but $w_1 \models_v \neg \exists x \exists \dot{x} K_i((x = a) \wedge (\mu(\dot{x}) = a))$. Here, i cannot name a due to an ambiguous concept. a may be either of d_1 or d_2, and can therefore not be identified precisely enough to ensure a correct answer.

Whether application entails inferential competence, and whether naming entails application is not discussed in [12]. In the present model, however, these are modeled as dissociated in the sense that (4) does not entail, nor is entailed by, either (3) or (5). However, the modeled dissociations are *single instances* of the various abilities. Once more instances are regarded simultaneously, implicational relationships arise, as will be utilized in the analysis of the Fregean argument below.

A Weak Competence: Correlation. A further, albeit very weak, competence type can be found in the formal framework. This type emerges when the agent is able to correlate a name with an entry in the semantic lexicon, but where the latter is not an unambiguous concept. The ability is given by

$$M, w \models_v K_i \left(\mu \left(n \right) = a \right) \tag{6}$$

Here, the agent knows that the referent of the name n is co-extensional with i's concept a, but may be unable to identify which object a in fact is. We will refer to this ability as *correlation*.

4.4   Default Properties

To familiarize the reader with the class of models defined, a few properties are worth noting. First, we note that

$$K_i \forall x \exists \dot{x} (\mu(\dot{x}) = x) \tag{7}$$

stating that agent i knows of every object that it is named, is invalid on the set of models defined. This follows as we have not assumed μ surjective. Permuting the quantifiers results in the validity

$$K_i \forall \dot{x} \exists x (\mu(\dot{x}) = x) \tag{8}$$

capturing the idea that i knows that all names refer. In regard to [12], the validity of (8) is preferable, as non-denoting names where not used in the case-studies. Though i knows that all names refer, it is not assumed that the agent knows *what they refer to*. Hence,

$$\forall \dot{x} \exists x K_i (\mu(\dot{x}) = x) \tag{9}$$

is invalid on the set of models. This is natural as competence types are made as substantial assumptions.

5   Reviewing Frege's Puzzle

We now return to the argument presented in the introduction. Recall that where (a) is the identity statement 'Hesperus is Hesperus' and (b) is 'Hesperus is Phosphorus', the Fregean argument can be given the following structure:

(A) (a) and (b) mean the same.

(A→B) If (a) and (b) mean the same, then a semantically competent speaker would know that (a) and (b) mean the same.

(B→C) If a semantically competent speaker would know that (a) and (b) mean the same, then they are equally informative to the speaker.

(¬C) (a) and (b) differ in informativeness to the competent speaker.

∴ Contradiction.

The four premises are jointly inconsistent, and, as was mentioned, the typical textbook choice is to reject the premise (A).

Given the formal machinery introduced, it is now possible to evaluate this argument in a formal setting. The strategy used to evaluate the argument is to assume that the initial premise (A) is satisfied at actual word w in a model M, while also assuming that the agent is semantically competent, in each of three relevant ways. This results in three different versions of the argument: one for inferential competence, one for application and one for correlation. In the first two cases, the assumptions lead to satisfied versions of the premises (A→B) and (B→C), while making it clear why the 'intuitive' premise (¬C) should be rejected in these cases. In the final case, (¬C) cannot be rejected. However, due to the weak competence type used, the argument does not result in a contradiction, why it does not force the abandonment of Millianism.

Due to the restriction to a first-order language, it is not possible to properly represent the first premise, namely that the identity statements (a) and (b) mean the same. A proper representation would amount to something like

$$\mu(n \simeq n) \leftrightarrow \mu(n \simeq n') \tag{10}$$

where '$\simeq$' represents the word 'is' from the agent's language. Since this is not possible in $\mathcal{L}$, it is assumed that the first premise is natural language-equivalent with '(The meaning of 'Hesperus' is identical to the meaning of 'Hesperus') is equivalent with (The meaning of 'Hesperus' is identical to the meaning of 'Phosphorus')'. Under this assumption, the first premise may be represented by

$$(\mu(n) = \mu(n)) \leftrightarrow (\mu(n) = \mu(n')). \tag{11}$$

Since the left-hand identity is a validity, the first premise only amounts to the assumption that the actual world w in model M satisfies

$$(\mu(n) = \mu(n')). \tag{12}$$

The second premise is that (12) implies that any competent speaker knows that $(\mu(n) = \mu(n)) \leftrightarrow (\mu(n) = \mu(n'))$. The truth of this premise depends on the type of competence meant. The last three premises of the argument will be run through using inferential competence, application and correlation. The ability to name objects is not relevant for the present.

5.1   Inferential Competence

Casting the argument in terms of inferential competence, the second premise states that if n and n' mean the same, i.e. that (12) is satisfied, and agent i is inferential competent with respect to the two names, then agent i would know that n and n' mean the same. Recall that i is generally inferentially competent with respect to n iff

$$\forall \dot{x}((\mu(n) = \mu(\dot{x})) \rightarrow K_i(\mu(n) = \mu(\dot{x}))) \tag{13}$$

The antecedent of the second premise for inferential competence therefore becomes the conjunction of (12) and (13), and the consequent that (12) is known by i, i.e. that

$$K_i(\mu(n) = \mu(n')). \tag{14}$$

The full resulting second premise, that the conjunction of (12) and (13) imply (14), is a validity in relation to the semantics defined. By the initial assumption that (12) is satisfied, it therefore follows that

$$M, w \models_v K_i(\mu(n) = \mu(n')). \tag{15}$$

The third premise states that (14) implies that the two identity statements are equally informative to the agent. 'Equally informative' is here taken to mean that the two statements would eliminate the same worlds from agent i's model *if truthfully announced to the agent*, in the sense of [18]. As $(\mu(n) = \mu(n))$ is a validity, it eliminates no worlds, so the third premise can be reduced to (15) implying that

$$\neg \exists w' \sim_i w : M, w' \models_v \neg(\mu(n) = \mu(n')). \tag{16}$$

That no $\neg(\mu(n) = \mu(n'))$ world exists follows directly from (15) and the semantics of the K_i operator. Hence this premise holds true as well.

This is not the case with the last premise, namely that the identity statements should *not* be equally informative, i.e. that

$$\exists w' \sim_i w : M, w' \models_v \neg(\mu(n) = \mu(n')). \tag{17}$$

This premise is false as a consequence of the assumption of Millianism and agent i's inferential competence with respect to n and n'. However, that the agent will not be informed by the identity statement does not seem all that counter-intuitive *given the assumption of inferential competence*. The inferential competence of agent i is constituted by i's ability to find synonyms when prompted with names. As this is a knowledge-based ability, the knowledge that the identity statement is supposed to provide is already assumed to be possessed by the agent.

In short, if we stick with Millian meaning and assume agent i inferentially competent, i does not learn anything new by being told that the two names co-refer because this was assumed to be already known by i. This conclusion seems far from puzzling. In particular, it does not seem paradoxical enough (if at all) to warrant a rejection of the Millian view.

5.2   Referential Competence: Application

Turning to the argument utilizing application as the relevant competence type, the assumption that agent i is semantically competent with respect to n and n' results in the assumption that i can apply both names. Recall that i can apply the name n at w iff $M, w \models_v \exists x K_i(\mu(n) = x)$, i.e., there is an object which i can identify as being the referent of n.

With the assumption that i can apply both n and n' in the antecedent, the second premise is captured by

$$(\mu(n) = \mu(n')) \wedge \exists x K_i(\mu(n) = x) \wedge \exists y K_i(\mu(n') = y) \rightarrow K_i(\mu(n) = \mu(n')). \quad (18)$$

The formula (18) is valid on the class of models defined, and is therefore also satisfied at w in M. As the antecedent is assumed satisfied, the consequent (B) from the second premise will, as in the previous case, follow. I.e., it is concluded that $M, w \models_v K_i(\mu(n) = \mu(n'))$.

The third premise can be formulated as it was in the previous case, and given that $M, w \models_v K_i(\mu(n) = \mu(n'))$ holds, it will again follow that the agent will not be informed by the identity statement, i.e. that the statement eliminates no worlds: $\neg \exists w' \sim_i w : M, w' \models_v \neg(\mu(n) = \mu(n'))$.

Hence, if one assumes that n and n' co-refer, and that the agent is able to apply both of these names, then one is forced to reject the the premise $(\neg C)$, that the agent will be informed.

Yet, one may still feel that this argument does not provide ample reason to give up the intuitions behind $(\neg C)$. In particular, one may object to the validity of (18). One argument can be based on exactly on the case involving Hesperus and Phosphorus. One could easily envision an agent able to identify Venus as the referent of 'Hesperus' in the evening and as the referent of 'Phosphorus' in the morning, while still being unaware that these two names co-refer. Exactly this objection is raised in [15], where it is argued that the objection contains an appeal to *contexts* not captured in the present models. However, if contexts are added to the formal setting and suitable, context-dependent competence types are defined, the objection can be avoided, cf. [15, ch. 7].

In the present work, the model is only constructed to deal with the mono-context case, fitting, e.g., the interview scenarios used when testing the linguistic abilities of various brain injured subjects. Within the same context, the validity of (18) is easy to justify. Assume a person in the presence of a number of items is given a name of one of them, and successfully applies the name, i.e., successfully identifies the object to which the name refers, using his knowledge-based identification skills regarding that name and object. The task performed to identify the proper object could for example be to place a note with the name on the object. Assume the same task is repeated with the same successful outcome, but a different name referring to the same object. Given suitable assumptions regarding short-term memory and minimal deductive abilities, the agent should now know that the two names refer to the same object. In fact, this should not be much harder for the agent than to realize that the two notes just placed are stuck on the same object.

To summarize, if we stick with Millian meaning and assume that the agent can identify both referents, then she does not learn anything new by being told that the two names co-refer. Further, that the agent is not informed is a natural consequence of the assumptions made regarding the agent's semantic competence. Therefore, the intuitively correct premise ($\neg$C) should be rejected.

5.3   Weak Competence: Correlation

For the third version of the argument, we turn to a weaker notion of semantic competence, namely correlation. Running through the argument using this weaker ability, the second premise becomes

$$K_i(\mu(n) = a) \wedge K_i(\mu(n') = b) \rightarrow K_i(\mu(n) = \mu(n')) \tag{19}$$

This formula is satisfiable, but not valid in the defined class of models. This means that $M, w \models_v K_i(\mu(n) = \mu(n'))$ will be true or false depending on the specific model. In case the consequent of (19) is satisfied, the agent will have knowledge of co-reference, and it will, like above, not be surprising that he is not informed by the identity statement.

In case the consequent fails, a new situation arises. In particular, this will imply that (16) likewise fails to be the true. From this it follows that the premise ($\neg$C)

$$\exists w' \sim_i w : M, w' \models_v \neg(\mu(n) = \mu(n'))$$

now holds, as opposed to the above cases. This in turn means that the agent *will* be informed by the identity statement. If a truthful announcement of the identity statement is made to the agent, any w' as specified in (17) can be eliminated, and the agent will thereby gain information.

By the truthful announcement, the agent is informed on both an *inferential* and a *conceptual* level. First, the agent will after the announcement have knowledge of co-reference with respect to the two names. Secondly, where the agent before had two distinct concepts, the agent's concepts of a and b will after the announcement have merged.

However, given the weaker notion of competence, that the agent is informed does not conflict with the assumption of Millian meaning of proper names. To see this, notice that the two premises (A→B) and (B→C) from the argument above are false when assuming this weaker form of semantic competence. As a result, the problematic contradiction no longer follows, and Millianism and the requirement that the agent should be informed by the identity statement can therefore be unified.

To sum up, neither of the three arguments provide a strong basis for rejecting Millianism. If inferential competence is assumed, then the knowledge supposedly provided by the identity statement is directly assumed already. If the agent is supposed to be able to apply both names, it should also be able to deduce that the names denote the same object, why the identity statement will not be informative. Finally, if one assumes that the agent is weakly competent enough to be informed, the contradiction problematic for the Millian cannot be derived.

6   Conclusions and Further Perspectives

The theory of lexical competence from [12] has been modeled, and the key elements of the structure preserved. In the model, the three types of lexical competence proposed in [12] were identified along with a fourth which had not been considered in the original text. When regarding Frege's Puzzle in a formal setting using the relevant types of competence, it was seen that each argument was far from all being as decisive against Millianism as has been the mainstream assumption in 20th century philosophy of language.

One issue for further research would be to investigate whether light can be thrown on other puzzles from the philosophy of language by focusing on the epistemic states of the language user, rather than on semantic theories of the language. It would further be interesting to investigate the model in more details, and compare this to newer literature from cognitive neuropsychology. One could suspect that a more fine grained view of semantic competence was required. One obvious way to gain such would be to use weaker operators like those presented in [1]. Using weaker modalities to model semantic competence could possibly result in levels where individual concepts contain no existing objects. This could possibly shed light on problems of reference to non-existing objects. Finally, a logic of language is not much fun in the mono-agent case. In order to investigate how lacking semantic competence influences communication and action in multi-agent settings, it would be interesting to move to a dynamic framework.

References

1. Baltag, A., Smets, S.: A Qualitative Theory of Dynamic Interactive Belief Revision. In: LOFT7, pp. 11–58. Amsterdam University Press (2008)
2. Collin, F., Guldmann, F.: Meaning, Use and Thruth. Automatic Press/VIP (2010)
3. Devitt, M., Sterelny, K.: Language and Reality: An Introduction to the Philosophy of Language, 2nd edn. Blackwell Publishers (1999)
4. Fagin, R., Halpern, J.Y., Moses, Y., Vardi, M.Y.: Reasoning about Knowledge. The MIT Press (1995)
5. Hillis, A.E.: The Organization of the Lexical System. In: Rapp, B. (ed.) The Handbook of Cognitive Neuropsychology, pp. 185–210. Psychology Press (2001)
6. Hintikka, J.: Knowledge and Belief: An Introduction to the Logic of the Two Notions. Cornell University Press (1962); Reprinted in 2005, prepared by Hendricks, V.F., Symons, J., King's College Publications
7. Hintikka, J.: Different Constructions in Terms of 'Knows'. In: Dancy, J., Sosa, E. (eds.) A Companion to Epistemology. Wiley-Blackwell (1994)
8. Hughes, G.E., Cresswell, M.J.: A New Introduction to Modal Logic. Routledge (1996)
9. Lycan, W.G.: Semantic Competence, Funny Factors and Truth-Conditions. In: Modality and Meaning. Springer (1994)
10. Lycan, W.G.: Philosophy of Language: a contemporary introduction. Routledge (2000)
11. Lycan, W.G.: Names. In: Devitt, M., Hanley, R. (eds.) The Blackwell Guide to The Philosophy of Language. Blackwell Publishing (2006)

12. Marconi, D.: Lexical Competence. The MIT Press, Cambridge (1997)
13. Rapp, B., Folk, J.R., Tainturier, M.-J.: Word Reading. In: Rapp, B. (ed.) The Handbook of Cognitive Neuropsychology, pp. 233–262. Psychology Press (2001)
14. Rast, E.H.: Reference & Indexicality. PhD thesis, Section for Philosophy and Science Studies, Roskilde University (2006)
15. Rendsvig, R.K.: Towards a Theory of Semantic Competence. Master's thesis, Roskilde University (2011), http://rudar.ruc.dk/handle/1800/6874
16. Soames, S.: Semantics and Semantic Competence. Philosophical Perspectives 3, 575–596 (1989)
17. Tainturier, M.-J., Rapp, B.: The Spelling Process. In: Rapp, B. (ed.) The Handbook of Cognitive Neuropsychology, pp. 263–290. Psychology Press (2001)
18. van Ditmarsch, H., van der Hoek, W., Kooi, B.: Dynamic Epistemic Logic. Springer (2008)

Comparing Inconsistency Resolutions
in Multi-Context Systems

Antonius Weinzierl*

Knowledge-Based Systems Group,
Vienna University of Technology
weinzierl@kr.tuwien.ac.at

Abstract. Inconsistency in heterogeneous knowledge-integration systems with non-monotonic information exchange is a major concern as it renders systems useless at its occurrence. For the knowledge-integration framework of Multi-Context Systems, the problem of finding all possible resolutions to inconsistency has been addressed previously and some basic steps have been proposed to find most preferred resolutions. Here, we refine the techniques of finding preferred resolutions of inconsistency in two directions. First, we extend available qualitative methods using domain knowledge on the intention and category of information exchange to minimize the number of categories that are affected by a resolution. Second, we present a quantitative inconsistency measure for inconsistency resolutions, being suitable for scenarios where no further domain knowledge is available.

1 Introduction

Knowledge integration frameworks are essential for combining information from different knowledge bases. Multi-Context Systems (MCSs) introduced in [2] are a powerful framework for non-monotonic information exchange between heterogeneous knowledge bases. They extend MultiLanguage systems of [11] by allowing non-monotonic information exchange. Information in the MCS framework is exchanged via bridge rules of the form

$$(k : s) \leftarrow (c_1 : p_1), \ldots, (c_j : p_j), \textbf{not } (c_{j+1} : p_{j+1}), \ldots, \textbf{not } (c_m : p_m)$$

which states that information s is added to knowledge base k whenever information p_i is present in knowledge base c_i (for $1 \leq i \leq j$) and information p_l is not present in knowledge base p_l (for $j < l \leq m$).

In this work we advance and refine previously introduced methods of finding preferred resolutions to inconsistency in MCSs (cf. [6] and [7]). Inconsistency is of major interest as it can render logic-based systems useless and it occurs easily due to unanticipated side effects of the information exchange established by bridge rules. Therefore we consider faulty information exchange, i.e., bridge

---

* This work has been funded by the Vienna Science and Technology Fund (WWTF) through project ICT 08-020.

D. Lassiter and M. Slavkovik (Eds.): ESSLLI Student Sessions, LNCS 7415, pp. 158–174, 2012.

rules, as reasons of inconsistency. Several strategies to cope with inconsistency have been developed. For example, para-consistent reasoning (cf. [5]), where inconsistency is often treated purely technically, i.e., no knowledge from the application domain is taken into account to find out whether one resolution of inconsistency is better than another. For real applications this might not be acceptable as inconsistencies have to be resolved respecting additional domain knowledge.

Consider the case of an MCS employed in a hospital to give decision-support on patient medication in addition to handling the billing process. Assume there is a patient needing a certain medication, say human insulin, because she has severe hyperglycemia (high blood sugar) and she is allergic to the alternative, say animal insulin. If the billing system refuses treatment with human insulin, because the patient's medical insurance does not cover this type of insulin, then the system becomes inconsistent. There are several resolutions of that inconsistency, either modify the information flow to the billing system or ignore the patient's needs and treat her with the wrong medication. Technically both resolutions are fine, but the patient may feel different.

Following common terminology, we call the resolution to inconsistency a diagnosis. In [7] the problem of finding preferred diagnoses is addressed in general by specifying general ways to compare diagnoses using domain knowledge, and defining a quantitative inconsistency value for bridge rules as a first step towards an inconsistency measure for diagnoses. We advance this work by:

a) introducing a preference relation on diagnoses using domain knowledge on the intention of bridge rules. We categorize bridge rules by their intention, e.g. rules that exchange information about medication make up the category of "treatment", while "billing" is another category in our above example. Furthermore, dependencies between categories are used to capture that modifications to bridge rules of one category may influence the results of another category. Preferred diagnoses then are those diagnoses that modify a least amount of categories.

b) extending the quantitative inconsistency value from bridge rules to diagnoses. We introduce a measure on diagnoses, show some of its properties, and discuss another alternative.

Thus the achievements of this paper are twofold.

 – First, the proposal of a concrete, qualitative method to resolve inconsistencies based on domain knowledge, which uses information that is (at least implicitly) present for every system.
 – Second, the introduction of a quantitative measure for selection of preferred diagnoses, which can be applied even if no domain knowledge is given.

The remainder of this paper is organized as follows: Section 2 defines MCSs and diagnoses, Section 3 introduces bridge rule categorization and a comparison relation for diagnoses based on this categorization, Section 4 defines a quantitative measure of inconsistency on diagnoses, and in Section 5 we conclude and discuss related and future work.

2   Preliminaries

A heterogeneous non-monotonic Multi-Context System [2] consists of *contexts*, each composed of a knowledge base with an underlying *logic*, and a set of *bridge rules*, which control the information flow between contexts.

Definition 1. *A logic* $L = (\mathbf{KB}_L, \mathbf{BS}_L, \mathbf{ACC}_L)$ *consists, in an abstract view, of the following components:*

- $\mathbf{KB}_L$ *is the set of well-formed knowledge bases of* L*, where each element* $kb \in \mathbf{KB}_L$ *is a set. Intuitively, the elements of kb are the "formulas" of the knowledge base, but for generality, they are not further restricted.*
- $\mathbf{BS}_L$ *is the set of possible belief sets, where the elements of a belief set are "theorems" possibly accepted under a knowledge base.*
- $\mathbf{ACC}_L : \mathbf{KB}_L \to 2^{\mathbf{BS}_L}$ *is a function describing the "semantics" of the logic by assigning to each knowledge base a set of acceptable belief sets.*

This concept of a *logic* captures many monotonic and non-monotonic logics, e.g., classical logic, description logics, modal, default, and autoepistemic logics, circumscription, and logic programs under the answer set semantics.

Example 1. To capture propositional logic, let Σ be an alphabet of non-logical symbols. For a boolean interpretation (valuation) $V : \Sigma \to \{t, f\}$ we identify each subset L of Σ with the interpretation $V(a) = t$ iff $a \in L$. Propositional logic then is represented by $L = (\mathbf{KB}, \mathbf{BS}, \mathbf{ACC})$ where

- **KB** is the powerset of well-formed propositional formulas over Σ using connectives $\wedge, \vee, \neg, \to$. Therefore each $kb \in \mathbf{KB}$ is a set of well-formed Σ-formulas.
- **BS** is the set of sets of atoms over Σ, so $\mathbf{BS} = 2^{\Sigma}$. Therefore each $bs \in \mathbf{BS}$ corresponds to an interpretation.
- **ACC** maps a set of well-formed Σ-formulas to its models, i.e., $\mathbf{ACC}(kb) = \{L \in \mathbf{BS} \mid L \models kb\}$ where the $\models$-relation is defined in the usual way.

Note that, although, a logic can formally rely on infinite sets, there usually are finite representations and algorithms to evaluate such a logic in finite time, i.e., for evaluation we usually do not need to rely on an explicit representation of the above sets.

For simplicity we will only use one kind of abstract logic in the examples throughout this work, namely disjunctive answer-set programs (ASP), whose formal definition is given by the following example.

Example 2. For a logic capturing answer set programs, $L_{ASP} = (\mathbf{KB}, \mathbf{BS}, \mathbf{ACC})$ over a signature Σ:

- **KB** is the set of normal disjunctive logic programs over Σ: Let $a_1, \ldots, a_n$, $b_1, \ldots, b_m \in \Sigma$, then a rule is defined as

$$a_1 \vee \ldots \vee a_n \leftarrow b_1, \ldots, b_i, not\, b_{i+1}, \ldots, not\, b_m$$

where where either n or m may be 0. A logic program is a set of rules and each $kb \in \mathbf{KB}$ is a logic program.

- **BS** is the set of Herbrand interpretations over Σ, i.e, each $bs \in \mathbf{BS}$ is a set of atoms from Σ.
- **ACC** maps a logic program kb to its answer sets. Let $P \in \mathbf{KB}$ be a logic program and $T \in \mathbf{BS}$ be an interpretation, then $T^P = \{r \in P \mid T \models r\}$ is the FLP-reduct (cf. [9]) of P wrt. T. Now $bs \in \mathbf{BS}$ is an answer set, i.e., $bs \in \mathbf{ACC}(kb)$, iff bs is the minimal model (under classical semantics) of bs^{kb}.

A more detailed introduction to ASP is available in [8]. Note that the original ASP semantics is based on the GL-reduct (cf. [14]), while we use the FLP-reduct above. This is because both notions coincide on the above notion of logic program.

Information exchange in an MCS is specified by *bridge rules*, where a *bridge rule* can add information to a context, depending on the belief sets which are accepted at other contexts. Let $L = (L_1, \ldots, L_n)$ be a sequence of logics. An L_k-bridge rule r over L is of the form

$$(k : s) \leftarrow (c_1 : p_1), \ldots, (c_j : p_j), \mathbf{not}\ (c_{j+1} : p_{j+1}), \ldots, \mathbf{not}\ (c_m : p_m) \quad (1)$$

which state that information s is added to knowledge base k whenever information p_i is present in knowledge base c_i (for $1 \leq i \leq j$) and information p_l is not present in knowledge base p_l (for $j < l \leq m$).

We denote by $head(r)$ the head $(k : s)$ of r and by $hd_b(r)$ the belief formula s in $head(r)$. Furthermore, $uncond(r)$ denotes the bridge rule stemming from r by removing all elements in its body, i.e., $uncond(r)$ is $(k : s) \leftarrow .$ and for a set of bridge rules R, $uncond(R) = \bigcup_{r \in R} uncond(r)$.

Definition 2. *A Multi-Context System $M = (C_1, \ldots, C_n)$ is a collection of contexts $C_i = (L_i, kb_i, br_i)$, $1 \leq i \leq n$, where*

- $L_i = (\mathbf{KB}_i, \mathbf{BS}_i, \mathbf{ACC}_i)$ *is a logic,*
- $kb_i \in \mathbf{KB}_i$ *a knowledge base, and*
- br_i *is a set of L_i-bridge rules over $(L_1, \ldots, L_n)$.*

Furthermore, for each $H \subseteq \{hd_b(r) \mid r \in br_i\}$ holds that $kb_i \cup H \in \mathbf{KB}_{L_i}$, i.e., bridge rule heads are compatible with knowledge bases.

Example 3. Let M be an MCS handling patient treatments and billing in a hospital; it contains the following contexts: a patient database C_1, a program C_2 suggesting proper medication, and a program C_3 handling the billing. Knowledge bases for these contexts are:

$$kb_1 = \{hyperglycemia.\ insurance\_B.\},$$
$$kb_2 = \{give\_human\_insulin \vee give\_animal\_insulin \leftarrow hyperglycemia.$$
$$\perp \leftarrow give\_animal\_insulin, \mathbf{not}\ allow\_animal\_insulin\}.$$
$$kb_3 = \{bill \leftarrow bill\_animal\_insulin.\ bill\_more \leftarrow bill\_human\_insulin.$$
$$\perp \leftarrow insurance\_B, bill\_more.\}$$

Context C_1 provides information that the patient has severe hyperglycemia, and her health insurance is from company B. Context C_2 suggests to apply either human or animal insulin if the patient has hyperglycemia and requires that the applied insulin does not cause an allergic reaction. Context C_3 does the billing and encodes that insurance B only pays animal insulin. Bridge rules of M are:

$$
\begin{aligned}
r_1 &= (2 : hyperglycemia) & &\leftarrow (1 : hyperglycemia). \\
r_2 &= (2 : allow\_animal\_insulin) & &\leftarrow \mathbf{not}\ (1 : allergic\_animal\_insulin). \\
r_3 &= (3 : bill\_animal\_insulin) & &\leftarrow (2 : give\_animal\_insulin). \\
r_4 &= (3 : bill\_human\_insulin) & &\leftarrow (2 : give\_human\_insulin). \\
r_5 &= (3 : insurance\_B) & &\leftarrow (1 : insurance\_B).
\end{aligned}
$$

A *belief state* of an MCS $M = (C_1, \ldots, C_n)$ is a sequence $S = (S_1, \ldots, S_n)$ such that $S_i \in \mathbf{BS}_i$. Given such a belief state S, a bridge rule r of form (1) is applicable in S, written $S \models r$, iff for all $1 \leq i \leq j$ holds $p_i \in S_i$ and for all $j < l \leq m$ holds $p_l \notin S_l$. For a set R of bridge rules, $app(R, S)$ denotes applicable bridge rules, i.e., $app(R, S) = \{r \in R \mid S \models r\}$.

Equilibrium semantics selects certain belief states of an MCS M as acceptable. Intuitively, an equilibrium is a belief state $S = (S_1, \ldots, S_n)$, where each context C_i takes the heads of all bridge rules that are applicable in S into account, and accepts S_i.

Definition 3. *A belief state* $S = (S_1, \ldots, S_n)$ *is an equilibrium of M, iff for all* $1 \leq i \leq n$:
$$
S_i \in \mathbf{ACC}_i\left(kb_i \cup \{hd_b(r) \mid r \in app(br_i, S)\}\right)
$$

Inconsistency in an MCS is the lack of an equilibrium.

Example 4. In our example, one equilibrium S exists:

$$
\begin{aligned}
S = (&\{hyperglycemia, insurance\_B\}, \\
&\{give\_animal\_insulin, allow\_animal\_insulin, hyperglycemia\}, \\
&\{bill, bill\_animal\_insulin, insurance\_B\}).
\end{aligned}
$$

Rules r_1, r_2, r_3, and r_5 are applicable in S.

Example 5. As running example, we consider a slightly modified version of Example 3, with the patient being allergic to animal insulin:

$$
kb_1 = \{allergic\_animal\_insulin, hyperglycemia, insurance\_B\}
$$

The MCS is inconsistent as r_2 becomes applicable, forcing C_2 to treat the patient with human insulin, which makes r_4 applicable and finally C_3 inconsistent.

We will use the following notation. Given an MCS M and a set R of bridge rules (compatible with M), by $M[R]$ we denote the MCS obtained from M by replacing its set of bridge rules br_M with R (e.g., $M[br_M] = M$ and $M[\emptyset]$ is M with no bridge rules). By $M \models \bot$ we denote that M has no equilibrium, i.e., that M is inconsistent, and by $M \not\models \bot$ that some equilibrium exists for M.

Diagnoses. A diagnosis identifies parts of the bridge rules that need to be changed to restore consistency. In non-monotonic reasoning, adding or removing knowledge can both cause and prevent inconsistency. Therefore, a diagnosis is a pair of sets of bridge rules such that if the rules in the first set are removed, and the rules in the second set are added in unconditional form, the MCS becomes consistent (i.e., it admits an equilibrium).

Definition 4. *Given an MCS M, a diagnosis of M is a pair (D_1, D_2) with $D_1, D_2 \subseteq br_M$ such that $M[br_M \setminus D_1 \cup uncond(D_2)] \not\models \bot$. By $D^\pm(M)$ we denote the set of all diagnoses.*

To obtain a more relevant set of diagnoses, pointwise subset-minimal diagnoses are preferred: we denote by $D_m^\pm(M)$ the set of all such diagnoses of an MCS M.

Example 6. In our running example,

$$D_m^\pm(M) = \{(\{r_1\}, \emptyset), (\{r_4\}, \emptyset), (\{r_5\}, \emptyset), (\emptyset, \{r_2\})\}.$$

Accordingly, deactivating one of r_1, r_4, r_5, or adding r_2 unconditionally, respectively, results in a consistent MCS. This means ignoring the illness of the patient, ignoring to bill human insulin, ignoring the inferior insurance, or considering the patient to be not allergic. Depending on one's values, some of those diagnoses are preferred while others are unacceptable. If the health of the patient is considered most important, then ignoring the illness or the allergy of the patient, i.e., diagnosis $(\{r_1\}, \emptyset)$ respectively $(\emptyset, \{r_2\})$, are clearly not preferred.

It is sometimes useful to restrict the scope of a diagnosis such that certain bridge rules are excluded from being modified in a diagnosis. Such protected rules are especially useful to analyze whether a diagnosis is modifying one of the remaining bridge rules. This information then can be used to reason about diagnoses within an MCS, i.e., it allows meta-reasoning on diagnoses and thus we can realize preferences over diagnoses.

Definition 5. *Let M be an MCS with protected rules $br_P \subseteq br_M$. A diagnosis excluding protected rules br_P is a diagnosis $(D_1, D_2) \in D^\pm(M)$, where $D_1, D_2 \subseteq br_M \setminus br_P$. We denote the set of all minimal such diagnoses by $D_m^\pm(M, br_P)$.*

As a direct consequence we obtain that every (minimal) diagnosis excluding protected rules is a (minimal) diagnosis, i.e., let M be an inconsistent MCS with protected rules br_P, then $D_{(m)}^\pm(M, br_P) \subseteq D_{(m)}^\pm(M)$.

3   Assessment with Categories

In this section we introduce categories as a method to compare diagnoses on qualitative terms. Intuitively, a category is a non-empty set of bridge rules which together ensure that the information flow about some entity is correct. For example, the bridge rules r_1 and r_2 of our running example convey necessary information about the patients condition, i.e., her illness and her allergy. Information about only one of these two leads to wrong conclusions and might be dangerous, e.g., if a diagnosis makes r_2 unconditional then the patient is given animal insulin, risking an allergic reaction. Thus it intuitively is better to not conclude anything about the patient than making wrong and dangerous conclusions.

For the realization of preference based on categories, we rely on preference orders as defined in [7], i.e., partial orders over diagnoses. Preference orders allow to compare diagnoses in general, based on the rules they modify. This covers statements like "proper treatment of patients is more important than correct billing", trust relations, or any other preference relation over diagnoses.

Definition 6 (cf. [7]). *Let M be an MCS, a preference order for M is a transitive binary relation $\preceq$ on elements of $2^{br_M} \times 2^{br_M}$.*

As usual, we write $\prec$ to denote the irreflexive version of $\preceq$.

In logic programming a rule by itself often is not useful, but only several rules together form a specific behaviour and cover an intended meaning. As syntax and semantics of bridge rules is inspired by logic programming rules, we assume that the same will also hold for bridge rules.

Example 7. In the running example, rules r_1 and r_2 carry the information of how to treat the patient correctly, while rules r_3, r_4, and r_5 carry information for accounting and billing. So one can identify two "types" or "categories" of bridge rules, e.g., "treatment" for r_1, r_2 and "billing" for r_3, r_4, r_5.

Category names in general are arbitrary, including the possibility of a syntactic derivation from the MCS, e.g., by a partitioning of beliefs.

Definition 7. *Let C be the set of category names, M an MCS, and for each $r \in br_M$ let $cat(r) \subseteq C$ be an association of bridge rules to (one or more) category names. $Cat_M = \bigcup_{r \in br_M} cat(r)$ denotes the set of categories of M.*

Example 8. We formalize the previous example using the set of category names $Cat_M = \{treatment, billing\}$ and associating bridge rules to categories as follows: $cat(r_1) = cat(r_2) = \{treatment\}$ and $cat(r_3) = cat(r_4) = cat(r_5) = \{billing\}$. This categorization naturally follows from what the bridge rules are intended to do.

If a bridge rule is modified by a diagnosis, it is likely that the behaviour of all categories where the bridge rule is part of, is modified and possibly corrupted. Furthermore, if the result of category A depends on another category B, then A gives wrong or unexpected results if B is modified, although A was not modified directly. Therefore categories may depend on each other and modifications of rules of the latter also change the result of the former. So we also consider dependencies among categories.

Definition 8. *Let Cat_M be the categories of an MCS M. Each $cat \in Cat_M$ is associated a set of categories $P_{cat} \subseteq Cat_M$ on which it depends. We write $dep(cat, cat')$ iff $cat' \in P_c$.*

Example 9. In our running example, if r_2 is modified, the patient not only is given a different treatment, but also the billing gives other results than expected – although its behaviour is correct under the then modified assumptions. So, category "billing" depends on category "treatment", formally *dep(billing, treatment)*.

Note that the dependency of categories as well as their names and associations are semantic information, so for an MCS several categorizations may be adequate. If we assume that each bridge rule of an MCS was added by the creator for some reason, then the creator intuitively knows the category this bridge rule belongs to, i.e., the reason(s) for a bridge rule to exist corresponds to its category(s). Therefore one can assume that categories are supplied by the creator of the MCS as they are at least implicitly known at the time of creation.

For dependencies among categories we also assume them to be specified explicitly by the creator of the MCS. Although, under certain restrictions, it is possible to derive them automatically. For example, if all contexts of an MCS consist of logic programs and those programs are openly known, then one could take the dependency graph G of the whole MCS to derive dependencies among categories. Here G could be the dependency graph over all bridge rules combined with the rules of all contexts (suitably renamed, if necessary). Then category ct_1 depends on ct_2, if there exist bridge rules r_1, r_2 with $ct_1 \in cat(r_1)$ and $ct_2 \in cat(r_2)$ such that there is a path in G from the head node of r_1 to the head node of r_2. In the case that the category of a constraint rule depends on two other categories, it is, however, not immediately clear if those two categories then mutually depend on each other. Therefore an automatic derivation of categories has to address further details which are beyond the scope of this paper.

As an alternative to automatic derivation, one could think of using an ontology to represent dependencies among categories (T-Box statements) and associations of rules to categories (A-Box statements). As each specific MCS will have its own category names and dependencies, it is unlikely that there exists a general ontology for all use cases of MCSs, however.

Different categorizations and dependencies may lead to other diagnoses being preferred, therefore we assume in the following that a categorization deemed correct for the given MCS is applied. Whether such a categorization can be derived automatically (at least to some extent) is an issue possibly addressed in the future.

Definition 9. *Let M be an MCS with category names Cat_M and dependencies dep. For a diagnosis $D = (D_1, D_2)$ of M, the set of possibly corrupted categories wrt. D is the smallest set $C_D \subseteq Cat_M$ such that for all $r \in D_1 \cup D_2$ holds $cat(r) \subseteq C_D$ and whenever $cat_1 \in C_D$ and $dep(cat_2, cat_1)$ then $cat_2 \in C_D$.*

Obviously, a diagnosis which modifies a smaller set of categories is always desirable, as it ensures that more parts of the diagnosed system still yield reliable results. This induces a preference order such that preferred diagnoses modify only a minimal set of categories

Definition 10. *Let $D, D' \in D^{\pm}(M)$ be diagnoses of an MCS M. D is at least as preferred as D' iff $C_D \subseteq C_{D'}$. We denote this preference order by $D \preceq_{sd} D'$.*

Example 10. Recall our example, where $Cat_M = \{treatment, billing\}$, $cat(r_1) = cat(r_2) = \{treatment\}$, $cat(r_3) = cat(r_4) = cat(r_5) = \{billing\}$, and dependency is given by $dep(billing, treatment)$, we obtain for diagnosis $D = (\{r_1\}, \emptyset)$ and $D' = (\{r_4\}, \emptyset)$ that $C_D = \{treatment, billing\}$ and $C_{D'} = \{billing\}$. Therefore $D \prec_{sd} D'$.

Assuming that all categories are of equal importance, one can strengthen the above notion by requiring that a preferred diagnosis modifies only the least amount of categories, i.e., select by cardinality minimality. Cardinality-based preference can drastically reduce the number of diagnoses to be considered. So it may be easier for a human operator, responsible for restoring consistency, to select the best diagnosis.

Definition 11. *Let $D, D' \in D^{\pm}(M)$ be diagnoses of an MCS M. D is preferred over D' iff $|C_D| \leq |C_{D'}|$. This is denoted by $D \preceq_{|sd|} D'$.*

Example 11. With $\preceq_{sd}$ (or $\preceq_{|sd|}$), most preferred diagnoses are $(\{r_4\}, \emptyset)$ and $(\{r_5\}, \emptyset)$.

3.1   Realization of Categories by Meta-reasoning

Preference orders in general and orders on categories may be realized following the very general approach of [7], which is based on a meta-reasoning transformation of the given MCS. In the remainder of this section we give a concrete instantiation of this transformation to realize preference orders on categories.

The approach can be sketched as follows: transform the given MCS M into an MCS M^t where one additional observer contexts ob import head formulas and body beliefs of all bridge rules in M. If those imports are realized using protected bridge rules, i.e., bridge rules which are not modified in the respective diagnosis, then the observer ob knows if a rule $r \in br_M$ is modified in a diagnosis (D_1, D_2), because if $r \in D_1$ then the body of r is fulfilled, but its head is not added to the respective context. Similarly, if $r \in D_2$ then the head is present in the respective context, while the body of r is not fulfilled. Based on the observed modification, ob may also become inconsistent therefore a diagnosis of M might not be a diagnosis of M^t.

On the other hand, however, if ob has some additional, seemingly unnecessary, bridge rules K then it can map a given preference $\preceq$ on diagnoses to those additional bridge rules in K. For $K = \{t_1, \ldots, t_m\}$ and $1 \leq i \leq m$ those additional bridge rules are of form $(ob : k_i) \leftarrow .$ so these rules are applicable in any belief state and the mapping of a preference then works as follows: Let $D = (D_1, D_2), D' = (D'_1, D'_2)$ be two diagnoses of M with $D \preceq D'$, furthermore $K_1, K_2 \subseteq K$ with $K_1 \subseteq K_2$. Now construct $\mathbf{ACC}_{ob}$ such that if ob observes D, then ob is inconsistent if one $k_i \in K_1$ is present, and if ob observes D' then it is inconsistent if one $k_j \in K_2$ is present. Effectively, D and D' are no diagnoses of the transformed MCS M^t, but $(D_1 \cup K_1, D_2)$ and $(D'_1 \cup K_2, D'_2)$ are diagnoses of M^t.

Now we consider bridge rules of K to have precedence over those of br_M using a notion of prioritized minimal diagnosis (i.e., a lexicographic ordering). So $(D_1 \cup K_1, D_2)$ is considered at least as minimal as $(D_1' \cup K_2, D_2')$ according to prioritized minimality, thus D is at least as preferred as D'. Therefore the prioritized minimal diagnoses of M^t correspond one-to-one to the most preferred diagnoses of M wrt. $\preceq$. Notably, this transformation works for all preference orders on diagnoses and leaves the choice of the actual logic of ob open for the creator of the system.

Notably, the transformation is efficient for many preference orders, specifically for $\preceq_{sd}$ and $\preceq_{|sd|}$, and the complexity of recognizing a prioritized minimal diagnosis with protected bridge rules does not increase compared to recognizing a minimal diagnosis. The transformation also works with multiple observer contexts where each observer uses its own logic and considers only a subset of the bridge rules of M. So this transformation not necessarily introduces a centralized observer. For presentation purposes, however, we introduce the transformation using one centralized observer context ob.

Meta-reasoning Transformation (cf. [7]). In general, to observe for a bridge rule r with head $(k : s)$ whether s is added to k, is not directly possible. First, because the semantics $\mathbf{ACC}_k$ of context k might simply not reflect the addition of s in the resulting belief sets, and second, because k could derive s on its own, regardless if s was also imported by an applicable bridge rule. To observe r properly, therefore the introduction of a relay context for k is necessary.

Given an MCS M and a set of bridge rules br_o to be observed, an observation context ob for br_o is a context with bridge rules $br_{ob} = br_b^{ob} \cup br_h^{ob}$ with $br_b^{ob} = \{r_b^{ob} \mid r \in br_o\}$ and $br_h^{ob} = \{r_h^{ob} \mid r \in br_o\}$, where r_b^{ob} is of the form

$$(ob : body_r) \leftarrow (c_1 : p_1), \ldots, (c_j : p_j), \mathbf{not}\ (c_{j+1} : p_{j+1}), \ldots, \mathbf{not}\ (c_m : p_m).$$

and r_h^{ob} is of the form

$$(ob : head_r) \leftarrow (relay_k : s).$$

for a bridge rule of form (1).

The relay context $relay_k$ is defined over a logic L_{ASP} with signature $\Sigma = \{s \mid (k : s) \in head(r) \wedge r \in br_o\}$. The knowledge base $kb_{relay_k} = \emptyset$ and for each rule of form (1) in br_o there is a rule in br_{relay_k} of form

$$(relay_k : s) \leftarrow (c_1 : p_1), \ldots, (c_j : p_j), \mathbf{not}\ (c_{j+1} : p_{j+1}), \ldots, \mathbf{not}\ (c_m : p_m).$$

Given a belief state S, the semantics of ASP then ensures that the head formula s of r is present in the accepted belief set of $relay_k$ if and only if r is applicable in S.

As the context C_k of M also must use the relay, we create its relayed version where all bridge rules are routed through C_{relay_k}. We associate with context $C_k = (L_k, kb_k, br_k)$ its relayed context $C_k^{rel} = (L_k, kb_k, br_k^{rel})$ where $br_k^{rel} = \{r_{rel} \mid r \in br_M\}$, and r_{rel} is for a bridge rule with $head(r) = (k : s)$ of the form

$$(k : s) \leftarrow (relay_k : s).$$

Example 12. In our running example, consider the case that context *ob* observes the bridge rules of the medication context C_2. The original bridge rules of C_2 are:

$$r_1 = (2 : hyperglycemia) \qquad \leftarrow (1 : hyperglycemia).$$
$$r_2 = (2 : allow\_animal\_insulin) \leftarrow \mathbf{not}\ (1 : allergic\_animal\_insulin).$$

The meta-reasoning transformation introduces relay context C_{relay_2} with bridge rules

$$(relay_2 : hyperglycemia) \qquad\qquad \leftarrow (1 : hyperglycemia). \tag{2}$$
$$(relay_2 : allow\_animal\_insulin) \quad \leftarrow \mathbf{not}\ (1 : allergic\_animal\_insulin). \tag{3}$$

while the relayed context C_2^{rel} of C_2 has bridge rules

$$(2 : hyperglycemia) \qquad\qquad \leftarrow (relay_2 : hyperglycemia).$$
$$(2 : allow\_animal\_insulin) \leftarrow (relay_2 : allow\_animal\_insulin).$$

So *ob* is now able to observe applicability of r_1 and r_2 by the following rules:

$$(ob : body_{r_1}) \leftarrow (1 : hyperglycemia).$$
$$(ob : head_{r_1}) \leftarrow (relay_2 : hyperglycemia).$$
$$(ob : body_{r_2}) \leftarrow \mathbf{not}\ (1 : allergic\_animal\_insulin).$$
$$(ob : head_{r_2}) \leftarrow (relay_2 : allow\_animal\_insulin).$$

Note that in this case the relay context actually is not necessary as the belief sets of C_2 contain *hyperglycemia*, respectively *allow_animal_insulin*, if and only if r_1, respectively r_2, are applicable. In such a situation, C_2 and its bridge rules can be kept as they are and *ob* imports the head beliefs of r_1 and r_2 directly from C_2.

Based on this rewriting, the meta-reasoning transformation of an MCS for one observer context is as follows.

Definition 12. *Given an MCS* $M = (C_1, \ldots, C_n)$, *let ob be a new observation context* $ob \notin M$. *The* meta-reasoning transformation M^t *of* M *is the MCS*

$$M^t = (C_1^{rel}, \ldots, C_n^{rel}, relay_1, \ldots, relay_n, ob)$$

where C_i^{rel} *and* $relay_i$ *are relayed contexts and relay contexts, respectively, and* $br_P = \bigcup_{i=1}^{n} br_i^{rel} \cup br_{ob}$ *are protected rules.*

To realize preferences based on categories, we use ASP for *ob* and let its knowledge base kb_{ob} consist of the following rules to detect which bridge rules of M are modified by a diagnosis. For each $r \in br_M$ the following rules are contained in kb_{ob}:

$$r_{removed} \leftarrow body_r, not\ head_r.$$
$$r_{unconditional} \leftarrow not\ body_r, head_r.$$
$$r_{unchanged} \leftarrow not\ r_{removed}, not\ r_{unconditional}.$$

The system M^t so far allows to monitor diagnoses $D = (D_1, D_2)$ with $D_1 \cap D_2 = \emptyset$. Note that for diagnoses where for some $r \in D_1 \cap D_2$, ob will not observe $r_{removed}$ correctly. For minimal diagnoses, however, it holds that $D_1 \cap D_2 = \emptyset$ and this will not be an issue.

For a given MCS M with categories $Cat_M = \{cat_1, \ldots, cat_m\}$ and dependency relation dep, the observer context additionally contains for each cat_i a bridge rule r_i^c of form $(ob : cat_i) \leftarrow$. Mapping the preference $\preceq_{sd}$ to those bridge rules finally is achieved by adding the following rules to kb_{ob}:

$$mod_t \leftarrow not\ r_{unchanged}. \qquad \text{for all } r \in br_M \text{ with } t \in cat(r)$$
$$mod_t \leftarrow mod_{t'} \qquad \text{for all } dep(t, t')$$
$$\bot \leftarrow mod_t, cat_t. \qquad \text{for all } t \in Cat_M$$

The resulting MCS, call it M^{Cat}, then exhibits $\preceq_{sd}$ on the bridge rules of ob.

Example 13. For the observer ob in our running example to exhibit the preference $\preceq_{sd}$ given by categories *treatment*, *billing* and *dep(billing, treatment)*, we have two additional bridge rules for ob:

$$(ob : cat_{billing}) \leftarrow . \qquad (4)$$
$$(ob : cat_{treatment}) \leftarrow . \qquad (5)$$

To detect if bridge rule r_2 is modified, the knowledge base kb_{ob} of ob contains the following rules:

$$r_{2removed} \leftarrow body_{r_2}, not\ head_r.$$
$$r_{2unconditional} \leftarrow not\ body_{r_2}, head_{r_2}.$$
$$r_{2unchanged} \leftarrow not\ r_{2removed}, not\ r_{2unconditional}.$$

Assuming that kb_{ob} contains above rules for $r_1, \ldots, r_5$ the mapping to categories is as follows:

$$mod_{treatment} \leftarrow not\ r_{1unchanged}.$$
$$mod_{treatment} \leftarrow not\ r_{2unchanged}.$$
$$mod_{billing} \leftarrow not\ r_{3unchanged}.$$
$$mod_{billing} \leftarrow not\ r_{4unchanged}.$$
$$mod_{billing} \leftarrow not\ r_{5unchanged}.$$
$$\bot \leftarrow mod_{treatment}, cat_{treatment}.$$
$$\bot \leftarrow mod_{billing}, cat_{billing}.$$
$$mod_{billing} \leftarrow mod_{treatment}.$$

Observe that the last rule establishes the dependency between categories *billing* and *treatment*.

Let br_H contain the additional bridge rules r_i^c of ob, then the following notion of a minimal prioritized diagnosis selects from M^{Cat} exactly those diagnoses that correspond to $\preceq_{sd}$-preferred diagnoses of M.

Definition 13. *Let M be an MCS with bridge rules br_M, protected rules br_P, and prioritized rules $br_H \subseteq br_M$. The set of minimal prioritized diagnoses is*

$$D_m^{\pm}(M, br_P, br_H) = \{\, D \in D_m^{\pm}(M, br_P) \mid \forall D' \in D_m^{\pm}(M, br_P) :$$
$$D' \cap br_H \subseteq D \cap br_H \Rightarrow D' \cap br_H = D \cap br_H \,\}.$$

where $(D_1, D_2) \cap S := (D_1 \cap S, D_2 \cap S)$.

Example 14. For our running example MCS M, all bridge rules of M^{Cat} are protected, except rules of form (2), (3) and similar rules representing the remaining bridge rules of M. Additionally, bridge rules (4) and (5) of M^{Cat} are prioritized and not protected. The set of minimal protected diagnoses then correspond directly to the most preferred diagnoses according to $\preceq_{sd}$.

4   Assessment with Quantitative Measures

The quantitative inconsistency measure for bridge rules is based on the notion MIV_C from [12], which employs cardinalities of the minimal inconsistent sets a certain formula belongs to. For MCSs an equivalent notion of a minimal inconsistent set is defined in [6] as inconsistency explanation. It is a pair of sets of bridge rules, whose presence resp. absence causes a relevant inconsistency.

Definition 14 (cf. [6]). *An* inconsistency explanation *of an MCS M is a pair $(E_1, E_2) \in br_M \times br_M$ s.t. for all (R_1, R_2) where $E_1 \subseteq R_1 \subseteq br_M$ and $R_2 \subseteq br_M \setminus E_2$, it holds that $M[R_1 \cup uncond(R_2)] \models \bot$. The set of all pointwise subset-minimal such (E_1, E_2) is denoted by $E_m^{\pm}(M)$.*

The intuition is that $M[E_1]$ is inconsistent, and this inconsistency is relevant for M, as adding more bridge rules from br_M never resolves that inconsistency. Moreover, the inconsistency of M entailed by E_1 cannot be avoided by adding bridge rules unconditionally, unless bridge rules from E_2 are used.

As a bridge rule r may introduce and prevent inconsistency, we define the inconsistency value m_{br} of r as a pair (I_1, I_2) where I_1 and I_2 measure the amount of inconsistency caused, respectively, prevented by r.

Definition 15 (cf. [7]). *Let M a MCS and $r \in br_M$, and let $A_r^i(M) = \{(E_1, E_2) \in E_m^{\pm}(M) \mid r \in E_i\}$, $i = 1, 2$. Then the* bridge-inconsistency mea*sure is defined by*

$$m_{br}(M, r) = \left(\sum_{(E_1, E_2) \in A_r^1(M)} \frac{1}{|E_1|}, \sum_{(E_1, E_2) \in A_r^2(M)} \frac{1}{|E_2|} \right).$$

Example 15. There is one minimal inconsistency explanation: $(\{r_1, r_4, r_5\}, \{r_2\})$. So the inconsistency values are: $m_{\mathrm{br}}(M, r_1) = \left(\frac{1}{3}, 0\right)$, $m_{\mathrm{br}}(M, r_2) = (0, 1)$, $m_{\mathrm{br}}(M, r_3) = (0, 0)$, $m_{\mathrm{br}}(M, r_4) = \left(\frac{1}{3}, 0\right)$, and $m_{\mathrm{br}}(M, r_5) = \left(\frac{1}{3}, 0\right)$.

Given a quantitative measure on bridge rules, we derive quantitative measures on diagnoses. This allows to select preferable diagnoses without additional domain knowledge as well as to select preferable diagnoses that are considered incomparable or equal by measures based on domain knowledge.

On the one hand, subset-minimal diagnoses which remove the most inconsistency are preferable as they yield a most "clean" system. This may be the method of choice for "stable" systems that should not give rise to inconsistency when further modifications are applied. On the other hand, potential inconsistencies still carry some kind of information which therefore should not be removed without the need to, i.e., subset-minimal diagnoses removing the least amount of inconsistency are then preferable.

Definition 16. *Let M be an MCS, π_i be a projection to the ith element of tuples, $m_{\mathrm{br}} : br_M \to \mathbb{R} \times \mathbb{R}$ the bridge-inconsistency measure, and $D_1, D_2 \subseteq br_M$. Then $m_d : 2^{br_M} \times 2^{br_M} \to \mathbb{R}$ is a measure on diagnoses with*

$$m_{\mathrm{d}}(D_1, D_2) = \sum_{r \in D_1} \pi_1\left(m_{\mathrm{br}}(r)\right) + \sum_{r \in D_2} \pi_2\left(m_{\mathrm{br}}(r)\right).$$

Indeed, m_{d} is a measure on $br_M \times br_M$, as the following properties hold:

- non-negativity: $m_{\mathrm{d}}(D_1, D_2) \geq 0$ for any D_1, D_2, as the resulting pair of numbers from m_{br} is always positive,
- null empty set: $m_{\mathrm{d}}(\emptyset, \emptyset) = 0$, as both summations of m_{d} are empty, and
- countable additivity: let $\{A_1, \ldots, A_n\}$ be a countable collection of disjoint pairs of sets of bridge rules, i.e., $A_k = (D_1^k, D_2^k)$ and $D_1^k \cap D_1^{k'} = \emptyset$ as well as $D_2^k \cap D_2^{k'} = \emptyset$ for $k, k' \in \{1, \ldots, n\}$ and $k \neq k'$. Then

$$m_{\mathrm{d}}\Big(\bigcup_{i=1}^{n} D_1^i, \bigcup_{i=1}^{k} D_2^i\Big) = \sum_{i=1}^{k} m_{\mathrm{d}}(D_1^i, D_2^i).$$

This holds directly by the definition of m_{d}, as it sums up m_{br} for each single bridge rule. Also note that there are only finitely many bridge rules, so any collection on pairs of bridge rules is countable.

From these properties, it also follows that m_{d} is monotonic.

Having a measure, one needs to decide which diagnoses are the most preferred ones. If diagnoses that remove the most inconsistency are preferred, one obtains

$$D_{C+} = \arg \max_{(D_1, D_2) \in D_m^{\pm}} \{m_{\mathrm{d}}(D_1, D_2)\}.$$

Preferring diagnoses that remove a least amount of inconsistency gives

$$D_{C-} = \arg \min_{(D_1, D_2) \in D_m^{\pm}} \{m_{\mathrm{d}}(D_1, D_2)\}.$$

Example 16. In our running example $D_{C^+} = \{(\emptyset, \{r_2\})\}$ and $D_{C^-} = \{(\{r_1\}, \emptyset)$, $(\{r_3\}, \emptyset), (\{r_5\}, \emptyset)\}$. Note that $(\emptyset, \{r_2\})$ removes the most inconsistency as r_2 alone makes the system consistent, while for D_{C^-} each rule r_1, r_3, r_5 only contributes one third to the cause of inconsistency, i.e., $m_d(\emptyset, \{r_2\}) = 1$ and $m_d(\{r_1\}, \emptyset) = m_d(\{r_3\}, \emptyset) = m_d(\{r_5\}, \emptyset) = \frac{1}{3}$.

Observe that we take into account how a bridge rule appears in a diagnosis, so either the value for removing or the value for adding it unconditional is counted. As removing a bridge rule also removes the ability to restore consistency with that rule, one may combine both values to obtain a different "measure":

$$m_d'(D_1, D_2) = \sum_{r \in D_1 \cup D_2} \pi_1\left(m_{br}\left(r\right)\right) - \pi_2\left(m_{br}\left(r\right)\right)$$

Note however, that one of the basic properties of a measure, namely monotonicity, fails for m_d'.

5   Related Work and Conclusion

In this paper we advanced the available methods of finding preferred resolutions of inconsistency in the Multi-Context Systems framework.

- We introduced categorizations of bridge rules for qualitative assessment of inconsistencies.
- Based on previous work, a realization of this assessment is presented and exemplified.
- Furthermore, an inconsistency measure for quantitative assessment of inconsistency is introduced.

Related Work. In [1] the problem of inconsistency in MCSs is addressed using defeasible rules which are applicable only if they do not cause inconsistency. In the presence of inconsistency defeasible rules are deactivated using additional trust information. Four algorithms to compute trust are given where the first uses a total order over contexts while the others also employ provenance information of increasing depth. Provenance, however, requires insight to context internals which is in conflict with our requirements of information hiding and privacy.

Work on distributed ontologies bears some similarities to our work, consider e.g., [13] where bridge rules represent ontology mappings and a notion of minimal diagnosis is used to repair inconsistent mappings. While our categorizations are similar to concepts in ontologies, the scopes of these works are different as we seek preference criteria for diagnoses on bridge rules between heterogeneous logics.

Inconsistency tolerance in peer-to-peer systems (e.g., [4]) considers homogeneous logics only and inconsistency resolution is local to each peer while our notion of minimal diagnosis is globally minimal.

In [3] the notion of MCS is extended such that bridge rules not only add information to a knowledge base but allow arbitrary manipulation of knowledge bases using so called context managers. These managers then can also do inconsistency management on a local level, e.g., for a context using propositional logic the manager can apply methods of classical belief revision. This revision, however, is again local and such methods can not prevent inconsistency of an MCS in all cases.

Concerning the MCS framework and global inconsistency management, no further work addressing inconsistency management is known to us, although finding preferred diagnoses is an ubiquitous task in inconsistency handling.

Future Work. Preferences to resolve inconsistency are an interesting issue with many open questions: for example, is it possible to resolve inconsistency in an MCS based on the belief sets obtained if all bridge rules are removed, i.e., keeping knowledge bases as close to their original semantics as possible? Other goals could be to improve the notion of categories for the aspects of: allowing arbitrary importance of categories, deriving categories automatically from a given MCS, or handling multiple categorizations for one MCS.

But as other investigations show, e.g. [10], the computation of equilibria of an MCS within reasonable time is still an issue; while finding diagnoses is an even more involved task.

References

1. Bikakis, A., Antoniou, G., Hassapis, P.: Strategies for contextual reasoning with conflicts in ambient intelligence. Knowl. Inf. Syst. 27(1), 45–84 (2011)
2. Brewka, G., Eiter, T.: Equilibria in heterogeneous nonmonotonic multi-context systems. In: AAAI, pp. 385–390. AAAI Press (2007)
3. Brewka, G., Eiter, T., Fink, M., Weinzierl, A.: Managed multi-context systems. In: Walsh, T. (ed.) IJCAI, pp. 786–791. IJCAI/AAAI (2011)
4. Calvanese, D., De Giacomo, G., Lembo, D., Lenzerini, M., Rosati, R.: Inconsistency Tolerance in P2P Data Integration: An Epistemic Logic Approach. In: Bierman, G., Koch, C. (eds.) DBPL 2005. LNCS, vol. 3774, pp. 90–105. Springer, Heidelberg (2005)
5. Damásio, C.V., Pereira, L.M.: A survey of paraconsistent semantics for logic programs. In: Handbook of Defeasible Reasoning and Uncertainty Management Systems, pp. 241–320. Kluwer Academic Publishers (1998)
6. Eiter, T., Fink, M., Schüller, P., Weinzierl, A.: Finding explanations of inconsistency in multi-context systems. In: Lin, F., Sattler, U., Truszczynski, M. (eds.) KR. AAAI Press (2010)
7. Eiter, T., Fink, M., Weinzierl, A.: Preference-Based Inconsistency Assessment in Multi-Context Systems. In: Janhunen, T., Niemelä, I. (eds.) JELIA 2010. LNCS, vol. 6341, pp. 143–155. Springer, Heidelberg (2010)
8. Eiter, T., Ianni, G., Krennwallner, T.: Answer Set Programming: A Primer. In: Tessaris, S., Franconi, E., Eiter, T., Gutierrez, C., Handschuh, S., Rousset, M.-C., Schmidt, R.A. (eds.) Reasoning Web. LNCS, vol. 5689, pp. 40–110. Springer, Heidelberg (2009)
9. Faber, W., Pfeifer, G., Leone, N.: Semantics and complexity of recursive aggregates in answer set programming. Artif. Intell. 175(1), 278–298 (2011)

10. Fink, M., Ghionna, L., Weinzierl, A.: Relational Information Exchange and Aggregation in Multi-Context Systems. In: Delgrande, J.P., Faber, W. (eds.) LPNMR 2011. LNCS, vol. 6645, pp. 120–133. Springer, Heidelberg (2011)
11. Giunchiglia, F., Serafini, L.: Multilanguage hierarchical logics or: How we can do without modal logics. Artif. Intell. 65(1), 29–70 (1994)
12. Hunter, A., Konieczny, S.: Measuring inconsistency through minimal inconsistent sets. In: Brewka, G., Lang, J. (eds.) KR, pp. 358–366. AAAI Press (2008)
13. Meilicke, C., Stuckenschmidt, H., Tamilin, A.: Repairing ontology mappings. In: AAAI, pp. 1408–1413. AAAI Press (2007)
14. Przymusinski, T.: Stable semantics for disjunctive programs. New Generation Computing 9(3), 401–424 (1991)

Vague Determiner Phrases and Distributive Predication[*]

Heather Burnett

University of California, Los Angeles
hburnett@ucla.edu

1 Introduction

The goal of this paper is to provide the formal basis for a new approach to modelling the application of vague predicates like *tall* and *bald* to plural subjects like *John and Mary* and *the men*. In other words, we are interested in developing a new logical analysis for natural language sentences like *Mary is tall* and *The men are bald*. In the past 30 years, much research has been devoted to finding the proper logical framework to model the application of non-vague predicates to pluralities (cf. [16], [21] among others). Additionally, there has been a lot of work on how to model the application of vague predicates to singular terms (cf. [8], [5] among many others). However, the question of how to apply vague predicates to plural subjects and what complexities may arise in doing so has yet to be examined. This paper is a contribution to filling this gap. In particular, I argue that extending an analysis of predicate vagueness to incorporate pluralities is not immediately straightforward; that is, I show that sentences with vague predicates and certain kinds of plural subjects give rise to additional vague effects that are not present with singular subjects. Extending previous work on both plural predication and vague language, I propose a new logical system (Plural TCS) that models these effects.

In the remainder of this section, I present a brief description of the data that an analysis of vagueness in the adjectival and determiner phrase domains aims to model. In section 2, I present a logical system based on [16] to treat (non-vague) plural predicates[1]. In section 3, I present a recent prominent framework for modelling sentences with vague predicates and singular subjects: [5]'s similarity-based *Tolerant, Classical, Strict* (TCS) logic. Finally, in section 4, I present a system that incorporates the main proposals of theses two frameworks and models both plural and singular predication with vague predicates.

---

[*] This research has been partially supported by a SSHRC doctoral grant to the author (#752-2007-2382) and the TELCAS grant (UCLA/École normale supérieure (Paris)) from the Partner University Fund. I thank Paul Égré, Thomas Graf, Ed Keenan, Friederike Moltmann, Dominique Sportiche, and Ed Stabler for helpful comments and discussion. Of course, all errors are my own.

[1] Link's *Logic of Plurals and Mass Nouns* (LPM) is generally viewed as the standard approach to modelling the semantics of plurals in linguistics (see, for example, [3] and references within).

D. Lassiter and M. Slavkovik (Eds.): ESSLLI Student Sessions, LNCS 7415, pp. 175–194, 2012.

1.1 Vagueness in the AP Domain

In this section, I provide a very brief overview of the vagueness-related patterns associated with predicates of the adjectival syntactic category. As is common in the literature (since at least [24]), I make a distinction between three principle subclasses of adjectives: *relative scalar* adjectives (RAs, as in (1)), *absolute scalar* adjectives (AAs, as in (2)), and *non-scalar* adjectives (NSs, as in (3)).

(1) **Relative Scalar Adjectives**
    a.   John is **tall**.
    b.   Mary is **short**.
    c.   This watch is **expensive**.

(2) **Absolute Scalar Adjectives**
    a.   This stick is **straight**.
    b.   The room is **empty**.
    c.   The table is **flat**.

(3) **Non-Scalar Adjectives**
    a.   This algebra is **atomic**.
    b.   This number is **prime**.
    c.   This shape is **hexagonal**.

Relative Adjectives. RAs like *tall, short, long, expensive*, and *young* are paradigm cases of vague predicates. Following many authors (ex. [7], [23], among others), I take vague language to be characterized by the presence of three (related) properties: *borderline cases* (objects for which it is difficult or even impossible to tell whether they satisfy the predicate), *fuzzy boundaries* (the observation that there appear to be no sharp boundaries between cases of a vague predicate and its negation), and *susceptibility to the Sorites paradox* (a paradox for classical logical systems that follows from the fuzzy boundaries property). In the vast majority (if not all) contexts, RAs, as a class, display these properties. Consider the following example with the predicate *tall* used in a context where we take the set of American males as the appropriate comparison class for *tallness*. In this situation, some men will be clearly tall: for example, anyone over 6 feet. Similarly, it is clear that anyone under 5ft9" (the average) is not tall. But suppose that we look at John who is somewhere between 5ft9" and 6ft. Which one of the sentences in (4) is true?

(4)   a.   John is **tall**.
       b.   John is **not tall**.

For John, it seems like the most appropriate answer is either "neither" or "both". Thus, *tall* permits borderline cases in this context. Furthermore, if we take a tall person and we start subtracting millimetres from their height, it seems impossible to pinpoint the precise instance where subtracting a millimetre suddenly moves us from the height of a tall person to the height of a not tall person. In principle, if we line all the individuals in the domain up according to height, we ought to be able to find an adjacent pair in the *tall*-series consisting of a tall person and a not tall person. However, it does not appear that this is possible. Thus, in this context, *tall* has fuzzy boundaries.

The observation that relative adjectives have fuzzy boundaries leads straightforwardly to the observation that these predicates gives rise to a paradox for systems like first (or higher) order logic (upon which most formal theories of the semantics of natural language are based) known as the *Sorites*, or the paradox of the 'heaper'. Formally, the paradox can set up in a number of ways. A common one found in the literature is (5), where $\sim_P$ is a 'little by little' or 'indistinguishable difference' relation.

(5)   **The Sorites Paradox**

    a.   **Clear Case:** $P(a_1)$
    b.   **Clear Non-Case:** $\neg P(a_k)$
    c.   **Sorites Series:** $\forall i \in [1,n](a_i \sim_P a_{i+1})$
    d.   **Tolerance:** $\forall x \forall y((P(x) \wedge x \sim_P y) \rightarrow P(y))$
    e.   **Conclusion:** $P(a_k) \wedge \neg P(a_k)$

Thus, in first order logic and other similar systems, as soon as we have a clear case of P, a clear non-case of P, and a Sorites series, we can conclude that everything is P and that everything is not P. We can see that *tall* (for a North American male) gives rise to such an argument. We can find someone who measures 6ft to satisfy (5-a), and we can find someone who measures 5ft6" to satisfy (5-b). In the previous paragraph, we concluded that the application of *tall* is insensitive to small changes in height (we call such a predicate a *tolerant* predicate, after [25]), so it satisfies (5-d), and, finally, we can easily construct a Sorites series based on height to fulfil (5-c). Therefore, we would expect to be able to conclude that this 5ft6" tall person (a non-borderline case) is both tall and not tall, which is absurd. Of course, the observations made in this section are, by no means, limited to *tall*. The entire class of relative adjectives display these properties across contexts. For example, consider the predicate *expensive* in the context of buying a large television (at which exact cent does a TV go from being *expensive* to *not expensive*?), or *long* in the context of a watching a movie (at which exact second does a movie go from being *not long* to *long*?), and so on.

Absolute Adjectives. As observed by [19] and [11] (among others), in many contexts, adjectives like *empty, straight, flat*, and *clean* do not have borderline cases, fuzzy boundaries, or give rise to the Sorites. As a first example, we might consider [11]'s discussion of the absolute predicate *straight*. He observes that, in some very special cases where our purposes require the object to be perfectly straight, it is possible to say something like (6).

(6)   The rod for the antenna needs to be **straight**, but this one has a 1mm
       bend in the middle, so unfortunately it won't work.
       [11] (p.25)

In this situation, *straight* has no borderline cases: even a 1 mm bend is sufficient
to move an object from *straight* to *not straight*. Similarly, the boundary between
straight and *not straight* is sharp and located between the perfectly straight
objects and those with any small bend. Thus, we have a context where *straight*
stops being vague. We can see the same pattern with *empty*. Suppose we are
describing the process of fumigating a theatre. In this case, since having even
a single person inside would result in a death, the cutoff point between empty
theatres and non-empty theatres would be sharply at 'one or more spectators'.
Additionally, we can construct similar examples with *flat* (think of situations
where an object is required to be perfectly flat), *clean* (think of situations where
a tiny speck of dirt makes a difference to our purposes), and the other members
of the AA class. In other words, unlike relative adjectives, absolute adjectives
can be used precisely.

    However, it has been long observed that, in very many contexts, adjectives
like *straight*, and *empty* display certain properties that are extremely similar
to the properties displayed by *tall* and *long*. For example, in most situations,
we can refer to objects with slight bends as *straight*, provided the bends are
not large enough to interfere with our purposes. Consider a context in which
we are talking about roads. A road that a few bends in it will most likely still
be called *straight*, but at which number of bends does a road go from being
straight to not straight? Indeed, it seems bizarre to think that there is some
point at which adding a single small bend to a road could take it from being
straight to not straight; therefore, *straight* is tolerant in this context. Thus, we
have the ingredients for a Sorites-type argument. We can see the same thing for
empty. Consider a context in which we are talking about theatres and whether
or not a particular play was well-attended. In this kind of situation, we often
apply the predicate *empty* to theatres that are not completely empty (i.e. those
with a couple people in them), and, in this context, *empty* has borderline cases,
has fuzzy boundaries, and is tolerant: If we are willing to call a theatre with a
couple of people in it *empty*, then at what number of spectators does it become
not empty? In summary, we can conclude that, at least in some contexts, absolute
adjectives can also display the characteristic properties of vague language, like
relative adjectives.

Non-scalar Adjectives. Finally, scalar adjectives like *tall* and *bald* are often
contrasted with non-scalar adjectives like *hexagonal, illegal, atomic, Canadian*
and *prime*, which are precise predicates. Consider the predicate *hexagonal*:
either a shape has six sides, and it is hexagonal, or it does not have six sides, and
it is not. The boundaries of this predicate are sharp. Likewise for *illegal*: either a

particular action is forbidden by laws of a community and it is illegal, or it is not forbidden, in which case the action is legal. And so on[2].

Summary. In summary, we have seen three kinds of vagueness-related patterns in the adjectival domain: some lexical items (like relative adjectives) are vague in all (or maybe almost all) contexts, some other items (like absolute adjectives) are vague in some contexts, but precise in others, and, finally, some other lexical items (like non-scalar adjectives) are precise in all contexts. In the next section, I argue that these basic patterns are replicated in the DP domain.

Table 1. Adjectival Vagueness Patterns

	Vague	Vague/Precise	Precise
APs	*tall, short, expensive...*	*empty, bald, straight...*	*prime, atomic, hexagonal...*

1.2   Vagueness in the DP Domain

In this section, I present a brief review of the vagueness patterns associated with determiner phrases. I argue that (following discussions in the literature), we see three main classes of DPs: *relative/'intensional'*, *non-maximal/imprecise*, and *precise* DPs.

(7) **Relative/'Intensional' DPs**
   a.   **Many girls** arrived.
   b.   **Few boys** left.

(8) **'Non-Maximal'/Imprecise DPs**
   a.   **The/these girls** are late.
   b.   **30 000 spectators** were at the game.

(9) **Precise DPs**
   a.   **All the girls** are late.
   b.   **No girls** are late.
   c.   **29 821 spectators** were at the game.

---

[2] Note that, as discussed by [15] among many others, there exist 'rough/imprecise' uses of non-scalar adjectives such as in (i), and we can observe that, in these uses, the predicates are vague (how many 'sides' does a country need to have to no longer be considered hexagonal? What exact degree of immorality is required to be considered really illegal?)

(i)   a.   France is hexagonal.
      b.   Jaywalking is not illegal (you only get a small fine).

However, as observed by [2], what appear to be vague uses of 'non-scalar' predicates are actually vague uses of scalar versions of these predicates.

(ii) a.   France is more hexagonal than Canada.
      b.   Jaywalking less illegal than murder.

'Intensional' DPs. It has often been observed that vagueness is a property that holds not only of scalar adjectives and nouns (like *heap*), but also of determiner phrases. The first category of DPs that display the characterizing properties of vague language are what are often called *intensional* quantifier phrases like *many people*, *few girls*, and *several boys* (cf. [10], [14], a.o.). Like relative adjectives, these constituents display borderline cases, fuzzy boundaries, and can be used in a Soritical argument in all (or almost all) contexts. For example, consider a context in which we are describing a party to which we expected about half the people (of a guest list of 100) to show up. In this context, (10) is clearly true if 90 or 80 people came, and clearly false if only 5 people came. However, what if 60 people came? 61?

(10)   Many people came to the party.

Furthermore, in this context, at which number of guests does the sentence go from being true to being false? Thus, with *many girls*, we can construct a Soritical series based on the number of guests at the party and form the appropriate paradoxical argument. We can easily think of other contexts in which *many people* displays the symptoms of vagueness, and, indeed, like adjectives such as *tall*, it is difficult to think of contexts in which this DP (or DPs like *few men* and *several people*) could be used precisely.

'Non-maximal' DPs. The second kind of pattern that we see in the DP domain is one that parallels the vague/precise pattern displayed by absolute scalar adjectives. As discussed in many works, such as [6], [26], [13], [1], [17], in contexts where it is important to be precise, sentences with definite descriptions and distributive predicates (like (11)) are true and appropriate just in case every member of the group denoted by the subject DP is affected by the predicate. Suppose (as in an example from [13] (p. 523)) that we are conducting a sleep experiment and that it is vital to our purposes that the people that we are studying actually fall asleep. In this context, not only is (11) true if all the subjects are asleep, but it is clearly false if one of the participants of the study is awake. In other words, like AAs such as *empty* and *straight*, definite plural DPs can be used precisely in some contexts.

(11)   The subjects are asleep.

Furthermore, as discussed in [6] and [1], the precise use of a definite plural can be enforced by the linguistic context. For example, when they are paired with a member of a certain class of collective predicate (what is known (after [6]) as a *pure cardinality* predicate), the predicate must hold of the entire group denoted by the subject for the sentence to be felicitous. This can be seen in (12), where the predicate *are a group of four* must apply the group composed of every single girl picked out by the definite description, regardless of the extra-linguistic context.

(12)   The girls are a group of four.

However, the aforementioned authors also observe that, in contexts where precision is not as important, sentences with definite plurals and distributive predicates can be said even if the plural predicate does not affect every single part of the subject. In the words of [1], these DPs give rise to *non-maximality* effects with distributive predicates. Consider the case (also from [13]) where, instead of describing an experiment, we are describing the state of a town at night. In this context, it is perfectly natural to use (13) even if a couple of insomniacs or night-watchmen are still awake.

(13)   The townspeople are asleep.

We can observe that, in the contexts where non-maximality is allowed, definite plurals display the hallmark properties of vague language. For example, (13) is clearly true when all the townspeople are asleep, and clearly false when less than half of the townspeople are asleep. However, what if 75% are asleep? 70%? It is not clear: these are the borderline cases. Furthermore, once the context allows us to tolerate exceptions with a definite plural, exactly how many exceptions are we allowed to tolerate before the sentence becomes clearly false? It seems bizarre to think that, in this context, subtracting a single townsperson could make a difference to whether we would assent to (13), so how is it that our reasoning with definite plurals is not paradoxical?

Finally, [12] and [23] have made similar observations about DPs containing 'round' numeral expressions like *30 000* and *100*. Although we can use these terms precisely, in many contexts, sentences like (14) can be said even if slightly fewer than 30 000 spectators attended the game or if the stop sign is not quite 100 meters away. As with absolute adjectives and definite plurals, in these contexts, the expression is vague with respect to how much deviation from the quantity denoted by the numeral phrase is allowed before the sentence is clearly false.

(14)   a.   There were 30 000 spectators at the football game.
        b.   There is a stop sign 100 meters down the road.

Note importantly that, in all these examples, it is not that the reference of the definite description/numeral phrase is, itself, vague. In fact, non-maximality effects can be found even with plural demonstrative phrases in cases where the precise group to which we are attributing the plural property is completely identified. For example, the sentence in (15) could be said in a situation where we know exactly who *the girls* are and what it takes to be Canadian, but in this situation, for our purposes, it is not necessary that all the girls have that property, and so we allow some exceptions.

(15)   These girls are Canadian.

In other words, what is vague in a sentence like (15) is the actual predication of the property *Canadian* to the parts of the plural subject. Therefore, in what follows, I will refer to the kind of vagueness displayed by definite plurals, demonstrative plurals, and round numeral phrases with distributive predicates as *part-structure* vagueness, in opposition to the simple *property vagueness* that we see with relative and absolute adjectives.

Precise DPs. Finally, a third pattern that we see in the DP domain is one that parallels the behaviour of non-scalar adjectives. Some DPs do not display the characteristic properties of vague language. As a first example, consider the contrast in the sentences in (16) (from [13]).

(16)   a.   The townspeople are asleep.
       b.   **All** the townspeople are asleep.

As discussed above, given an appropriate context, (16-a) is a vague utterance. However, as observed by [6] and [13], (16-b) is precise: it is true just in case every single townsperson is asleep. Other DPs that force a precise use[3] are those headed by logical expressions like *every* and *no*, and explicit co-ordination structures like (18).

(17)   a.   Every girl in this room is asleep.
       b.   No one is asleep.

(18)   John and Mary are asleep.

Finally, as discussed in [12], very small and 'unround' numeral phrases like those in (19) also enforce precision.

(19)   a.   Three girls are asleep.
       b.   29 871 spectators were at the game.
       c.   There is a stop sign 103 meters down the road.

Summary. In this subsection, we have seen three vagueness-based patterns in both the adjectival and DP domains: certain constituents (like RAs and 'intensional DPs') can only have vague uses, other constituents (like AAs, definite/demonstrative descriptions, and 'round' numeral phrases) can have both vague and precise uses, and, finally, other constituents (like NSs, logical DPs, and 'unround' numeral phrases) have only precise uses.

---

[3] It should be noted that it may still be possible to find some exceptional context in which logical expressions and expressions like *all the girls* can be used vaguely, particularly in cases of very high granularity (consider a situation where two people are in a 3 000 seat theatre for 3).

(i)   No one was in the theatre.

However, as discussed in [13], it is markedly more difficult to find such contexts than with simple definite descriptions. I believe that vague uses of logical expressions bear some similarity to cases of vague 'coerced' non-scalar adjectives discussed in footnote 3. However, the analysis of these phenomena is out of the scope of this paper.

Table 2. AP/DP classes relevant for vagueness

	Vague	Vague/Precise	Precise
APs	*tall, short, expensive...*	*empty, bald, straight...*	*prime, atomic, hexagonal...*
DPs	*many girls, few girls ...*	*the girls, these girls, 100 meters...*	*all the girls, no girls, 103 meters ...*

1.3   The Scope of the Paper

Compared to the size and complexity of the data set described in above, the analytical goal of this paper is very modest. In particular, it consists in, firstly, presenting a mereological extension of one of the logics that has been applied to the analysis of vague adjectival predicates ([5]'s *Tolerant, Classical, Strict* (TCS)) and, secondly, showing how part-structure vagueness can modelled in this framework. Thus, the formal part of this paper serves as a small illustration of the potential that this style of approach has to be developed into an analysis of the full range of data concerning vagueness and precision in the DP domain.

In what follows, I will restrict my attention to how to combine two kinds of subject DPs (singular DPs and plural definite descriptions) with singular/plural vague/precise predicates.

(20)   a.   Mary is Canadian. (Singular subject/Precise singular predicate)
         b.   Mary is tall. (Singular subject/Vague singular predicate)
         c.   The girls are Canadian. (Vague plural subject/Precise plural predicate)
         d.   The girls are tall. (Vague plural subject/Vague plural predicate)

Since even this small fragment will present a fair amount of complexity, I will leave many of the constructions discussed above to future work. Importantly, I will not make a distinction between relative and absolute adjectives, nor will I present an in depth analysis of intensional DPs like *many girls*. For how to integrate the relative/absolute distinction and the different vagueness patterns associated with this distinction into TCS, see [2]. Furthermore, for simplicity, I will essentially treat all subject DPs as syntactically atomic, setting aside (for the moment) problems of the semantic composition of DPs and the effects of the composition process on the vagueness of syntactically complex constituents. Finally, I will not provide an analysis of vagueness and precision associated with DPs paired with predicates of other plural predication classes besides (stubbornly) distributive predicates. That is, although, as discussed above, the predicate makes an important contribution to the presence/absence of the symptoms of vagueness, the contrast between examples (12) and (13) will also be left to future research.

2   Plural Predication: LPl

In this section, I present a simple logic for modelling non-vague plural predication based on [16]'s system. The basic idea is that, instead of containing structureless individuals in an unordered domain like in classical first order logic (FOL), the domain for the interpretation of plural individuals is (partially) ordered, and pluralities denote sums/joins of singular individuals. The vocabulary and syntax of the *Logic of Plurals* (LPl) are given below.

Definition 1. *Vocabulary. The vocabulary of LPl is that of first order predicate logic with the usual logical connectives and quantifiers ($\neg$, $\wedge$, $\forall$), singular individual constants ($A = \{a_1, a_2 \ldots\}$), singular individual variables ($V = \{v_1, v_2 \ldots\}$), and 1-place predicate symbols ($Pr = \{P, Q \ldots\}$). For ease of exposition, I restrict my attention to unary predicates. Additionally, there is another series of plural individual constants ($G = \{g_1, g_2 \ldots\}$) and variables ($S = \{s_1, s_2 \ldots\}$), a distinguished binary predicate: $\leq$, and a function on Pr: $*$.*

Definition 2. *Syntax. The syntax of LPl is given as follows:*
1. i) *If $\underline{x} \in V \cup A$, then $\underline{x} \in$ I-term.* **ii)** *If $\underline{x} \in G \cup S$, then $\underline{x} \in$ P-term.*
2. *If $P \in Pr$, then $P^* \in PlurP$.*
3. Atomic Formula: i) *If $\underline{x} \in$ I-term and $P \in Pr$, then $P(\underline{x})$ is an atomic formula,* **ii)** *If $\underline{x} \in$ P-term and $P^* \in PlurP$, then $P^*(\underline{x})$ is an atomic formula,* **iii** *If $\underline{x}, y \in$ P-term, then $\underline{x} \leq y$ is an atomic formula.*
4. Well-Formed Formula (wff): *Defined as in FOL.*

With respect to the semantics of LPl, we first define the structure into which pluralities are interpreted.

Definition 3. *Plural Model Structure. A plural model structure $\mathcal{M}$ is a tuple $\langle D, \leq \rangle$, where D is a finite set of singular/plural individuals, $\leq$ is a binary relation on D^4.*

Furthermore, we stipulate that $\langle D, \leq \rangle$ satisfies the axioms of classical extensional mereology (CEM).[5] First, some definitions:

Definition 4. *Overlap ($\circ$). For all $g_1, g_2 \in D$, $g_1 \circ g_2$ iff $\exists g_3 \in D$ such that $g_3 \leq g_1$ and $g_3 \leq g_2$.*

Definition 5. *Fusion (Fu). For $g_1 \in D$ and $X \subseteq D$, $Fu(g_1, X)$ ('g_1 fuses X') iff, for all $g_2 \in D$,*

(21) $g_2 \circ g_1$ iff there is some g_3 such that $g_3 \in X$ and $g_2 \circ g_3$.

We now adopt the following constraints on $\langle D, \leq \rangle$:

1. **Reflexivity.** For all $g_1 \in D$, $g_1 \leq g_1$.
2. **Transitivity.** For all g_1, g_2, g_3, if $g_1 \leq g_2$ and $g_2 \leq g_3$, then $g_1 \leq g_3$.
3. **Anti-symmetry.** For all $g_1, g_2 \in D$, if $g_1 \leq g_2$ and $g_2 \leq g_1$, then $g_1 = g_2$.

---

[4] Note that I use the non-bolded $\leq$ for the distinguished binary predicate in the language and the bolded $\leq$ for the part structure relation in the model. I trust this will not cause confusion.

[5] This particular axiomatization is taken from [9] (p.81). The version of *fusion* used here is what Hovda calls 'type 1 fusion'.

4. **Strong Supplementation.** For all $g_1, g_2 \in D$, for all g_3, if, if $g_3 \leq g_1$, then $g_3 \circ g_2$, then $g_1 \leq g_2$.
5. **Fusion Existence.** For all $X \subseteq D$, if there is some $g_1 \in X$, then there is some $g_2 \in D$ such that $Fu(g_2, X)$.

We can note that, in CEM, for every subset of D, not only does its fusion exist, but it is also unique (cf. [9], p. 70). Therefore, in what follows, I will often use the following notation:

Definition 6. *Join/sum/fusion* ($\bigvee$). *For all $X \subseteq D$, $\bigvee X$ is the unique g_1 such that $Fu(g_1, X)$.*

- *Occasionally, we will write $g_1 \vee g_2$ for $\bigvee \{g_1, g_2\}$.*

Finally, since we stipulated that every domain D is finite, every structure $\langle D, \leq \rangle$ is atomic. Thus, the structures that we are interested in are those of atomistic CEM. We define the notion of an *atom* as follows[6]:

Definition 9. *Atom.* $g_1 \in D$ *is an atom iff there is no $g_2 \in D$ such that $g_2 < g_1$.*

- *We write $AT(D)$ for the set of atoms of $\langle D, \leq \rangle$.*

Finally, we can observe that, in atomistic CEM, there is a very simple condition on the identity of individuals: two individuals are identical iff they have the same atoms.

Proposition 1. *[22]'s SF8 (p. 87).* *For all $g_1, g_2 \in D$,*

(22) $g_1 = g_2$ *iff for all atoms a_1, $a_1 \leq g_1$ iff $a_1 \leq g_2$.*

We now define a plural model.

Definition 10. *Plural Model. A plural model M is a tuple $\langle D, \leq, m \rangle$, where $\langle D, \leq \rangle$ is a plural model structure and m is a mapping on the non-logical vocabulary such that: If $\underline{a_1} \in A$, then $m(\underline{a_1}) \in AT(D)$; If $\underline{g_1} \in G$, then $m(\underline{g_1}) \in D$; and if $P \in Pr$, then $m(P) \in \mathcal{P}(AT(\overline{D}))$.*

Note that I will often write a_1 for $m(\underline{a_1})$ and g_1 for $m(\underline{g_1})$.

A major insight of Link's paper is to propose that there exists a non-arbitrary link between the interpretation of a singular predicate and its plural counterpart; in particular, he proposes that plural distributive predicates are derived from singular predicates through a * operator which generates all the individual sums/joins of members of the extensions of P.

---

[6] Where identity and proper part are defined as follows:

Definition 7. *Identical (=). For all $g_1, g_2 \in D$, $g_1 = g_2$ iff $g_1 \leq g_2$ and $g_2 \leq g_1$.*

Definition 8. *Proper part (<). For all $g_1, g_2 \in D$, $g_1 < g_2$ iff $g_1 \leq g_2$ and $g_1 \neq g_2$.*

Definition 11. *Interpretation of* *. *For all* $P \in Pr$, $m(P^*) = \{g_1 : Fu(g_1, X),$
for some $X \subseteq m(P)\}$.

The interpretation of variables is given by assignments.

Definition 12. ***Assignment.*** *An assignment in a model* M *is a function* $g :$
$\{x_n : n \in \mathbb{N}\} \to D$ *(from the set of variables to the domain* D*)*.

- *If* v_1 *is a singular variable, then* $g(v_1) \in AT(D)$.
- *If* s_1 *is a plural variable, then* $g(s_1) \in D$.

A model together with an assignment is an interpretation.

Definition 13. ***Interpretation.*** *An interpretation* $\mathcal{I}$ *is a pair* $\langle M, g \rangle$, *where*
M *is a model and* g *is an assignment.*

We first associate an element from the domain D with every interpretation $\mathcal{I}$
and every term t.

Definition 14. ***Interpretation of terms.***

1. *If* v *is a (singular or plural) variable, then* $\mathcal{I}(v) = g(v)$.
2. *If* $\underline{a}$ *is a (singular or plural) constant, then* $\mathcal{I}(\underline{a}) = m(\underline{a})$.

Finally, the satisfaction relation ($\vDash$) is defined as in definition 15. In what follows,
for an interpretation $\mathcal{I} = \langle M, g \rangle$, a (singular or plural) variable v, and $\underline{a}$ a
(singular or plural) constant, let $g[\underline{a}/v]$ be the assignment in M which maps
v to a and agrees with g on all variables that are distinct from v. Also, let
$\mathcal{I}[\underline{a}/v] = \langle M, g[\underline{a}/v] \rangle$.

Definition 15. *Plural Satisfaction. For* $\mathcal{I}$ *an interpretation,*

1. $\mathcal{I} \vDash P(\underline{a_1})$ *iff* $\mathcal{I}(\underline{a_1}) \in m(P)$
2. $\mathcal{I} \vDash P^*(\underline{g_1})$ *iff* $\mathcal{I}(\underline{g_1}) \in m(P^*)$
3. $\mathcal{I} \vDash \underline{g_1} \leq \underline{g_2}$ *iff* $\mathcal{I}(\underline{g_1}) \leq \mathcal{I}(\underline{g_2})$
4. $\mathcal{I} \vDash \neg\phi$ *iff* $\mathcal{I} \nvDash \phi$
5. $\mathcal{I} \vDash \phi \wedge \psi$ *iff* $\mathcal{I} \vDash \phi$ *and* $\mathcal{I} \vDash \psi$
6. $\mathcal{I} \vDash \forall v_1 \phi$ *iff for every* $a_2 \in AT(D), \mathcal{I}[\underline{a_2}/v_1] \vDash \phi$
7. $\mathcal{I} \vDash \forall s_1 \phi$ *iff for every* $g_2 \in D, \mathcal{I}[\underline{g_2}/s_1] \vDash \phi$

We can prove that all predicates in this system are distributive; that is, when a
plural property P^* holds of a plurality g_1, the corresponding singular property
P holds of all the singular individuals that make up g_1.

Theorem 1. *Distributivity. For* $\mathcal{I}$, *a plural interpretation,* $g_1 \in D$, *and* $P \in Pr$,
$\mathcal{I} \vDash P^*(\underline{g_1})$ *iff for all atoms* $a_1 \leq g_1$, $\mathcal{I} \vDash P(\underline{a_1})$

Proof. $\Rightarrow$ Suppose $\mathcal{I} \vDash P^*(\underline{g_1})$ and let a_1 be an atom such that $a_1 \leq g_1$. Suppose,
for a contradiction that $\mathcal{I} \nvDash P(\underline{a_1})$. Since $\mathcal{I} \vDash P^*(\underline{g_1})$, by definition 11, there is
some set of atoms $X \subseteq P$ such that $Fu(g_1, X)$. Since $\mathcal{I} \nvDash P(\underline{a_1})$, $a_1 \notin X$. So
$X \neq X \cup \{a_1\}$. Therefore, by proposition 11, $\bigvee X \neq \bigvee(X \cup \{a_1\})$. However,
since, by assumption, $a_1 \leq g_1$, and $\bigvee X = g_1$, by the definition of Fusion,
$\bigvee X \cup \{a_1\} = g_1$. So $\bigvee X = \bigvee X \cup \{a_1\}$. $\bot$ Therefore $\mathcal{I} \vDash P(\underline{a_1})$. $\Leftarrow$ Suppose
that, for all atoms $a_1 \leq g_1$, $\mathcal{I} \vDash P(\underline{a_1})$ to show $\mathcal{I} \vDash P^*(\underline{g_1})$. Immediate from
definition 11. $\qquad\square$

In summary, with LPl, we can analyze sentences with non-vague predicates that have both singular and non-vague plural subjects. However, the system does not provide a way for modelling the properties of vague language (borderline cases etc.) with either singulars or plurals. Furthermore, Theorem 1 shows that LPl is not equipped to treat part-structure vagueness: all its predicates are fully distributive.

3   Vague Predication: TCS

In this section, I outline [5]'s *Tolerant, Classical, Strict* framework. This system was originally developed as a way to preserve the intuition that vague predicates are *tolerant* (i.e. satisfy $\forall x \forall y [P(x) \ \& \ x \sim_P y \rightarrow P(y)]$, where $\sim_P$ is an indifference relation for a predicate P), without running into the Sorites paradox. [5] adopt a non-classical logical framework with three notions of satisfaction: classical truth, tolerant truth, and its dual, strict truth. Formulas are tolerantly/strictly satisfied based on classical truth and predicate-relative, possibly non-transitive *indifference relations*. For a given predicate P, an indifference relation, $\sim_P$, relates those individuals that are viewed as sufficiently similar with respect to P. For example, for the predicate *tall*, $\sim_{tall}$ would be something like the relation "not looking to have distinct heights". In this framework, we say that *John is tall* is tolerantly true just in case John has a very similar height to someone who is classically tall (i.e. has a height greater than or equal to the contextually given 'tallness' threshold). The framework is defined (using the notation adopted in this paper) as follows:

Definition 16. *Language. The language of TCS is that of first order predicate logic with neither identity nor function symbols.*

For the semantics, we define three notions of truth: one that corresponds to truth in classical FOL (*c-truth*), and two that are novel: *t-truth* and its dual *s-truth*.

Definition 17. *C(lassical) Model. A c-model is a tuple $\langle D, m \rangle$ where D is a non-empty domain of individuals and m is a mapping on the non-logical vocabulary: for a constant $\underline{a_1}$, $m(\underline{a_1}) \in D$; for a predicate P, $m(P) \in \mathcal{P}(D)$.*

Definition 18. *T(olerant) Model. A t-model is a tuple $\langle D, m, \sim \rangle$, where $\langle D, m \rangle$ is a c-model and $\sim$ is a function that takes any predicate P to a binary relation $\sim_P$ on D. For any P, $\sim_P$ is reflexive and symmetric (but possibly not transitive).*

A non-empty set with a reflexive, symmetric relation on it is often called a *tolerance space* (ex. [20]). Thus, for any P, the structure $\langle D, \sim_P \rangle$ is a tolerance space.

Assignments, interpretations (in either c-models or t-models ($\mathcal{I} = \langle \langle D, m, \sim \rangle, g \rangle$)) and the interpretation of terms are defined in a manner parallel to classical FOL. Furthermore, *c-truth/c-satisfaction* is defined as classical truth in either a c-model or a t-model.

Definition 19. *c-truth. Let M be either a c-model such that $M = \langle D, m \rangle$ or a t-model such that $M = \langle D, m, \sim \rangle$. For an interpretation $\mathcal{I}$ of M:*

1. $\mathcal{I} \vDash^c P(\underline{a_1})$ *iff* $\mathcal{I}(\underline{a_1}) \in m(P)$
2. $\mathcal{I} \vDash^c \neg\phi$ *iff* $\mathcal{I} \nvDash^c \phi$
3. $\mathcal{I} \vDash^c \phi \wedge \psi$ *iff* $\mathcal{I} \vDash^c \phi$ *and* $\mathcal{I} \vDash^c \psi$
4. $\mathcal{I} \vDash^c \forall v_1 \phi$ *iff for every a_1 in D,* $\mathcal{I}[\underline{a_1}/v_1] \vDash^c \phi$

T-truth and s-truth are defined as follows.

Definition 20. *t-truth and s-truth. Let $\mathcal{I}$ be an interpretation of a t-model.*

1. $\mathcal{I} \vDash^t P(\underline{a_1})$ *iff* $\exists a_2 \sim_P a_1 : \mathcal{I} \vDash^c P(\underline{a_2})$
2. $\mathcal{I} \vDash^t \neg\phi$ *iff* $\mathcal{I} \nvDash^s \phi$
3. $\mathcal{I} \vDash^t \phi \wedge \psi$ *iff* $\mathcal{I} \vDash^t \phi$ *and* $\mathcal{I} \vDash^t \psi$
4. $\mathcal{I} \vDash^t \forall x \phi$ *iff for every a_1 in D,* $\mathcal{I}[\underline{a_1}/v_1] \vDash^t \phi$

5. $\mathcal{I} \vDash^s P(\underline{a_1})$ *iff* $\forall a_2 \sim_P a_1 : \mathcal{I} \vDash^c P(\underline{a_2})$
6. $\mathcal{I} \vDash^s \neg\phi$ *iff* $\mathcal{I} \nvDash^t \phi$
7. $\mathcal{I} \vDash^s \phi \wedge \psi$ *iff* $\mathcal{I} \vDash^s \phi$ *and* $\mathcal{I} \vDash^s \psi$
8. $\mathcal{I} \vDash^s \forall v_1 \phi$ *iff for every a_1 in D,* $\mathcal{I}[\underline{a_1}/v_1] \vDash^s \phi$

In summary, TCS models sentences with singular subjects and both vague and non-vague predicates (i.e. *Mary is tall* and *Mary is Canadian*).

4   Vague Language and Plural Predication: PTCS

In this section, I enrich the framework above with the structure of LPl in order to treat sentences with plural subjects. The language of this new system, *Plural Tolerant Classical Strict* (PTCS), is that of LPl, and c-truth is defined in the same way as truth in LPl as well.

Definition 21. *Plural c-model. A plural c-model is a tuple $\langle D, \leq, m \rangle$ where $\langle D, \leq \rangle$ is a plural model structure (as defined above) and m is a mapping on the non-logical vocabulary such that: $m(\underline{a_1}) \in AT(D)$; $m(\underline{g_1}) \in D$, $m(P) \in \mathcal{P}(AT(D))$. Also, $m(P^*)$ is defined as in definition 11.*

Definition 22. *C-truth in a plural model for formulas involving mereological relations (c-truth for logical connectives is the same as truth in FOL/LPl). For $\mathcal{I}$ be an interpretation of a plural model,*

1. $\mathcal{I} \vDash^c P(\underline{a_1})$ *iff* $\mathcal{I}(\underline{a_1}) \in m(P)$
2. $\mathcal{I} \vDash^c P^*(\underline{g_1})$ *iff* $\mathcal{I}(\underline{g_1}) \in m(P^*)$
3. $\mathcal{I} \vDash^c \underline{g_1} \leq \underline{g_2}$ *iff* $\mathcal{I}(\underline{g_1}) \leq \mathcal{I}(\underline{g_2})$

First of all, since classical truth and c-truth coincide, (Classical) Distributivity is also a theorem of PTCS:

Theorem 2. *Classical Distributivity. For M, a plural c-model or a plural t-model (to be defined below), and an interpretation $\mathcal{I} = \langle M, g \rangle$, $g_1 \in D$, and $P \in Pr$, $\mathcal{I} \vDash^c P^*(\underline{g_1})$ iff for all atoms $a_1 \leq g_1$, $\mathcal{I} \vDash^c P(\underline{a_1})$ (Proof is immediate from Theorem 1.)*

T-models are defined as follows:

Definition 23. *Plural t-model. A plural t-model M is a tuple $\langle D, \leq, m, \sim \rangle$ such that $\langle D, \leq, m \rangle$ is a plural c-model and $\sim$ is a function that takes any predicate P to a binary relation $\sim_P$ on $AT(D)$ that is reflexive and symmetric, but possibly not transitive.*

With respect to defining indifference relations with plural predicates, a first option might be to have $\sim_{P*}$ be given as part of the model (i.e. have them given entirely based on context), like $\sim_P$.

Definition 24. $\sim_*$ *(First try). For all P^*, $\sim_{P*}$ is a binary relation on D that is reflexive and symmetric (but possibly not transitive).*

T/S-truth for the formulas involving mereological relations is defined below (t/s-truth for logical connectives is the same as in TCS).

Definition 25. *T-truth and s-truth. Let M be a plural t-model and $\mathcal{I} = \langle M, g \rangle$ be an interpretation.*

1. $\mathcal{I} \vDash^t P(\underline{a_1})$ iff $\exists a_2 \sim_P a_1 : \mathcal{I} \vDash^c P(\underline{a_2})$
2. $\mathcal{I} \vDash^t P^*(\underline{g_1})$ iff $\exists g_2 \sim_{P*} g_1 : \mathcal{I} \vDash^c P^*(\underline{g_2})$
3. $\mathcal{I} \vDash^t g_1 \leq g_2$ iff $\mathcal{I} \vDash^c g_1 \leq g_2$

4. $\mathcal{I} \vDash^s P(\underline{a_1})$ iff $\forall a_2 \sim_P a_1 : \mathcal{I} \vDash^c P(\underline{a_2})$
5. $\mathcal{I} \vDash^s P^*(\underline{g_1})$ iff $\forall g_2 \sim_{P*} g_1 : \mathcal{I} \vDash^c P^*(\underline{g_2})$
6. $\mathcal{I} \vDash^s g_1 \leq g_2$ iff $\mathcal{I} \vDash^c g_1 \leq g_2$

Firstly, note that the interpretation of formulas involving $\leq$ is the same regardless of which type of satisfaction we are considering. This reflects the fact that mereological relations are part of the model structure[7].

Note secondly that the definition of $\sim_{P*}$ is very weak. In fact, I argue that the definition 24 is insufficient to account for how the tolerant truth of sentences with non-vague plural subjects is calculated. In particular, it seems that we want a link between the tolerant truth of a sentence like *The three girls are tall*, where *the three girls* refers to the group of Mary, Sarah and Isabelle, and the tolerant truth of the sentences *Mary is tall; Sarah is tall* and *Isabelle is tall*. In other words, we want the tolerant truth of sentences with vague distributive predicates and non-vague plural subjects to be calculated on the basis of whether

---

[7] See [5] for the same 'crisp' approach to *indifference predicates*: predicates in the language that express the $\sim$ relations in the model. This is not a necessary feature of the system; in fact, allowing for part structure relations to be vague may have some empirical explanatory potential (cf. [4]'s analysis of the non-countability of mass nouns). However, exploring this possibility is out of the scope of this work.

the predicate tolerantly applies to the subjects' atoms. However, if we allow $\sim_{P*}$ to be just any reflexive and symmetric relation between pluralities, this dependency is not there, even though, as shown by theorem 2, the predicates of PTCS are all classically distributive. The fact that, with no further restrictions on plural indifference relations, classical distributivity does not imply tolerant distributivity is shown by theorem 3[8].

Theorem 3. *c-distributivity $\not\to$ t-distributivity. It is not the case that, for all interpretations $\mathcal{I}$, $g_1 \in D$, and $P \in Pr$,*

- *If $\mathcal{I} \vDash^c P^*(\underline{g_1})$ iff for all atoms $a_1 \leq g_1$, $\mathcal{I} \vDash^c P(\underline{a_1})$, **then** $\mathcal{I} \vDash^t P^*(\underline{g_1})$ iff for all atoms $a_1 \leq g_1$, $\mathcal{I} \vDash^t P(\underline{a_1})$.*

Proof. Let M be a plural t-model $\langle D, \leq, m, \sim \rangle$, where D is a mereological structure generated by the atoms $\{a_1, a_2, a_3\}$ and let $m(P) = \{a_1, a_2\}$. Therefore, by definition 21, $m(P^*) = \{a_1, a_2, a_1 \vee a_2\}$. Furthermore, let $\sim_P = \{\langle a_1, a_2 \rangle, \langle a_2, a_1 \rangle\}$ + reflexivity, and let $\sim_{P*} = \{\langle a_1 \vee a_3, a_1 \vee a_2 \rangle, \langle a_1, a_2 \rangle, \langle a_2, a_1 \rangle\}$ + reflexivity. Finally, let $m(g_1) = a_1 \vee a_3$.

Clearly, P^* is classically distributive. However, $\mathcal{I} \vDash^t P^*(\underline{g_1})$, but $\mathcal{I} \not\vDash^t P(\underline{a_3})$. Therefore, P^* is not tolerantly distributive. $\square$

Therefore, in order to reflect the relationship between plural tolerant distributive predication and singular tolerant predication, I propose that plural indifference relations are constructed out of singular ones through closure under pointwise join, the binary operation over pairs defined below.

Definition 26. *Pointwise join. ($\vec{\vee}$) For $\langle w, x \rangle$ and $\langle y, z \rangle$, $\langle w, x \rangle \vec{\vee} \langle y, z \rangle = \langle w \vee y, x \vee z \rangle$*

Definition 27. *$\sim_*$ (final). For all P^*, $\sim_{P*}$ is the closure of $\sim_P$ under $\vec{\vee}$.*

We first verify that $\sim_{P*}$ has the required properties to be an indifference relation: it is reflexive and symmetric.

Theorem 4. *For all P^*, $\langle D, \sim_{P*} \rangle$ is a tolerance space.*

Proof. Since, by assumption, D is non-empty, we must show that $\sim_{P*}$ is reflexive and symmetric. Let P be a singular predicate. **Reflexivity.** Let $g_1 \in D$ to show $\langle g_1, g_1 \rangle \in \sim_{P*}$. Let A be the set of atoms under g_1. By the reflexivity of $\sim_P$, for all $a_1 \in A$, $\langle a_1, a_1 \rangle \in \sim_P$. By definition 27, the pointwise join of all the pairs $\langle a_1, a_1 \rangle$, for $a_1 \in A$, is in $\sim_{P*}$, i.e. $\langle \bigvee A, \bigvee A \rangle \in \sim_{P*}$. Since, by assumption and the atomicity of $\langle D, \vee \rangle$, $\bigvee A = g_1$, $\langle g_1, g_1 \rangle \in \sim_{P*}$. **Symmetry.** Let $\langle g_1, g_2 \rangle \in \sim_{P*}$ to show $\langle g_2, g_1 \rangle \in \sim_{P*}$. Call the set of atoms under g_1, A and the set of atoms under g_2, B. Because $\langle D, \vee \rangle$ is atomic, $\langle g_1, g_2 \rangle = \langle \bigvee A, \bigvee B \rangle$. Since $\langle g_1, g_2 \rangle \in \sim_{P*}$, it is the pointwise join of some subset R of $\sim_P$. Since $\sim_P$ is symmetric, the inverse of R, R^{-1} is also a subset of $\sim_P$. Consider the pointwise join of R^{-1}: $\langle \bigvee B, \bigvee A \rangle$, a.k.a $\langle g_2, g_1 \rangle$. By definition 27, $\langle g_2, g_1 \rangle \in \sim_{P*}$. $\square$

---

[8] This result is somewhat surprising, given that it is a theorem of singular TCS that classical validity implies tolerant validity ([5]'s Corollary 1).

With this new definition of $\sim_{P*}$, we can prove that tolerant distributivity holds in PTCS:

Theorem 5. *Tolerant Distributivity. Let M be a plural t-model, let P be a predicate, and let $g_1 \in D$. $\mathcal{I} \vDash^t P^*(\underline{g_1})$ iff for all atoms $a_1 \leq g_1$, $\mathcal{I} \vDash^t P(\underline{a_1})$.*

Proof. $\Rightarrow$ Suppose $\mathcal{I} \vDash^t P^*(\underline{g_1})$ and let a_1 be an atom such that $a_1 \leq g_1$. Since $\mathcal{I} \vDash^t P^*(\underline{g_1})$, by definition 25, there is some group g_2 such that $g_2 \sim_{P*} g_1$ and $\mathcal{I} \vDash^c P^*(\underline{g_2})$. By definition 27, there is some atom $a_2 \leq g_2$ such that $a_2 \sim_P a_1$. Furthermore, by classical distributivity (Theorem 2), $\mathcal{I} \vDash^c P(\underline{a_2})$. Therefore, by definition 25, $\mathcal{I} \vDash^t P(\underline{a_1})$.
$\Leftarrow$ Suppose for all atoms $a_1 \leq g_1$, $\mathcal{I} \vDash^t P(\underline{a_1})$ to show $\mathcal{I} \vDash^t P^*(\underline{g_1})$. Call the set of atoms under g_1 A. Since P tolerantly holds on all the members of A, by definition 25, they are all related to some other atom for which P classically holds. Let $B = \{a : x \sim_P a \mid x \in A\}$. Now consider the group $\bigvee B$, call it g_2. By Theorem 2, $\mathcal{I} \vDash^c P^*(\underline{g_2})$. Furthermore, by definition 27, $g_1 \sim_{P*} g_2$. So, $\mathcal{I} \vDash^t P^*(\underline{g_1})$. $\qquad\square$

In summary, the mereological extension of TCS that I have presented correctly assigns interpretations to sentences with singular subjects and both vague and non-vague predicates (*Mary is tall/Canadian*), and non-vague plural subjects with both vague and non-vague predicates (*John and Mary are tall/Canadian*). However, we still cannot model sentences like *The girls are tall/Canadian*: although we need it to create the proper interpretation for sentences with vague predicates and non-vague plural subjects, definition 27 enforces universal (tolerant) distributive quantification over the atoms of the subject (this fact is reflected in Theorem 5). Thus, we have not yet accounted for the vague effects created by subjects like *the girls*.

4.1   Vague Subjects

To account for vagueness associated with the subject DP, I add to the language a generalized quantifier lifter: I.

Definition 28. *Syntax. 1) If $\underline{g_1} \in P\text{-}Term$, then $I_{\underline{g_1}} \in GQ\text{-}term$. 2) If $I_{\underline{g_1}} \in GQ\text{-}term$ and $P^* \in PlurP$, then $I_{\underline{g_1}}(P^*)$ is an atomic formula.*

For the classical semantics, the proposal is essentially that of [10] (p.48), based on a proposal by [18]: rather than denoting in D, subject DPs can be viewed as denoting generalized quantifiers; that is, they denote second order properties as defined below.

Definition 29. *Semantics. For all $g_1 \in D$, I maps g_1 to the family of properties containing it: 1) $m(I_{\underline{g_1}}) = \{P^* : M \vDash^c P^*(\underline{g_1})\}$ 2) C-truth is defined as: $\mathcal{I} \vDash^c I_{\underline{g_1}}(P^*)$ iff $P^* \in \{Q^* : \mathcal{I} \vDash^c Q^*(\underline{g_1})\}$*

It is easily proven from the definitions above that $\mathcal{I} \vDash^c I_{\underline{g_1}}(P^*)$ iff $\mathcal{I} \vDash^c P^*(\underline{g_1})$.

For the tolerant/strict semantics: just like how properties of individuals are associated with indifference relations by $\sim$, I propose that properties of properties are also associated with indifference relations that express how similar they are with respect to an individual. For example, in the same way that $\sim_{tall}$ relates elements of $AT(D)$ that have an irrelevant difference in height, $\sim_{I_{g_1}}$ relates elements of $^*\mathcal{P}(D)$ that map the relevant parts of g_1 to true.

Definition 30. *T/S-truth in a plural t-model. Add to definition 25:*

1. $\mathcal{I} \vDash^t I_{\underline{g_1}}(P^*)$ *iff* $\exists Q^* \sim_{I_{g_1}} P^*: \mathcal{I} \vDash^t Q^*(\underline{g_1})$
2. $\mathcal{I} \vDash^s I_{\underline{g_1}}(P^*)$ *iff* $\forall Q^* \sim_{I_{g_1}} P^*: \mathcal{I} \vDash^s Q^*(\underline{g_1})$

To see how this new system works, consider the following example.

Example 1. Let M be a plural t-model $\langle D, \leq, m, \sim \rangle$ such that $D =$ a mereological structure generated by the atoms $\{a_1, a_2, a_3\}$. Let $m(P) = \{a_1, a_2\}$ and $m(Q) = \{a_1, a_2, a_3\}$. Therefore, by the definition of *, $m(P^*) = \{a_1, a_2, a_1 \vee a_2\}$ and $m(Q^*) = \{a_1, a_2, a_3, a_1 \vee a_2, a_2 \vee a_3, a_1 \vee a_3, a_1 \vee a_2 \vee a_3\}$. Let $m(g_1) = a_1 \vee a_2$ and $m(g_2) = a_1 \vee a_2 \vee a_3$. By definition 29, $m(I_{g_1}) = \{m(P^*), m(Q^*), \{a_1 \vee a_2\}, \{a_1 \vee a_2, a_1\}, \{a_1 \vee a_2\} \ldots \}$ and $m(I_{g_2}) = \{m(Q^*), \{a_1 \vee a_2 \vee a_3\}, \{a_1 \vee a_2 \vee a_3, a_1\}, \{a_1 \vee a_2 \vee a_3, a_2\} \ldots \}$ (note $m(I_{g_2}) \subset m(I_{g_1})$). Let $\mathcal{I}$ be an interpretation: $\langle M, g \rangle$. So $\mathcal{I} \vDash^c I_{\underline{g_1}}(P^*)$ but $\mathcal{I} \nvDash^c I_{\underline{g_2}}(P^*)$.

Now, let $\sim_P = \{\langle a_1, a_1 \rangle, \langle a_2, a_2 \rangle, \langle a_3, a_3 \rangle\}$ (i.e. P is a non-vague predicate), so by definition 27, $\sim_{P^*}$ is the point-wise join of $\sim_P$. Therefore, $\sim_{P^*}$ has no members beyond what is required for reflexivity. Finally, let $\sim_{I_{g_2}} = \{\langle m(P^*), m(Q^*) \rangle, \langle m(Q^*), m(P^*) \rangle\} +$ reflexivity. By definitions 25 and 30, $\mathcal{I} \vDash^t I_{\underline{g_2}}(P^*)$.

The example can be summarized as follows: Suppose that *the girls* refers to the group $a_1 \vee a_2 \vee a_3$. Then *the girls* does not classically map P^* to true in the model because P^* does not affect a_3. However, since P^* is indifferent from Q^*, and Q^* tolerantly maps $a_1 \vee a_2 \vee a_3$ to true, *the girls* will tolerantly hold of P^*. In other words, *the girls* tolerantly maps P^* to true even though P does not tolerantly hold of a_3 because cases where the predicate holds of two members of the group are 'just as good' as cases where the predicate holds of all three members, i.e. a_3 is an irrelevant member. Thus, this example illustrates how a sentence with a vague subject and a non-vague predicate could be tolerantly true even if the predicate does not hold of the entire subject.

Furthermore, the example above can serve as the required case to prove that tolerant distributivity does not hold between I_{g_1}s and their atoms.

Theorem 6. *Non-maximality. Let $\mathcal{I}$ be an interpretation of a plural t-model, let P be a predicate, and let $g_1 \in D$. $\mathcal{I} \vDash^t I_{\underline{g_1}}(P^*) \nrightarrow$ for all atoms $a_1 \leq g_1$, $\mathcal{I} \vDash^t P(\underline{a_1})$.*

Proof. In example 1, $\mathcal{I} \vDash^t I_{\underline{g_2}}(P^*)$, but a_3 is an atom under g_2, and it is not the case that $\mathcal{I} \vDash^t P(\underline{a_3})$. $\qquad\square$

Theorem 6 is the result that we need to reflect the observation that bare definite plural (i.e. vague) subjects tolerate exceptions. An interesting corollary of this fact is that, at the tolerant level, the equivalence between a group and the corresponding Montagovian individual breaks down: in particular, in some models, I_{g_1} will tolerantly map more properties to true than will hold of g_1.

Corollary 1. $\mathcal{I} \vDash^t I_{\underline{g_1}}(P^*) \nrightarrow \mathcal{I} \vDash^t P^*(\underline{g_1})$

Proof. Immediately from theorems 5 and 6. $\qquad\square$

Although, for ease of exposition, the example features a non-vague predicate, the recursion in definition 30 allows for sentences with borderline subjects to be tolerantly true even if they only tolerantly satisfy the predicate. Thus, we capture 'double vagueness' cases like *The girls are tall.*

In conclusion, I presented a new system, PTCS, that combines the insights from Link's LPM and Cobreros et al.'s TCS to model distributive predication with singular and plural vague and non-vague predicates. The empirical scope of this paper was limited to certain kinds of definite plurals combined with distributive predicates; however, the analysis outlined above provides a basis for extending this approach to vague DPs with other kinds of predication and opens a new line of research into the distribution and properties of vague constituents outside the adjectival domain.

References

1. Brisson, C.: Plurals, ALL and the Non-uniformity of Collective Predication. Linguistics and Philosophy 26, 129–184 (2003)
2. Burnett, H.: The Grammar of Tolerance: On Vagueness, Context-Sensitivity, and the Origin of Scale Structure. PhD Thesis. University of California, Los Angeles (2012)
3. Champollion, L.: Parts of a Whole: Distributivity as a Bridge between Aspect and Measurement. PhD Thesis, University of Pennsylvania (2011)
4. Chierchia, G.: Mass Nouns, Vagueness and Semantic Variation. Synthese 174, 99–149 (2010)
5. Cobreros, P., Égré, P., Ripley, D., van Rooij, R.: Tolerant, Classical, Strict. Journal of Philosophical Logic (2011) (forthcoming)
6. Dowty, D.: Collective predicates, Distributive predicates, and *all*. In: Marshall, F. (ed.) Proceedings of the 3rd ESCOL, pp. 97–115. Ohio State University, Ohio (1987)
7. Fara, D.: Shifting Sands: An interest-relative theory of vagueness. Philosophical Topics 20, 45–81 (2000)
8. Fine, K.: Vagueness, Truth and Logic. Synthese 30, 265–300 (1975)
9. Hovda, P.: What is Classical Mereology? Journal of Philosophical Logic 38, 55–82 (2009)

10. Keenan, E., Faltz, L.: Boolean Semantics for Natural Language. Riedel, Dordrecht (1985)
11. Kennedy, C.: Vagueness and Grammar: The study of relative and absolute gradable predicates. Linguistics and Philosophy 30, 1–45 (2007)
12. Krifka, M.: Approximate Interpretation of Number Words: A Case for Strategic Communication. In: Bouma, G., Krämer, I., Zwarts, J. (eds.) Cognitive Foundations of Interpretation, Koninklijke Nederlandse Akademie van Wetenschapen, Amsterdam, pp. 111–126 (2007)
13. Lasersohn, P.: Pragmatic Halos. Language 75, 522–571 (1999)
14. Lappin, S.: An Intensional Parametric Semantics for Vague Quantifiers. Linguistics and Philosophy 23, 599–620 (2000)
15. Lewis, D.: Score-keeping in the Language Game. Journal of Philosophical Logic 8, 339–359 (1979)
16. Link, G.: The Logical Analysis of Plurals and Mass Nouns. In: Bauerle, R., Schwartze, C., von Stechow, A. (eds.) Meaning, Use and the Interpretation of Language, pp. 302–322. Mouton de Gruyter, The Hague (1983)
17. Malamud, S.: Non-Maximality and Distributivity: A Decision-Theoretic Approach. In: The Proceedings of Semantics and Linguistic Theory 16, Tokyo, Japan (2006)
18. Montague, R.: The Proper Treatment of Quantification in Ordinary English. In: Thomason, R. (ed.) Formal Philosophy: Selected Papers of Richard Montague, pp. 247–270. Yale University Press, New Haven (1974)
19. Pinkal, M.: Logic and Lexicon. Kluwer Academic Publishers, Dordrecht (1995)
20. Pogonowski, J.: Tolerance Spaces with Applications in Linguistics. Poznan University Press, Poznan (1981)
21. Rayo, A.: Word and Objects. Noûs 36, 436–464 (2002)
22. Simons, P.: Parts. MIT Press, Cambridge
23. Smith, N.: Vagueness and Degrees of Truth. OUP, Oxford (2008)
24. Unger, P.: Ignorance. Clarendon Press, Oxford (1975)
25. Wright, C.: On the Coherence of Vague Predicates. Synthese 30, 325–365 (1975)
26. Yoon, Y.: Total and Partial Predicates and the Weak and Strong Interpretations. Natural Language Semantics 4, 217–236 (1996)

The Syntax and Semantics
of Evaluative Degree Modification*

Hanna de Vries

Utrecht University

1   Introduction

Evaluative adverbs - a large and open class of adverbs that express the attitude
of the speaker towards the information she is conveying - can systematically
modify gradable adjectives as well as complete sentences. The different positions
are associated with a clear difference in meaning:

(1)   a.   Maxwell is $\left\{\begin{array}{l} \text{surprisingly} \\ \text{remarkably} \\ \text{shockingly} \end{array}\right\}$ tall.

   b. $\left\{\begin{array}{l} \text{Surprisingly} \\ \text{Remarkably} \\ \text{Shockingly} \end{array}\right\}$, Maxwell is tall.

The sentences in (1a) do not entail those in (1b) (Morzycki 2004, Nouwen 2005):
if we were expecting Maxwell to be tall, but just not *that* tall, we could utter
(1a) but not (1b).

   The semantics of the (b)-sentences seems uncomplicated: the adverb simply modifies the proposition expressed by *Maxwell is tall*. But what exactly
do the adverbs modify in an evaluative degree construction (henceforth EDC)
like *Maxwell is remarkably tall*? Do they similarly modify propositions, and if so,
what do these propositions express? Where does the semantic difference between
(1a) and (1b) come from?

1.1   Degree Semantics

I will adopt the following (fairly uncontroversial) assumptions about degree and
degree phrases, following a line of research developed in e.g. von Stechow (1984),
Heim (2000) and the first chapters of Kennedy (1997), though some details may
vary.

   Degree constructions, like *Vernon is six feet tall* or *Vernon is taller than
Maxwell*, are uniformly analysed as involving (1) a degree predicate G that relates

---

* I would like to thank Rick Nouwen, three anonymous reviewers and the audience
of the ESSLLI Student Session 2010 in Copenhagen for many useful discussions,
comments and questions on this paper and previous versions of it.

D. Lassiter and M. Slavkovik (Eds.): ESSLLI Student Sessions, LNCS 7415, pp. 195–211, 2012.

individuals and degrees (such that $G(d)(x)$ means that x has a property G to a degree d), and (2) a comparison between d and some other degree of G, d'. For example, a sentence like *Vernon is six feet tall* can be paraphrased as 'There is a degree d such that Vernon is d-tall and d equals or exceeds six feet'[1]. Similarly, *Vernon is taller than Maxwell* may be paraphrased as something like 'There is a degree d such that Vernon is d-tall and d exceeds Maxwell's height' (meaning '...d exceeds all degrees d' such that Maxwell is d-tall'). We capture this by assuming the following type and denotation for gradable adjectives like *tall*:

(2) $[\![tall]\!]_{\langle d,\langle e,t\rangle\rangle} = \lambda d\lambda x[\text{HEIGHT}(d)(x)]$

So gradable adjectives denote degree predicates. The comparison function, then, is provided by degree morphology: *-er*, for example, indicates a greater-than relationship between d and d'. Finally, the value of d' is provided by elements like *six feet* or *than Maxwell*.

While the above ingredients all need to be present in the semantics, they may be absent from overt syntax. The 'positive form' (*Vernon is tall*) intuitively involves Vernon's height being favourably compared to some contextually defined standard degree, but neither the comparison nor the standard are overt. Similarly, *Vernon is six feet tall* lacks an overtly stated greater-than-or-equal-to-relationship between Vernon's height and the degree of six feet, yet this meaning cannot be compositionally derived from just the denotations of *tall* and *six feet* (at least not without additional assumptions). For this reason, Cresswell (1976) and many people after him have assumed that the standard here is provided by a covert degree morpheme POS (where s_G is the contextually defined standard of G); its measure phrase-introducing cousin first appeared in Kennedy (1997) and was baptised MEAS in Svenonius & Kennedy (2006):

(3) a. $[\![\text{POS}]\!] = \lambda G_{\langle d,et\rangle}\lambda x_e\exists d_d[G(d)(x) \wedge d \geq s_G]$
     b. $[\![\text{MEAS}]\!] = \lambda G_{\langle d,et\rangle}\lambda x_e\lambda d'_d\exists d[G(d)(x) \wedge d = d']$

In (3), the three ingredients of a degree construction - degree predicate, comparison function and comparison degree - are explicitly present. Both denotations involve existential closure of the degree argument of the predicate.

Finally, following Heim (2000), we take it that gradable predicates are *monotone* in the following sense:

(4) A function f of type $\langle d, \langle e, t\rangle\rangle$ is monotone iff
     $\forall x\forall d\forall d'[f(d)(x) = 1 \ \& \ d' < d \rightarrow f(d')(x) = 1]$

In words: If x has a certain property to a degree d, it also has this property to all lower degrees d'. This means, for example, that every person who is tall to some degree $d \geq s_G$, is also tall to the standard degree s_G. 'Being tall' may thus be defined as 'being tall to the standard degree s_G', which is true for everyone who

---

[1] For those who are not convinced that 'being six feet tall' is compatible with an actual height of over six feet, consider *You have to be four feet tall to be allowed to ride this rollercoaster* (cf. Klein 1980)

meets or exceeds this standard but false for everyone who does not. Similarly, 'being six feet tall' is true for everyone who meets or exceeds this height.[2]

1.2   Degree Syntax

I furthermore assume that the syntax of degree constructions is best described using a Degree Phrase, DegP (Abney 1987, Corver 1991, 1997), which looks as follows:

(5)

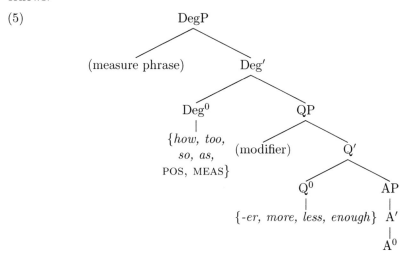

If Q^0 is empty or contains -er, head movement from A^0 to Q^0 takes place (Corver 1997). Modifiers like *very* and *extremely* are located in SpecQP, and measure phrases in SpecDegP.

2   The Semantics of Evaluative Degree Constructions

One of the most intuitive ways to paraphrase an EDC like *Vernon is remarkably tall* is something like 'the degree to which Vernon is tall is remarkable' or 'it

---

[2] As one reviewer noted, this means that the denotations of both POS and MEAS can be simplified in the following way:

(i) a. $[\![\text{POS}]\!] = \lambda G \lambda x [G(s_G)(x)]$
     b. $[\![\text{MEAS}]\!] = \lambda G \lambda d \lambda x [G(d)(x)]$

When we get to our analysis of EDCs, however, it will be necessary to have an existential quantifier over degrees. For that reason I am leaving the more complex definition of POS as it is.

Note also that if MEAS is reduced in this way, it essentially becomes superflous - the measure phrase could compose directly with the degree predicate (Heim 2000). Doing away with MEAS entirely, however, would leave us with the syntactic problem of a phrase without a head (see (5)). Possibly, MEAS has additional semantic content - for example, as Svenonius & Kennedy 2006 propose, to ensure that measure phrases can only compose with *measurable* predicates (compare *Vernon is six feet tall* to #*Vernon is six hours tired* or #*Maxwell is 110 IQ-points intelligent*.)

is remarkable that Vernon is as tall as he is' (cf. Cresswell 1976, Katz 2005, Nouwen 2005). The semantic difference between (1a) and (1b), then, could be captured in terms of quantifier scope:

(6)   a. Remarkably, Vernon is tall:
         It is surprising that $\exists d$ [Vernon is d-tall and $d \geq s_{tall}$]
     b. Vernon is remarkably tall:
         $\exists d$ [Vernon is d-tall and $d \geq s_{tall}$ and it is surprising that Vernon is d-tall]

However, in an early and influential account of both the syntax and semantics of EDCs, Morzycki (2004) explicitly rejects this paraphrase as a correct representation of the semantics of EDCs. Consider a situation in which Vernon is in fact remarkably short - surely, we would be able to claim that 'the degree to which Vernon is tall is remarkable'. However, we would not call the remarkably short Vernon *remarkably tall*. In another scenario envisioned by Morzycki, Vernon was born at precisely 5:09 in the morning, on the fifth day of the ninth month of 1959 - and to our amazement, his height happens to be exactly five feet and nine inches. This is remarkable indeed, and yet, again, we would not be able to claim that Vernon is *remarkably tall*. This leads Morzycki to analyse EDCs as embedded exlamatives, which he takes to denote sets of true propositions, just like questions. For *Vernon is remarkably tall* to be true, one of the propositions in the set must be remarkable (see (7b)). For current purposes, this amounts to the denotation in (7c), in which reference is made to sets of degrees rather than sets of propositions.

(7)   a. $[\![$*How tall Vernon is!*$]\!] = \{p : p$ is true and there is a degree of height d such that p is the proposition that Vernon is d-tall$\}$
     b. $[\![$*Vernon is remarkably tall*$]\!] = [\![$*It is remarkable [how tall Vernon is!]*$]\!] =$ $\exists p[p \in \{$'V. is 6 feet 1 inch tall', 'V. is 6 feet 2 inches tall', 'V. is 6 feet 3 inches tall', ... 'V. is n feet m inches tall'$\} \wedge$ REMARKABLE$(p)]$
     c. $=$ REMARKABLE($^\wedge\exists d[d \in \{$'6 feet 1 inch', '6 feet 2 inches', '6 feet 3 inches', ... 'n feet m inches'$\} \wedge$ Vernon is d-tall$])$

Following Zanuttini & Portner (2003), Morzycki argues that a crucial property of exclamatives is *domain widening*. To see the effect of this, consider the different implications about Maxwell's eating habits in (8a-b):

(8) a. Maxwell eats everything.
    b. What things Maxwell eats!

Arguably, the domain of *everything* in (8a) is restricted by the context such that we do not expect it to include "lightbulbs, his relatives, or presidential elections" - or, in general, anything but ordinary food. For (8a) to be true, it is not necessary that Herman's eating habits include things like live locusts for breakfast; it merely suggests that Herman is a particularly easy dinner guest. In contrast, (8b) does suggest that the domain of things eaten by Herman also includes the extraordinary, like live locusts or raw serrano chillies. This is the effect of domain widening. Morzycki's semantics for EDCs, which takes into account both domain widening and factivity (essentially, the entailment of the positive form[3]) is given in (9):

(9) $[\![EDC]\!] = R(\,\hat{}\,\exists d \exists C'[C' \supset C \wedge d \in C' - C \wedge G(d)(x) \wedge d \geq s_G])]$ (for some gradable adjective G, evaluative adverb R, domain C and individual x)

However, I want to argue that this analysis of EDCs as embedded exclamatives is not only conceptually inelegant, it does not always give the right predictions either (section 2.1). Moreover, as Nouwen (2005) already shows, Morzycki's scenarios can be ruled out independently if the monotonicity of gradable predicates is taken into account (section 2.2).

2.1 EDCs Are Not Embedded Exclamatives

First, I would like to observe that there is something redundant about the domain widening part of the denotation in (9). It guarantees that the degree to which x is G is somehow so 'extreme' that it falls outside of the range of degrees we would naturally consider. But that is just another way of saying that what is going on is 'remarkable', or 'surprising', or 'unbelievable'. As an illustration, take a sentence like *Maxwell is remarkably tall*. Paraphrasing Morzycki's denotation, the semantics of this would boil down to something like 'It is remarkable that Maxwell's degree of tallness is such that it is somehow unexpected'.

This is, in fact, a general problem of analysing EDCs as embedded exclamatives. An exclamative (*How tall Maxwell is!*) can itself be paraphrased as something roughly like 'Maxwell is unexpectedly tall'. To quote Morzycki himself:

> [The] idea [of domain widening] elegantly gathers together several otherwise slippery and elusive intuitions about what exclamatives mean. Among these are the intuition that exclamatives somehow involve an 'extreme' value for something, and that exclamatives convey that something is unexpected in a particular way.

Embedding this under a modifier that *also* conveys a sense of unexpectedness or surprise, then, leads to a strange kind of redundancy. After all, it suggests that the 'unexpectedness' of Maxwell being d-tall is the case even before the contribution of *remarkably* to the semantics. All in all, resorting to domain widening

---

[3] On the other hand, Nouwen (2005) claims that *Vernon is remarkably tall* does not entail the positive form *Vernon is tall*. If Vernon's parents and siblings are all tiny but Vernon is of average height, the first statement would be true but the second would presumably be false. Alternatively, we could claim that the second statement *is* true in this case, if we let s_{tall} be determined by the family's height ('Vernon is tall *for a member of this family*'). Nothing hinges on this in either Morzycki's or Nouwen's analysis, but I am following Morzycki in claiming that EDCs entail the corresponding positive form (and as we will see, this will turn out quite important for my particular adaptation of Nouwen's analysis).

seems merely a clever way to smuggle the semantics of *remarkable* into the scope of the existential quantification over degrees, rather than something independently motivated.

Considering the above, we can test empirically whether the embedded-exclamative analysis is true: we would expect the sense of unexpectedness or extremeness caused by domain widening to be there, regardless of the meaning of the modifier. This expectation is not borne out, however. The evaluative adverbs in (10) themselves do not express anything 'extreme', and indeed, the sentences in (10) do not seem to suggest unexpectedness or extremeness in any way.

(10) Maxwell is $\left\{\begin{array}{l} \text{disappointingly} \\ \text{arousingly} \\ \text{satisfyingly} \end{array}\right\}$ tall.

In short: the apparent domain widening effect of certain EDCs, like *Maxwell is remarkably tall*, seems to be a consequence of the semantics of the particular adverb, rather than a property of this kind of construction in general. If domain widening is a crucial part of the semantics of exclamatives, this strongly suggests that EDCs do not involve embedded exclamatives.

An additional problem for Morzycki is his assumption that evaluative adverbs can modify sets of propositions. This is not only the type of exclamatives, but also of questions. However, evaluative adverbs are unable to modify questions (11a-b). Morzycki claims that the inability to modify questions is a general property of speaker-oriented expressions, but as (11c) shows, this does not seem to be true. This means that the exceptional status of evaluatives in this respect requires additional explanation.

(11) a. *Remarkably, is Maxwell tall?
      b. *Surprisingly, how tall is Maxwell?
      c. $\left\{\begin{array}{l} \text{Actually} \\ \text{Honestly} \\ \text{According to Vernon} \end{array}\right\}$, is Maxwell tall?

2.2 In Which Monotonicity Saves the Day

I propose that the intuitive paraphrase we saw earlier, which was rejected by Morzycki, is in fact the right one. The nonexistent interpretations involving freakish heights are ruled out by an independent reason: the monotonicity of gradable predicates (Nouwen 2005). I summarise Nouwen's argument here.

Recall the definition in (4), repeated here:

(4) A function f of type $\langle d, \langle e, t \rangle \rangle$ is monotone iff
    $\forall x \forall d \forall d' [f(d)(x) = 1 \ \& \ d' < d \rightarrow f(d')(x) = 1]$

How does it follow from this that *Maxwell is remarkably tall* cannot be an appropriate description of a situation in which Maxwell's height equals his birthday?

The crucial factor here is that *remarkable* is also monotone - downward monotone, to be precise. A downward monotone operator O, when applied to some proposition p, reverses p's entailments: if $p \models p'$, then $O(p') \models O(p)$. It is easy to verify that this holds for *remarkable* and other evaluatives:

(12) a. Vernon is reading a Booker Prize-winning novel $\models$ Vernon is reading a novel.
   b. It is remarkable for Vernon to be reading a novel $\models$ It is remarkable for Vernon to be reading a Booker Prize-winning novel.

Similarly, as the monotonicity of *tall* implies that $\text{TALL}(d)(x) \models \text{TALL}(d')(x)$ where $d \geq d'$,

(13) $\text{REMARKABLE}(\hat{}\,\text{TALL}(d')(x)) \models \text{REMARKABLE}(\hat{}\,\text{TALL}(d \geq d')(x))$

In other words, the monotonicity of both *remarkable/remarkably* and *tall* ensures that if it is remarkable that x is d'-tall, x being $d \geq d'$-tall must also be remarkable. This cannot be true in a situation in which Maxwell is remarkably short or has a height corresponding to his birthday. Imagine that Maxwell is four feet tall, which is remarkably short for a grown man, but not *remarkably tall* - the truth conditions for *remarkably tall* require that Maxwell having any height $d' > 4'0''$ would also be remarkable, but this includes completely unremarkable heights of, for example, $5'7''$ or $5'9''$. So *Maxwell is remarkably tall* is not true of this situation. Similarly, if Maxwell's height of $5'9''$ is remarkable because it corresponds precisely to his date and time of birth, we still cannot say that *Maxwell is remarkably tall*: if he were, he would still be remarkably tall at $6'0''$, but since $6'0''$ is again a rather unremarkable height (to the eyes of this Dutch linguist, at least!), our assertion is falsified in this case as well.

Following Nouwen (except for my assumptions about the entailment of the positive form) and contra Morzycki, then, I propose that the the the truth conditions of EDCs are accurately captured by the following semantics:

(14) $[\![\textit{is remarkably tall}]\!] = \lambda x.\exists d[\text{TALL}(d)(x) \wedge \text{REMARKABLE}(\hat{}\,\text{TALL}(d)(x)]$

Thus, we have arrived at a semantics for EDCs that is both empirically more accurate and quite a bit simpler than Morzycki's. Unlike Morzycki, we do not need to assume that evaluative sentential adverbs are ambiguous between a propositional modifier and an operation on sets of propositions. Moreover, our semantics defines the relationship between the different semantics associated with different adverb positions in an elegant, intuitive way that mirrors their syntactic difference, namely in terms of quantifier scope:

(15) a. Maxwell is remarkably tall:
      $\exists d[\text{REMARKABLE}(\hat{}\,\text{TALL}(d)(\text{m})) \wedge \text{TALL}(d)(\text{m})) \wedge d \geq s_{tall}]$
   b. Remarkably, Maxwell is tall:
      $\text{REMARKABLE}(\hat{}\,\exists d[\text{TALL}(d)(\text{m}) \wedge d \geq s_{tall}]) \wedge \exists d[\text{TALL}(d)(\text{m}) \wedge d \geq s_{tall}]$

In (15a), *remarkably* is located inside the DegP, and existential closure of the degree argument of TALL takes place higher up in the derivation. In (15b), *remarkably* enters the derivation only after the degree argument has been existentially closed. In section (3), I will give a syntax (and compositional semantics) for EDCs that gives precisely these results. But first, let us have a look at one remaining question.

2.3   Adverbial Gradability and the Various Uses of Evaluatives

So far, we have only encountered evaluative adverbs in the role of propositional modifiers, which I (like Nouwen and Morzycki troughout most of his paper) have simply taken to denote constants of type $\langle\langle s,t\rangle,t\rangle$. But this ignores the fact that an evaluative like *remarkable* is itself a gradable predicate headed by a DegP:

(16)   a. Vernon is $\left\{\begin{array}{l}\text{remarkable.}\\\text{quite remarkable.}\\\text{less remarkable than I thought.}\end{array}\right\}$

   b. $\left\{\begin{array}{l}\text{Quite remarkably}\\\text{Even more remarkably}\\\text{Most remarkably}\end{array}\right\}$, Vernon is tall.

How we want to analyse this depends on two different but related questions. First, how are the noun-modifying and the sentence-modifying uses of evaluatives related? Second, to what extent are we dealing with two different kinds of DegP here - do we need to assume a separate adverbial DegP with its own adverb-specific degree morphology, or can we use the same DegP we have assumed for adjectives?

The simplest answer to both questions is that there is no *semantic* difference between adjectives and their corresponding adverbs. Semantically, both function as predicates over entities, but due to syntactic restrictions on their distribution, they differ in which particular entities they may take as arguments. In the case of adjectives, those entities may be individuals ('Vernon') or individual correlates of propositions ('that Vernon is tall'; cf. Chierchia 1984); in the case of adverbs, they may be individual correlates of propositions or events. This proposal is very close to (and indeed partly inspired by) an informal suggestion in Morzycki (2004), who speculates (building on a suggestion from Kratzer 1999) that individual correlates of propositions are formed from propositions by a type-shifting operator, covert in the case of adverbial and overt in the case of adjectival modification, where this typeshift is performed by *that*.

The apparent advantage of this proposal is that it enables us to use precisely the same DegP for both adverbs and adjectives, including the full range of degree morphology, without needing to assume any additional ambiguity or type shifting. However, it turns out that not all degree morphology is compatible with adverbial sentential modifiers, which suggests that we do not need or even want a full-fledged DegP in this case. Compare the data in (16) to the following:

(17)   a. It is $\left\{\begin{array}{l}\text{so remarkable}\\\text{too remarkable to be true}\\\text{just as remarkable as I had hoped}\end{array}\right\}$ that Vernon is tall.

   b. $\left\{\begin{array}{l}\text{*So remarkably}\\\text{*too remarkably to be true}\\\text{?as remarkably as I had hoped}\end{array}\right\}$, Vernon is tall.

(18) a. Verrassend genoeg is Herman lang.   (Dutch)
          Surprising enough is Herman tall
          'Surprisingly, Herman is tall.'

$$\left.\begin{cases} \text{*Verrassend} \\ \text{*Nogal verrassend (genoeg)} \\ \text{*Verrassender (genoeg)} \\ \text{*Te verrassend (genoeg) om waar te zijn} \\ \text{*Zo verrassend (genoeg)} \end{cases}\right\} \text{ is Herman lang.}$$

b. (positioned at left of brace)

'Surprisingly/Quite surprisingly/More surprisingly/Too surprisingly to be true/So surprisingly, Herman is tall.'

In English (and also in Dutch), the full range of degree morphology is available for adjectival sentential modifiers ((17a)), but the same does not hold for adverbials. While we have seen in (16) that English proposition-modifying adverbs can combine with QP-associated morphology (*more, less, enough* and degree modifiers in SpecQP), Deg-heads like *so, too* and *as* seem to be out (17b). In Dutch, the options are even more limited: sentential evaluative adverbs obligatorily combine with the Q-head *genoeg* 'enough', anything else is ungrammatical.

There are two ways to account for this. The first one is to keep our analysis above and treat the incompatibility of sentential evaluative adverbs with DegP-associated degree morphology as an independent syntactic issue. The second one is to abandon the idea that sentential evaluative adverbs are equivalent to their adjectival, individual-modifying counterparts. Instead, they are derived from the latter by a type-shifting operation, that takes place at Deg^0-level in English and perhaps even lower in Dutch.

In English, this typeshift could be performed by a covert operator akin to POS; this explains why overt Deg-heads are unable to combine with sentential evaluative adverbs (their position is occupied by another element). This operator, which we might call POS_{adv}, would denote something along the following lines:

(19) $[\![\text{POS}_{adv}]\!]_{\langle\langle d,et\rangle,\langle st,t\rangle\rangle} = \lambda R_{\langle d,et\rangle}\lambda p_{st}\exists d_d[R(d)(p) \wedge d \geq s_R]$

The type-shifting matter is less clear in Dutch. It seems that *genoeg* might do the job; this would explain why all the examples in (18b) are out (*verrassend genoeg*, being of type $\langle st, t\rangle$, is of the wrong type for any further degree morphology and modifiers to combine with), and fits with the intuition that *genoeg* does not have its usual meaning here:

(20) a. Verrassend genoeg is Herman lang.
          'surprisingly *genoeg*, Herman is tall' $\nLeftrightarrow$
      b. Het is verrassend genoeg dat Herman lang is.
          'it is surprising enough that Herman is tall'

On the other hand, we would then expect *genoeg* to show up in EDCs as well, which it does not: *Herman is verrassend genoeg lang* 'Herman is surprisingly *genoeg* tall' only has the interpretation equivalent to *Surprisingly, Herman is tall*. So perhaps Dutch also has something like POS_{adv} and *genoeg* here is merely a syntactic dummy, required for some reason if the adverb is in sentence-modifying position.

I am leaving the rest of the discussion open, because it requires a more in-depth review of the interplay between morphosyntax and semantics in the adverbial domain than I am able to provide here (for example, I have entirely ignored the possible contribution of -*ly*). For present purposes, little hinges on the precise composition of evaluative sentential adverbs - the crucial point of the analysis presented here is that whatever the adverb denotes in [ADVERB] *Vernon is tall*, it has the same denotation in *Vernon is* [ADVERB] *tall*. For this reason (and for the sake of simplicity and readability), I will use the simple denotation in (21a) in the remainder of this paper. However, the reader may keep in mind that this is a shorthand form of either (21b), if we take the first of the approaches above, or (21c), if we go for the typeshifting analysis.

(21) a. $[remarkably]_{st,t} = \lambda p_{st}[\text{REMARKABLE}(p)]$
      b. $[remarkably]_{et} = \lambda p_e \exists d[\text{REMARKABLE}(p)(d) \wedge d \geq s_{remarkable}]$
      c. $[remarkably]_{st,t} = \lambda p_{st} \exists d[\text{REMARKABLE}(p)(d) \wedge d \geq s_{remarkable}]$

3 Syntactic Movement, *much*-Support and Agreement

We now turn to the syntax of EDCs in order to see how the denotation in (16) (repeated here) is arrived at.

(15) Maxwell is remarkably tall:
      $\exists d[\text{REMARKABLE}(\hat{}\text{TALL}(d)(\text{m})) \wedge \text{TALL}(d)(\text{m}) \wedge d \geq s_{tall}]$

First, I propose that evaluative adverbs, like other degree modifiers, are located in SpecQP. For one, they are not heads: we have already seen that they are themselves phrases. Secondly, they pattern with SpecQP degree modifiers like *very* and *extremely*, which (as Corver (1991, 1997) extensively argues) are located in SpecQP (data adapted from Corver 1991):

(22) a. How very/surprisingly interesting!
      b. Zo heel/ongelofelijk knap is ze anders niet.   (Dutch)
         that very/incredibly pretty is she however not
         'She's not that very pretty at all'
(23) a. Too/how/that big a car
      b. *Very/extremely/remarkably big a car
(24) a. Though the house is very/amazingly expensive...
      b. Very/amazingly expensive though the house is...
      c. Though Mary is too shy for her own good...
      d. *Too shy for her own good though Mary is...

Semantically, this is supported by the fact that evaluatives can gradually lose their meaning and flexibility and turn into 'proper' degree modifiers; for example, Dutch *ontzettend* has mostly lost its original meaning of 'shocking, horrifying' and is nowadays used almost exclusively as a degree modifier; English *terribly* is a similar case.

Now, consider the following examples of *so*-pronominalisation in English (from Corver 1997):

(25)   a.   John is *fond of Mary*. Bill seems [less *so*].
       b.   John is *fond of Mary*. *Maybe he is [too *so*].

When the whole AP is replaced by the pro-form *so*, there is no A^0 to raise to Q^0. Corver notes that this results in ungrammaticality when Q^0 is empty (25b). To make the $Deg^0 + so$ combination grammatical, we need to insert the syntactic dummy *much* into Q^0 ('*much*-support'):

(26)   John is *fond of Mary*. Maybe he is [too **much** *so*].

Now, consider the data in (27):

(27)   a.   Vernon is tall, even very *(much) so.
       b.   Vernon is tall, even $\left\{\begin{array}{l} \text{remarkably} \\ \text{surprisingly} \\ \text{eerily} \\ \dots \end{array}\right\}$ (*much) so.

In (27a), Q^0 is empty, so the sentence needs *much*-support. In (27b), however, *much*-insertion is ungrammatical, which can only be explained by assuming that the Q^0-position is not available. I propose that it is not empty, but occupied by a covert element which I will call EVAL[4]. EVAL is a null degree morpheme that applies to an evaluative and a gradable adjective to yield a lambda term with exactly the same semantic type as the adjective itself, to which POS (in Deg^0) is then applied in the usual way.

(28)   a.

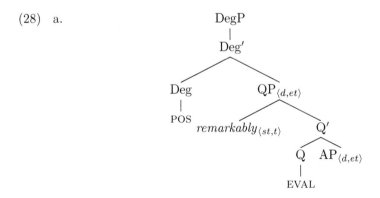

---

[4] Not to be confused with Rett's (2008) operator of the same name; her use of the term *evaluative* is different from the sense in which it is used here.

b.

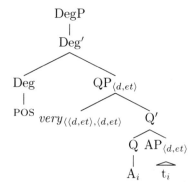

As the trees in (28) illustrate, this analysis defines the difference between evaluative modifiers and 'true' degree modifiers (e.g. *very, pretty*) in terms of their ability to modify degree directly - the latter can, while the former need the mediation of EVAL. EDCs and degree constructions with 'true' degree modification are syntactically parallel, apart from the presence or absence of EVAL (and its direct consequences, i.e. whether the adjective is able to move to Q^0).

In English, this claim is supported by the presence or absence of *much*-support in the case of *so*-pronominalisation (*very* and *pretty* do need *much*-support). Dutch does not have *so*-pronominalisation, but it does offer some interesting independent evidence in the form of gender agreement between adjective and modifier.

Dutch has two grammatical genders, neuter and nonneuter. While adjectives always agree with the noun (29a-c), adjectival modifiers, in turn, generally show no agreement with the adjective (in fact, prescriptive grammars forbid the presence of agreement morphology on adjectival modifiers). Nevertheless, (29b-c) shows that in some cases speakers prefer to use the inflected form of the modifier. (*Fiets* 'bike' is nonneuter.)

(29)   a. Een belachelijk(*-e)/ongelofelijk(*-e) dur-e fiets
           'a ridiculously(-NONN)/incredibly(-NONN) expensive-NONN bike'
       b. Een ontzettend(?-e) mooi-e fiets
           'an extremely(-NONN) beautiful-NONN bike'
       c. Een ?heel/hel-e mooi-e fiets
           'a very/very-NONN beautiful-NONN bike'

Belachelijke 'ridiculous-NONN' and *ongelofelijke* 'incredible-NONN' in (29a) cannot receive a degree-modifying interpretation; only their non-inflected forms *belachelijk* and *ongelofelijk* can. The use of the inflected form *onzettende* 'extremely-NONN' as a degree modifier, however, is relatively common; finally, degree-modifying *hele* 'very-NONN' has an overwhelming tendency to agree with the adjective, in spite of the prescriptivists. The table below shows the number of Google hits for several combinations of modifier and adjective (other evaluatives pattern with *belachelijk*):

	dure	*mooie*
belachelijk	13,900	3,210
belachelijke	1,610	262
ontzettend	5,520	23,100
ontzettende	351	27,300
heel	8,900	257,000
hele	27,200	873,000

Assuming that agreement reflects a Spec-Head relationship, the difference follows naturally from our assumptions as illustrated by the trees in (28): EDCs do not involve a Spec-Head relationship between the modifier and the adjective, as the presence of EVAL in Q^0 prevents the adjective from raising there. In contrast, *heel/hele* 'very', as a proper degree modifier, does not need the mediation of an element like EVAL in Q^0, so the adjective can raise to this position, ending up in a Spec-Head relationship with the degree modifier. Finally, the mixed behaviour of *ontzettend* is exactly what we would expect of an evaluative that is diachronically turning into a 'real' degree modifier.

The account presented here is similar in spirit to that of Morzycki (2004), who also deals with EDCs in terms of covert morphology; however, the syntactic and semantic details are quite different, as Morzycki locates evaluatives in SpecDegP and collapses the semantic contributions of POS and (his rather different version of) EVAL into one covert morpheme located in Deg^0. Neither of these choices, however, is compatible with the syntactic data presented here.

4 Assembling the Pieces

The denotation I assume for EVAL is the following:

(30) $[\![\text{EVAL}]\!] = \lambda G \lambda R \lambda d \lambda x [G(d)(x) \wedge R(\hat{}\,G(d)(x))]$

Here, G is a gradable adjective and R an evaluative adverb (again, I am abstracting away from its internal structure). The semantics of a sentence like *Vernon is surprisingly tall*, then, is built up according to the structure in (32), as follows:

(31) a. $[\![surprisingly \text{ EVAL } tall]\!]$
$= \lambda G \lambda R \lambda d \lambda x [G(d)(x) \wedge R(\hat{}\,G(d)(x))]([\![tall]\!])([\![surprisingly]\!])$
$= \lambda G \lambda R \lambda d \lambda x [G(d)(x) \wedge R(\hat{}\,G(d)(x))](\lambda d \lambda x [\text{TALL}(d)(x)])([\![surprisingly]\!])$
$= \lambda R \lambda d \lambda x [\text{TALL}(d)(x) \wedge R(\hat{}\,\text{TALL}(d)(x))](\lambda p [\text{SURPRISING}(p)))$
$= \lambda d \lambda x [\text{TALL}(d)(x) \wedge \text{SURPRISING}(\hat{}\,\text{TALL}(d)(x))]$

b. $[\![Vernon \text{ is POS } surprisingly \text{ EVAL } tall]\!]$
$= \lambda G \lambda x [\exists d [G(d)(x) \wedge d \geq s_G]]([\![surprisingly \text{ EVAL } tall]\!])([\![Vernon]\!])$
$= \lambda G \lambda x [\exists d [G(d)(x) \wedge d \geq s_G]](\lambda d \lambda x [\text{TALL}(d)(x) \wedge \text{SURPRISING}(\hat{}\,\text{TALL}(d)(x))])$
$\quad ([\![Vernon]\!])$
$= \lambda x [\exists d [\text{TALL}(d)(x) \wedge \text{SURPRISING}(\hat{}\,\text{TALL}(d)(x)) \wedge d \geq s_{tall}]](\text{v})$
$= \exists d [\text{TALL}(d)(x) \wedge \text{SURPRISING}(\hat{}\,\text{TALL}(d)(\text{v})) \wedge d \geq s_{tall}]]$
$= (15a)$

(32)

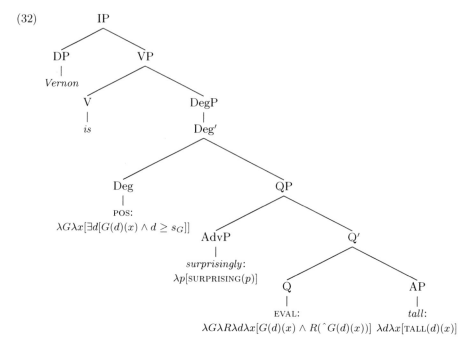

So far, we have only discussed EDCs headed by POS, but note that the above analysis (unlike Morzycki's) leaves room for EDCs to be headed by other degree morphemes. It seems that this correctly predicts the existence of constructions like (33a-c):

(33) a. How remarkably tall Maxwell is!
      b. Maxwell is so remarkably tall that all tourists want to take a picture with him.
      c. Maxwell is just as remarkably tall as Vernon.

However, as *remarkably* is itself part of a DegP, the degree heads *how*, *so*, and *as* in (33) might also be heading this DegP rather than the main *tall* DegP ((34)).

(34) a.   b.

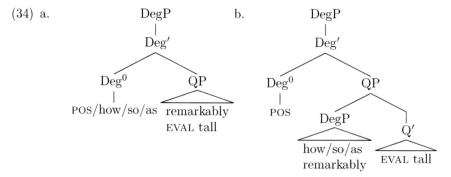

This predicts that the sentences in (33) are actually ambiguous, which it seems they are, even though the truth-conditional differences this ambiguity leads to are so subtle that it is hard to separate the two readings from each other. But consider for example that both (35b(i)) and (35b(ii)) are valid answers to the question in (35a):

(35)   a. *How* remarkably tall is this Vernon you keep talking about?
        b. (i) - Very.
           (ii) - Almost seven feet.

How here can be interpreted as either inquiring after the degree of remarkableness or the degree of tallness, suggesting that the structure of (35a) is ambiguous in the way shown in the trees above. In particular, under the analysis argued for in this paper, the possibility of (35b(ii)) is crucially predicted.

Similarly, the inferences in (36a) and (36b) seem to be equally valid, each based on a different reading of the second premise:

(36) Maxwell is 6′5″ tall. Maxwell's wife is just as remarkably tall as Maxwell.
       a. $\overset{1}{\Rightarrow}$ Maxwell's wife is 6′5″ tall.
       b. $\overset{2}{\Rightarrow}$ Maxwell's wife is less than 6′5″ tall.

The entailment in (36a) follows if it is Maxwell's height and his wife's height that are equated[5], whereas (36b) follows if the equation concerns the remarkableness of their heights - women being on average shorter than men, for any degree of remarkableness d, a d-remarkable height for a woman should be lower than a d-remarkable height for a man.[6]

Thirdly, it is well-known (cf. Kennedy 1997) that comparative and equative constructions are semantically anomalous if the adjectives that are compared are not measured along the same dimension ((37a) vs. (37b)). We can use this fact to determine which element is compared to which in the sentences in (38). If (38b) may have the structure in (34a), we expect it to have a reading in which it is as anomalous as (37b). According to my intuitions, this is indeed the case:

---

[5] The entailment may be formulated more strongly than the sentence *Maxwell's wife is as tall as Maxwell* actually merits - according to my intuition, this can still be true if Maxwell's wife is less tall than Maxwell, if both of their heights are evaluated according to a different comparison class. However, I believe that the stronger reading for *Maxwell's wife is as tall as Maxwell*, according to which they have equal heights, exists as well, and that is the one I am trying to force here.

[6] Attentive readers may have noticed that the structure in (34b) seems to be at odds with certain parts of the discussion in section 2.3, where it was suggested that evaluative adverbs in sentence-initial position cannot be modified by Deg-heads. So if (35) and (36) do indeed have readings that correspond to the structure in (34b), in which evaluative adverbs *are* combined with Deg-heads, we need to explain why degree-modifying evaluatives (which we have also analysed as propositional modifiers) are different from their sentence-modifying counterparts in this respect. Perhaps our final account of the relation between individual- and proposition-modifying evaluatives should be a hybrid between Morzycki's suggestion and my own tentative typeshifting account, according to which evaluative adverbs sometimes take individual correlates of propositions as their argument and sometimes typeshift into true propositional modifiers.

(37) a. Maxwell is just as tall as Vernon is wide.
      b. #Maxwell is as tall as he is arrogant.
(38) a. Maxwell is as remarkably tall as Vernon is remarkably wide.
      b. #Maxwell is as remarkably tall as Vernon is remarkably arrogant.

The difference between (38a) and (38b) under this reading would be hard to explain if the first instance of *remarkably* were compared with the second one, or with *wide/arrogant*. Under the present account, though, we can easily explain why (38b) is anomalous while (38a) is not: (38b) compares *tall* and *arrogant*, which do not have identical dimensions, whereas (38a) compares *wide* and *tall*, which do. This means that *tall*, and not *remarkably*, is the complement of *as* here, showing that (34a) is indeed a possible structure for (38a-b).

In conclusion, it seems that other degree heads than POS are able to co-occur with an evaluative modifier in SpecQP, which is at odds with the account in Morzycki (2004) but predicted by our present analysis.

One exception, however, is MEAS. There seems to be no semantic reason to rule out a combination of MEAS and EVAL; yet, as (39) shows, evaluative modifiers are incompatible with measure phrases (a property they share with ordinary degree modifers like *very*):

(39) *Vernon is seven feet very/remarkably tall.

However, this structure can be ruled out on independent syntactic grounds: it is argued in Corver (1997, 2009) that measure phrases originate in SpecQP, which explains why they are in complementary distribution with modifiers.[7]

5   Conclusions

In this paper, I have argued that an analysis of EDCs as embedded exclamatives runs into several conceptual and empirical problems, and subsequently, that an analysis in which evaluative degree modification is analysed in terms of ordinary propositional modification is in fact perfectly valid if we assume that gradable adjectives and evaluatives are monotone.

Furthermore, I have proposed a syntax for EDCs based on evidence involving *much*-support and Dutch gender agreement; this syntax allows EDCs to be headed by POS or any other degree head in Deg^0, nicely parallelling other degree constructions.

It also allows words like *very* and *pretty* to be treated syntactically like degree modifiers (occupying SpecQP), while still explaining why they occasionally behave differently from evaluatives that occupy the same position: *very*, *pretty* and

---

[7] As one of the reviewers of this paper pointed out, it is possible to get approximately the intended semantics ('There is a degree d such that $d=7'0''$ and Maxwell is d-tall and it is remarkable that Maxwell is d-tall') by using a slightly different construction: *Maxwell is a remarkable seven feet tall*. This suggests that the *semantics* of evaluatives and measure phrases are by no means incompatible. Constructions like these are a test case for the semantics presented in this paper, but I will leave this issue for future study.

other 'true' degree modifiers can directly modify the adjective without needing an intervening element.

Finally, I have offered some suggestions for further study, including the relation between individual-modifying and proposition-modifying uses of evaluative adjectives and adverbs.

References

Abney, S.: The English Noun Phrase in its Sentential Aspect. PhD dissertation. MIT, Cambridge, MA (1987)

Chierchia, G.: Topics in the syntax and semantics of infinitives and gerunds. PhD dissertation, Umass, Amherst (1984)

Corver, N.: Evidence for DegP. In: Proceedings of NELS 21, Umass, Amherst (1991)

Corver, N.: Much-support as a last resort. Linguistic Inquiry 28(1), 119–164 (1997)

Cresswell, M.: The semantics of degree. In: Partee, B. (ed.) Montague Grammar, pp. 261–292. Academic Press, New York (1976)

Heim, I.: Degree operators and scope. In: Proceedings of SALT X. CLC Publications, Ithaca (2000)

Katz, G.: Attitudes towards degrees. In: Maier, E., Bary, C., Huitink, J. (eds.) Proceedings of Sinn und Bedeutung 9 (2005)

Kennedy, C., McNally, L.: Scale structure, degree modification, and the semantics of gradable predicates. Language 81(2), 345–381 (2005)

Kennedy, C.: Projecting the Adjective: The Syntax and Semantics of Gradability and Comparison. PhD dissertation, University of California, Santa Cruz (1997)

Klein, E.: A semantics for positive and comparative adjectives. Linguistics and Philosophy 4, 1–45 (1980)

Kratzer, A.: Lecture notes, seminar on the semantics of clausal embedding, Umass, Amherst (1999)

Morzycki, M.: Evaluative adverbial modification in the adjectival projection. Ms, Université du Québec à Montréal (2004)

Nouwen, R.: Monotone amazement. In: Dekker, P., Franke, M (eds) Proceedings of the Fifteenth Amsterdam Colloquium. University of Amsterdam (2005)

Rett, J.: Degree Modification in Natural Language. PhD dissertation, Rutgers, The State University of New Jersey (2008)

von Stechow, A.: Comparing semantic theories of comparison. Journal of Semantics 3, 1–77 (1984)

Svenonius, P., Kennedy, C.: Northern Norwegian degree questions and the syntax of measurement. In: Frascarelli, M. (ed.) Phases of Interpretation, pp. 133–161. Mouton de Gruyter, Berlin (2006)

Zanuttini, R., Portner, P.: Exclamative clauses: At the syntax-semantics interface. Language 79(1), 39 (2003)

A Kripkean Solution to Paradoxes of Denotation

Casper Storm Hansen*

University of Aberdeen, Aberdeen, UK
casper_storm_hansen@hotmail.com

Abstract. Kripke's solution to the Liar Paradox and other paradoxes of truth is generalized to the paradoxes of denotation. Berry's Paradox and Hilbert and Bernays' Paradox are treated in detail.

Keywords: Paradoxes of Denotation, Kripke, Berry's Paradox, Hilbert and Bernays' Paradox, Fixed Point Construction.

1 Introduction

Priest (2002) has demonstrated that all of the semantical paradoxes share a common structure and has argued that the solution to this class of paradoxes should, therefore, also be shared. According to him, this is a reason to reject Kripke's (1975) famous solution to the paradoxes of truth, as it is indeed *only* a solution to these paradoxes and not to the paradoxes of denotation. In this paper I will show that this critique is misplaced; Kripke's solution can be generalized. I will just treat two of the paradoxes of denotation, namely Berry's and Hilbert and Bernays', but the approach can be applied to them all.

Berry's Paradox (Russell 1908) results from the definite description

> Berry's description: the least integer not describable in fewer than twenty syllables

which is a description of nineteen syllables. So the least integer not describable in fewer than twenty syllables is describable in only nineteen syllables.

Hilbert and Bernays' Paradox (originally presented in (Bernays 1939), natural language formulation in (Priest 2006)) also results from a definite description, namely this:

> Hilbert and Bernays' description: the sum of 1 and the referent of Hilbert and Bernays' description

If we let n be the referent of Hilbert and Bernays' description, then it also refers to $n + 1$. As the referent of a definite description is unique, it follows that $n = n + 1$.

I will assume familiarity with Kripke's paper.

---

* I would like to express my gratitude to Vincent Hendricks for his encouragement and assistance in the work that lead to this paper and to the anonymous reviewers for their valuable comments.

D. Lassiter and M. Slavkovik (Eds.): ESSLLI Student Sessions, LNCS 7415, pp. 212–220, 2012.

2   Informal Presentation of the Theory

In Kripke's theory sentences become true and false in a recursive process where a sentence is given a truth value when there is, so to speak, enough information to do so. For instance, a sentence of the form "sentence S is true" is made true after it has been decided that S is true, false after it has been decided that S is false, and is left undecided as long as S is. Further, a disjunction is made true at such time as one of the disjuncts is, since the information about the (eventual) truth value of the other disjunct is irrelevant.[1]

To formulate Berry's description we need two linguistic resources that are not in the formal language of Kripke's paper: The ability to form definite descriptions and a binary predicate expressing that a given term refers to a given object. However, when we equip the formal language with these resources the principle in Kripke's theory can be transfered to them. We let a definite description refer to a given object when it is determined that this is the unique object that satisfies the description; and if it is decided at some point in the iterative process that there are no objects, or more than one object, that satisfy the description, it is decided that the definite description fails to refer. Additionally, a sentence of the form "T refers to O" is made true if at some point it is decided that the term T indeed does refer to the object O, and made false if it is decided that T refers to something different from O or if T fails to refer.

In Kripke's theory, the Liar Sentence, "this sentence is false", is neither true nor false: It is "undefined". The reason is that it could only receive a truth value after it itself had received a truth value, so at no point in the iterative process does that happen. When the semantics of definite descriptions and the object-language reference predicate works as described, something similar is the case for Berry's description. Prior to the determination of the referent of Berry's description, the predicate "is an integer not describable in fewer than twenty syllables" is false of a lot of integers, for example 3 and 11 which are the referents of "the square root of 9" and "the number of letters in 'phobophobia'" respectively. However, it is not true of any integers; for given any integer for which the predicate is not yet false, it is not yet ruled out that Berry's description might refer to that integer. Ergo, the unique object satisfying Berry's description cannot be identified prior to this identification itself, so Berry's description is never assigned a referent and is hence undefined in the fixed point.

Obviously, as formulas of formal languages do not have syllables we have to be a little creative in formalizing Berry's description. But a suitable formal equivalent of "more than nineteen syllables" can be defined with just a standard predicate (see below), so adding further machinery on that account is not necessary.

In formalizing Hilbert and Bernays' Paradox, we will also use definite descriptions and the reference relation. Yet, we need one more thing, namely functions.

---

[1] What is described here is in fact just one version of Kripke's theory, namely the minimal fixed point, strong Kleene scheme version. This is the version which the theory of this paper is modeled on. The different ways in which Kripke considers tweaking this basic version of the theory could be similarly applied here.

As is standard, the interpretation of a function symbol will be specified by the interpretation function, and the function symbol can take terms as its arguments. However, the value of a function for given arguments may be undetermined for a while in the evaluation process since it may be undetermined what the terms acting as arguments refer to. We will treat this similarly to the truth functions which constitute the semantics of the connectives and the quantifiers: When there is sufficient information the function value will be determined. To take an example, consider $f(t_1, t_2, t_3)$ where f is a function symbol and t_1, t_2, and t_3 are terms, and suppose that at some stage in the evaluation process the referents of t_1 and t_2 but not t_3 have been determined. Then $f(t_1, t_2, t_3)$ will get a referent at this stage iff the referent of t_3 does not matter; i.e. if $I(f)(r_1, r_2, d)$, where I is the interpretation function and r_1 and r_2 are the referents of t_1 and t_2, respectively, has the same value for every value of d.

It is easy to see intuitively that also Hilbert and Bernays' description does not have a referent in the fixed point; a referent of the description cannot be determined prior to this determination itself.

As I plan on showing in a forthcoming longer paper, the Kripkean approach can be used to solve all the known paradoxes of denotation, for example the paradoxes of König and Richard. Here, however, I will focus on the paradoxes of Berry and Hilbert and Bernays and present a formal language that has just the resources needed to formalize them. Another thing that has been left for future work, because it would distract from the main point here, is the ability to handle "the present king of France is bald" in the Russellian way (making it false) if one so chooses. In that respect, the theory of this paper is Fregean (the sentence is undefined (clause 2 and 8 below)).

In Kripke's theory, the evaluations at the various levels consist of a set of true sentences and a set of false sentences. The extension of the theory here envisaged means that an evaluation must also contain a reference relation from the set of terms to the domain (supplemented with something to indicate that it has been decided that a given term fails to refer). However, it is not necessary to complicate things by making an evaluation a triple. Instead, we can take a cue from Frege (1892) and identify a sentence *being* true/false with the sentence *referring* to Truth/Falsity. This way an evaluation can simply *be* a reference relation: a relation from the union of the set of sentences and the set of terms to the union of the domain and $\{\top, \bot, *\}$, where $\top$, $\bot$, and $*$ are symbols for Truth, Falsity, and failing to refer respectively.

We will use a standard first-order predicate language with function symbols supplemented with three things: a unary predicate T for "is true", a binary predicate R for "refers to", and a definite description operator: "$\imath v(\phi)$" is to be read as "the v such that ϕ".

In order to keep technical complexity at a minimum, self-reference is made possible simply by letting the domain include all sentences and terms of the language and by making certain assumptions about the denotation of specific constants when the "paradoxical" terms are formalized. That way, the complications of Gödel coding and a diagonal lemma can be avoided.

3   Syntax

We now turn to the precise specification of the syntax (this section) and semantics (next section) of a formal language. For each $n \in \mathbb{N}$ let there be a countable set $\mathcal{P}_n$ of **ordinary n-ary predicates** and a countable set $\mathcal{F}_n$ of **n-ary function symbols**. In addition, there are two **extra-ordinary predicates**, one unary, T, and one binary, R. We also have a set $\mathcal{C}$ of **constants** and a set of **variables**, both of cardinality $\aleph_0$.

The set of **well-formed formulas (wff)** and the set of **terms** are defined recursively thus:

- Every constant and variable is a term.
- If P is an ordinary n-ary predicate and $t_1, \ldots, t_n$ are terms, then $P(t_1, \ldots, t_n)$ is a wff.
- If ϕ and ψ are wff's, then $\neg\phi$ and $(\phi \wedge \psi)$ are wff's.
- If ϕ is a wff and v a variable, then $\forall v \phi$ is a wff.
- If t_1 and t_2 are terms, then $T(t_1)$ and $R(t_1, t_2)$ are wff's.
- If ϕ is a wff and v a variable, then $\imath v(\phi)$ is a term.
- If f is an n-ary function symbol and $t_1, \ldots, t_n$ are terms, then $f(t_1, \ldots, t_n)$ is a term.
- Nothing is a wff or term except by virtue of the above clauses.

The connective $\rightarrow$ is used as an abbreviation in the usual way.

Variables, constants, predicates (ordinary as well as extra-ordinary), function symbols, connectives, quantifiers, parenthesis, and commas are called **primitive symbols**.

When ϕ is a wff, v a variable, and c a constant, $\phi(v/c)$ is ϕ with all free occurrences of v replaced with c.

A wff is a **sentence** and a term is **closed** if it does not contain any free variables. Let $\mathcal{S}$ and $\mathcal{CT}$ be the set of sentences and the set of closed terms respectively.

We will make use of a notion of **complexity** of a formula, but a precise definition can be dispensed with. Any reasonable definition will do.

4   Semantics

A **model** is defined as a pair $\mathfrak{M} = (D, I)$, where D, the **domain**, and I, the **interpretation function**, satisfy the following:

- D is a superset of $\mathcal{S} \cup \mathcal{CT} \cup \mathbb{N}$ such that
  - $* \notin D$, and
- I is a function defined on $\bigcup_{n \in \mathbb{N}} (\mathcal{P}_n \cup \mathcal{F}_n) \cup \mathcal{C}$ such that
  - for every $P \in \mathcal{P}_n$, $I(P) \subseteq D^n$,
  - for every $f \in \mathcal{F}_n$, $I(f)$ is a function from D^n to D,
  - for every $c \in \mathcal{C}$, $I(c) \in D$, and
  - $I[\mathcal{C}] = D$.

Let a model be fixed for the remainder of this paper. We now define an **evaluation** to be a relation $\mathcal{E}$ from $\mathcal{S} \cup \mathcal{CT}$ to $D \cup \{\top, \bot, *\}$ such that elements of $\mathcal{S}$ are only related to elements of $\{\top, \bot\}$ and elements of $\mathcal{CT}$ are only related to elements of $D \cup \{*\}$. $\mathcal{E}$ is **consistent** if every sentence and closed term is related by $\mathcal{E}$ to at most one element. An evaluation $\mathcal{E}'$ **extends** $\mathcal{E}$ if $\mathcal{E} \subseteq \mathcal{E}'$.

The semantics is built up in levels as in Kripke's theory. We first specify how to get from one level to the next: The **evaluation with respect to the evaluation** $\mathcal{E}$, $\mathrm{E}_{\mathcal{E}}$, is defined by recursion on the complexity of the formula[2]:

1. If t is a constant, then
   - $t \, \mathrm{E}_{\mathcal{E}} \, I(t)$.
2. If s is of the form $P(t_1, \ldots, t_n)$ where P is an ordinary n-ary predicate and $t_1, \ldots, t_n$ are closed terms, then
   - $s \, \mathrm{E}_{\mathcal{E}} \, \top$ if there are $d_1, \ldots, d_n \in D$ satisfying $t_1 \, \mathrm{E}_{\mathcal{E}} \, d_1, \ldots, t_n \, \mathrm{E}_{\mathcal{E}} \, d_n$ such that $(d_1, \ldots, d_n) \in I(P)$, and
   - $s \, \mathrm{E}_{\mathcal{E}} \, \bot$ if there are $d_1, \ldots, d_n \in D$ satisfying $t_1 \, \mathrm{E}_{\mathcal{E}} \, d_1, \ldots, t_n \, \mathrm{E}_{\mathcal{E}} \, d_n$ such that $(d_1, \ldots, d_n) \notin I(P)$.
3. If s is of the form $\neg \phi$ where ϕ is a sentence, then
   - $s \, \mathrm{E}_{\mathcal{E}} \, \top$ if $\phi \, \mathrm{E}_{\mathcal{E}} \, \bot$, and
   - $s \, \mathrm{E}_{\mathcal{E}} \, \bot$ if $\phi \, \mathrm{E}_{\mathcal{E}} \, \top$.
4. If s is of the form $(\phi \wedge \psi)$ where ϕ and ψ are sentences, then
   - $s \, \mathrm{E}_{\mathcal{E}} \, \top$ if $\phi \, \mathrm{E}_{\mathcal{E}} \, \top$ and $\psi \, \mathrm{E}_{\mathcal{E}} \, \top$, and
   - $s \, \mathrm{E}_{\mathcal{E}} \, \bot$ if $\phi \, \mathrm{E}_{\mathcal{E}} \, \bot$ or $\psi \, \mathrm{E}_{\mathcal{E}} \, \bot$.
5. If s is of the form $\forall v \phi$ where v is a variable and ϕ is a wff with at most v free, then
   - $s \, \mathrm{E}_{\mathcal{E}} \, \top$ if for all $c \in \mathcal{C}$, $\phi(v/c) \, \mathrm{E}_{\mathcal{E}} \, \top$, and
   - $s \, \mathrm{E}_{\mathcal{E}} \, \bot$ if there exists a $c \in \mathcal{C}$ such that $\phi(v/c) \, \mathrm{E}_{\mathcal{E}} \, \bot$.
6. If s is of the form $T(t)$ where t is a closed term, then
   - $s \, \mathrm{E}_{\mathcal{E}} \, \top$ if there is an $s' \in \mathcal{S}$ such that $t \, \mathrm{E}_{\mathcal{E}} \, s'$ and $s' \mathcal{E} \top$,
   - $s \, \mathrm{E}_{\mathcal{E}} \, \bot$ if there is an $s' \in \mathcal{S}$ such that $t \, \mathrm{E}_{\mathcal{E}} \, s'$ and $s' \mathcal{E} \bot$, and
   - $s \, \mathrm{E}_{\mathcal{E}} \, \bot$ if there is a $d \in D$ such that $t \, \mathrm{E}_{\mathcal{E}} \, d$, but no $s' \in \mathcal{S}$ such that $t \, \mathrm{E}_{\mathcal{E}} \, s'$.
7. If s is of the form $R(t_1, t_2)$ where t_1 and t_2 are closed terms, then
   - $s \, \mathrm{E}_{\mathcal{E}} \, \top$ if there is a $d \in D \cup \{*\}$ and a closed term t_1' such that $t_1 \, \mathrm{E}_{\mathcal{E}} \, t_1'$, $t_1' \mathcal{E} d$ and $t_2 \, \mathrm{E}_{\mathcal{E}} \, d$,
   - $s \, \mathrm{E}_{\mathcal{E}} \, \bot$ if there are $d_1, d_2 \in D \cup \{*\}$, such that $d_1 \neq d_2$, and a closed term t_1' such that $t_1 \, \mathrm{E}_{\mathcal{E}} \, t_1'$, $t_1' \mathcal{E} d_1$ and $t_2 \, \mathrm{E}_{\mathcal{E}} \, d_2$, and
   - $s \, \mathrm{E}_{\mathcal{E}} \, \bot$ if there is a $d' \in D \cup \{*\}$ such that $t_1 \, \mathrm{E}_{\mathcal{E}} \, d'$, but no closed term t_1' such that $t_1 \, \mathrm{E}_{\mathcal{E}} \, t_1'$.

---

[2] The clauses make reference to $\mathrm{E}_{\mathcal{E}}$, but only with respect to less complex formulas than the one under consideration. By clause 6 and 7, a formula may "gain" its reference from a more complex formula, but here it is only the relation $\mathcal{E}$ that is used. In short, the reference of a formula only depends on the previous level and formulas of lower complexity. Hence, as stated, the definition is simply by recursion on the complexity of the formula.

8. If t is of the form $\imath v(\phi)$ where v is a variable and ϕ is a wff with at most v free, then
   - $t \, \mathrm{E}_{\mathcal{E}} \, d$ if d is an element of D such that for some $c \in \mathcal{C}$, $I(c) = d$ and $\phi(v/c) \, \mathrm{E}_{\mathcal{E}} \, \top$ and for all other elements d' of D, every $c' \in \mathcal{C}$, such that $I(c') = d'$, satisfies $\phi(v/c') \, \mathrm{E}_{\mathcal{E}} \, \bot$,
   - $t \, \mathrm{E}_{\mathcal{E}} \, *$ if there are two different elements d_1 and d_2 of D such that for some $c_1, c_2 \in \mathcal{C}$, $I(c_1) = d_1$, $I(c_2) = d_2$, $\phi(v/c_1) \, \mathrm{E}_{\mathcal{E}} \, \top$ and $\phi(v/c_2) \, \mathrm{E}_{\mathcal{E}} \, \top$, and
   - $t \, \mathrm{E}_{\mathcal{E}} \, *$ if for all elements d of D, there is a $c \in \mathcal{C}$ such that $I(c) = d$ and $\phi(v/c) \, \mathrm{E}_{\mathcal{E}} \, \bot$.
9. If t is of the form $f(t_1, \ldots, t_n)$ where f is a n-ary function symbol and $t_1, \ldots, t_n$ are closed terms, then
   - $t \, \mathrm{E}_{\mathcal{E}} \, d$ if d is an element of D and satisfies $I(f)(d_1, \ldots, d_n) = d$ for any $d_i \in D$ $(i = 1, \ldots, n)$ such that if t_i is related to anything by $\mathrm{E}_{\mathcal{E}}$ then it is d_i.

Now we iterate the process by defining for all ordinals α the **evaluation with respect to the level** α, written E^{α}, by recursion:

$$\mathrm{E}^{\alpha} = \begin{cases} \emptyset & \text{if } \alpha = 0 \\ \mathrm{E}_{\mathrm{E}^{\alpha-1}} & \text{if } \alpha \text{ is a successor ordinal} \\ \bigcup_{\eta < \alpha} \mathrm{E}^{\eta} & \text{if } \alpha \text{ is a limit ordinal} \neq 0 \end{cases}$$

The following two lemmas show that the process is monotonic and does not result in any inconsistency:

Lemma 1. *For all ordinals α, β, if $\alpha < \beta$ then $\mathrm{E}^{\alpha} \subseteq \mathrm{E}^{\beta}$.*

Proof. By induction on the complexity of formulas it is seen that for each bullet in each of the nine clauses above, if the condition in that bullet is satisfied for some evaluation $\mathcal{E}$ it is also satisfied for every extension of $\mathcal{E}$. Ergo if $\mathcal{E} \subseteq \mathcal{E}'$ then $\mathrm{E}_{\mathcal{E}} \subseteq \mathrm{E}_{\mathcal{E}'}$. As it also holds that $\mathrm{E}^0 = \emptyset$ is a subset of every evaluation, the lemma follows. □

Lemma 2. *For every ordinal α, E^{α} is consistent.*

Proof. By outer induction on α and inner induction on the complexity of formulas, considering clause 1–9. □

For every ordinal α and every $x \in \mathcal{S} \cup \mathcal{CT}$ we define $[\![x]\!]^{\alpha}$ to be the unique y such that $x \, \mathrm{E}^{\alpha} \, y$, when there is a such. We say that x is **determined at level** α, if α is the first level where $[\![x]\!]^{\alpha}$ is defined.

We now come to the important fixed point theorem:

Theorem 3. *There is a unique consistent evaluation $\mathcal{E}$ such that for some ordinal α it holds for all ordinals $\beta \geq \alpha$ that $\mathrm{E}^{\beta} = \mathcal{E}$.*

Proof. As there are only countably many sentences and closed terms, the monotonic process must reach a fixed point. Consistency of the fixed point follows from lemma 2. □

Letting $\mathcal{E}$ and α be as in the theorem, we define the **evaluation**, E, as $\mathcal{E}$, and for all $x \in \mathcal{S} \cup \mathcal{CT}$ set $[\![x]\!]$ equal to $[\![x]\!]^\alpha$ when this is defined. The value of $[\![x]\!]$ is to be thought of as *the* referent of x.

5   Expressibility of the Reference Relation

Kripke's theory is famous for validating the Tarskian T-schema in the sense that if (in the notation of this paper) s is a sentence and c is a constant such that $I(c) = s$, then $[\![s]\!] = \top$ if and only if $[\![T(c)]\!] = \top$. In other words: If a sentence is true, this can be expressed in the object language. In this theory a similar result holds for reference: If a closed term refers to a given object, then this can be expressed in the language itself. That is the content of the following theorem.

Theorem 4. *Let t be a closed term, d an element of D, and c_1 and c_2 constants such that $I(c_1) = t$ and $I(c_2) = d$. The following biimplication holds: $[\![t]\!] = d$ iff $[\![R(c_1, c_2)]\!] = \top$.*

Proof. From clause 1 it is seen that for all ordinals α we have $c_1 \, \mathrm{E}^\alpha \, t$ and $c_2 \, \mathrm{E}^\alpha \, d$. So it follows from bullet 1 of clause 7 that $[\![t]\!] = d$ iff $t \, \mathrm{E}^\beta \, d$ for some ordinal β iff $R(c_1, c_2) \, \mathrm{E}^{\beta+1} \, \top$ iff $[\![R(c_1, c_2)]\!] = \top$. $\square$

6   Solution to Berry's Paradox

In formalizing Berry's description we have to get around the fact that in the formal language, any natural number can be defined with a definite description of just one symbol, namely a constant. We can do this by defining the length of a term not in the obvious way, as the number of primitive symbols in the term, but slightly differently. Reflecting the fact that in natural languages there are only finitely many primitive symbols, let Φ be a function from the set of primitive symbols of our formal language to $\mathbb{N}$ which sends only a finite number of primitive symbols to each $n \in \mathbb{N}$. Then, define the length of a term to be the sum of $\Phi(x)$ for every occurrence x of a primitive symbol in the term.

Now we can formalize Berry's description. Let n, m, and x be variables and let N and L be unary predicates and $\geq$ a binary predicate, such that $I(N)$ is the set of natural numbers and $I(\geq)$ the relation "larger than or equal to" on the set of natural numbers. L is to be interpreted as "long", but we postpone the precise specification of $I(L)$ until we know just what "long" should mean to make our formalization "paradoxical".

We can formalize "x is a definite description of the natural number n" like this:

$$N(n) \wedge R(x, n)$$

So "the natural number n does not have a short definite description" can be formalized

$$N(n) \wedge \forall x (R(x, n) \rightarrow L(x)) \ ,$$

and "n is the least natural number that does not have a short definite description"

$$(N(n) \wedge \forall x(R(x,n) \to L(x))) \wedge$$
$$\forall m((N(m) \wedge \forall x(R(x,m) \to L(x))) \to \geq(m,n)) \ .$$

Ergo, Berry's description in a version with length of formal expressions instead of number of syllables, "the least natural number that does not have a short definite description", can be formalized as (B):

$$m((N(n) \wedge \forall x(R(x,n) \to L(x))) \wedge$$
$$\forall m((N(m) \wedge \forall x(R(x,m) \to L(x))) \to \geq(m,n))) \quad \text{(B)}$$

Now we can set $I(L)$ to be the set of terms which are longer than (B).

That (B) fails to refer, i.e. that there is no $d \in D$ such that $[\![(B)]\!] = d$, is proved as follows: Assume *ad absurdum* that there is such a $d \in D$. Then it follows by clause 8 that for a constant c with $I(c) = d$, we have

$$[\![(N(c) \wedge \forall x(R(x,c) \to L(x))) \wedge$$
$$\forall m((N(m) \wedge \forall x(R(x,m) \to L(x))) \to \geq(m,c))]\!] = \top \ .$$

Using clause 4 twice, it can be inferred that

$$[\![\forall x(R(x,c) \to L(x))]\!] = \top \ ,$$

and consequently by clause 5 that

$$[\![R(c',c) \to L(c')]\!] = \top$$

where c' is a constant such that $I(c') = (B)$. It is already determined at level 1 that $L(c')$ is false. This follows from the specification of $I(L)$. Ergo, we must have $[\![R(c',c)]\!] = \bot$. So, at some level, bullet 2 or 3 of clause 7 is satisfied. However, bullet 3 can not be, for c' refers to (B) and since the referent of a constant is unique, not to some object which is not a term. And bullet 2 can not be satisfied either, for then (B) would have to refer to something different from d, but by assumption, this is not the case. This is a contradiction.

7   Solution to Hilbert and Bernays' Paradox

The Hilbert and Bernays description can be formalized

$$+(\bar{1}, \imath v(R(h,v))) \qquad \text{(HB1)}$$

where v is a variable, h is a constant such that $I(h) = (\text{HB1})$, and $+$ is a binary function symbol such that $I(+)$ is the function that sends every pair of numbers to their sum and every other pair to 0. $\bar{1}$ is a numeral for 1.

⟦(HB1)⟧ is undefined as we will proceed to prove. As the sum of 1 and n is not the same for every natural number n, (HB1) will get a referent, only if

$$w(R(h, v)) \tag{HB2}$$

gets a referent (clause 9). By clause 8, this happens only if there is a constant c such that

$$R(h, c) \tag{HB3}$$

is related to $\top$. We have $h\, \mathrm{E}_\emptyset(\text{HB1})$ from which it follows by bullet 1 of clause 7 that this can only be the case if (HB1) gets a referent. We have come full circle and can conclude that neither (HB1), (HB2), nor (HB3) become related to anything.

References

Bernays, P., Hilbert, D.: Grundlagen der Mathematik (zweiter Band). Verlag von Julius Springer (1939)

Frege, G.: Über Sinn und Bedeutung. Zeitschrift fur Philosophie und Philosophische Kritik 100, 26–60 (1892)

Kripke, S.: Outline of a theory of truth. The Journal of Philosophy 72, 690–716 (1975)

Priest, G.: Beyond the limits of thought, 2nd edn. Oxford University Press (2002)

Priest, G.: The paradoxes of denotation. In: Bolander, T., Hendricks, V.F., Pedersen, S.A. (eds.) Self-reference. CSLI Publications (2006)

Russell, B.: Mathematical logic as based on the theory of types. American Journal of Mathematics 30, 222–262 (1908)

Trust Games as a Model for Requests

Jason Quinley

University of Tübingen , Tübingen, Germany
jason.quinley@student.uni-tuebingen.de

Abstract. We apply of Game Theory to linguistic politeness, considering requests as the canonical speech act where polite expressions factor in. As making a request is necessarily both strategic and asymmetric, we adapt *Trust Games*, modifying them by the notions of reputation, *face*, and repetition. Given this framework, our results show that although some polite requests may not be rational under one-shot situations, they may become so under assumptions of reputation or observation. We also derive constraints for the levels of politeness that are necessary and sufficient for cooperative behavior.

Keywords: politeness theory, trust games, game–theoretic pragmatics.

1 Introduction

Instances of linguistic politeness seem to defy what we know about rational communication. Were speakers to always follow pragmatic constraints like those of Grice (1975), we might end up with very different conversations than we see on a day to day basis. Consider the following utterances, paired with appropriate maxims:

BE CLEAR

- **Aaron:** Can you take out the garbage this week?
- **Bert:** I can. But I won't.

BE RELEVANT

- **Aaron:** Don't you know that buying wine after 22:00 is illegal?!
- **Bert:** Did I ask you? I think not.

BE INFORMATIVE

- **Aaron:** Hey how's it going buddy?
- **Bert:** Really terrible. My girlfriend left me for the Prince of Kashmir.
- **Aaron:** Well at least we can say she's in a better place now.

BE TRUTHFUL

- **Aaron:** Do these pants make my behind look fat?
- **Bert:** No. Your behind makes your behind look fat.

D. Lassiter and M. Slavkovik (Eds.): ESSLLI Student Sessions, LNCS 7415, pp. 221–233, 2012.

What we see in each of these examples is an instance of communication seemingly gone awry. Why? The interlocutors have placed brutal honesty or informativity as their foremost priorities. While Grice also said that we violate maxims strategically to highlight an implicated meaning, these examples show a clear disregard for what we term *politeness*.

As a language universal, politeness governs the strategic use of utterances when the relevance of more than simply the information content of a discourse is in play; i.e., social relationships and their accompanying expectations can make the difference between two utterances with equivalent semantic content. Untangling the fibers of context from content is a key to understanding pragmatic strategies in general, for it is these variables that spur the diversity of linguistic utterances seen under permutations of social situations. It is, then, to the former variable, social context, that we focus our attention.

In particular, let us focus on requests. Requests arise as speakers seek to address their own needs through the aid of another. As such, they derive from a problem central to economics: scarcity. This means that speakers are at a necessary disadvantage when making them. Further, hearers, should they grant the request, may endure a cost in opportunity or resources. So what rationale is there for granting a request in the first place?

To address this, we turn to another problem central to economics: cooperation. Cooperation exists not only despite the rigors of competition but also often because of them. Societies of cooperators fare well against those who more myopically turn against one another (Nowak, 2006). This strain of cooperation runs deep, and, I claim, steers discourse to not only be cooperative in the information-centric way of the Gricean Cooperative Principle, but also in terms of politeness, the relation-centric prong of pragmatic reasoning.

This economic perspective, in particular Game Theory, applied to Gricean implicatures has been successful of late for its ability to incorporate rationality, theory of mind, and context into what determines optimal pragmatic strategies (e.g. Franke, 2009). These studies, by and large, have omitted politeness and requests. To remedy this in part and address the parallels between making a request and the previously mentioned hope for cooperation while disadvantaged, we consider Trust Games (e.g. McCabe et al., 2003) as an avenue for formalizing requests.

In this paper, I will connect Game-Theoretic Pragmatics with Politeness Theory via Trust Games. Section 2 will give a brief overview of some concepts from Game Theory, Game-Theoretic Pragmatics, and Politeness Theory. Section 3 will outline games of Trust and some of their extensions. Section 4 will discuss how these trust games and their extensions mirror polite linguistic behavior.

2   Game-Theoretic Pragmatics

Grice's central principle outlined communication as strategic. In the wake of this work, the field of Pragmatics has endeavored to pin down these strategies more concretely. Recently, linguists, philosophers, economists, and political scientists (inter alia) have turned their attention to *Game Theory* as a tool with promise to explicate communicative strategies. To acquaint ourselves with some of this methodology, we take a diversion into classical game theory.

2.1 Basic Game Theory

Consider the well-known *Prisoner's Dilemma* given in the table below. The numbers reflect the respective utilities of the players in choosing their strategies. A rational player has a higher incentive to choose strategies leading to higher utilities. The utility of the Row Player (A) is given first, the Column Player (B) second.

Table 1. Prisoner's Dilemma

	C	D
C	3;3	0;5
D	5;0	1;1

Two criminals are arrested by the police, with the options to COOPER-ATE(C) with the police or DEFECT(D) on each other and deny their complicity in the crime. What will they do?

Consider A's situation. If B Cooperates, A can obtain a payoff of 5 if he Defects vs. 3 if he also Cooperates. If B Defects, A would rationally choose the higher payoff of 1 vs. 0 for Cooperation. No matter what action B chooses, it behooves A to defect on him. But the situation for B is symmetric. Thus rationality would lead them to both Defect on each other and thus earn lower payoffs than if they Cooperated. This outcome is known as a *Nash equilibrium*, a situation where no player stands to profit from unilateral deviation. Observe that this only holds however for a one–shot scenario and that if we repeated the game, new strategies emerge. Defection now becomes irrational when other players know of our past via direct observation or even word of mouth. So repetition and reputation, therefore, are innately tied together and form one of the bases for building cooperative social structures.

Deriving a rationale for cooperation has long been a thorn in the side of economists, political scientists, and biologists (Fehr & Fischbacher 2003). Nonetheless, cooperation occurs on every level of the biological, political, and economic strata. Mechanisms like reputation, reciprocity, repetition, and selection increase the likelihood of its emergence, as seen in works like Nowak(2006). Like cooperation in the Prisoner's Dilemma, polite language seemingly confounds theories of rational communication. Yet it bears the same flavor of reciprocal exchange and tit-for-tat standards of repeated behavior. For this reason, some of the games similar to the Prisoner's Dilemma may hold promise for investigating requests, and some of the mechanisms found to induce cooperation may also play a role in encouraging linguistic politeness.

2.2 Pragmatics and Language Evolution

Games like the Prisoner's Dilemma point to the dual nature of strategic interaction. We can think of games as occurring between players simultaneously rationalizing their decisions or as contests between populations of organisms. In the latter case, rationality is replaced by various notions of evolutionary stability subject to permutations of selective pressures. These notions are made formal in the biology literature, but it is only their intuitions that are important here.

This dual nature means that game-theoretic modeling lends itself to both studies of language in context and language evolution. Much of this work revolves around signaling games, a framework first seen in Lewis (1969) and designed to answer the question of how conventions arise in a society. Since then, work such as Franke (2009) and Van Rooij (2004), among others[1], have shown pragmatic implicatures arise as equilibria of signaling games, both in the rational and evolutionarily stable senses. For example, Van Rooij (2004) shows that the pragmatic strategy of choosing a longer expression to indicate an atypical situation is an evolutionarily stable state of a signaling game with costly messages. This idea of language being costly brings us to politeness, and one conclusion drawn from the aforementioned paper will soon be a point of contention.

2.3 Politeness Theory

Politeness phenomena cut across language groups and cultures. While each language may have a different way of expressing politeness, its wide range makes it an obvious target of research. One thing that has yet to arise, however, is a rigorous mathematical backbone in which we can ground politeness phenomena.

In their ur-text on polite language, Brown and Levinson (1978) argued for a strategic theory of politeness. Their theory spoke of *face* as the medium through which we recognize the potential status/ needs/ autonomy of our hearer. To be more specific, they claim that agents have two distinct sets of face needs, termed *positive* and *negative* face. An agent's positive face represents his desires for acceptance within a group, whereas an agent's negative face represents his need to be autonomous and unencumbered. As the preferences of agents' often conflict, especially in communicative scenarios, utterances can threaten the face of potentially both participants in a discourse.

Consider the utterance *Get out of here!* without context. In the presence of a bomb, this is useful instruction. However, as a dinner guest, this is hardly polite language. The source of the utterance might be the intention to remove unwanted visitors, and doing so challenges their autonomy. Brown and Levinson denote utterances like these in the latter context as *face-threatening acts* or FTAs. Politeness serves as a way to maintain social stability through redressing potential FTAs. For instance, redressing the FTA involving the guests might involve saying *I hate to bother you, but we have to ask you to leave.* Some examples follow in Figure 1.

---

[1] Cf. Jäger (2008) for examples and a source on game theory for linguists.

	Person	
	Hearer	Speaker
Negative Face	Orders Advice Threats	Accepting Offers or Thanks Forced Promises
Positive Face	Complaints Disagreements	Apologizing Taking Compliments

Fig. 1. Examples of FTAs

Brown and Levinson's model envisions a strategic tree of possible utterances, with inaction, indirect speech, polite speech, and direct speech forming the branches. As speakers perceive lower potentials for face threat, the likelihood of them using direct speech increases.

Fig. 2. Brown and Levinson's decision tree for a strategic speaker considering a Face-Threatening Act(FTA). A speaker begins with an intention and weighs the potential consequences of his actions against the value of the communication. As we move vertically up the chart, potential for face threat increases.

Requests are a canonical example of an FTA. As making a request is necessarily asymmetric, the speaker should pay the hearer face proportional to the gravity of the request and the social distance between the conversants. This emphasis on strategic interaction makes politeness an inviting ground for testing the merits of game-theoretical models.

Requests need not be direct however, as utterances like "It sure would be nice if someone would open the window," attest. Such indirect utterances increase in usage when speakers value the preservation of face over the actual information content contained in the speech act. Pinker et al. (2008) treated the rationales behind indirect speech using game theory, and argued that indirect speech has three sources of incentives: plausible deniability under threat of action, relationship negotiation, and direct speech's role in evoking common knowledge or eliminating context-dependence. The second factor, relationship negotiation, also serves as an incentive towards rationalizing politeness.

The first notable treatment of politeness from a game-theoretic perspective, Van Rooy (2003) used ideas similar to Van Rooij[2] (2004) in that the longer formulations of polite requests may indicate a costly message parallel to the phenomenon of the *Peacock's Tail*, a reproductive strategy outlined via the Zahavian Handicap Principle. I.e. just as costly, wasteful biological signals lead to the emergence and evolution of honest communication between groups with conflicting preferences on selection, so should costly language like politeness indicate a form of honesty. While this approach has merit, it captures neither the spirit nor the dynamics of making a request. Why not? First, for a request to succeed, there must be sufficient incentive for the requester to grant the favor. Assuming the speaker and hearer are not in a dominance relationship, the speaker must acknowledge the potential autonomy/ need for acceptance of the hearer in said request. This is typically done through some sort of face payment. It is not done by using speech as a marker of fitness, but rather as a medium of exchange. Second, the exchange in general is one of reciprocity when speakers make requests, so the rewards are levied not through selection, but rather through the payoffs in the game itself and the maintenance of a reciprocal society. Third, the Handicap Principle can also explain impolite speech used among groups with selection criteria geared toward counterculture movements. Its ability to seemingly account for both politeness and impoliteness suggests that costly speech (e.g. learning jargon) does play a role in group selection, but that this phenomenon is orthogonal to making a request by paying someone face. Just as Nowak (2006) details that the mechanisms enabling cooperation fall under selection and reciprocity, we turn from the selection-oriented Handicap Principle to games focused on reciprocal behavior, i.e. those of trust and exchange.

3   Games of Trust and Exchange

We provide here a formal model of making a request through the mechanism of asymmetric bargaining and exchange games. An exchange game can be thought of as a formal model of two or more agents sending gifts to one another; the Prisoner's Dilemma is an example of a symmetric exchange game. However, the asymmetric component is crucial here, as we place our fate in the hands of the hearer when making a request. To model this, we incorporate the literature on the burgeoning field of *trust games* as seen in e.g. Lev-On et al. (2010).

Trust games depict a scenario where Player X has an initial option to defer to Player Y for a potentially larger payoff for both. However, similar to the Prisoner's Dilemma, Player Y could defect on Player X and keep more money for himself. For a one-shot game, this act of deference will not occur for a rational Player X. Hence, a signal granting yes-no power to a hearer would not be rational; i.e. politeness would not emerge as an optimal strategy in a single dialogue. To account for the emergence of polite language, we will extend the game in several ways. Before we do that, however, let us take a preliminary look

---

[2] These are the same author.

at the game's decision and payoff structure, the motivations for using it, and the optimal strategy for one round of play.

3.1   Vanilla Trust Game

Motivation and Utility Structure. Two questions must be addressed when considering the trust game depicted above. One, why is it appropriate, and two, why are the parameters as such? Accounting for the dynamics of making requests necessarily involves asymmetry. Were every individual fully self-sufficient, speech itself might be unnecessary. The problem of coordination under uncertainty and diversity of talents, addressed by Skyrms(2010), requires communication of some sort. Unlike the classic example of the *Stag Hunt* however, asking for help involves agents with different abilities, decision processes, and timing. This means that a proper model would depict the person asking for help as surrendering control to the other player to resolve the game. Further, a proper model would incorporate the conflict between asking for help and risking a loss of face or opportunity. This financial language is no coincidence, as the notion of paying face accords with the theory of social exchange posited by Homans(1958). Thus, the model should derive from games of bargaining and exchange, of which trust games are a subset. Last, the game should be amenable to modifications like repetition or additions to its payoff structure.

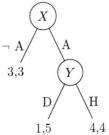

- Player X can Ask(A) or be Not Ask(¬ A)
- Player Y can Defect(D) or Help(H)
- If Player X does Not Ask, Utilities are 3,3
- If Player X Asks Y for help, Y has control
- If Player Y Defects, Utilities are 1,5
- If Player Y Helps, Utilities are 4,4

To answer the second question regarding the payoff structure, we consider each player at a time. X not asking for help simply means leaving the status quo in place. When X asks Y for help via a polite request, Y should experience a raise in self-esteem (+1) based on the attention he is now receiving and the fact that X is attending to his face needs through his language(+1). Hence his utility goes up. These values would be lower and possibly even negative if the request were to be issued in the imperative or with disdain for the listener's needs, e.g. *Hey! Help me out now you imbecile!* While requests of this form occur as well, this model assumes an implicit face payment. Such a face-threatening request would lower Y's utility of responding positively to it due to the loss of both dignity and effort.

If Y helps X, then Y incurs a time/energy cost (−1), and thus his utility is not as high as if he had defected. Now consider X. If Y does not help him, he might feel dejected and has not only spent time/ energy (−1) on the request but has also lost the opportunity to ask someone else (−1). Hence his utility is two steps lower if Y defects on him. However, if Y helps him, then X would obviously experience an increase in utility. This is, after all, the reason for X to ask for Y's help. To connect these this situation to the tree from Brown and Levinson, observe that just as there are a multitude of linguistic variations for making a request, so are there multiple trust games that we could use. Consider the requests below, seen with escalating politeness markers and their accompanying games in Figure 3.

a. *Help me out now you imbecile!*

b. *Can you help me?*

c. *Pardon me, sir. Can you help me?*

d. *Pardon me, sir. Can you please help me?*

Last, we set the initial values to 3, 3 so as to not obscure the cancellation of values when performing the calculations in equilibrium. This is also done in concert with literature in trust games where the participants begin with a nonzero amount.

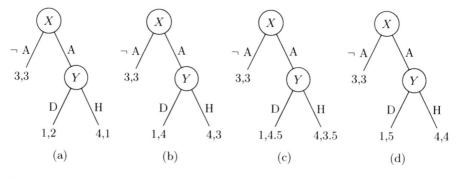

Fig. 3. Trust Games with various payoffs mirroring the utterances above. Note that as the utterances become more polite, we see an increase in the utility for Y. This also assumes a cost–free set of messages for X.

Behavior in Equilibrium. What is rational for the players to do? To answer this question, we will proceed by backward induction. First, think of Y's options. Given the choice, it makes sense for him to choose Defect, as this leads to a higher payoff. But if Y were to defect, then X would never ask for Y's help in the first place. Hence, we need ways to sweeten the pot for cooperative behavior to emerge.

3.2   Repetition, Reputation, and Observation

Here we consider games with *Reputation* induced by a history of play or by observation. The paragraphs below consider conditions that could lead to equilibria(optimal strategies for all players) favoring the emergence of deferential or cooperative players.

Reputation and History. In this next example, we take on the assumption that players are consistent with their past behavior. In economics, this is one of the variegated notions of *reputation*. Consider the expected utility EU_x of Player X. One way that he might be inclined to asking for Y's help is if he knows something about the probability of Y's rate of Helping. If this probability is high enough, X has an incentive to Ask. The following details a constraint on the minimum level of Helping that Y can demonstrate if he wants X to Ask. Realize that Y has an interest in this action, as it allows him a payoff higher than if X did not ask. Here I use a for $Pr(A)$, d for $Pr(d)$, etc. Observe also that d + h = 1.

$$EU_x = 3(1-a) + a(1d + 4h)$$
$$= 3 - 3a + a - ah + 4ah \qquad (1)$$
$$= 3 - 2a + 3ah$$

What do we want here? X has an incentive to Ask iff $EU_x > 3$. This happens if

$$3ah > 2a$$
$$h > \frac{2}{3} \qquad (2)$$

What does this show? It demonstrates that Y must help more than $\frac{2}{3}$ of the time (or defect less than $\frac{1}{3}$ of the time) in order for X to have incentive to ask for help. This action is rational if Y plays a probabilistic strategy consistent with his history of past play.

But what about Y? What behavior should X display in order to foster his cooperation? Consider Y's expected utility function, EU_y below.

$$EU_y = 3(1-a) + a(5(1-h) + 4h)$$
$$= 3 - 3a + 5a - 5ha + 4ha \qquad (3)$$
$$= 3 + 2a - ha$$

What does Y want? He would like the opportunity to have an expected utility of at least 4. What should be true of X then?

$$EU_y > 4$$
$$3 + a(2-h) > 4$$
$$a(2-h) > 1$$
$$2 - h > \frac{1}{a} \qquad (4)$$
$$h < 2 - \frac{1}{a}$$

From before, we know a lower bound on h. Now we have an upper bound as well. Using this tells us more about X's behavior.

$$\frac{2}{3} < h < 2 - \frac{1}{a}$$
$$\frac{2}{3} < 2 - \frac{1}{a}$$
$$2a < 6a - 3$$
$$\frac{3}{4} < a$$

(5)

As shown above, we now see incentives for both X and Y to behave in a fashion similar to the *tit-for-tat* exchanges observed in games like the Prisoner's Dilemma. How this differs is that this dynamic is self-reinforcing. Why? X has an incentive to ask Y again only if Y maintains a record of helping. So strangely enough, if X controls whether the game will continue, then X's vulnerability becomes a source of power.

Reputation and Observation. What if we have no guarantee that future behavior is consistent with past behavior? Moreover, what if we lack information on our partner, or there is no chance of repetition? We would need extra incentive to ask for help, or for that matter, to provide help. Consider the social pressure induced by an outside observer, in front of whom defectors stand to lose face. In this case, we introduce values f_x and f_y that affects the utilities as seen below. [3]

- Player X can Ask(A) or Not Ask($\neg$ A)
- Player Y can Defect(D) or Help(H)
- If Player X is Silent, Utilities remain $3, 3$
- If Player X asks Y for help, Y has control
- If Player Y defects, Utilities are $1 - f_x, 5 - f_y$
- If Player Y Helps, Utilities are $4 - f_x, 4 + f_y$

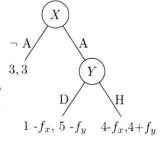

Why do the utilities change as such? First, consistent with accounts in Politeness Theory, requests necessarily involve a loss of face to the requester. So X loses face regardless of whether Y helps him or not. Second, Y can gain face in the presence of an observer if he shows himself to be cooperative, whereas he can lose face if he shows himself to be a defector.

Here we see there is a minimum amount of face that must be paid to the hearer. There is also a maximum level of face that can be accorded, beyond which anything would be counter-productive. Notice that in the left diagram, an

---

[3] These parameters are, as far as we know, novel to the literature on trust games and connect them more intimately to the ideas in Politeness Theory

f_y value of 0.5 would make defection and helping equally attractive. Anything further would push the hearer in the direction of helping. In the right diagram, we see the ceiling on f_x, as any further face paid to the hearer would be less effective than simply not asking.

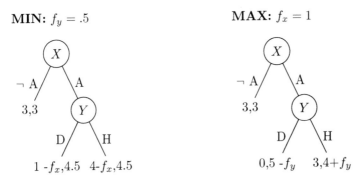

MIN: $f_y = .5$ **MAX:** $f_x = 1$

3.3   Repetition and Observation Combined

Combining the previous two approaches gives intuitive results that link the model to a more realistic language setting. Derivations from the last two lines in the following calculation reveal the intimate connections between face and helpful responses. Here we see a more general result on a ceiling for how much face a speaker is willing to risk and a higher lower bound on the helpfulness of the listener.

$$
\begin{aligned}
EU_x &= (1-a)(3) + a((1-h)(1-f_x) + h(1-f_x)) \\
&= 3 - 3a + a(1 - h - f_x + hf_x + 4h - hf_x) \\
&= 3 + a(3h - 2 - f_x)
\end{aligned}
\tag{6}
$$

Once again, a positive probability of X playing A arises when $EU_x > 3$. How does this happen? Notice that this probability is strictly greater than before, leading to the natural result that reputation and observation strengthen further the incentive for interaction.

$$
\begin{aligned}
3 &< 3 + a(3h - 2 - f_x) \\
0 &< a(3h - 2 - f_x) \\
f_x &< 3h - 2, \ i.e. \\
h &> \frac{2 + f_x}{3}
\end{aligned}
\tag{7}
$$

4   Conclusion

Politeness is the gateway to further conversation and dialogue that can align interest, reveal preferences, or negotiate relationships. It unites speakers together under an implicit social code, removes boundaries, and enables communality and cooperation. However, there is a clear distinction between player types in this game for the same reason that there exists a clear distinction in communicative roles. The asymmetry seen in the diagram mirrors the asymmetry in the nature of making requests, and the utility structures mirror the value we place in the potential outcomes. But what do these outcomes suggest about language?

4.1 Discussion

The first observation to make is that, given a one-shot scenario, no observation, and strictly rational players, the game predicts that speakers stand to lose from making requests and so will not make them. Nonetheless, people make requests everyday, and others help them, often without being seen or recognized again. The results above show two variables that increase this likelihood of deferential and helpful behavior. Behavior consistent with one's past and common knowledge of this behavior accelerate this process. The same occurs for actions under observation, particularly when combined with repetition and reputation. When X risks losing face with the possibility of repetition, Y's likelihood of helping is even higher than with repetition alone.

The second item to be gleaned from these examples is that the model also includes a conflict between stability and informativity. Not asking is not only the equilibrium strategy in a single play, it is also stable to irregularities in the behavior of Y, should he choose to defect. But this stability comes at a cost: Informativity. Every time X makes a request, he gets information about Y. This bent towards the informativity of choosing A also runs counter to the patterns of risk aversion attested in the economic literature (Morgan 2003).

Last, we consider Y's perspective. Even without social pressure, individuals act in altruistic ways on a daiy basis (Fehr and Fischbacher 2003). This places this study within the context of examining the sources and patterns of human altrusim. Further incentive may also exist for Y in the potential for him to play the role of requester later.

4.2 Outlook

In concurrence with Brown & Levinson, politeness is strategic, and we have shown it has both a floor and a ceiling. Furthermore, we have shown that under these assumptions politeness is not always rational, but that it can arise out of repeated interaction or observation. Reputation makes it rational to ask politely, and observation makes it rational to respond politely.

Much of the work on Game-Theoretic Pragmatics revolves around Lewisean Signaling Games. Is there a way to model games of trust with Signaling Games different from the ones in Van Rooy(2003)? Future directions on this topic should also include network models of information spread, link formation, and adoption. E.g. when a critical mass of speakers adopts polite utterances, it pays off for the other members of the society to follow suit. The mechanisms of network reciprocity or dynamic link formation also provide a more realistic setting in which to test the effects of cooperative behavior. While we have mentioned risk-aversion and risk as informative, finding a tractable way to combine the two will also lead to further aligning a strategic theory of politeness with real-world data.

References

1. Lev-On, A., Chavez, A., Bicchieri, C.: Group and dyadic communication in trust games. Rationality and Society 22 (2010)
2. Brown, P., Levinson, S.: Politeness: Some Universals in Language Use (1978)
3. Fehr, E., Fischbacher, U.: The Nature of Human Altruism. Nature 425 (2003)
4. Franke, M.: Signal to Act. PhD Dissertation, University of Amsterdam (2009)
5. Homans, G.: Social Behavior as Exchange. The American Journal of Sociology 63(6) (1958)
6. Jäger, G.: Game-Theoretical Pragmatics. In: Handbook of Logic and Language, 2nd edn. Elsevier (2008)
7. McCabe, K., Rigdon, M., Smith, V.: Positive reciprocity and intentions in trust games. Journal of Economic Behavior & Organization 52 (2003)
8. Morgan, J., Steiglitz, K., Reis, G.: The Spite Motive and Equilibrium Behavior in Auctions. Contributions to Economic Analysis and Policy 2(1) (2003)
9. Nowak, M.A.: Five rules for the evolution of cooperation. Science 314(5805), 1560–1563 (2006)
10. Pinker, S., Nowak, M.A., Lee, J.J.: The logic of indirect speech. Proceedings of the National Academy of Sciences USA 105(3), 833–838 (2008)
11. Van Rooy, R.: Being polite is a handicap: Towards a game theoretical analysis of polite linguistic behavior. TARK 9 (2003)
12. Van Rooy, R.: Signalling games select Horn strategies. Linguistics and Philosophy (2004)

Author Index